The Hitchhiker's Guide

To

Big History

David Baker
Macquarie University

Diabolical Press

2019

Dedicated to the young generation upon whose shoulders the heaviest burdens of the 21ˢᵗ Century will fall. I have absolute confidence they will fight bravely in the wars to come, toil ceaselessly with mounting strength, and deliver the countless generations that follow them to a glorious future where the sky will clear once again and humanity will escape the darkness for a new golden age.

This book is also dedicated to the programmers of this simulation, if the Universe is one, for being so clever. You should have left an instruction manual for the players. Or have you, somewhere?

If not, this book will have to do.

Preface

Don't panic! This textbook will help you understand the entire history of the Universe and your place within it, without danger of your head exploding. Big History charts the rise of complexity, the continuum of change of all the "stuff" around us in the cosmos, right from the Big Bang to the formation of planets, the evolution of life, and the long thrust of human history. While the whole story may not be distilled to "bite-sized" history for the newcomer, it certainly is pleasantly streamlined to a "summer barbecue steak with cold beers" or "Sunday roast dinner" sized history.

Looking at history from the widest lens, even the incomprehensible tangle of human affairs begins to straighten out and become clear in its direction and context. Through Big History we can also look into the prospects for humanity in the short term (the next century) and the long term (trillions and trillions of years to the end of the Universe). In that sense this textbook serves as both a tome of history and a harbinger of things to come.

Big History is neither just a history nor a science course. It is both. For the sciencephobic, please rest assured that no equations will be used, and the purpose of telling the story of the cosmos as history is to boil things down as far as possible into plain speech. The inevitable result is people come out of Big History a little less phobic of the sciences than before.

For the history buff eager to "get to humans", you won't be disappointed. First, the scientific story is entirely historical in the sense that we use empirical evidence to decipher events of the past. Second, humans may only inhabit the "thinnest chip of paint at the top of the Eiffel Tower" in terms of the Universe's total chronology, but due to theme of rising complexity in Big History there is very good reason to get to humans quite soon. For human society is one of the most complex things we know of in the Universe – and how could it not be, given it is a network of billions of whirring brains each with more nodes and connections than there are stars in the galaxy?

For the indifferent among you, while I cannot guarantee your eyes will never glaze over, I can guarantee this Big History is naturally more interesting than most subjects you could have chosen. We shall try to augment the experience by presenting it well.

Each chapter will end with a list of suggested readings for any Big History essays or research you may perform, along with chasing up any questions that interest you personally. Periodically, some essay writing exercises will be included to hone your skills. It should also be noted that this textbook is supplemented by video lectures on Big History that can be found within the course taught at Macquarie University and also online on Youtube.

Table of Contents

CHAPTER 1

BIG HISTORY & THE BIG BANG

Or,

ON ALL THINGS BIG:

HISTORY, BANGS, & OTHERWISE...

What is Big History?

The Universe is big. *Really big*. The Universe is also old. *Really old*. 13.8 billion years old.

It can be a rather difficult thing to conceptualise at first. And for many people across the world, the awareness of the scope and size of the cosmos sits on the periphery of their thinking. Barely factoring into their identities and how they live their daily lives. But this could not be further from the truth.

Big History takes the whole of space and time, identifies a continuum of connected events, and presents everything as a digestible historical narrative presented in plain language. The continuum of connected events covers the origin of matter and energy after the Big Bang, the coalescing of matter and energy into the first stars, the creation of new chemical elements from those stars, the arrangement of those new chemical elements into planets and organisms, the evolution of those organisms on Earth, the accumulation of learning over a few thousand years of one species of organisms, *Homo sapiens*, and their creation of increasingly complex societies. If you thought providing a history of the Universe was impossible, consider that in these few short lines I have already delivered the major beats and arc of the story.

Big History is important because it helps humans understand their place in the Universe. Just as conventional history helps us understand our place in the ongoing drama of national and international affairs. However, Big History is not overly concerned with the clash of tribes, ethnic groups, dynasties, classes, or political ideologies. As Fernand Braudel said, those things are the insignificant bubbles and swirling foam atop an ocean of deep time. Here today, gone tomorrow. Instead Big History focuses on the everlasting and more crucial drama of existence. Humanity's wider context is being played out with the rise and fall of complexity in the Universe, a trend that has been ongoing since the Big Bang, and, if it continues, may eons from now impact the fate of the Universe itself. The trend toward rising complexity created us, continues to change us, and will ultimately determine our fate.

Big History derives its narrative from empirical evidence, just like any other credible historical narrative. In the case of Big History, this involves cosmological evidence like the observation of supernovas, geological evidence like the radiometric dating of rocks, biological evidence like fossils and DNA, archaeological evidence like long buried ancient ruins and collections of ancient pottery, as well as the classic historical sources like written archival documents. In many ways, all academic disciplines are historical in nature, and so history can remorselessly plunder all of them to construct a narrative.

Big History seeks to explain how things began from the very beginning of time, and in that respect it mirrors the religious mythologies that many cultures across thousands of years also used to deliver such a story of beginnings. Humans are pattern seeking animals, and as such we are driven to try and explain the world around us – even when we don't have the best methods or evidence. Consider the Palaeolithic tribesman living 100,000 years ago. He could not explain the lightning or earthquakes or the spread of disease. So a religious mythology sprang up to explain how those things worked, and by extension where all those things began. The same practice was initiated by ancient civilisations and the architects of the world's great religions in the Bronze and Iron Ages. Explanations for lightning and earthquakes might be written off as vengeful gods, explanations for origins might include a deity summoning the Earth from a dark netherworld. And much of this mythology would inform a culture's identity, decision-making, morality, and worldview.

Big History, on the other hand, exists in a period of time where we know much more about the natural world and its mechanics than ever before. Since the 17th century, the scientific method has slowly developed to use hypothesis, experimentation, and observation to construct increasingly accurate models of reality. We know that lighting is caused by a collision of positive and negative electrical charges in a rain cloud, we know that earthquakes are caused by the Earth's shifting tectonic plates. And we know that the galaxies of the Universe are speeding away from each other and if you calculate backward must have been compressed at an ultra-hot, ultra-dense point.

Where Big History is different is the fact it is based on the scientific method which constantly critiques and demolishes theories and replaces them with ones that better describe reality. Unlike a religious dogma which claims to be irrefutable truth, or a traditional religious narrative which may be taken literally at first and then as the years go by be considered allegorical, Big History constantly updates itself to meet new evidence. For example, Big History courses used to state that the Universe was 13.7 billion years old, but more accurate measurement of the Cosmic Microwave Background by the Planck satellite in 2013 determined the age was closer to 13.8 billion. For another example, we used to think modern humans (*Homo sapiens*) were around 200,000 to 250,000 years old as a species, but fossil remains discovered in Morocco in 2017 determined that *Homo sapiens* are at least 315,000 years old and probably closer to 350,000 years old as a species. This will not be the last time the story is updated. For instance, as we learn more about Dark Matter and Dark Energy (substances that make up 95% of the entire Universe) that version of Big History is liable to look much different from the one that exists today.

All historical genres have a cultural role to play. And the role of Big History is fairly straightforward. Modernity has not created a void where the ancient stories used to be, but rather it has created a new story to be learned and explored. And it is our job to learn this story, let it inform our identity, and to seek within it the meaning and purpose we sought in the stories of old.

The Big History Course Timeline

The overall timeline of Big History can be divided in several ways. The simplest way of dividing 13.8 billion years is into three parts:

- The Inanimate Phase: *13.8 billion to 3.8 billion years ago*
- The Animate Phase: *3.8 billion to 315,000 years ago*
- The Cultural Phase: *315,000 years ago to the Present*

These three phases correspond to the major increases in complexity as the timeline progresses and we narrow down our spatial scope from the Universe, to the Earth, to humanity. In each phase the new form of complexity takes centre stage.

In the Inanimate Phase, we are concerned with the non-living cosmos, from the Big Bang, to stars, to asteroids, to planets. This spans from the Big Bang 13.8 billion years ago to the appearance of life on Earth 3.8 billion years ago. That is not to say that the subsequent phases are devoid of inanimate complexity – obviously the galaxy keeps spinning and the Sun keeps shining as we approach the 21st century in our story. But up until 3.8 billion years ago we are not aware of inanimate complexity in the Universe being surpassed by anything else (unless of course life arose elsewhere in the cosmos before then, but we'd need to see some evidence first!).

In the Animate Phase, life takes centre stage, from the first organic chemicals that started to self-replicate and evolve 3.8 billion years ago, to the Cambrian Explosion 541 million years ago, to the extinction of the dinosaurs 65 million years ago, and the evolution of *Homo sapiens* approximately 315,000 to 350,000 years ago. Even the simplest life is a much more complex tangle of chemicals than anything found in the inanimate cosmos, thus it gets its own separate phase of Big History. And once we move on to the Cultural Phase that is not to say that animate life ceases to exist! Obviously humans are a form of animate life that produce culture and interact with the entire biosphere in a complex relationship that is growing increasingly lopsided.

In the Cultural Phase, suddenly the ideas generated by human brains take centre stage. Why? Because these ideas gradually generate higher and higher complexity. The biological miracle that is a human brain is certainly very complex, but a network of billions of them exchanging information is a much more complex structure even then. What distinguishes the Cultural Phase from the Animate Phase is the process of "collective learning" which is the accumulation of more innovation by one generation than is lost by the next. As such in the blink of an eye in evolutionary time humans have gone from stone tools to skyscrapers and created some truly unique forms of complexity. Instead of the blind process of evolution by natural selection, this phase is driven by invention and then tinkering and improvement on those inventions over thousands and thousands of years to the point that we arrive at the 21st century.

A slightly more detailed way of looking at the overall timeline of Big History is by eight thresholds, also rooted in complexity. When looking at the grand narrative of 13.8 billion years, certain pivotal moments that set off an explosion of new change and complexity can be noted. These are by no means all the pivotal moments that can be identified. One could identify 20 or 2000 such moments. And this framework by no means forms the basis of a scientific theory, as some naïve people have thought in the past, trying to seek a pattern in a selection of events that were simply selected by a couple authors to best structure a history course. Thresholds are simply a device to allow you to bite off a reasonable mouthful of Big History without choking on the Industrial Revolution while you are still trying to swallow the formation of the first stars.

1) **The Big Bang (13.8 billion years ago):** *wherein matter and energy appear within an expanding cosmic bubble of space, with each clump of matter and energy holding the potential to create endless forms of complexity. Your family tree starts here with a goopy clump of sub-atomic particles.*

2) **The First Stars (13.7 billion years ago):** *wherein billions of those clumps of matter and energy get sucked together, and fuse together atoms in perpetual nuclear explosions to create light, heat, and new chemical elements. You may not be the spoiled child of a movie actor, but you are definitely the descendant of stars.*

3) **New Chemical Elements (13.6 billion years ago):** *wherein those stars die, blow up horrifically in supernovas, and fling those new elements across the galaxy to form new molecules. Congratulations, you are now a bunch of carbon and a few droplets of water.*

4) **The Solar System (4.5 billion years ago):** *wherein a bunch of those new molecules accrete together by static electricity and collisions of proto-planets to form gigantic balls of interacting chemicals. Welcome home, please watch out for oceans of lava and that giant ball of rock that is going to hit us and create the moon.*

5) **Life (3.8 billion years ago):** *wherein some of those interacting chemicals start self-replicating and evolving into creatures, at first microscopic, then very large and multi-celled. Congratulations, your great-great-great-grand-pappy was a fish.*

6) **Collective Learning (315,000 years ago):** *wherein a species like* Homo sapiens *evolves the ability to accumulate more information with one generation than is lost by the next, leading to*

increased tinkering, improvement, and new inventions in a very short period of a few thousand years. Some invented the wheel, some invented controlled use of fire, and some invented story-time vlogs and mullets. Which is the most historically-significant? You be the judge.

7) **Agriculture (12,000 years ago):** *wherein our species (Homo sapiens) uses their collective learning to domesticate plants and animals in order to have food to support more people who continue to tinker and invent more things. Congratulations, you now get to be a farmer for the next 12,000 years.*

8) **Industrial Revolution (250 years ago):** *wherein our species has been tinkering and improving for so long that we harness the fossil fuels of long buried dead things to set off an explosion of production, population growth, and further innovation, delivering us to modernity, the Anthropocene, and societies full of technology, an ocean full of plastic, and countries full of fast-food restaurants and endangered species.*

Please note how one threshold lays the groundwork for the one that follows it. The Big Bang creates unequal distributions of matter and energy that clump together into billions of stars, stars create the elements, the elements create planets and life, that life evolves on the planet until it can use collective learning, and that collective learning sets off a plethora of historical change that delivers us to the current era.

Need I point out again that we've just traveled through the major beats and arc of the history of the Universe again? Far from being impossible, Big History is quite easy. And, as will become increasingly clear, it is also essential to know if you want to figure out what the heck you are doing in this Universe or where all these existential shenanigans are going.

Speaking of which there will one day be another threshold to add:

9) **Unknown (? years from now)** *wherein our species or something that follows us will undergo another revolution in complex on the scale of the invention of agriculture or heavy industry. There are some indications that collective learning is accelerating and it is possible that the next threshold will occur soon. Or it is possible humanity will decline or disappear, in which case the ninth threshold may be delayed or cancelled completely.*

And so long as complexity is not completely destroyed by some sort of natural or manmade disaster, then there really is no limit to the number of thresholds that could emerge. One could be looking at humans or their descendants moving out beyond the solar system, harnessing the power of stars, macro-engineering galaxies, or becoming all-powerful manipulators of spacetime. So long, that is, as we don't completely screw things up this century…

But that's where you come in, my young bright-eyed student. Your generation gets to clean up the mess of earlier generations and pay for their sins. Or make entirely new messes of your own to similarly hand down to your children and grandchildren. The next chapter of Big History is up to you to decide. That is at once an empowering and intimidating thought.

Why Historians are Thirsty for Dates

In order for history to have any physical meaning, it needs to be structured as a sequence of events happening within the spacetime continuum. These events are measured by dates just as distance can be measured by miles. *And the concept of time itself is really just a coordinate in the Universe like distance.* Time allows you to find yourself in the fabric of the ever-expanding and changing cosmos. Let's say that Mr. Jenkins is looking for his top hat. It is not enough to say "I saw the top hat on the table." When was it on the table? Now? Yesterday? A thousand years ago? Or has the top hat been on the table for 13.8 billion years since the beginning of the Universe? If the top hat emerged sometime after the Big Bang, how was it created? From a cloud of hydrogen? From a pile of loose fabric on a factory floor? What forces propelled it to be on the table? Without the coordinate of time, it is virtually impossible to locate anything in the Universe. That top hat (or the materials it is made from) literally travelled across the cosmos to get to that table. Without the coordinate of time, the top hat was always on the table, was never on the table, and is potentially in every other place in the Universe besides the table. Without the coordinate of time, you might as well throw that GPS into the dustbin while the very fabric of reality collapses around you.

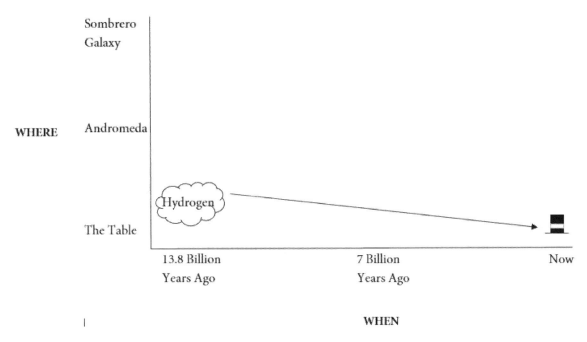

So it is unsurprising that historians are so desperate to find dates, and not just because they are a lonely sort of people. Imagine being able to say that the Universe began with the Big Bang, but being unable to say whether it happened billions of years ago or yesterday. Or being unable to say whether the Napoleonic Wars happened before or after you had your morning coffee. Imagine being able to say that you live on the planet Earth but being unable to say whether you are older or younger than Adolf Hitler. A history without dates would be a pretty useless thing, just as a road map without miles or kilometres wouldn't tell us much about the location of the nearest town.

Prior to the 20th century, we lacked accurate dates to make Big History possible. Without accurate dates unworldly events like the start of the Universe, the formation of the first atoms, the first stars flaring into life, all fade into a haze. Some vague notion of "a long time ago". But to humans a thousand, million, or a billion years all fit into that category. Without a sense of the magnitude of the scale of time involved in taking the first flash of energy in the cosmos and transforming it into stars, planets, and life, history loses the majority of its clarity and educational value. Or, as mentioned, it loses an entire dimension and coordinate of where it belongs on the map.

When pre-modern cultures had a numerical date for the creation of the world at all, it was usually expressed in the thousands of years. Probably because even a thousand years seems like an inconceivably long passage of time to the average human being. For instance, a literal interpretation of the Old Testament would imply the world is approximately 6000 years old. In 1650 AD the Archbishop of Armagh, James Ussher, added up the ages of all the patriarchs in the Bible and calculated that humans were created one fine evening on October 23 4004 BC.

Interestingly enough, 6000 years ago is just a few centuries before the first city-states and writing systems came into being. But we now know, however, that humans had existed for hundreds of thousand years before that point (at least 315,000 years according to current evidence) but did not have complex writing systems to keep track of the passage of time. And even the most devoted of oral traditions can only keep track of so many ancestors.

Even if you only mentioned your direct bloodline, and each person only by name and no further information, it would take approximately 24 hours without breaks to name everyone going back 315,000 years. So it is not surprising that pre-modern humans seriously underestimated how long we've been kicking around.

Indeed prior to the modern age, written documents like the Anglo-Saxon Chronicle, for example, were our only way of confirming that events happened at all. If it wasn't written down, if it wasn't dated, an event would disappear from the collective memory. It is quite likely that there are thousands, if not millions, of noteworthy events that happened in human history that will forever be lost to us, as Rutger Hauer's character says in *Blade Runner*, "like tears in rain".

Even today, conventional academic history is still largely associated with finding written accounts or evidence in a dusty archive. But what of the histories that humans did not see with their own eyes, or chose not to write down? We had no writing for most of the 315,000 years of human existence (roughly 98.4% of it). Writing only started approximately 5000 years ago, and then only in places where there were city-states (ignoring much of the rest of the world).

Further still, until the dawn of modernity 200 years ago, written accounts of historical events were patchy at best, with many things left out, and many historians more interested in producing political propaganda than in delivering a recreation of the past (it is true that many historians today still seem interested in only producing propaganda, but that is a different story).

And even then, what about the 13.8 billion years of history that happened before humans even existed? How do we construct a narrative of the natural world without witnesses or documents?

The Birth of Big History

Enter something called the "Chronometric Revolution" that came to fruition in the 20th century. There are a few ingredients to this. Cosmologically, we discovered in 1920s that the Universe wasn't eternal but had a birthdate several billion years ago – the Big Bang. The Universe had a starting point and thus a history. We also began to estimate the ages of various stars, galaxies, and quasars. Geologically, we discovered in the 1940s and 1950s that the Earth hadn't sat unchanged for billions of years, but thanks to plate tectonics was forever changing and moving, allowing us to date fossils in various rock layers. Biologically, we discovered in the 1960s that looking at the DNA between two species could allow us to determine when those two species had a common ancestor in both their family trees. For instance, the ancestor of both chimpanzees and humans lived within the range of 5 and 7 million years ago, and the last common ancestor of humans and daffodils lived somewhere between 1.6 and 1.8 billion years ago.

Most crucial to the Chronometric Revolution was the practice of "radiometric dating". This one is a bit tricky to understand, so let us boil it down. All the "stuff" around us is made up of atoms. The nucleus of each atom was fused together in the belly of stars via immense pressure. But over enough time the ingredients in these nuclei "jiggle loose" again like a loose tooth and the atoms "decay". When you change the ingredients in an atomic nucleus, you change the type of atom the thing is. When atoms decay, they turn into a different isotope/element that is further down the rung of the periodical table. On a long enough timescale, uranium turns into lead, carbon turns into nitrogen, and so on. Eventually all elements in the Universe will decay back into hydrogen gas (the simplest element) and then the hydrogen gas itself will decay back into energy and disappear. Essentially, all atoms have an expiry date like a bottle of milk. That, of course, includes the atoms in your body.

While it is impossible to predict the precise moment when an individual atom will decay, if you have a batch of those atoms, you can predict with startling accuracy when half of them will decay. This is called a "half-life". It takes 4.5 billion years for half a batch of uranium-238 to decay into lead-206, which makes it good for dating extremely old rocks on the Earth (which is also about 4.5 billion years old). It takes 1.3 billion years for half of potassium-40 to decay into argon-40. It takes 80,000 years for half a batch of uranium-234 to decay into thorium-230. And it takes 5,730 years for half of carbon-14 to decay into nitrogen, making it ideal for assigning dates to a lot of human artifacts. Rapidly we began to establish dates for the creation of everything around us. By the 1970s, it became possible to write a Big History supported by increasingly accurate dates. And that unsurprisingly is precisely when Big History began to emerge.

Thanks to the Chronometric Revolution, the natural sciences became historical, and it simultaneously became possible for history to embrace the natural sciences. For the first time in human existence, we are able to piece together an unambiguous sequence of events and map historical change from the very beginning of time and space itself.

Not only can we say definitively when we saw Mr. Jenkins's top hat on the table, but we can tell with considerable accuracy the story of the hydrogen cloud, stars, supernova explosions, planetary accretion, and the patchwork of human cultural and economic history from which it sprang. Thus we have Big History and Mr. Jenkins's top hat has not destroyed the spacetime continuum, causing a T-Rex to attack King's Cross, the Titanic to collide with the top of Sydney Tower, and the Mongols to pick fights with Nazi soldiers while you are trying to enjoy a day at the beach.

Banging "Big"

Threshold 1: The Big Bang – 13.82 billion years ago

- *Wherein all the "junk" discussed in this book appeared.*
- *Space appeared and gave us somewhere to put all our "junk".*
- *Time appeared and made it possible for that "junk" to change form (i.e. have a history).*
- *All "junk" is energy and matter which transformed into all known forms of complexity.*

Timeline

- **Big Bang (13.82 billion years ago):** Appearance of spacetime continuum and the extremely hot, densely-packed energy within it. Nothing exists outside of it. All the ingredients for everything in the Universe were inside it. They simply changed form. Universe is small as heck. Smaller than an atom, smaller than a proton in the nucleus of that atom, smaller than a quark that makes up part of that proton.

- **The Primordial Date (10^{-43} seconds after the Big Bang):** The passage of the smallest possible chunk of time after the Big Bang. What happened before this chunk of time is virtually indistinguishable from it. Nothing can move fast enough. That tiny sliver of a second is the time it takes a photon of light to shift 1.6 x 10^{-35} meters. Thus it marks the first date on our calendar. The Universe is still a tiny red hot ball that couldn't be seen with the naked eye or even the most super-powerful microscopes.

- **Guthian Cosmic Inflation (10^{-36} to 10^{-32} seconds after the Big Bang):** The Universe rapidly expands from a size much smaller than one tiny sliver of one tiny proton in the centre of an atom to about the size of a grapefruit. As a result, the Universe grows from the quantum level to the Newtonian level. Gravity, electromagnetism, and the strong and weak nuclear forces that run all the physics of our Universe become coherent. The unequal distribution of matter and energy appears, laying the groundwork for all the complexity that would emerge in the next 13.82 billion years. The clock is wound, the rules are set, groundwork is laid for everything to develop and evolve. And the rest, as they say, is history.

- **Annihilation of Matter and Anti-Matter (10 seconds after the Big Bang):** Universe was swirling full of positively and negatively charged matter (quarks and anti-quarks, positrons and electrons) that bumped into their oppositely charged partner and exploded in a flash turning back into energy. Only 1 billionth of the quarks and electrons could not find a partner, and thus some matter survives to create complexity in the Universe. A close shave.

- **Formation of Hydrogen and Helium Nuclei (3 minutes after the Big Bang):** Universe continues to expand, though slower than Guthian Cosmic Inflation period, and cools to allow the nucleus of an atom to form from the surviving quarks. Those quarks coalesce into protons and neutrons that make up the cores of hydrogen and helium (the simplest elements). It is still too hot for the nuclei of hydrogen and helium to capture electrons and become fully fledged atoms. And the Universe cools down too quickly for much of the other elements to be created (only trace amounts of lithium and beryllium).
- **Cosmic Background Radiation (380,000 years after the Big Bang):** The Universe continues to expand and cool for a period longer than *Homo sapiens* has existed. Finally, the Universe becomes cool enough for hydrogen and helium nuclei to capture electrons and become fully-fledged atoms. The Universe is no longer as hot or dense, and this allows photons of light to move freely through the cosmos for the very first time, which creates a huge flash of light, the remnants of which can still be detected in every direction in the Universe today.

Notes on Scale:

The first few dates deal with a lot of negative exponents to express tiny slivers of a second. To give you a better idea of the extremely small fragments of time with which we are dealing, 10^{-43} seconds looks like this: 0.0000000000000000000000000000000000000000001 seconds. To human eyes that is an absurdly small decimal.

One must also consider the size of the Universe as it expanded. At 10^{-43} seconds the Universe would have been around 10^{-35} metres across. A hydrogen atom is 10^{-10} metres across. Then after Guthian Cosmic Inflation, the universe was about the size of a grapefruit or 0.1 m (10^{-1} metres). That is an extremely fast expansion to happen in just 10^{-36} to 10^{-32} seconds!

It is difficult to estimate how large the Universe would have been at 3 minutes after the Big Bang, but odds are it would already have grown to be larger than our Milky Way Galaxy (which is 100,000 light years across). We do have a better idea of how large the Universe would have been 380,000 years after the Big Bang – roughly 86 million light years across, or almost as large as the entire Virgo Supercluster (110 million light years) which contains 47,000 galaxies, including our own.

The Big Bang Makes My Brain Hurt

Within Big History, the Big Bang is probably the most difficult thing to understand. And given the chronology of the course, it is unfortunately the first hurdle we must overcome. Rest easy, however, that once you get across this, the worst is over. And I will endeavour to boil this down as effectively as possible for you. Once you get your head round it, Big Bang cosmology is not such a scary thing.

The reason why the Big Bang is so mind boggling is that we humans lack a proper frame of reference that is friendly and digestible to our primate brains. We can come up with metaphors for something like plate tectonics (skin floating on top of a boiling pot of soup) or why the Earth orbits the Sun (marbles slowing circling a funnel). But it is not so easy for an event that _precedes_ the establishment of the physics of our Universe. As a result, so much of what we understand about the Big Bang seems counter-intuitive, leading to questions like "How do you get something from nothing?" and "What happened before the Big Bang?"

After all, we are talking about the event that started the physical rules of this Universe. It wound up the clock. At the moment of the Big Bang, concepts like time, space, and gravity didn't exist as we know them. Humans evolved within this Universe, and are programmed to respond to the physics of that Universe in order to survive. And so, our intellectual and more importantly _instinctual_ understanding of how things work don't quite match with the bizarre physics of the first few seconds of the Universe.

Bearing that in mind, I want you to imagine a speck. A tiny speck that you can't even see with the naked eye. This is the Big Bang singularity 13.8 billion years ago. All energy and matter are contained within that speck. All the ingredients for the rest of our story. The speck is all the space there is, and time has not yet started ticking and things have not yet changed or evolved. The speck is so hot that not even the forces of physics like gravity can operate coherently.

Don't imagine that there is anything outside the speck. No space exists outside the speck, the only space that exists is within the speck, and as the Universe expands the amount of space will grow. Don't even imagine pitch blackness outside the speck, like we see at night between the stars. That blackness would imply a void, or in other words, space. There is nothing but the speck. If you need to, draw a little dot on a piece of paper. That is the Big Bang singularity. _Now take a pair of scissors and cut off all the extra paper outside the speck._ There is no "background", there is no void, and there is no space. All you are left with is the speck. That is our Universe. If you can wrap your head around this, you've taken an important leap toward understanding the Big Bang.

The Cosmic "Players"

There are four players that concern us here: *space, time, matter,* and *energy.* So where were they at the moment of the Big Bang? Matter and energy are easy. They were contained within the speck. They are also the reason why the Big Bang was so unbelievably hot. When you lump a bunch of stuff on top of each other, the pressure heats things up. That is why the core of the Earth is molten. It is why stars (which are just big lumps of hydrogen, helium, and other elements) are so hot and constantly letting off nuclear explosions in their cores. The same applies to the Big Bang.

All the stuff around us in the cosmos, all of those billions of stars, all of the planets, all of the asteroids, *all of it,* was compressed into a space so small that it was at the quantum level. All was packed densely in a space millions and millions of times thinner than the width of a single strand of hair. This made normal physics impossible, which is why the Big Bang still remains so mysterious and on the frontier of scientific understanding. We need to devise a whole new way of looking at things, a whole new vocabulary, to fully understand what happened here at the beginning of things.

Matter and energy at the Big Bang also allow us another consideration. All the ingredients for all the stuff we see around us was there at the beginning. No new matter and energy were added. This is First Law of Thermodynamics. Nothing new is created, nor is anything old totally destroyed. Over the life of the Universe, they just endlessly change form. That means the atoms that make up your body existed in some form at the beginning of the Universe, and have continued to exist and evolve across the cosmos over 13.8 billion years. And after you die, those atoms will split off in different directions and continue to evolve in the Universe again. From a certain point of view, we are the Universe, one totality, and are blessed to briefly be one conscious part of it. As if the Universe were looking at itself through a looking glass.

It actually goes a little deeper than that still. Matter and energy are to some degree interchangeable. Meaning we have one core "dramatic actor" here rather than two. At the moment of the Big Bang, it is highly unlikely that matter existed. Matter is actually a more congealed form of energy. You read that correctly, the atoms in your body are just a goopier version of the original. It was most likely during Guthian Cosmic Inflation 10^{-36} to 10^{-32} seconds after the Big Bang that energy clumped together into sub-atomic particles of matter, and those clouds of particles were distributed unequally across the fledgling Universe, sowing the seeds for the first stars. As if to prove the point, consider that at the end of the Universe, the atoms of matter will actually decay back into energy and enter a long and eternal sleep.

What Happened Before the Big Bang?

Space and time existed within the Big Bang singularity. Again, please remember, *there was nothing but the speck*. In that sense, space is easy. Space came into being as a physical property 13.8 billion years ago and immediately began to expand – first to the size of a grapefruit after Guthian Cosmic Inflation, then within a few minutes to the size of a galaxy, then within 380,000 years to a realm approximately 86 million light years across. Space continues to expand today, and that expansion is accelerating, so that now our Universe is approximately 93 billion light years across. On some distant day, we will have to update that number. And keep updating it – until the end of things. And the one thing that makes the gradually accelerating expansion of space possible is, you guessed it, *time*. Without time, space cannot be the size of a grapefruit at one moment, and then the size of a galaxy supercluster the next, in the same way Mr. Jenkins's top hat cannot be on the table at one point and not another.

Time is a bit trickier to understand because it is even more fundamental a concept to the human mind than space. We can get the idea of something starting small and then growing. It is a bit more difficult to imagine time not being here and then suddenly starting. Nevertheless, time also existed within the speck and started rolling from the moment the Big Bang singularity flickered into being. No wonder this is harder for the human brain to conceptualise – think of a period in time where time didn't exist. It is complete and utter paradox. The great ape brain balks and breaks down.

But that is how it happened. This is because time and space are relative. If there is no space to move, there is no space for anything to change or evolve. And if there is no change, there are no events, and no history. As such, time requires space in order to exist. Thus we can fairly confidently say that time did not exist "before" the Big Bang created space.

If this is more difficult for you to digest, you are not alone. Humans are evolved to firmly grasp something as fundamental as time. It is such a vital concept in the existence of any animal. Our brain tracks events for survival, even when they pass at the most insignificant level. To miss a trick might mean death. Like not noticing the moment when a car is hurtling down the road as we try to cross. As such we are very good at monitoring change and the passage of time. It makes us good historians, it keeps us going as a species, but it makes us rather sluggish at understanding that even time has its limits. To our limited neurological hardware, it simply does not compute.

As you may have predicted, this completely annihilates the question, "What happened before the Big Bang?" because time did not exist yet. There literally was no "then" back then. Without time, you cannot have a sequence of events. You cannot have causality, with one thing leading to another. There was no "before" the Big Bang, because the Big Bang created time. Ultimately you have to trace things back to a prime mover, or first cause, which got busy when time first began.

So we can definitely talk about things happening "at the moment of the Big Bang". But we can't talk about something happening "before". The grammar of the question simply doesn't make sense. It would be like talking about your role in your own conception. Like you introduced your mother and father to each other at a bar. It is nonsensical.

Instead, if we can't ask what happened "before" the Big Bang, what have we got? We can investigate the physics of the Universe as they existed at the moment of the Big Bang. They would have been different to ours, and it will take some time for even physicists to get their heads round it. But we shall do so. Currently humanity is capable of recreating the conditions that prevailed 10^{-10} seconds after the Big Bang. We simply have to keep pushing further back.

There are three considerations to come out of this. All of them pertain to the human mind wrestling with the ostensibly absurd:

1) If the secrets of the start of the Universe are completely divorced from how our primate brains make sense of things, then the answer to the start of existence may sound like gibberish to us. As a result of this, the scientific answer may not fill the emotional void left empty by human secularism. At the moment of discovery, whether in 100 years or 1000 or more, if our primate brains are wired in the same way, it may not fill us with any greater sense of calmness, enlightenment, or truth. The same baffled emptiness with which we glare at current cosmological theories may continue.

2) It is possible that we are missing a piece of the puzzle that would satisfy the human brain, but it is probably beyond the tales of mysticism and magic with which we have filled that void and comforted ourselves in the past. It will involve forces we have not yet imagined.

3) It is possible that in order to find meaning in our existence, while these things remain uncovered, that we must stop looking for answers and satisfaction at the beginning of things and focus our thoughts entirely on how we'd like things to end. Not only in our own lives, but in the Big History of the Universe itself.

Much Ado about Nothing

Another question is how you get "something from nothing". First of all, people might raise the point that it contradicts the First Law of Thermodynamics – that matter and energy are neither created nor destroyed, they simply change form. Except that at the moment of the Big Bang the physical laws of the Universe as we know them were not yet coherent. It was so hot that even the four fundamental forces of physics (gravity, electromagnetism, and the strong and weak nuclear forces) weren't operating yet.

Further still, at the moment of the Big Bang, the singularity was about the size of a quantum particle. At the quantum scale, things don't operate quite as they do at the larger Newtonian level. And we *do* know that at the quantum level we have virtual particles popping in and out of existence all the time. They just don't register on larger "Newtonian" levels. In fact, the idea of quantum physics being responsible for the appearance of the Universe in the first place is one of the leading hypotheses in this area. Finally, there is nothing to confirm that the Big Bang singularity was "created" at the moment of the Big Bang. It may already have existed. And if we stretch further back, we run into the same problem of time not existing yet. So with a breakdown in causality, how can we say that anything was created before the actual bang?

Putting the First Law of Thermodynamics to one side, we also have to confront the idea that we really don't know what "nothing" is. As a shorthand, idiomatic expression in the English language, nothing just means the absences of something. But within our existing Universe, we know that it is impossible for absolutely *nothing* to even exist – even in the deepest reaches of space. Everywhere in the cosmos has either "stuff" whether stars, planets, or clouds of hydrogen, or at the very least a bath of weak radiation hovering a few degrees above Absolute Zero. We can't even artificially create a space where there is nothing. Physicists have tried. It is theoretically impossible to create what is called a "zero energy vacuum" or essentially a void of space that doesn't even have radiation.

As such, the common concept of nothing as a black void (reminiscent of space in the night's sky – which is full of radiation) is not the same as the concept of "nothing" existing. No radiation, and not even time or space. It is difficult for scientists to even define that concept. If it could even possibly exist. The question "how do you get something from nothing?" also comes with a massive presumption that before the Universe there was indeed nothing. *How do you know that?* What empirical evidence has indicated that fact? It is only indicated by the logic of the human mind that if you don't have a Universe, you've got "nothing". Yet we've already encountered the limits of the human mind dealing with a period in Big History before the physics it evolved in even existed.

What Does the Universe Look Like?

If your mind has successfully moved past the obstacles of there not being a "before" the Big Bang, not being anything "outside" the Big Bang or the expanding Universe, and there not necessarily having been "nothing" into which the Big Bang singularity just popped, then it pays to get oriented in the Universe we *do* know.

As noted, the Universe started off as a tiny subatomic speck. It then expanded. Not into anything. It just expanded like a balloon expands when inflated. This brings us to the question of the "shape" of the Universe. There are several answers to this.

The first is the most simple and pertains to the shape of the "observable Universe" or that part of the Universe that we can observe from Earth. The shape of the Universe is a sphere, because we can observe stuff in all directions. Does that mean we are at the centre of the Universe? No. Because if you existed on a planet on Andromeda 2 million light years away, you'd still be able to see stuff in all directions. It is just that the light from the furthest stuff has only had 13.8 billion years to reach us. So in that respect, saying the "observable Universe" is a sphere is a perfectly valid assertion. And imagining the Universe as a cosmic bubble is much less intimidating.

Moving onward to "size" the question for the observable Universe is quite simple. We have some idea of the rate of the expansion of the Universe, and its acceleration. The Universe expands much faster than the speed of light and is accelerating all the time. So the most distant objects from us that we can see, which first shone their light over 13 billion years ago are not just 13 billion light years away. They are an estimated 46.5 billion light years away in all directions, meaning our cosmic bubble (the observable Universe) is about 93 billion light years across.

But what about the "unobservable Universe" or parts from which we can see no light? There are a number of possibilities. It could be that the observable Universe is all there is, but this is unlikely. The shape of the wider Universe that we can't see depends on how it is expanding. Looking at the nature of its acceleration, we have determined that the Universe in total has "zero curvature". Meaning that the Universe beyond the observable may well be like a flat table top that is expanding outward forever. That does not mean that the Universe is "two-dimensional" but rather that it does not curve in any direction as it expands. To simplify, the Universe as a whole expands "east and west" but does not go up or down to the "north and south". If the Universe was curved, the Universe would either be shaped like a bell, forever heading outward, or would be curved back in on itself ultimately forming a sphere. Instead current measurements indicate the Universe has zero-curvature and thus is shaped like a table top. But these observations are currently being debated among cosmologists, so watch this space (no pun intended)!

If the wider "unobservable Universe" is flat like a table top, then it is also possible that our observable Universe is only one patch on it. Essentially our little sphere is like a coffee cup ring on the table. That little coffee cup ring came out of Guthian Cosmic Inflation approximately 10^{-32} seconds after the Big Bang with its current arrangement of physical forces. It is possible that other regions of space (aka other coffee rings on the table top) did not come out of Guthian Cosmic Inflation at the same time. As such, it is possible that there are other patches of the Universe with completely different physical laws to our own.

In other words, the table top may represent a Multiverse, with each patch having different physical laws and with each patch separated by trillions of light years of inflationary space. In fact, according to Guth's only theory and the idea of "eternal inflation" this idea of a Multiverse isn't even just a possibility, it is implied by the theory. The only thing is that currently we have no direct observable evidence for the Multiverse existing.

Size gets more complicated if we look at the table top model beyond the observable Universe. No precise measurement can be given, because we cannot be sure whether different regions of space stayed in Guthian Cosmic Inflation for longer (and thus expanded faster), or how far from the edges of the Universe observable from Earth there is more stuff. It could be that the "unobservable Universe" does not go much beyond 93 billion light years across, but it is much *more* likely that the Universe beyond our sight stretches much, much further than that. Into the hundreds of billions or even trillions or quadrillions of light years, or more.

Finally, there remains the question of "colour". And this one is entirely dependent on light and human perceptions. If you were to look at the mixture of light from all the stars in the observable Universe blended together, as if you were viewing it from a distance, the colour of our cosmic bubble would be beige. Or as cosmologists have tried to jazz it up by calling it "cosmic latte".

So there you have it. The observable Universe is a beige ball that is 93 billion light years across. The unobservable and unknowable Universe/Multiverse may be quite different, but that will take our efforts in future years to uncover. For now the stage of our narrative is the beige ball we call home.

An Age Before Anyone Knew How to Bang

When it comes to figuring out the Universe, humans are very much in the same position as we were 300,000 years ago: despite advances in science, we are still tasked with looking up into the sky and making sense of the awe-inspiring display of lights above us, only a sliver of those mysteries have been unravelled, and only a small segment of the population claims to halfway understand them. One can only imagine what the first *Homo sapiens* with no scientific methodology to aid them must have thought of the sky at night. A multitude of explanations would have been given for the heavens. Perhaps the stars were ancestors, perhaps the stars were gods. These stories are lost to us. But a most beautiful comparison is derived from the medieval Tatars who roamed the grassy landscapes of Eurasia. As they sat in their camps and looked up at the sky at night, they believed that the cluster of stars that form the Milky Way were the pole to a giant tent, for which the black void was the canopy, and with stars being holes in the tent, letting the light of the heavens twinkle down to Earth.

Slowly, but surely, methodical work and observation began to join speculation and myth. The origin of modern cosmology did not occur overnight. Rather it was a process of thousands of years of accumulating knowledge by generations of innovators, or, *collective learning.*

Ptolemy

We start our story with Claudius Ptolemy (c.90/100-170 AD), a mathematician and astronomer in Roman Egypt. His work on astronomy was considered some of the best even as late as the 1500s CE. That's how much of an impact he had on European and Islamic science. In his *Almagest*, Ptolemy was able to present a model that could predict the movement of the planets. Or tell you where those planets were at some point in the past. The fact that his model's predictions worked out fairly well made him admired for centuries. Ptolemy also preserved the earliest map of the constellations of stars in the sky, making him one of the founders of astronomy and the art of mapping the Universe.

But where did Ptolemy fall short? He thought that the Earth was the centre of the Universe and that the planets, Sun, and stars all revolved around it. The geocentric model created some flaws in Ptolemy's mathematics. So he calculated in that occasionally the planets briefly go "in reverse" or retrograde, just to make the calculations work.

Ptolemy also miscalculated that the visible Universe, in our terms, was about 1/75,000th of a light year, or about 7 "light minutes". That would make the entire Universe smaller than the distance between the Earth and the Sun. Instead of the 93 billion light years we know the visible Universe to be today. He also thought the mere movement of the planets could affect the events of people's lives on Earth or even the health of people who were sick. Got a little bit of a cough? The movements of Mars or Venus might have something to do with it. Ptolemy also mapped the world known to the Romans at the time, depicting a large part of Europe, Africa, and Asia. The Americas were then unknown to the Romans. And Ptolemy estimated the Earth was a lot smaller than it actually is. Still, Ptolemy's geography was also applauded throughout the centuries and, no, he did not believe the Earth was flat (contrary to the old myth about ancient peoples) but knew that it was curved.

Ptolemy was also known for his studies of the movement of light and its different coloured rays. A study that would also be built upon by Isaac Newton and many other scientists. And that is the point. Ptolemy formed much of the scientific bedrock of human collective learning, which was built upon and improved by later generations. Ptolemy is also representative of how humans viewed the Universe in the ancient and medieval periods.

Copernicus

Nicolaus Copernicus (1473-1543 AD) was born roughly 1300 years after the death of Claudius Ptolemy. For over a thousand years Ptolemaic ideas of the Earth being the centre of the Universe had prevailed. Nicolaus Copernicus lent his life's work to the eventual overturning of this view of the Universe.

Copernicus became increasingly skeptical of the flaws in Ptolemy's mathematics. Ptolemy's model for the rotation of the planets around the Earth seemed to fit, but not quite, and the idea that they occasionally went in reverse just seemed strange. It is also fairly clear that Copernicus rejected the idea that the movement of the planets affected people's fates or their medical health. Or at the very least Copernicus showed no interest in studying it.

Copernicus discovered that if you placed the Sun in the centre, instead of the Earth, then you avoided a lot of the flaws and inconsistencies in Ptolemy's model. But Copernicus had to work carefully. At the time, the Catholic Church could be skeptical of anything that departed from established knowledge. If a writer claimed something that ran contrary to church doctrine, especially something as big as how the solar system worked, it could undermine the church's authority. Anything that did that ran very near to heresy.

In 1514, Copernicus wrote *Commentariolus* where he outlined in layman's terms a model for the Sun being the centre of the solar system instead of the Earth. He only made a few copies for his friends. Copernicus did not intend for it to circulate any wider, or it could endanger his life.

However, as the decades went by, Copernicus's ideas gradually circulated amongst Europe's elite. Eventually in 1533 it got as far as Pope Clement VI. But the Pope did not consider it heresy. Far from it. He was intrigued by the idea. Nevertheless, Copernicus's friends could not convince him to publish his ideas. At this point, the Protestant Reformation was in full swing, and there was talk enough of excommunications, persecutions, and heretics. Copernicus seemed hesitant to reveal himself to the full gaze of the public, even if Clement VII thought the ideas were interesting. Moods could change. As it did for later astronomers, to dangerous effect.

In fact, Copernicus would not publish his master work, *De revolutionibus orbium coelestium*, until the year of his death in 1543. While Copernicus' idea of the Earth rotating around the Sun had been thought of for centuries by other scholars, he probably arrived at the conclusion independently. His book was also the first to start the overthrow of Ptolemy's astronomy on the eve of the Scientific Revolution.

Galileo

Galileo Galilei (1564-1642 AD) continued what Copernicus started. The controversy and persecution that Nicolaus Copernicus eluded all his life, hit Galileo hard when he tried to expound a model where the Sun was at the centre of the solar system. That is because by Galileo's time, the heliocentric model had grown from an interesting notion to a "dangerous idea" that threatened the established order.

During his early career, Galileo gained a reputation for inventing an early thermometer, developing very early versions of telescopes, discovering that Jupiter had moons, and writing on the laws of motion. In1609, Galileo got into Copernicus' theory of a heliocentric solar system, which was an area of growing debate. Galileo's intuition led him into accepting the idea that the Earth moved around the Sun, and soon became a staunch advocate. However, he rushed into some inaccurate ideas, like the tides being caused by the Earth's movement as proof, rather than being caused by the Moon.

The fact that Galileo was a strong advocate for Copernicus' ideas alienated many elites and the clergy. The problem was that heliocentricism seemed to contradict some passages in the Bible which imply the Earth is stationary and the Sun moves around it. Without too much tact, Galileo dismissed the idea that the Bible was the authority on science. Word got around about this.

In 1615, Galileo was targeted by the Inquisition. Members of the Italian clergy implied he was a heretic, or a blasphemer, or even a Protestant. Bear in mind that Europe was on the verge of yet another devastating war of religion where millions would perish as Catholics and Protestants tried their best to wipe each other out. These were tense times.

Galileo went to Rome to defend himself, but the clergy were already dead-set against him. The Inquisition denounced heliocentrism and the Pope ordered Galileo to no longer hold those ideas as true. Or to teach or defend them. Such were the times where dangerous ideas could not even be believed, much less by taught or asserted.

Galileo was effectively gagged, Copernicus's work was banned, and so the matter rested. Eventually Galileo was given papal permission to print a book, the *Dialogue*, that presented both geocentric and heliocentric models and not to come down on the side of heliocentrism.

However, in the book Galileo mercilessly lampooned theories that the Earth was the centre of the Universe and mocked those who believed in it. The brutality of the Vatican's response surprised even Galileo. In 1633, Galileo was charged with heresy, threatened with torture, had his book banned, and was placed under house arrest for the remainder of his life.

Galileo's works remained controversial well into the 1700s. But by that time more and more educated people accepted the idea that the Earth revolved around the Sun. By the height of the Enlightenment, it became the dominant view. Nevertheless the papal ban on Galileo's work remained until 1835.

Try as they might, those in charge were not able to suppress the spread of so-called dangerous ideas. Ideas rise and fall by their merits, regardless of whether they are censored. If anything, ideas become all the more tantalising because they are forbidden. Galileo's fiery defense of those ideas landed him in a great deal of trouble. But our understanding of the Universe changed. Suddenly the Earth was not the centre of the Universe, garnished by the orbit of stars and planets. The Earth was just one planet among several, in a cosmos that had become a larger and stranger place.

Newton

Isaac Newton (1643-1727 AD) was from a farming family in a small hamlet in Lincolnshire. He was well educated enough and his family wealthy enough to send him to Cambridge. But only with some supplementary aid and a special arrangement with the university, where Newton had to wait tables and clean the student rooms. Over the following 9 years (including a 2 year hiatus when Cambridge shut down due to the threat of plague) Newton studied the works of the ancients and the great minds of the early Scientific Revolution. This included Copernicus and Galileo.

Newton developed infinitesimal calculus and gradually developed his laws of motion, which are still used in many forms of physics and engineering today. These laws were also the pinnacle of scientific understanding of physics until the 20th century.

Newton's interests extended across the physics of light, the use of lenses, the nature of chemistry, and, of course, mathematics. Newton so impressed people at Cambridge with his work that he was made a professor of mathematics in 1670.

In 1687, Newton published the *Principia Mathematica*. It was the sum of his work on the laws of motion. In particular, it laid forth his explanation of the law of gravitation. It also was one of the first works to use mathematics to underpin these laws. When it came to explaining the movement of planets in the solar system, Newton was revolutionary in boiling it down to a few simple equations. All of it was driven, in his estimation, by a universal force called gravity. Newton had just provided humanity with the key to understanding the Universe. It had a huge influence on how humanity viewed the Universe even in Newton's own time. By 1700, most scientists (or natural philosophers as they were then called) accepted the idea that the Earth revolved around the Sun, and were developing better and better models for how the Universe worked.

Newton also discovered that light falls into a spectrum by shining it through prisms. It looks like a rainbow. This understanding would be developed in later decades and would prove key to the development of the Big Bang Theory. His research into optics came at a price, however. Newton once stuck a small needle in his eye to understand how eyes interacted with light.

Newton was also obsessed with theology, argued bitterly against the existence of Satan and the Trinity, and spent much of his time predicting when the end of the world would occur. Additionally, Newton devoted a great deal of study and experimentation into figuring out how to turn metal into gold. Needless to say, without much success. Newton also took an interest in ancient history and believed in the existence of Atlantis.

Newton was very much a man of his time. Natural philosophy did not have a clear division between the disciplines as modern science does. As a result Newton's interests ranged across a great many subjects, leading to work that was sometimes genius, sometimes strange.

Newton gave the world proof that the heliocentric solar system was the correct model. More significantly, he showed how the entire Universe ran on laws that could be expressed through the highly accurate language of mathematics. His laws of motion opened up the door to accurate prediction and calculation as scientists laboured to figure out how the Universe worked. As a result, the past three centuries since Newton have been a blizzard of highly accurate models and a rapidly increasing understanding of the cosmos.

Before Newton, we had but a tiny glimmer of understanding of how the Universe worked. After Newton, our notions of the cosmos became ironclad with the laws of physics.

Cosmologists Learn How to Bang

With the groundwork laid by hundreds of generations over two thousand years, in a form of collective learning, modern cosmology was ready to spring upon the scene. In the 19th century, Galileo and Copernicus's model for the solar system was widely accepted. As was Newton's theory of gravitation. Yet the scientific community had several shortcomings in knowledge relative to our own. Firstly, they thought that the Milky Way was the entire Universe, and that the distant galaxies that dot the sky outside of our galaxy were just 'nebulae' or stellar clouds, rather than hundreds of billions of galaxies millions of light years from our own. Secondly, there was little to suggest that the Universe was anything but infinite and eternal. That is to say, we had no reason to suspect the Universe had an edge or that it had a start date. Yet as we shall see, a few key discoveries in the 20th century changed all of that.

Leavitt

Henrietta Leavitt (1868-1921 AD) lived at a time when scientists had limited means of figuring out how far away other stars were. Leavitt's contribution was to help map the cosmos and pave the way for the Big Bang theory.

Leavitt was an American astronomer from Massachusetts, born into the family of a rich church minister. She was fortunate enough to attend university, first in Ohio, and later at the women's collegiate at Harvard. Late in her academic career Leavitt developed an interest in astronomy. She then did the first part of a graduate degree, but never completed and instead took a job working for astronomer Edward Charles Pickering. The wages were slim, but Leavitt was able to support herself due to her social position in American society.

During this time an illness was damaging Leavitt's hearing, which became increasingly impaired. This did not impede her ability to do astronomy, and she threw herself furiously into her work. Pickering's all-female team was tasked with going through picture after picture of the constellations, writing down the brightness of various stars. Leavitt was assigned to those stars that seemed to flicker and have their brightness vary at intervals.

The grueling work of looking through hundreds of photographs revealed an intriguing pattern. There was a specific kind of star first discovered in the Cepheus constellation. The star type's brightness varied in a pattern. So-called Cepheid variables were so consistent that Leavitt correctly deduced that a Cepheid variable's period of brightness was determined by its size. This work was hammered home by Leavitt compiling a database of nearly 2000 stars.

Here's the important part. If a star's brightness varied depending on its size, you could calculate how big the star was. From there you could calculate how bright the star would be if you were viewing it in the same solar system, rather than thousands of light years away. Astronomer Ejnar Hertzsprung built on Leavitt's data and figured out you could use this to determine distance. Because a star's light gets dissipated the further it is away from Earth, you could use those calculations to figure out how far away the star actually was. Which Hertzsprung actually did for several stars in the Milky Way galaxy.

A star that shines so predictably made Cepheid variables perfect milestones in the Universe from which astronomers could measure their distance from Earth. The result of Leavitt's work was astronomers could now map distances in the galaxy, and later, the Universe.

Leavitt published her data and discovery between 1908 and 1913, at a time when scientists still thought the Universe was infinite. Leavitt died from cancer in 1921. It was only three years later that Edwin Hubble depended on her work to make some startling discoveries…

Through Henrietta Leavitt's dedication and landmark discovery, our view of the Universe was radically changed. We entered a cosmos where we were one galaxy among hundreds of billions, and where the Universe had a history with a beginning, a middle, and (one day) an end.

Hubble

Edwin Hubble (1889-1953 AD) was born in the United States and went to University of Chicago. Originally distinguishing himself with his athletic prowess, this jock also had a love for science. But keeping his word to his father, Hubble studied law instead.

When his father died in 1913, Hubble taught physics, math, and Spanish at a high school instead of becoming a lawyer. Being a high school teacher didn't stick, however, and Hubble quickly pivoted to a path in graduate school studying astronomy. He was able to finish his PhD by 1917. The Americans entered World War I, in which Hubble served but never saw combat. Then in 1919, Hubble got hired at the Mount Wilson Observatory in California.

The Observatory had one of the largest telescopes in the world at the time. Hubble set about a project mapping the Universe, which people still thought was infinitely large at the time. People also thought the Milky Way was the only galaxy there was, and that other galaxies were just nebulae (essentially "clouds"). Hubble made use of Henrietta Leavitt's Cepheid variable stars to plot the distance of these nebulae. He discovered that they were millions of light years away, way too distant to be just clouds in the Milky Way. Instead they were galaxies with billions of stars of their own. Hubble first published his findings in 1924, to the great shock and amazement of the scientific community. Our Universe suddenly got a whole lot bigger.

More astounding discoveries were to come. But this will require a little backstory. Isaac Newton had experimented with glass prisms, which revealed white light could be split into a rainbow-like spectrum. Joseph von Fraunhofer did the same thing in the early 19th century with a spectroscope. Fraunhofer also discovered that between these different rays of light there were "absorption lines". In the late 19th century Vesto Slipher discovered these lines were either "redshifted" or "blueshifted" depending on where the object that emitted the light was moving. If the star was moving away, its light was "redshifted", if it was moving toward us, its light was "blueshifted".

This is because light works much like sound in a Doppler Effect. When an ambulance moves toward you, the sound waves get squished in between, raising the tone of the siren. When the ambulance moves away, the sound waves get stretched out, lowering the tone. The same thing happens with light, except squished lightwaves appear blue and stretched lightwaves appear red.

Hubble built upon all this collective learning. He observed at Mount Wilson that the most distant galaxies were all redshifted. This meant that all the furthest galaxies from the Milky Way were moving further and further away. Hubble published his observations in 1929. The trajectory of most galaxies in the Universe implied something significant. It implied that the Universe was expanding.

Galaxies aren't like ships. They don't have a captain that can suddenly change course. So logically, through the blind march of physics, it would imply that far enough back in time, those galaxies were all crushed together. This dove-tailed nicely with a 1927 hypothesis by George Lemaitre, who stated that the Universe could have begun as a primeval atom.

Now Hubble's conclusions weren't universally accepted at first. Even Albert Einstein rejected it, in what he would later call his "biggest blunder". However, there were a few predictions that could be made in the Big Bang scenario that, if proven true, would confirm the theory.

Proof for the Big Bang Theory

I. **Nothing is older than the age of the Universe.** If the Universe has a starting point 10-15 billion years ago, and we'd be able to find nothing older than 10-15 billion years old. We've now narrowed the age of the Universe down to 13.8 billion years, and indeed we can find nothing older than that. If we find an object that is older than 13.8 billion years, like the Methuselah star might be, we would need to adjust our estimated age of the Universe by a few million years. But we certainly cannot find any outliers that are 20 billion or 100 billion years old, which we would expect to find if the Universe was ageless and eternal.

II. **The Majority of Atoms in the Universe are Hydrogen and Helium.** If the Universe began as a tiny speck 13.8 billion years ago, then all that pressure must have made it immensely hot. During the first few years of expansion, it would still be hot enough to fuse together atoms of hydrogen and helium. These are the simplest elements. But the Big Bang model implies that the Universe would have expanded and cooled much too rapidly for the rest of the elements to form. Perhaps a few smidges of lithium and beryllium, the next elements along the line of the periodic table, but not much of them. The rest of the elements would have to wait for another heat source to form (i.e. stars). So all of those elements would be dwarfed by the amount of hydrogen and helium out there. Indeed, today we know that the majority of the Universe is 74% hydrogen and 24% helium, and the rest of the elements in the periodic table make up the remaining 2%. This is precisely what we would expect to see if the Big Bang model were true.

III. **Scientists Predicted then Discovered Cosmic Background Radiation.** In the Big Bang model, the early Universe would have been so hot and thick that not even light could travel freely. Physicist George Gamow in the 1940s calculated that approximately 380,000 years after the Big Bang, the Universe would have expanded enough for a brilliant flash of light to erupt as it was finally able to move. They predicted we should see it everywhere in the Universe. Then in 1964, Arno Penzias and Robert Wilson discovered the remnants of this flash of light. They were working on an ultra-sensitive radio antenna for the Bell Telephone company and trying to get rid of all the static. No matter where they pointed the antenna, they still picked up a signal. Hilariously, they at one point though it might be the heat from pigeon shit causing the static. It wasn't until they contacted Robert Dicke, a physicist at Princeton, that they realised this was the long sought after relic of the Big Bang that was released 380,000 years after the start of the Universe. This piece of evidence is so decisive because it was predicted than observed, and still can be directly observed to this day. A small percentage of any static picked up by a radio is the sound of the Universe being born.

IV. **Hubble's Redshift.** As mentioned in the previous section, the fact that the majority of galaxies are "redshifted" indicates that the Universe is expanding. Those galaxies are "moving away from us" because the space between us is expanding. To visualise this, take a deflated balloon and draw a bunch of galaxies on it. Then inflate the balloon. As the metaphor for the Universe inflates, the space between galaxies increases and so does the distance between them. Work this all the way back, and we arrive at a point where space is infinitesimal and all the stuff in all the galaxies would be crushed on top of each other. This is the Big Bang singularity.

Problems with the Big Bang Theory

It is a long-standing tradition in Big History to close the section discussing the Big Bang with a brief profile of some of the problems with the Big Bang theory.

This is not because the Big Bang theory is "just a theory" as I've seen in several dozen student essays over the years. In common parlance, a theory can mean a "guess" or "hypothesis". As in, "I have a theory that if she ever met me Margot Robbie would fall madly in love with me." This is a way of differentiating it from we would commonly call "fact". There is an important distinction with how the term "theory" is used in science. In science, you have a "hypothesis" which is then tested by experimentation and observation. Once you have enough data and proof to back up your "hypothesis" it can be classified as a "theory". The wider scientific community with whom you are in competition will then try to tear strips off your theory. If your theory is accurate, then all this accomplishes is a greater mountain of evidence in favour of your theory.

The scientific use of the term "theory" means an evidence-based model of reality that is widely accepted by the scientific community. In common parlance, this is akin to what we would describe as a "fact". But in the scientific community it is rarely referred to as such. In science, we can never be sure that our model of reality is the most accurate possible, so we try to avoid describing things as 100% true or an undeniable fact. Even if our models are correct and heading in the right direction, there will always be another scientist who comes up with a more accurate version of it a few years later. In science, we never have absolute truth but increasingly accurate models of reality.

The idea that I could fly if I flapped my wings really hard is an untested hypothesis. The idea that if I jumped off a cliff I would fall to my death is derived from a model put forward by the theory of gravity. One would never jump off a cliff because gravity is "just a theory". That is the distinction.

With all that said, it is clear that our current Big Bang model will be refined and expanded in coming years. It is not 100% accurate and does not explain a great many things. And no, the fact it cannot satisfactorily answer "what happened before" is not one of them, since to discuss a "before" the existence of spacetime would be even more inaccurate a model.

I. **It is possible that the age of the Universe is slightly older than our current estimates.** Hubble's original estimate for the age of the Universe placed its age between 10 and 20 billion years. For much of the 20th century, the estimate was very vague between 10 and 15 billion years. Much of the work done presently on refining the age of the Universe is done by observing Cosmic Background Radiation – a snapshot of the early Universe when light was first released approximately 380,000 years after the Big Bang. In 2003, the Wilkinson Microwave Anisotropy Probe (WMAP) closely examined Cosmic Background Radiation and established that the age of the Universe was 13.77 billion years old, with some margin for error. Then in 2013, the Planck Satellite refined this age to 13.82 billion years old, with again some margin for error. In 2019, analysis of the age of an ancient star just 190 light years from Earth found the age to be between 13.66 and 14.46 billion years old. While the youngest age of the star might just fit within the current estimated age of the Universe, something like 14.46 billion years old would mean the Universe is much older and that the estimates of both WMAP and Planck are inaccurate. Along with the age published in this book, and every other piece of Big History material. I am not looking forward to it!

II. **We cannot see any further back than 380,000 years after the Big Bang.** Cosmic Background Radiation is great scientific evidence because it can be directly observed. But it is difficult to see much further back in cosmic history beyond when light could move freely. Prior to the 380,000 year mark, we rely heavily on simulations and calculations based on what we know of physics. CBR is predicted by the Big Bang theory, which means much of what we promulgate happened before then is probably accurate. Furthermore, the prevalence of hydrogen and helium in the Universe means that Big Bang chemistry is probably right. However, things get more uncertain the further back in time we go because, as mentioned earlier, the earlier we go the more messed up physics becomes. This is particularly true of when the Universe was still extremely small at the quantum scale in the first split second after the Big Bang. And that is one reason why quantum physics is so important to modern cosmology. The Large Hadron Collider which runs underneath France and Switzerland is a particle accelerator that allows us to smash together bits of matter into their most fundamental particles, and this allows us to simulate the conditions of the early Universe. However the LHC is only really able to push back the clock to around 10^{-10} seconds after the Big Bang. In order to simulate how the Universe might have existed at 10^{-43} seconds after the Big Bang, you would need a particle accelerator that went 4.2 light years to Proxima Centurai (the nearest solar system to our own) and back. At least with current technology. Another method that may allow us to see back into the early Universe is "gravitation lensing" which essentially is the method of seeing waves in spacetime caused by major events in the past. This method of astronomy is just starting to bear fruit and is much vaunted to uncover a great many mysteries in the future.

III. **There are a lot of subatomic particles that are difficult to detect and we haven't discovered.** In 2012, the Large Hadron Collider made history by discovering the Higgs Boson. This was a particle first proposed by Peter Higgs in 1964 which made particle physics work coherently in various calculations. People didn't know it existed but presumed it existed for decades simply because of how beautifully it worked. Finally we had observation evidence of its existence decades later. This is, however, just the tip of the iceberg. There are numerous other subatomic particles that likely exist that we have not yet detected. The existence of many of these are implied by various working models of physics. For instance, the "supersymmetry" model pioneered by the likes of Sylvester James Gates Jr. implies that for every known subatomic particle, there is likely an opposite version. Whatever these particles are, they would have had a role in Big Bang cosmology.

IV. We still haven't got an accurate model which combines the fundamental forces of physics. There is also the problem that gravity is not fully understood and isn't even accounted for by the Standard Model of Physics. Still less is there much hope at present of finding a Grand Unified Theory that combines gravity, electromagnetism, and the strong and weak nuclear forces into one elegant theory that explains the fundamental forces of our Universe.

V. We have no frigging idea what Dark Matter is. Much publicized and mysterious, the prevalence of Dark Matter in our Universe will require some sort of revision to the Big Bang theory – once we figure out what the hell it is. We can detect it, but we don't understand it. Dark Matter was discovered when physicists realised that their models for the rotation of galaxies don't work. Galaxies are spinning too fast, than if they were just made up of normal matter like hydrogen and helium. In fact the stars seem to have a much heavier mass – approximately 20 times heavier than the models predict. So that leaves two possibilities: that all our theories for gravity are completely inferior and inaccurate (which may be true), or that there is something exerting a force on these galaxies that we cannot detect. If the latter, there is a bunch of matter in the Universe which forms about 25% of the total mass of the cosmos, but it does not reflect light nor does it interact with normal matter. In fact, there would be a bunch of Dark Matter in the room with you right now, it is just that the atoms of your body do not interact with them. One possible theory is Dark Matter is made up of "Weakly Interacting Massive Particles" (WIMPs) that exist in the Universe but don't interact with normal matter unless at large scales like galaxies.

VI. We have no frigging idea what Dark Energy is. Meanwhile, studies of redshifted galaxies imply that the expansion of the Universe is accelerating. Type Ia supernovas occur in pretty much any galaxy, so make a great "standard candles" to measure the expansion of the Universe, and these confirm the observation. The problem is we would not expect to see the expansion of the Universe accelerate in our current models. So either our current Big Bang models are terrible, or else there is an unseen force that forms about 70% of the Universe that is provoking accelerated expansion.

If Dark Matter and Dark Energy form about 95% of the Universe, then the stuff we can see like stars, planets, and life, only constitute about 5% of it. Currently, Big Bang cosmology explains with reasonable accuracy where this 5% came from. But that's a heck of a lot that isn't covered. Combined together, these problems imply there will be major revisions to our story of the beginning of things. You can fully expect future editions of this book to look profoundly different.

The Unifying Theme of Big History

So what about that 5% of stuff that we can explain? There's a unifying theme that ties its 13.8 billion year story together. That unifying theme is the "increase of complexity" from the Big Bang to today. From stars to salamanders to submarines. But what is complexity?

Complexity can be defined as anything with an ordered structure that is created and sustained by flows of energy. An atom of hydrogen is a form of complexity, with one proton and one electron forming its structure. A molecule of water is a form of complexity, with its structure involving two hydrogen and one oxygen atoms. A human brain is a form of complexity, as is a toaster that humans invented. The society of trade and information exchange that houses 7.5 billion humans is one of the most complex structures of all. The only way these things differ is their level of complexity. The more intricate the structure, the more energy flow it uses, the more complex it is.

There are two approaches to discussing complexity:

1. **By reference to its structural intricacy.** This is the less precise, shorthand way of describing complexity. Essentially it boils down to how many "puzzle pieces" the form of complexity has, and how tangled up together they are. A complex object tends to have an intricate patchwork of diverse building blocks and connections. The number of things in the structure is not the measure – but the variety of things in the structure and how closely together they are bound. A star has a lot of hydrogen atoms in it, but it is not particularly complex, it is just a big disordered lump of them. Contrast that to a dog, which has a much more complex tangle of chemicals, DNA, liver cells, brain cells, blood vessels, and highly complex respiratory, circulatory, and nervous systems. Move a few thousand atoms of hydrogen from the core of the Sun to its surface, and it keeps running as if nothing happened. Replace a dog's brain cells with its liver cells, and the dog is not going to be chasing birds anymore. While this form of discussing complexity is less precise, it is more intuitive and more commonly used to quickly gauge the increase of complexity in Big History.

2. **By reference to its energy flows.** This is the more precise, quantifiable way of describing complexity. One requires energy flows to create, sustain, and increase all forms of complexity. You need energy flows to fuse new atoms in a star, energy flows to keep a pigeon from starving and dying, energy flows to keep a car engine running, and so on. Even objects that don't have a great deal of energy flow, like a napkin sitting on a table, nevertheless required a huge amount of energy flow to be manufactured in a factory in the first place. And without future energy flows, the napkin is liable to decay and be destroyed. When it comes to a star, it contains a lot of energy overall but not a huge *density* of energy flow across its vast structure to keep going.

Meanwhile a significantly smaller structure like a dog requires many thousands of times denser energy flows to sustain its complexity, to keep barking and chasing birds. It is why a dog needs to constantly find and eat food to live for another week, while a star does not need float around the cosmos munching down more hydrogen clouds but nevertheless lives for a few billion years. Complexity in this sense can be measured by the amount of energy flowing through a certain amount of mass in a certain amount of time, or roughly 2 erg/g/s for the Sun and approximately 20,000 erg/g/s for a dog. "Free energy rate density" is harder to wrap your head around, but it is the cause of all forms of complexity in the Universe, whereas structural intricacy is only the symptom.

System Complexity (ranked from lowest to highest)	Free Energy Rate Density (Averages)
The Milky Way	0.1
The Sun	2
A Red Giant Star near to supernova	120
Algae (photosynthesizing)	900
Cold-Blooded Reptiles	3000
Fish and Amphibians	4000
Multi-celled plants (e.g. trees)	5000-10,000
Warm-Blooded Mammals (average)	20,000
Australopithecines	22,000
Human Foragers (Africa)	40,000
Agricultural Society (average consumption)	100,000
19th century textile machine	100,000
Industrial Society (average)	500,000
A Model-T Automobile (c.1900)	1,000,000
A Vacuum Cleaner (present)	1,800,000
Modern Society (average consumption)	2,000,000
Average Airplane	10,000,000
A Jet Engine (F-117 Nighthawk)	50,000,000

As you can see above, there are some important trends in energy flows that mirror the course of Big History. Either the more structurally intricate a form of complexity is, the greater the amount of free energy rate density it requires and/or the further down the line of cosmic evolution we go, the greater the amount required. The simplest and oldest complexity in the Universe like a star doesn't require that much energy, whereas the products of billions of years of biological evolution, and thousands of years of collective learning and invention require a great deal of energy. While space is vast and mostly cold and quiet, there are tiny pockets of complexity like ours where energy flows are getting more intense, and the structures they produce more complex.

Emergent Properties

With every increase of complexity, there comes an increase in what a form of complexity "can do". A simple cloud of hydrogen can't do much but float in space. A simple star can fuse atoms and generate heat, but still just floats in space. A DNA strand made up of billions of interlocking chemicals is able to self-replicate and evolve. A brain is capable of calculating, generating consciousness, and adapting to its environment in a single lifetime. A jet engine that brains invented is capable of soaring through the sky faster than the speed of sound. These sudden flashes of new behaviour are referred to as "emergent properties" or new phenomena that arise as a result of a new arrangement of "puzzle pieces". At every new stage of Big History, there is an emergence of new phenomena where complexity can do things that were previously impossible.

Take two simple examples. Firstly, water is wet. Made of two parts hydrogen and one part oxygen, neither hydrogen nor oxygen alone are "wet". Neither are a universal solvent, neither can be used as an environment in which to create life. The second example is salt. Salt is one part sodium, one part chloride. But you would not want to put sodium alone on your French fries. Not unless you wanted to burn off your tongue. The emergent property of sodium chloride is "saltiness" which is good for preserving meats, enhancing taste of food, and in small amounts part of a healthy diet. Salt also played a tremendously important role in ancient, medieval, and modern history. For example, Gandhi's "March to the Sea" which emboldened the Indian independence movement was protesting the British imperial tax on salt. In a roundabout way, and with many other component parts, even that was an "emergent property". In Big History, everything is connected.

Emergent properties are greater than the sum of their parts. Not only is a structure like a brain a complex mixture of living cells and connections, with more stars than there are in the galaxy, the brain spawns consciousness. The consciousness is the emergent property that goes beyond just an intricately woven lump of flesh. And that consciousness can yield all sorts of further emergent properties like agriculture, inventions, airplanes, and artificial intelligence. Since emergent properties add a new variable to the mix that didn't exist previously, they usually instigate further changes in Big History. And so the cycle continues for 13.8 billion years.

The Birth and Death of Complexity

Birth

There is a reason why complexity is mentioned in the same chapter as the Big Bang. During Guthian Cosmic Inflation, approximately 10^{-35} to 10^{-32} seconds after the Big Bang, when the Universe grew from the quantum scale to the Newtonian scale, there were slight ripples in spacetime (quantum fluctuations) that created clumps of energy unequally distributed across the cosmos. You can see these clumps recorded in a "snapshot" in Cosmic Background Radiation 380,000 years after the Big Bang. As a result of these clumps, energy congealed into the first particles of matter. If it weren't for this unequal distribution of energy, complexity would not exist.

In order for complexity to exist, you need energy flows to create and sustain it. In order to have energy flow, *you need to have flow from where there is more energy to where there is less energy*. And if all energy were equally distributed at the start of the Universe, there would be no need for energy to move. Nothing would have changed. Nothing would have happened. And the Universe would have been born "dead". No complexity, just a blank cosmos of thinly distributed radiation from start to finish. In a nutshell, there would have been no history.

Instead, the first clumps of unequally distributed matter and energy created the first stars. These stars created all the other naturally occurring elements in the periodic table. These elements came together to form molecules and planets. On one such planet, Earth, more of these molecules came together to create life. And some of that life evolved consciousness and the ability to invent stuff and continually tinker and improve upon those inventions.

All the while, from stars, to life, to technology, we required more energy flows to create, sustain, and increase complexity. And so tiny pockets of the cosmos have been getting more complex over 13.8 billion years. That is the unifying theme of Big History. The Big Bang created unequal amounts of energy across the cosmos, then for 13.8 billion years energy has been evening itself out again, and as a result of that we had energy flow and all the wondrous things that emerge from that.

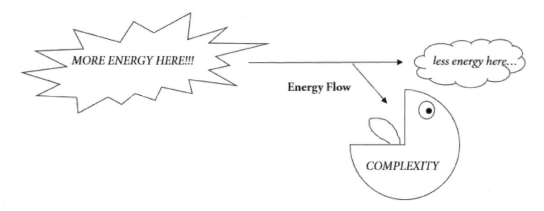

Death

There is some irony, however, to the increase of complexity in Big History. The reason why energy flows from stars, to feed plants, which nourish animals, to give energy to brains in the human web, is because of the 2nd Law of Thermodynamics. That law compels energy to want to "even itself out" and it can only do that by flowing from where there is more energy to where there is less. In the short term, this energy flow can create complexity. But ultimately that energy flow evens itself out so there can be no more energy flow, which kills complexity.

It is only in tiny pockets of the Universe where there has been an unequal distribution of energy that complexity continues to rise. The rest of the Universe, about 99.9999999999999% of space is already dead, unable to generate more complexity. This is why the clumping of energy in the first split second of the Universe was so crucial to our existence.

In those tiny pockets of complexity, we continue to use up energy flows and actually speed up the process by which energy becomes evenly distributed and the ultimate death of complexity. And the more complex something is, the more energy flow it requires, and the faster it uses up energy flows. For example, a dog requires more energy flow per day than a tiny colony of bacteria. And a car requires so much energy that it needs to use the stockpiled energy of millions of years of organic material crushed underground and transformed into oil and petrol. Dogs poop, cars spew smoke out of their exhaust pipes, and some of the energy cannot be used again. Ever. So we are actually speeding up the end of complexity in the Universe!

So in reality, complexity is just a by-product of a longer tale in Big History where the Universe is trying to revert back to a realm of equally distributed energy. The endgame of which is a Universe that is nothing more than a weak orb of radiation. A quiet cosmos with no history, no change, and no complexity. This is a state referred to as Heat Death. In the long term, "winter is coming" to wipe us all out.

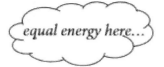  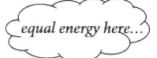

But Heat Death would take trillions upon quadrillions upon quintillions of years to finally use up all the energy flows in the Universe. Yet complexity is at risk all the time. Stars use up all their fuel and flicker out. Animals die either naturally, violently, through starvation, or by mass extinction. Ancient civilisations collapse into ruins and ashes. The ruins of ancient Egypt, the skeleton of a dinosaur, the remnants of a dead star, all have something in common. They are forms of complexity that no longer have as much energy flow. And their structures have decayed as a result. Now very frequently, the ashes of dead stars can form new stars, the fossils of dead animals can be converted into energy, and the resources of ancient civilisations can be repurposed to build new ones. That is another lesson of complexity: only death can pay for life, and only life creates death.

Every stage of increasing complexity in Big History comes at a price, and very frequently comes at the cost of destruction and, where there is consciousness, suffering. And that is something that we should bear in mind before we think complexity is completely synonymous with "progress" or get too complacent thinking we are at the peak of the process of rising complexity in the Universe – especially considering the challenges awaiting us in the 21st century.

Essay Writing Exercise

In a Big History course, you will also receive a lot of training about how to write academic essays. These skills are particularly important if you are going to try to make clear and cohesive arguments about things as massive as the story of 13.8 billion years. This chapter's exercise is on *thesis statements*. A thesis statement should sum up the argument of your paper. The best thesis statements are clearly worded (even bluntly worded) and let the reader know what to expect from the body of your essay and your research. It is best to drop the thesis statement right off the bat, in the first few sentences of the introduction without too much preamble. In fact, it is easy to get carried away in a history paper writing far too much preamble, so it might be best to make your thesis statement the very first sentence of your introduction.

Usually the thesis statement is responding to an essay question provided to you. For this chapter, try writing a thesis statement to the following question:

Why is the Big Bang theory the most widely accepted explanation for the origin of the Universe?

Remember, the thesis statement should *directly* answer the essay question. It should contain the central message that the remaining paragraphs of your essay would strive to support by evidence and argumentation. Consult the evidence provided for the Big Bang in this chapter because you may wish to list it in your thesis statement.

The thesis statement should have a "concentrated" amount of strength. It may be the most powerful sentence in your entire essay. Imagine someone sidled up to you in the pub and asked you this question. You probably wouldn't get to answer it in 2000 words. So what would your one sentence response be to sum up your answer? That is the same spirit in which you should think of your thesis statements.

Further reading

Alvarez, Walter. A Most Improbable Journey: A Big History of Our Planet and Ourselves. New York: W.W. Norton, 2016.

Blackwell, Richard J. Behind the Scenes at Galileo's Trial. Notre Dame: University of Notre Dame Press, 2006.

Brown, Cynthia. Big History: From the Big Bang to the Present. New York and London: The New Press, 2007.

Bryson, Bill. A Short History of Nearly Everything. New York: Broadway Books, 2003.

Chaisson, Eric. Epic of Evolution: Seven Ages of the Cosmos. New York: Columbia University press, 2006.

Chaisson, Eric J. Cosmic Evolution: The Rise of Complexity in Nature. Cambridge: Harvard University Press, 2001.

Christian, David. "The Evolutionary Epic and the Chronometric Revolution" in Genet et al. (eds) The Evolutionary Epic: Science's Story and Humanity's Response. Santa Margarita: Collingswood Foundation Press, 2009.

Christian, David. Maps of Time: An Introduction to Big History. Berkeley: University of California Press, 2004.

Christian. David. Origin Story: A Big History of Everything. London: Allen Lane, 2018.

Christian, David and Cynthia Stokes Brown and Craig Benjamin. Big History: Between Nothing and Everything. New York: McGraw Hill, 2014.

Christianson, Gale. Edwin Hubble: Mariner of the Nebulae. Chicago: University of Chicago Press, 1996.

Copernicus, Nicolaus. "De hypothesibus motuum coelestium a se constitutis commentariolus" in Three Copernican Treatises. 2nd ed. trans. Edward Rosen. New York: Dover Publications, 2004.

Copernicus, Nicolaus. De revolutionibus orbium coelestium. ed. trans. Edward Rosen. Baltimore: Johns Hopkins University Press, 1992.

Ellis, Walter. Ptolemy of Egypt. London: Routledge, 1994.

Galilei, Galileo. Dialogue Concerning Two Chief World Systems: Ptolemaic and Copernician. trans. Stillman Drake. ed. Stephen Jay Gould. Berkeley: University of California Press, 2001.

Gingerich, Owen. Copernicus: A Very Short Introduction. Oxford: Oxford University Press, 2016.

Hawking, Stephen. A Brief History of Time: From the Big Bang to Black Holes. New York: Bantam, 1988.

Hawking, Stephen and Leonard Mlodinow, The Grand Design. New York: Bantam Books, 2010.

Hawking, Stephen. The Universe in a Nutshell. New York: Bantam, 2001.

Heilbron, John. Galileo. Oxford: Oxford University Press, 2010.

Hubble, Edwin. "A Relation between Distance and Radial Velocity among Extra-Galactic Nebulae" Proceedings of the National Academy of Sciences vol. 15, no. 3 (1929) pg. 168-173.

Johnson, George. Miss Leavitt's Stars: The Untold Story of the Woman Who Discovered How to Measure the Universe. New York: W.W. Norton, 2005.

Krauss, Lawrence. A Universe from Nothing: Why There is Something Rather than Nothing. New York: Simon and Schuster, 2012.

Leavitt, Henrietta S. "1777 Variables in the Magellanic Clouds" Annals of Harvard College Observatory vol. 60, no. 4 (1908) pg. 87-108.

Newton, Isaac. The Mathematical Principles of Natural Philosophy. trans. Andrew Motte. London: Benjamin Motte, 1729.

Ptolemy, Claudius. Ptolemy's Almagest. trans and ed. G. Toomer. Princeton: Princeton University Press, 1998.

Ptolemy, Claudius. Ptolemy's Geography: An Annotated Translation of the Theoretical Chapters. trans and eds J. Berggren and Alexander Jones. Princeton: Princeton University Press, 2000.

Sharratt, Michael. Galileo: Decisive Innovator. Cambridge: Cambridge University Press, 1994.

Weinberg, Steven. The First Three Minutes: A Modern View of the Origin of the Universe. New York: Basic Books, 1977.

Westfall, Richard. The Life of Isaac Newton. Cambridge: Cambridge University Press, 1993.

CHAPTER 2

GALAXIES, STARS, AND SOLAR SYSTEMS

Or,

THE O.G. STARS:

LIKE A HOLLYWOOD ACTOR

BUT WITH 1,989,000,000,000,000,000,000,000,000

MORE KILOGRAMS OF ULTRA HOT PLASMA

AND A TRILLION TIMES

GREATER USEFULNESS TO SOCIETY

Stars are, like, so HAWT! lol :)

> **Threshold 2: The First Stars – 13.7 billion years ago**
>
> - *Wherein the first hydrogen and helium atoms got sucked together into clouds.*
> - *Those clouds became so tightly packed that the atoms fused together.*
> - *Fusion created big-ass nuclear explosions and birthed the first stars.*
> - *Stars are terrifying H-bombs in the sky exploding for millions or billions of years.*

Timeline

- **Inequalities in Matter and Energy Form (10^{-36} to 10^{-32} seconds after the Big Bang):** Quantum fluctuations as the Universe grows from the quantum scale to about the size of a grapefruit create tiny inequalities in energy that would eventually create the first stars. Without this happening, no stars could have formed. Big History books would then be rather short, not that there actually would have been books or anyone to read them.

- **Release of Cosmic Background Radiation (380,000 years after the Big Bang):** Light is finally able to travel freely through the Universe unleashing a huge flash that we can still detect today. We can see the little inequalities that bred stars in the hot and cold spots of CBR. At the same time, hydrogen and helium nuclei were able to capture electrons, creating the hydrogen and helium gas that would "soon" fuel stars.

- **Formation of the First Stars (50 to 100 million years after the Big Bang):** Gravity sucks hydrogen and helium gas together into increasingly dense clouds. Eventually the pressure at the core of these clouds becomes so intense that hydrogen atoms are "smushed" together, and their nuclei "fuse" together. Nuclear fusion lets off a huge burst of energy and suddenly the cloud is transformed into a gigantic fireball generating heat and throwing it out into the Universe as energy flows. Fusion continues as long as stars have gas to guzzle.

- **Formation of the Milky Way (13.7 to 10 billion years ago):** Groups of stars attracted to each other by gravity cluster together in groups. These groups then "merge" with each other to create even larger groups. And over a few billion years the mergers continue until the Milky Way galaxy is formed. The same process occurs to form the 400 billion other known galaxies in the Universe.

The Fire-Soaked Origins of Complexity

So hopefully after reading Chapter 1 a few times and perhaps banging your head up against a conveniently placed wall, you've gotten to grips with the Big Bang and the big beige cosmic orb that we call home. From this point forward, the narrative grows increasingly familiar. Which is exactly what you'd expect to see as we move through space and time and slowly zero in on where we are in the here and now.

After the release of Cosmic Background Radiation 380,000 years after the Big Bang, light was able to move freely through the Universe and hydrogen and helium were able to capture electrons becoming gas. The Universe continued to expand and cool, at this point being roughly 3000 Kelvin. It would continue to cool to just a few fractions above Absolute Zero. The vast majority of space from this point forward remained simple and cold. It was only in tiny pockets that where inequalities in matter and energy reigned that things began to heat up.

For millions of years, enormous clouds of hydrogen and helium floated through the ever-expanding cosmos. There was not much else amongst the gloom and the Universe seemed pretty homogenous. Dull, dead, and without much change or history. Unless you would find the history of a hydrogen cloud floating through deep space to be riveting reading. No doubt there is someone out there who would.

The Intervention of Gravity

Then gravity got to work. It is worthwhile for some readers to review exactly what the heck gravity is. Gravity is one of the four fundamental forces of our Universe which became coherent just a split second after the Big Bang (the other three are electromagnetism, the strong nuclear force, and the weak nuclear force). Gravity essentially is the force that attracts all matter and energy toward each other. Which is why gravity was so crucial for continuing the survival of those tiny inequalities that first emerged after the Big Bang.

The modern theory of gravity was first expressed by Isaac Newton in the *Principia Mathematica* (1687) where he displayed calculations proving that gravity is what drew objects with mass to the Earth (such as falling apples though this story about Newton may be apocryphal) and what kept the planets orbiting the Sun with its tremendous mass enacting a gravitational pull despite the long distances between it and the planets. In 1915, Albert Einstein improved upon Newton's theory by introducing the concept of "general relativity". Rather than a "force" attracting objects together, this theory boils down to the idea that an object like the Sun "bends" spacetime around it. The curvature of spacetime thus causes nearby objects to drift toward it. This curvature of spacetime can move not only matter, but can even bend rays of light.

For our purposes, it is simply enough to understand gravity as a force that pulls things together. So don't worry if the idea of "bending spacetime" messes with your head. Essentially, the thing about gravity is it grows stronger the closer something is, and grows weaker the greater the distance between objects. It is why all the planets are not all immediately sucked into the Sun, or why all the stars in the galaxy are not immediately sucked together into one inferno. So thankfully, gravity grows weak over distances!

What all this means for our story is that locally, clouds of hydrogen and helium became increasingly attracted to each other. The more hydrogen and helium got sucked together, the more mass it had, and the greater attraction it wielded, sucking in even more clouds of hydrogen and helium. But because gravity weakens over long distances, this process happened in pockets of the cosmos, rather than sucking all the hydrogen and helium into the same place. And thanks to the continued expansion of the Universe, giant clumps of hydrogen and helium that would one day form galaxies grew more and more distant from each other.

Nuclear Fusion & the Birth of Stars

And so the Universe was transformed from tiny pockets of *slightly* more matter and energy into greedy areas which sucked up all the matter and energy in their neighbourhoods. Instead of hydrogen clouds spread over millions of light years, these clouds got packed into a few hundred thousand light years (which is roughly the size of an average galaxy). At billions of points in one of these gigantic clouds, things began to heat up. That is because with increasing pressure, comes increased heat. Just like at the ultra-hot singularity of the Big Bang, or the heated up centre of the Earth. Temperatures in the core of these clouds began to rise, and pockets of the Universe which had long since cooled began to heat up again.

Heat caused the hydrogen and helium atoms in the core of these clouds to start moving faster and bouncing off of each other. Their electron shells at first repelled them from each other. But as heat and speed increased, these atoms began to smash together with increasing violence. When heat increased to roughly 10 million degrees Celsius (about 25,000 times the temperature of a hot summer's day in Sydney, though when I'm walking to the shops it feels about the same), the atoms of hydrogen began smashing together so hard that it overcame the repulsion of the electron shells, which were stripped away, and the nuclei of hydrogen fused together into new helium atoms. For the first time since the first three minutes after the Big Bang, some new elements were being created. This process is known as nuclear fusion, or stellar nucleosynthesis (stella = star, and synthesis = bringing things together).

Now, in Chapter 1 we discussed how matter is really just a more congealed form of energy. The first tiny particles of matter congealed from energy roughly a split second after the Big Bang. We know that they are basically the same thing because particles of matter are converted into energy all the time! Try throwing another log on the fire, or eating a hamburger, and you'll get the idea.

This idea was epitomised by Albert Einstein with the equation $E=mc^2$. And this may be the first time it is actually relevant for you to know exactly what that means. When matter is converted into energy, the amount of energy released (E) is equal to its mass (m) multiplied by the speed of light or roughly 300,000km/second (c) squared (multiplied by itself). So even a tiny amount of matter (like a few hydrogen atoms colliding) can great a massive burst of energy. And when you consider just how many atoms of hydrogen were in these gigantic clouds, those explosions were quite staggering. And there was so much hydrogen for fuel that these explosions continued for millions and millions of years. Thus the stars emerged from these gigantic clouds of gas.

Billions of stars were born, and not a single one of them needed to land a leading part in a superhero movie or to mysteriously "leak" a sex-tape. Though if a big ball of hydrogen gas had done either, it would probably have looked hilarious. Please someone do a movie about "star-man" in a little spandex uniform trying to stop a bank robbery by smashing into the planet the bank is on.

At any rate, fusion continued to happen at the core of these stars. New helium atoms were fused from hydrogen. Energy released from the explosion was beamed out into the Universe. Meanwhile the dense ball of fusing hydrogen in the cores stopped the stars from collapsing completely. Gravity shaped the stars into the roundish balls of fire that we see in the night's sky. If there is enough mass in a celestial object, gravity tends to round its shape.

It probably doesn't come as a surprise that the energy flows beamed out by stars into the rest of the Universe are useful for other forms of complexity. Nearly everything on Earth, for instance, owes its continued complexity to the existence of the Sun. Whether it be the plants that collect solar energy, the animals that eat the plants, the humans that eat the plants and animals, and the humans the burn the coal and oil from animals that died millions of years ago:

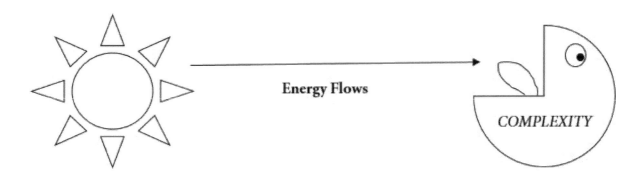

The first generation of stars that emerged 50 million to 100 million years after the Big Bang were *huge* by virtue of the fresh supply of gas in their neighbourhoods. And there weren't yet heavier elements to dilute the gas and keep their sizes in check. As such the first stars would have been 100 or even 1000 times as massive as our Sun. Different stars would form into clusters that were 30 to 300 light years across. Slowly, these clusters merged with each other into larger structures held together by gravity. Over 3 billion years, these mergers continued in our region of space to create the Milky Way, which is roughly 100,000 light years across. And in a few billion years our galaxy will merge with Andromeda to create an even larger galactic structure.

Stars live as long as there is fuel in their cores to keep up their energy flows which maintain their structure. These huge stars would have existed for a few million years before running out of fuel and collapsing in on themselves in gigantic supernova explosions. The remnants of these gigantic stars would then be gathered together by gravity again to form "second generation stars" and the cycle would continue.

Exploring the Universe

We now arrive at a point in our history where the wider Universe is growing increasingly familiar to us. A vast cosmic bubble filled with the blackness of space, dotted by other stars and galaxies. But what kind of galaxies are there out there?

1. **Spiral Galaxies.** These are the most common kind of galaxies out there in the Universe, forming approximately 60% of the *estimated* 400 billion of them. A spiral galaxy is characterised by a huge bulge in the centre, where there are billions of densely packed stars. Some of these stars are extremely old. The centre of a galaxy definitely isn't friendly for complexity because there are so many supernovas happening all the time as massive stars explode right next to each other. This would wipe out any life that tried to form there. Not that there is much chance of planets forming in the galaxy's core either, since the dust required to form a planet is highly likely to get sucked back into one of the nearby stars, or else get blown out into the wider galaxy.

Outside the core of the galaxy are the spiral arms. These take the shape of a flat disk around the galaxy's core. The spiral arms are created by the centrifugal force created as the galaxy spins. Stars are thrown out from the core, but is still held within its orbit. It is here on the arms that there is the possibility for dust to gather into planets, and for life to potentially form without supernovas going off as frequently to wipe it out. Spiral galaxies tend to hold young stars, and have abundant star formation, which is good for complexity.

Famous examples of spiral galaxies are the Milky Way, Andromeda, the Pinwheel Galaxy, the Phantom Galaxy, and the Whirlpool Galaxy.

2. **Lenticular Galaxies.** These are very similar to spiral galaxies in that they have a bulge, disk, but no spiral arms. This is because most of the matter in their disks have already coalesced into stars. They have very little star formation. They amount to roughly 15% of all the galaxies in the observable Universe. They are a halfway category between spiral galaxies and elliptical galaxies (see below). One famous lenticular galaxy is the Sombrero Galaxy, which looks oddly like its namesake.

3. **Elliptical Galaxies.** These are huge diffused galaxies that have no bulge at their centre, a more equal distribution of very old stars, and with very little new star formation. Consider these effectively "dead" or "dying" as far as generating new complexity is concerned. Elliptical galaxies form about 5% of all the galaxies in the Universe. They can be round globs or long and thin. Some of them can be quite small, even smaller than the Milky Way, but some of them are

giant galaxies. For instance, with its radio jets Hercules A is approximately 1.5 million light years from end to end.

4. Irregular Galaxies. This category holds the remaining 20% of galaxies that we can see in the night's sky. They are so-called because odd occurrences in their formation (of various kinds) messed up their shape from being easily categorised into spiral, lenticular, or elliptical. One way a galaxy could have its shape messed up would be the passage of a nearby galaxy that exerted a gravitational force and deformed its more classical structure. This is more than possible considering most irregular galaxies are quite small. Famous examples of irregular galaxies are the Large Magellanic Cloud which is nearby to the Milky Way and Hoag's Object, a bizarre little "ring galaxy" that is several million light years away.

The Hubble Deep Field surveys have yielded an estimate that there are approximately 200-400 billion galaxies in the known Universe. This has been the prevailing estimate since the 1990s. However, more recent estimates have placed the number as high as 1 trillion or even 10 trillion galaxies in the known Universe. A number that is considerably higher that increases the odds that complex life might be evolving somewhere else out there. Remember, each galaxy can contain millions, billions, or even trillions of stars.

In one region of the Universe, however, there seems to be an absence of stars and galaxies. This great void is reflected in Cosmic Background Radiation, and is known as the "cold spot". One hypothesis for why the cold spot formed in the early Universe was because it was a place of contact during Guthian Cosmic Inflation between our Universe and another universe. Then our two universes raced rapidly away from each other. That other universe would have physical laws different to our own, but if it also had light like ours, that light might travel the fast distances of inflationary space and reach our Universe in about 3 trillion years.

There is no way to prove that there is a Multiverse out there, though the mathematics of Guthian Cosmic Inflation implies there is. Our patch of the Universe may have come out of Guthian Cosmic Inflation at 10^{-32} seconds, other regions of space would not have, and indeed there may be areas of space that are eternally in Guthian Cosmic Inflation. New patches would come out of our inflation just like ours did. Each of them would have physical properties different to our own. And, it probably goes without saying, with different big histories to our own.

The number of possible sets of physical laws that could possibly exist is currently estimated to be 10^{500} a ridiculously large number. And the number of different universes that could emerge based on those sets of physical laws approaches the infinite. But if a Multiverse exists, bear in mind that out there somewhere is a person a lot like you who is reading this book at the exact same time, but whose skin looks more like pizza. And there is another Universe where no books, humans, or complexity exist at all.

Check out the Stars! (no sexy Instagram pics, sorry)

Meanwhile, our Universe was gradually filling up with stars. These came in various types and sizes. The first thing to note about all trillions upon trillions upon trillions of stars out there is that they can be divided into three main populations.

- **Population III:** The oldest stars in the Universe, and the first to form approximately 50 to 100 million years after the Big Bang. These stars have virtually no metal content because they formed in an age when the only elements in the Universe were hydrogen, helium, and a pinch of lithium and beryllium. As far as we know, they are all dead because they would have been huge and consequently have blown up billions of years ago. Additionally, astronomers have yet to detect and confirm the light of any very distant Population III stars by looking into the furthest reaches of the Universe.

- **Population II:** These are fairly old stars that formed from the remnants of the exploded first stars. We know this because they have some metallic content, which means that the iron that fused together in the core of the largest oldest stars, along with the many different types of metals created in their supernova, all gathered when the second generation of stars formed. While the largest Population II stars have long since died, there are still many of these stars detectable in the Universe. There are even some within the Milky Way.

- **Population I:** These are relatively younger stars that possess a great deal of metal, gathered from the numerous supernova from older stars flung out in the first few billion years of the Universe. These stars can either be second or third generation stars. If they are third generation, it is because they are the recipient of a long line of stellar nucleosynthesis. If they are second generation, it is because they have formed in areas where there have been numerous supernova. Our Sun is assumed to be either a second or third generation star. Population I stars also are more likely to have planets orbiting them, because of the abundance of heavier elements that would have formed a ring of dust orbiting them, which eventually would have accreted into planets. It is the Population I stars that are the best bet for complexity.

Star size and surface temperature also determine how they are classified and how they die. Stars that are over 8 times the size of the Sun go supernova. Stars that are smaller than that die without exploding and creating those heavier metals. The largest stars burn for only a few million years, larger stars might burn for a few hundred million years, and smaller stars might burn for a few billion years, and the smallest slowest burning stars can burn for a potential 100 billion to several trillion years.

In the Universe, 90% of stars fit into what the Hertzprung-Russell Diagram calls "main sequence stars". The model was conceived in 1910 by Ejnar Hertzprung and Henry Russell in an effort to categorise the great variety of stars out there. Within the main sequence stars there are:

- Red Dwarfs: Tiny slow burning stars that are between 5 and 50% the mass of the Sun. Their surface temperature is relatively cool. They make up roughly 70% of the stars in the Universe. They have a lifespan of billions, hundreds of billions, or perhaps even trillions of years, depending on how small they are. They don't fuse elements very high up the periodic table and so aren't as useful for generating complexity, however if a chemical rich planet orbits close enough to them it could be enough for them to support life.

- Yellow Dwarfs: The category that includes our Sun. They are always roughly the mass of our Sun, perhaps a little below or a little above. They make up roughly 10% of the stars in the Universe. They live for roughly 4 to 15 billion years, depending on their size. When they are dying they turn into Red Giants and engulf the planets closest to them (which is unfortunate for Earth). There after they gradually shrink back, become white dwarfs, and then flicker out. These stars also don't generate very many heavy elements in their life cycles (they don't go supernova and rarely get as far as iron) but are, as you might have guessed, ideal for supporting life for planets within their habitable zone.

- Orange Dwarfs: These are usually slightly smaller to one half the mass of our Sun. They represent another 10% of the stars in the Universe and live for approximately 15 to 30 billion years. This longer life cycle is a good increase of the odds for life on any habitable planets that may surround them, and they emit less deadly solar radiation than something like our Sun, which means that such a planet would not require as much protection from an ozone layer.

- Blue Stars: These hefty fellows are usually somewhere between 5 and 100 times the mass of our Sun and burn very hot indeed. These are the rarest of the main sequence stars, comprising a tiny fraction of 1% of the stars in our Universe. They are the only main sequence stars that are large enough to go supernova, which means that they are quite good for spreading the 92 naturally occurring elements across the galaxy to nourish complexity in other solar systems, once the materials arrive there.

Then we arrive at stars that are outside of the "main sequence":

- **White Dwarfs:** The most common of all stars outside the main sequence, which comprise roughly 5% of the stars in the Universe. These are essentially dead stars which no longer have fusion in their cores. They are essentially the skulls and bones of stellar complexity. This is what happens to smaller stars like the Sun, which do not go supernova when they die. They last for a million to a few billion years before finally yielding to darkness.
- **Red Giants:** The intermediate stage of a dying star, when its fuel stars to get used up and it stars fusing heavier and heavier elements. When that happens, the star "bloats up" like a dead cow in a wet field and grows to considerable sizes. They last for a few hundred million to billion years before shrinking into the White Dwarfs described above.
- **Red Supergiants:** These stars are also exhausting their fuel, and have bloated up to immense sizes, and may begin fusing iron in their cores. They are also large enough to explode in supernovas, which can pepper the nearby regions of a galaxy with heavier elements that may be used for complexity. Usually Red Supergiants last only a few million years before exploding.
- **Blue Giants:** These highly irregular stars burn extremely hot and tend to be large and capable of fusing heavier elements in their cores. They tend to live for only 10 to 100 million years before dying in brilliant explosions. They are not common, comprising only a tiny fraction of a fraction of a percent of the stars in the Universe.
- **Blue Supergiants:** Even rarer, larger, and hotter burning stars than Blue Giants, they tend to use up all their fuel extremely early in their life-cycles and live only a few million years before blowing up.
- **Neutron Stars:** These are the dead remnants of stars that have gone supernova. They are extremely dense and heavy stars that have very little luminosity. They are also extremely tiny, being only a few dozen kilometres across. All that mass in such a small space makes them very vulnerable to turning into black holes. When two smash together they create heavier elements.

When a star goes supernova, sometimes the remnant left behind is so dense that gravity sucks it in on itself. When that occurs it forms a black hole. These are essentially piles of matter with such a high mass that spacetime pulls in on itself, and no light can escape from it. While they might just be sloppy piles of matter, there are some hypotheses that predict that black holes warp space time to such an extent that they may have bizarre properties, like breaking down the laws of physics, making the passage of time seem incoherent, and perhaps even linking to other dimensions or universes. Essentially if you want to promulgate a far-fetched sounding theory in cosmology, you need look no further than black holes.

Finally, there are the brown dwarfs, which are wannabe stars that didn't quite grow big enough to start the process of nuclear fusion of hydrogen in their cores. Lots of hydrogen and helium gas got sucked into the brown dwarf's gravitation pull. But no fusion of hydrogen. This differentiates it from a gas giant like Jupiter, which has a lot of hydrogen and helium gas, but formed as part of the process of planetary accretion in our solar system, and is about 1/65th the mass necessary to form a brown dwarf.

Yet it is a terrifying thought to think what horrors would have been unleashed had Jupiter somehow had enough mass to become a second star in our solar system! As it was, Jupiter was massive enough to mess up the accretion of its nearby neighbour, and so instead of a planet existing between Jupiter and Mars we just have the planetary shrapnel of the Asteroid Belt. But it was not massive enough to become a star, nor even a brown dwarf.

Elementary, my dear Mendeleev! *puffs on pipe*

> **Threshold 3: New Chemical Elements – 13.6 billion years ago**
>
> - *Wherein the first stars fuse all their hydrogen and helium into heavier elements.*
> - *They start fusing carbon, nitrogen, oxygen, and continue to the 26th element, iron.*
> - *The stars collapse and blow up creating heavy elements like gold, silver, and uranium.*
> - *The 92 elements of the periodic table are created, boring everyone who isn't into chemistry.*

Timeline

- **The First Hydrogen and Helium Nuclei Form (3 minutes after the Big Bang):** The first major particles to emerge a split second after the Big Bang were quarks, which are the ingredients of protons and neutrons. Over the course of three minutes, the Universe expanded and cooled sufficiently to allow those protons and neutrons to form – they were the nuclei of hydrogen and helium atoms. These are the first complex structures of Big History, in the sense that they are made up of smaller ingredients (quarks) in the same way a wall is made up of bricks or a politician's career is made up of lies.

- **Hydrogen and Helium Nuclei Capture Electrons (380,000 years after the Big Bang):** For a length of time roughly equivalent to the period in which *Homo sapiens* has existed, radiation was too overwhelming in the Universe for the nuclei to capture electrons. The heat was still making the particles zip around too fast, smashing off each other, but without enough heat for them to fuse into heavier elements (hence the predominance of hydrogen and helium in the Universe). But by 380,000 years after the Big Bang, the Universe had cooled to the point that matter became dominant over radiation and hydrogen and helium snagged electrons, becoming "fully fledged atoms". Here was a slightly more complex structure, with the emergent properties that hydrogen and helium still possess today.

- **Formation of the First Stars (50 to 100 million years after the Big Bang):** As explained in the previous threshold section, stars formed as gravity sucked all that hydrogen and helium gas together into increasingly dense pockets. Eventually those pockets grew so dense again that the hydrogen atoms fused into helium (a slightly more complex atom with more component parts) and stars flared into life. As the giant first generation stars used up all the hydrogen they could fuse in their cores, they began fusing helium into stuff like carbon, nitrogen, oxygen, fluorine, neon, sodium, magnesium, aluminium, silicon, phosphorus, sulfur, chlorine, argon, potassium, calcium, scandium, titanium, vanadium, chromium, manganese, and finally iron inside their bellies. Each atom with more component parts than the last.

- **First Stars Blow Up (200 million to 1 billion years after the Big Bang):** Even the biggest stars cannot fuse iron into the next heaviest element (cobalt) which would prolong the star's life. And without any further fusion, the star rapidly collapses, letting off a huge explosion that can be seen thousands or even millions of light years away. It is in this huge explosion that even hotter temperatures are reached, which can fuse more elements. In 2019, there were clear indications that the neutron stars left over from supernovas can actually create heavier elements as well when two neutron stars smash together. These processes enable the fusion of the rest of the 92 naturally occurring elements on the periodic table. That's an additional 66, which would be too obnoxious to list here. But, to hell with it, here's some of the most familiar ones: copper, arsenic, silver, tin, iodine, tungsten, platinum, gold, mercury, lead, thorium, and uranium. Each of them have more protons and neutrons and electrons in their structure. And with each addition, they have new emergent properties (unless you think a chunk of copper is the same as a chunk of gold or uranium!). Because these heavier elements require not simply fusion in the core of a star, but explosions from the largest and rarest stars, these elements are the rarest on Earth and in the rest of the Universe (hence why something like gold is highly sought after by humans and used as a form of currency).

- **Supernova Kick-starts Birth of Solar System (4.6 billion years ago):** Just prior to the formation of the Sun from a nebular cloud, there was a supernova from a larger star approximately 1 light year away from where our solar system now is. This triggered the formation of the Sun from the cloud, and also peppered the solar system with heavier elements, all of which would one day be utilised to form higher complexity. Fortunately, there are no longer any stars about to go supernova that close to our solar system now! Naturally, there would also have been heavier elements in the nebula from which the Sun formed, which is why your body in all probability has atoms created from at least two different star lifecycles, and probably separated by billions of years.

The Death of Stars (not involving drugs, cars, or auto-erotic asphyxiation)

All complexity in the Universe is created, sustained, and increased by energy flows. Stars are no exception. It is the fusing of hydrogen atoms that create stars in the first place, and those same energy flows over millions or billions of years are what sustain its structure from collapsing. And as stars exhaust all their hydrogen, they begin fusing heavier elements, which further increases their complexity. But eventually all this must come to an end, just like any other form of complexity in the Universe.

Once a star is born, the explosions from nuclear fusion in its core throws matter and energy outward, preventing gravity from crushing the star completely and causing it to collapse. Otherwise you'd expect something as massive as a star to be crushed by gravity almost immediately. This is what happens to create white dwarfs, neutron stars, and black holes when those fusion explosions stop.

Why do the fusion reactions stop? Because stars can starve to death just like an animal, or to put it another way, they run out of fuel just like a car. Without energy flows, complexity cannot survive. It usually takes millions or billions of years for stars to fuse all their hydrogen into helium, but the supply isn't infinite. What happens next depends on the star's size.

If the star is relatively small, like a red dwarf, it fuses all of its hydrogen into helium, but it is too small to heat up enough to be able to fuse helium atoms into heavier elements. So all that happens is fusion reactions stop, and gravity crushes the star into a white dwarf. This can still emit light and heat, but only as a remnant of the fusion reactions that had happened long ago. From there, the dwarf will continue to shine for a few billion years, thereafter becoming a "black dwarf", which is essentially a skeletal corpse of a star that emits neither heat nor light. The older the Universe gets, the more its landscape will be scattered with these ruins.

Stars that are slightly larger, like yellow and orange dwarfs, also wind up as white dwarfs. But after a slight deviation in destiny. Stars 40% to 8 times the size of our Sun can achieve temperatures hot enough to fuse helium into heavier elements. During this phase, the star bloats up to become a red giant (which is bad news for any closely orbiting planets like Mercury, Venus, Earth, and Mars!). These stars can produce elements as high as iron in their bellies. The amount of each heavier element also depends upon its size. Then, higher temperatures eluding them allow fusion of iron, the fusion reactions stop and the stars become white dwarfs, then black dwarfs.

But if the star is over 8 times the size of our Sun, it has a different fate – that of the dreaded, catastrophic, but ultimately fertile, supernova. Once a large star has fused to the point of a red giant phase and then has filled up its belly with iron, fusion will also stop.

Gravity gets to work crushing the star. But the immense mass of these stars causes a collapse with such force that it causes an explosion in reaction to the collapse. Within this explosion, the heavier elements between cobalt and uranium form, and are blown rapidly out into the rest of the galaxy. The remnants of the star are crushed by gravity into an extremely small and dense neutron star, which are dead stars only a few dozen kilometres across. And if the star was large enough, then that remaining mass is crushed into a space even denser than a neutron star. Instead that pile of matter is so massive that it bends spacetime and creates a black hole, from which light cannot escape, and which may contort spacetime and the laws of physics beyond recognition, just like the singularity did at the moment of the Big Bang.

It should be noted that with each fusion of heavier elements, the star becomes not only more structurally complex by holding a greater diversity of building blocks, its energy flows also increase. Thus by both conceptions of complexity, a star's complexity increases over its lifetime before it runs out of energy flows and dies. In a way, a star is a microcosm of the Universe, in that its higher complexity is actually an offshoot of its slow winding path toward entropy and death. Or put another way, the star's higher complexity comes as a result of the dissipation of energy, just like the complexity of the Universe overall does. Only death can pay for life, only life can create death.

Professor Mendeleev Predicts the Unknown

Russian scientist Dmitri Ivanovich Mendeleev (1834-1907 AD) unravelled how the building blocks of the Universe behaved and interacted. He predicted the existence of elements and their traits even before they were discovered! And Mendeleev left humanity with a vital piece of knowledge – the periodic table, which still forms the backbone of chemistry today.

Since ancient times, we'd known about elements such as gold, silver, tin, copper, lead, and mercury. Then in Hamburg in 1669, Hennig Brand discovered phosphorus. Over the next two centuries, more elements were discovered. Scientists put the elements on a list, ordered by how much each element weighed – their atomic mass. But from the lightest to the heaviest, there was no clear pattern that governed their properties. The light ones were different from each other, and the heavy ones were different from each other. This was a puzzle.

In 1817, German chemist Johannes Dobereiner noticed that the elements in that list followed patterns. Elements with similar properties appeared in starts and jumps down the list. Calcium has similar traits to strontium and barium despite their having very different weights. The pattern down the list was periodic (defined as "appearing or occurring at intervals"). By 1860, about 56 elements had been discovered. In 1862 French geologist, de Chancourtois tried to show the periodic pattern in the atomic list. In 1864 John Newlands an English chemist figured out that similar traits occurred at periodic intervals of eight.

But the pattern of similar traits occurring periodically every eight elements was not perfect. It failed the further you went down the old list. Was the periodic similarity of elemental traits in the early part of the periodic table just a coincidence?

Enter Dmitri Ivanovich Mendeleev! He was born to a family in Siberia an academic family that had fallen on hard times. His father, Ivan, was an academic who died when Dimitri was 13. This left Dmitri's mother, Maria, to support her large number of children. She came from the merchant class and was able to reopen an old glass factory, but it burned down a year later.

Dmitri attended school in Siberia and showed a lot of potential. So when Dmitri was 15, his mother saddled up a horse and they rode hundreds and hundreds of miles across Siberia and through the Ural Mountains to Moscow where Maria pleaded with the university to let Dmitri study. They rejected him. So Maria and Dmitri rode all the way from Moscow to the university in St. Petersburg, his father's old university, where Dmitri was accepted. Maria died shortly after her mission was complete.

Dmitri graduated, caught tuberculosis, and had to go to the Crimea to recuperate. While Dmitri was there, he gained a Masters degree at a school in Simferopol. Dmitri returned to St. Petersburg in 1857 to start his career as a scientist.

Ten years passed as Dmitri Mendeleev worked as a teacher and researcher. Mendeleev was familiar with the periodic nature of the traits of elements. Yet he was distressed by the fact the pattern was imperfect. While preparing a new textbook in 1867, Mendeleev concluded that the reason why the pattern was not perfect is because there were elements that had not been discovered yet! He inserted gaps in his periodic table where the missing elements would be. He even predicted what the traits of those missing elements would be.

Mendeleev published and presented his theory on numerous occasions over the years, but many of his fellow chemists remained skeptical. Then in 1875 French chemist Paul Emile Lecoq de Boisbaudran discovered Gallium – a soft metal that melted at low temperatures – exactly on the periodic table where Mendeleev predicted it would be. And Gallium possessed many of the traits Mendeleev predicted.

However, Lecoq de Boisbaudran measured the density of Gallium to be lighter than Mendeleev had predicted. And so, without even seeing Gallium before, Mendeleev wrote him and told him that his measurements were incorrect. Lecoq de Boisbaudran measured it again, and Mendeleev's prediction was 100% accurate. Such was the power of Mendeleev's periodic table!

Over the next 30 years, Mendeleev's predictions were proven right again and again as new elements were discovered. Mendeleev's periodic table spread across the world and became the standard model for scientists. Meanwhile, Mendeleev was given many awards and honours for his work. He remained at the University of St. Petersburg until 1890 and held a job at the Bureau of Weights and Measures from 1893 until his death from illness in 1907.

By the time of his death, Mendeleev's periodic table had enabled countless discoveries in chemistry in a magnificent example of collective learning. And he had so changed the world of chemistry that in 1955 a newly discovered radioactive metallic element was named "Mendelevium" after him.

Stars with "Chemistry" (oof, what a terrible pun, I should be "pun"-ished)

The periodic table currently holds 118 elements, with more hypothetical elements that have not been created yet. While 92 elements are found naturally around the Universe, the remaining elements do not live for very long before decaying because they are so intricate in structure and complex. Any of the higher elements that form in nature would almost immediately degenerate into lower forms. That said, higher elements have been created in human laboratories, the most recent one being #118, Oganesson, created by a Russian-American team of boffins in 2002.

The number of protons in an atom corresponds to its atomic number. So hydrogen has one proton, and uranium has 92. Thus in the most fundamental of ways, heavier atoms are more structurally complex. The number of neutrons and electrons in an atom also increases the higher up the periodic table you go, but the number of these can vary depending on their isotope and ion status. Different numbers of neutrons determine isotopes and electrons determine whether the atom is an ion respectively. Change the number of protons, however, and you change the type of atom. Whether an atom becomes a type of isotope or ion depends on what happens to it during its lifetime. If that is starting to get a bit too granular for the sciencephobic amongst you, rest assured that is about as deep as we have to go to understand Big History.

The upshot is this. Complexity rose within stars as they went through their lifecycles. Then they died and flung those elements out into the Universe again. They would form the building blocks for further complexity. An almost innumerable amount of combinations of chemicals. To date, there are an estimated 60-100 million chemicals out there. A chemical is built upon a combination of elements strung into a higher structure: a *molecule*. This can create a liquid structure like H_2O (two hydrogen atoms and one oxygen atom to make water), or it create a mineral structure like SiO_2 (one silicon and two oxygen to make quartz, the most common mineral on Earth), or it can create a manmade structure like C_2H_4 (two carbon, four hydrogen to make polyethylene, the world's most common plastic).

Then there's more complex chemicals like organic proteins which are immense tangles of thousands of atoms, like the protein dubbed "Titin", the chemical formula of which is $C_{169723}H_{270464}N_{45688}O_{52243}S_{912}$ and which gives your muscles their elasticity. The technical name of this chemical is roughly 190,000 letters long and takes somewhere between 3 to 4 hours to fully read out loud.

Such is the immense scope for complexity once elements start forming into molecules! Same goes for the chemical formulas for the bases of DNA (adenine $C_{10}H_{12}O_5N_5P$, guanine $C_{10}H_{12}O_6N_5P$, cytosine $C_9H_{12}O_6N_3P$, and thymine $C_{10}H_{13}O_7N_2P$) which encode genetic traits, and allow organic material to self-replicate, evolve, and become "alive".

The Sun and 8 Planets, because Pluto is a loser and can't sit with us

> **Threshold 4: The Solar System – 4.567 billion years ago**
>
> - *Wherein the Sun forms and greedily sucks in 99% of the matter in the solar system.*
> - *The remaining 1% forms a ring of dust around the Sun over a light year wide.*
> - *Rings of that dust accrete into planets, dwarf planets, asteroids, and comets.*
> - *In one such orbit, the Earth forms from a series of terrifying collisions.*

Timeline

- **Formation of the Sun (4.567 billion years ago):** Triggered by a supernova about 1 light year from our current solar system, which seeded the region with even more heavier elements, our Sun emerged from a solar nebula. Due to the Sun's massive gravitational pull, the overwhelming majority of matter in the solar system was sucked into the Sun. The remaining 1% formed a disk of dust around the Sun around a lightyear wide, in side of which there were about 60 different chemical molecules formed from elements. The Sun's first fusion ignitions blast the majority of hydrogen and helium to the outer solar system, with what are called T- Tauri Winds. These create the division between the rocky and gassy planets. Slowly over a few million years dust accreted into rocks, rocks into planetesimals, and planetesimals into the eight planets, creating over 250 chemical molecules. Failed planet formation thrown off by Jupiter's gravity form the asteroid belt. Further out in the Kuiper Belt and the Oort Cloud planetary shrapnel exists as planetesimals, asteroids, and comets that are extremely distant but still held in thrall by the Sun's gravitational pull.
- **Formation of the Earth (4.54 billion years ago):** Earth accretes from the tremendous impact of planetesimals, and grows so massive that the core melts from the pressure setting off differentiation, where the heaviest elements sank to the core, except for rare traces that were trapped in the Earth's crust. Thanks to T-Tauri winds, Earth's chemical composition is much more diverse than the gas giants, proving fertile ground for rising complexity. The number of natural chemical combinations increased to over 1500. The early Earth, however, was still molten and extremely inhospitable for life.
- **Formation of the Moon (4.51 billion years ago):** An estimated 30 million years later, a final planetesimal called 'Theia' by scientists smashed into Earth in a cataclysmic event that sent shards of both planets, about 1.2% of Earth's current mass, back into orbit. These shards also accreted and became Earth's unusually sized Moon.

In the Name of the Father, the Sun, and Holy Crap an Asteroid is Coming!!!

In the first chapter of this book, we discussed how radiometric dating made Big History possible. This is quite true concerning the unravelling of the mystery of the origins of the solar system. Radiometric dating, again, monitors the decay of certain elements to establish highly accurate ages. While one can never predict exactly when one atom will decay, we can predict with startling accuracy how quickly half a sample can decay, coining the term "half-life". Different elements have different half-lives, which provides a range of different date ranges for radiometric dating. Uranium-238 has a half-life of 4.5 billion years, potassium-40 has a half-life of 1.3 billion years, all the way down to carbon-14 which has a half-life of 5,730 years. By capturing asteroids called chrondites that likely existed from the start of the solar system, we've been able to extract isotopes and establish the Sun is 4.567 billion years old.

Looking at the way those elements formed in the asteroids also tell us the conditions in which the Sun formed – whether it was a cold and gradual accumulation of gas or whether it was born in the firestorm of a stellar nebula. It appears that our Sun formed in the latter. Roughly 5 billion years ago, a stellar nebula formed in our area of the galaxy. This cloud would have been "second" or "third" generation, meaning that it already would have contained all 92 naturally occurring elements. A supernova approximately a light year away would have peppered the nebula with even more heavy elements.

The supernova flung more material into our solar nebula, increasing its mass, and causing gravity to rapidly collapse the cloud. This created fusion in the centre and the Sun began to flare into life. The gravitational pull of the Sun would have sucked in quite a bit of matter in the solar system, an estimated 99%. Further away from the Sun, to the tune of 57 million kilometres (where Mercury now is) to nearly a light year away (where the Oort Cloud now is) gravity's pull was weaker. This remaining 1% of cosmic dust didn't get pulled into the Sun but was still forced to orbit it. The dust formed into a flat rotating disk, much in the same way the rings of Saturn orbit that planet but on a much larger scale.

The earliest fusion blasts of the young Sun are called T-Tauri winds. These blasts of energy have the effect of carrying matter outward into the outer solar system. The most important effect was that the majority of hydrogen and helium were blasted out. Meanwhile in the regions closest to the Sun, there was a much greater proportion of silicates and iron compared to hydrogen and helium. The upshot of this is that the planets that formed closest to the Sun were small and rocky (Mercury, Venus, Earth, and Mars) and the planets that formed further outward had a lot more matter and were quite gassy (Jupiter, Saturn, Uranus, and Neptune).

But for now, in the early solar system these materials remained as small dust particles, still yet to accrete into planets.

Making Planets

The flat disk of dust orbiting the Sun avoids being sucked into it because of "centrifugal force". This is the momentum that causes the disk to spin in circles around the Sun. An appropriate comparison is a marble in a funnel. If you were to shoot the marble directly toward the hole in the centre, it would fall through relatively quickly. However, if you shoot the marble to trace around the sides, it travels all the way around the funnel, delaying the time it falls through the centre. The key difference with the solar system are the vast distances involved. Millions upon millions of kilometres that keeps the marble circling the funnel component but delays by eons the possibility of a planet "falling in". The disk orbits the Sun and might drift slightly in its direction, but is in no immediate danger of falling in, and will actually continue spinning until the death of the Sun.

The disk spins around the Sun and then static electricity manages to clump some of the dust in one orbital "track" together in a process called "accretion". In each and every orbital track where there is now a planet, the dust would rapidly become the size of rocks, and then the size of boulders, and then the size of mountains. Within 15,000 years, the solar system was full of millions of objects that were over 10 kilometres across. Then the collisions became decidedly less gentle. The smashing together of these objects generated heat, which pasted the two colliding objects together. After about 10 million years, the solar system was full of about 30 or so proto-planets, each roughly the size of the Moon or Mars. The exception would be the asteroid belt, where the gravitational pull of nearby Jupiter prevented numerous asteroids from colliding with each other and accreting. Within the short space of a few million years, these proto-planets also collided in terrifying crashes forming just 8 planets in each orbital track.

- Mercury: Approximately 3 light minutes from the Sun (a light minute is the amount of time it takes for light to travel from the Sun to the planet) the planet is about 5% the size of Earth. It suffers from extreme temperatures, with -170 degrees Celsius at night to 427 degrees Celsius during the day. Problem is, because Mercury is tidally locked with the Sun, one side of the planet faces the Sun for much longer than Earth, and therefore a single day or night can last months. In terms of chemical composition, it is very similar to Earth in terms of a predominance of metals and silicates, but with the surface conditions being brutal, being too small for much of an atmosphere, and with no liquid water being able to survive on the planet's surface it makes for a very poor candidate for complexity.

- **Venus:** Approximately 6 light minutes from the Sun, the planet is a very similar size to that of Earth. It also could have potentially have been habitable despite being closer to the Sun. Except for the planets horrific thick atmosphere which is overwhelmingly carbon dioxide. This traps a lot of heat from the Sun and makes surface temperatures so hot that it could melt lead. Venus was victim of a runaway greenhouse effect much more powerful than anything experienced on Earth. And this unfortunately also makes Venus an unlikely candidate for further complexity.

- **Earth:** Approximately 8 light minutes from the Sun, in terms of distance it is definitely within the habitable zone from the Sun. Naturally we know that conditions were right for higher complexity. But that certainly would not have been the case in the early solar system, where the surface of the Earth was still molten and it also possessed a fairly carbon dioxide heavy atmosphere. There are perhaps separate timelines in reality out there were it was Venus which spawned life, Earth that experienced a runaway greenhouse effect, or where both Venus and Earth became habitable and humans began laying plans to travel to Venus to explore and create settlements.

- **Mars:** Approximately 12.5 light minutes from the Sun, it exists on the very edge of the habitable zone in terms of distance from the Sun. It is roughly 10% the size of Earth which means it cannot capture much of an atmosphere, with it being quite thin – roughly 1% as thick as Earth's. This also means that it cannot maintain water in liquid form. Most of it is encased in ice, which makes life less likely. That said it is possible that small microbial life existed (or once existed) on Mars. If it were to be discovered, we'd encounter for the first time life that evolved separately from the ancestors of life on Earth, and would in turn teach us many things about the different conditions in which life could arise.

- **Jupiter:** Approximately 43 light minutes from the Sun, it is 99% hydrogen and helium. It is 11 times the diameter of Earth and roughly 320 times Earth's mass. Jupiter wasn't large enough to become a brown dwarf star, but is about as big as a planet can get before it starts verging on star-status. Obviously, Jupiter is unlikely to be able to support life, due to its violent weather patterns, chemical composition, and the amount of pressure that gravity would exert on the planet's surface. In fact it is hypothesized underneath all that thick cloud that the surface may be composed of a lot of "solid hydrogen", or that is hydrogen gas that is so compressed that it takes on a solid appearance. The moons of Jupiter possess less gravity, and given the right chemical composition could have formed life (so long as it could have stood the extreme cold) with the leader of the pack being Europa, with its frozen ice and oxygen atmosphere. But in all likelihood life never formed there – at least not in the same way it formed on Earth.

- **Saturn:** Approximately 78 light minutes from the Sun, Saturn is the second gas giant that is 9 times the size of Earth and has 95 times its mass. It similarly would not make a very good prospect for life. Saturn has, however, managed to capture 62 moons and a ring of ice and rock which is its signature (Jupiter also has a ring but it is much smaller). The most likely candidate for life is Titan, but it would have to have evolved very differently from life on Earth. The temperatures are so cold that water is always frozen solid and methane gas takes the form of liquid. So if life evolved in methane oceans, it would have to have a completely different form of respiration than the life that evolved in Earth's oceans.

- **Uranus:** Approximately 155 light minutes (or 2.5 light hours) from the Sun, Uranus is another gas giant about whom many grade schoolers (and a few adults) have made jokes. Uranus is four times the size of Earth (giggle) and it is the coldest in the solar system. Wind speeds are horrific, and in many ways the atmosphere and immense pressure resemble the other gas giants, making higher complexity extremely unlikely to have arisen there.

- **Neptune:** Approximately 4 light hours from the Sun, Neptune is the farthest planet in the solar system. It is so distant that it takes 165 years to make one orbit of the Sun. Much like Uranus, Neptune is extremely cold with a hydrogen and helium atmosphere and a core made up mostly of ice and rock.

The Moon

During the final phases of accretion in Earth's orbital track, there were two proto-planets. Earth and another about the size of Mars dubbed "Theia". About 4.51 billion years ago, these two proto-planets collided. The Earth absorbed much of the material from this other planet into its own makeup, but about 1.2% of the matter drifted into Earth's orbit as shrapnel from the collision. The process of accretion took hold again, and these shards then accreted into what is today the Moon. The evidence for this is that the Moon has neither much of an atmosphere (it is not big enough) nor plate tectonics. Which means much of the surface of the Moon is as it was 4.51 billion years ago. By collecting rocks from the Moon, scientists have been able to fairly accurately age it, and also see that the chemical composition is precisely what we would expect to see if a collision occurred in such a way at this time in Earth's history.

Poor Old Pluto

The result of these tremendous collisions was the formation of the eight rocky and gassy planets. Pluto used to be considered a planet since its discovery in 1930 as the furthest planet-like object we could see with telescopes at the time, approximately 333 light minutes (or 5.5 light hours) from the Sun. It was only decades later with the discovery of the Kuiper belt that scientists confirmed the existence of other planet-like objects and asteroids out there. The Kuiper belt itself starts approximately 4 light hours from the Sun, not far from Neptune, extends as far as 7 light hours from the Sun, and contains many other celestial objects besides Pluto. Some of them, like the dwarf-planet Eris, are actually bigger than Pluto.

So clearly the number of planets in our solar system had to be revised, either increased or reduced. And all depended on the squishy definition of what we classify as a planet. For the sole reason that Pluto has not managed to clear the other planetary shrapnel around its orbit it has been disqualified as a planet by the International Astronomical Union and declared a "dwarf-planet". Though in the hearts of many, Pluto will always remain a planet with underdog status. Not least because many people still grew up with Pluto being considered a planet and it shares its name with an adorable Disney dog. But those people better be reading to include many other dwarf-planets and planetesimals out there as planets, and the number could balloon to dozens or even hundreds depending on the criteria.

The Edges of the Solar System

Beyond Neptune lies of the aforementioned Kuiper Belt, of which Pluto is part, along with a number of other dwarf planets like Eris, Charon, Albion, Haumea, and Makemake. The Kuiper Belt also contains a number of asteroids, and simple frozen balls of water, ammonia, and methane. The formation of the Kuiper belt at the start of the solar system is currently hypothesized to be from a lack of material for the same process of planetary formation to complete itself. For instance, despite the vast amount of small objects out there spread out over many billions of kilometres, the total mass of all of them put together are unlikely to weigh much more than 10% the mass of Earth. Not enough matter quite plainly was flung out that far for full blown planets to emerge. This ring of planetary shrapnel is an example of failed accretion. Yet this ring of material is still held in by the Sun's gravity, despite the outer reaches being over 7 light hours away.

But if you think that is impressive, check out the Oort Cloud. It is a thick sphere at the furthest edges of our solar system composed of icy planetesimals and comets. It begins at approximately 27 light hours from the Sun (over an entire day for light to travel there!) and ends approximately 1 light *year* from the Sun. Some estimates hold that the Oort Cloud could extend as far as 3 light years from the Sun, or three-quarters of the way to the next nearest star, Proxima Centurai, which is 4.2 light years away. Like the Kuiper belt, the Oort Cloud is hypothesised to have formed from the residue of the proto-planetary disk flung out by the first fusion explosions of the Sun, but without enough material to coalesce into planets. But this sphere of comets and icy planetesimals represents the very edges of our solar system, and the border between us and the rest of the galaxy.

Life in the Rest of the Galaxy?

The Milky Way galaxy is 100,000 light years across and is an estimated 200 to 400 billion stars. Many of them exist in the core of the galaxy, which would be uninhabitable by life. In the flat disk of the galaxy (also created by centrifugal force) where our solar system lies, things are more habitable because we don't have a cluster of stars setting off supernovas as frequently. It is here that astronomers begin their search for other planets that could potentially foster life. Given that Earth forms our solar system's only decent real estate, the existence of life on "exoplanets" (planets outside of our solar system) seems the likelier possibility than its evolution on Mars, Europa, or Titan. Even if life did evolve in the solar system, it most likely was single cell, and may well be dead.

Life is somewhat finicky about the conditions in which it can arise. At first glance, this may lead one to the conclusion that we on Earth are alone in the Universe. Indeed the formation of a planet, the right distance from the Sun, in the right part of the galaxy, while conditions in planetary formation can be so brutal, might make life seem rare. However, once you lump the huge numbers on the scale, life suddenly appears much more likely elsewhere in the cosmos.

Until 1995, we had merely presumed that planets orbited other stars in the galaxy. Then Swiss astronomers discovered the first exoplanets. They did this by looking at the changes in a star's light as a planet passed in front of it. This can tell you a lot about the planet's size, distance from its star, and even allow you to make a few educated guesses about its chemical composition. Since 1995, numerous observations have discovered approximately 4000 confirmed and suspected exoplanets (I am being deliberately vague about the number at time of writing because more are being rapidly discovered and I may not immediately remember to return to this page in future editions!). And this has been from looking at 150,000 of the nearest solar systems, or roughly 0.0000000000000000009% of the total number of stars in the galaxy. As a result, we have discovered hundreds of Earth-sized planets within the habitable zones from their stars. Extrapolating from the small patch of the sky we have surveyed, we can estimate that there may be as many as 40 billion planets in the Milky Way capable of sustaining life. These are tremendously good odds.

Mind you, we are talking about planets that are light years from us. Until space-faring technology is millennia more advanced than it is now, it is unlikely that we shall ever encounter them. Many of these planets may have life which is now extinct, or else has life that is single cell.

Only a small sliver of those planets would have multi-celled life, or life that is capable of collective learning like humans. But consider that there may even be species that are far advanced from humans in terms of their overall technological evolution. Multiply the odds by the 400 to 10 trillion galaxies out there and the odds are that we are definitely not alone in the Universe.

Essay Writing Exercise

For this chapter's essay writing exercise, write a list of the evidence for the Big Bang. Try to be as comprehensive as possible. Then compose a thesis statement for the same question as the last chapter:

Why is the Big Bang theory the most widely accepted explanation for the origin of the Universe?

Try to incorporate the list of evidence (which may or may not have been provided for you explicitly in a couple pages of chapter 1) into your one sentence thesis statement. Then create an outline which lists each piece of evidence individually and provide brief explanations for their significance. Try to get each piece of evidence to reinforce your thesis statement – which is what all pieces of evidence in the body of an essay should try to do.

Then try to write a single sentence describing each piece of evidence at a time. Arrange these sentences into a paragraph, with the thesis statement followed by the sentences for each piece of evidence. You now have an essay introduction. Feel free to end the introduction with a rhetorical flourish, witty statement, or idea that underlines the significance of the topic. And congratulations, you now have the formula for the introductions of standard academic essays.

Further Reading

Asimov, Isaac. Beginnings: The Story of Origins – of Mankind, Life, the Earth, the Universe. New York: Walker, 1987.

Barrow, John. The Book of Universes: Exploring the Limits of the Cosmos. London: W.W. Nortion and Company, 2011.

Bucciantini, Massimo and Michele Camerota and Franco Gudice. Galileo's Telescope: A European Study. trans. Catherine Bolton. Cambridge, Mass.: Harvard University Press, 2015.

Chambers, John, and Jacqueline Morton. From Dust to Life: The Origin and Evolution of Our Solar System. Princeton: Princeton University Press, 2014.

Ghorsio, A. et al. "New Elements Einsteinium and Fermium, Atomic Numbers 99 and 100" Physical Review vol. 99, no. 3 (1955) pg. 1048-1049.

Gordin, Michael. A Well Ordered Thing: Dmitrii Mendeleev and the Shadow of the Periodic Table. New York: Basic Books, 2004.

Hoskin, Michael. Discoverers of the Universe: William and Caroline Herschel. Princeton: Princeton University Press, 2011.

Karol, Paul. et al. "Discovery of the element with atomic number $Z = 118$ completing the 7th row of the periodic table (IUPAC Technical Report)" Pure Applied Chemistry vol. 88 (2016) pg. 155-160.

King, Henry. The History of the Telescope. New York: Dover Publications, 2003.

Mendeleev, Dmitri. "Remarks Concerning the Discovery of Gallium" in Mendeleev on the Periodic Law: Selected Writings, 1869-1905. ed. William Jensen. New York: Dover Publications, 2005.

Watson, Fred. Stargazer: The Life and History of the Telescope. Cambridge, Mass.: Da Capo Press, 2006.

CHAPTER 3

THE EARTH & ORIGIN OF LIFE

Or,

HOW THE EARTH
BECAME LESS DEADLY
TO ENABLE LIFE
BUT IS STILL TRYING
TO KILL US

Mother Earth Needs to Put Down the Xbox Controller and Get a Life

---

Threshold 5: The First Life – 3.8 billion years ago

- *Wherein conditions on Earth became slightly less deadly giving life a fighting chance*
- *Differentiation and bombardments created the world's first oceans*
- *Within those oceans, long strands of organic chemicals were able to form*
- *These organic chemicals began to self-replicate, kicking off the origin of life*

Timeline

- **The Great Bombardment (4.5 to 4 billion years ago):** The pelting of Earth by asteroids, comets, (and one proto-planet) ranging between 5 to 500 kilometres in diameter (6000 kilometres in diameter for Theia) continued throughout this period, intensifying in the "Late Heavy Bombardment" around 4.1 billion years ago, when millions of asteroids and comets hit the Earth. While horrific, this had the friendly effect of bringing a lot more frozen water to Earth, which evaporated upon impact and entered the atmosphere. This would have a very important effect on life in a few hundred million years.

- **The First Oceans (4 to 3.8 billion years ago):** After the surface temperature of the Earth cooled to below 100 degrees Celsius (the boiling point of water), all the water vapour that had built up in the atmosphere was able to fall back to Earth. This process took millions of years, but the lowest lying areas of the Earth's crust were suddenly filled with deep and vast oceans, making it unique in the solar system. The vast world of liquid water is a crucial environment for fairly fragile organic chemicals to form into early life.

- **The First Life (3.8 billion to 3.5 billion years ago):** Sometime after the appearance of the first oceans (our best chemical evidence suggests 3.8 billion years ago, with confirmed fossil evidence from 3.5 billion years ago) organic chemicals began self-replicating. This meant that organic chemicals had a reaction that caused the long strands of proto-DNA and proto-RNA to copy itself. Shortly thereafter the chemicals evolved the ability to adapt and process energy flows through a metabolism. The earliest life would have likely evolved at the bottom of the oceans, and fed off of geothermal energy from underwater volcanoes and the fertile soup of chemicals down there.

A Squishy Earth: Differentiation

Approximately 4.54 billion years ago, our planet had rolled up the majority of matter in our previously dusty orbital track around the Sun. With a few notable exceptions – the other proto-planet, Theia, and countless millions of smaller asteroids. The Earth at this time remained extremely hot. This was because the solar system was still young and the Earth only recently formed from extremely violent collisions of proto-planets. The bombardment of asteroids, with each impact being as devastating as a nuclear holocaust, also kept the Earth molten. Finally, there was so much matter being gathered by the Earth that the pressure from all that mass generated heat and caused the insides of the Earth to *melt*.

While nowhere near the same scale as the Big Bang or fusion in a star, the amount of pressure from all that matter did generate heat. This kicked off another complexity building process, known as "differentiation". The Earth was a molten ball of squishy semi-liquid rocks, through which material could pass reasonably freely. Gravity took hold and much of the heaviest elements like iron and gold sank through the scorching soup down to the very core of the Earth. Only tiny traces of these heavier elements remained trapped in the cooling Earth's crust. To give you an idea of the disparity, throughout history gold has been a highly sought after material – largely due to its rarity. Yet if you were to somehow be able to burrow into the mantle and core of the Earth, you would find enough gold to coat the entire Earth's surface, gilding the continents from sea to sea. The same goes for iron, which was even more abundant due to the fact it does not require supernovas to be produced, but instead can form in the bellies of the biggest stars. Iron sank down into the core of the Earth, creating a ball 3400 kilometres thick which gave the Earth its magnetic field. As we shall see later, the magnetic field is an important guardian of higher complexity.

Meanwhile, differentiation also made the inverse occur. As the heavier elements sank, lighter elements rose toward the surface. To the top of this soup, bubbled forth a crust of silicon (silicates have a majority share of Earth's chemical composition) and also aluminium, sodium, and magnesium. The lightest of all elements, like carbon, oxygen, and hydrogen, were ejected as gasses to form the Earth's early atmosphere. As the primitive crust cooled at the top of the Earth, it trapped just trace amounts of iron and gold, along with silver, lead, uranium, and all the other naturally occurring heavy elements. Yet the cooling of the crust was frequently interrupted by cosmic impacts with asteroids and that pesky proto-planet, Theia. No sooner did the crust begin to congeal at the top of molten soup, but more impacts destroyed the thin layer, and heated the world up again. It was only around 4 billion years ago that the bombardments were over, and the crust was able to fully solidify.

Taking Mother Earth's Measurements

Even today, the crust is tiny and pathetic according to the standards set by the rest of the Earth's structure. This may be surprising when you consider how thick the rocky edifices of mountains and the dark stony halls of mineshafts appear to be to human perceptions. But it is quite apt to call it the "skin that forms at the top of a pot of soup". The crust, which contains a lot of the Earth's lighter elements and just smidges of the heavier ones, is only about 35 kilometres thick and in some places at the bottom of the oceans about 7 kilometres thick.

Below the crust is the upper mantle, where there is so much pressure that temperatures increase to over 1000 degrees Celsius, producing the horrific lava that occasionally spews to the surface from volcanoes. The upper mantle runs about 650 kilometres deep, in a sea of molten igneous rock. Below that is the lower mantle which runs down to 2900 kilometres deep, where it is so hot that rocks take a fully liquid form, but due to the immense pressure of everything on top of it, tends to be stiffer than the goopy lava.

Further down is the core. The outer core is composed primarily of liquid iron and nickel which flows down to 5200 kilometres below the surface, and then the inner core which runs down to 6370 kilometres to the very middle of this hell, experiences so much pressure that the extremely hot molten core nevertheless behaves as if it were solid. Just like the hydrogen below the clouds of Jupiter are thought to do. At the core of the Earth, temperatures increase to 6700 degrees Celsius.

These are quite extreme temperatures compared to the balmy -60 to +60 degrees Celsius we experience in the most extreme weather conditions on the surface. But to place things in perspective, the temperature on the surface of the Sun is about 5500 degrees Celsius and the core of the Sun where fusion happens is about 15 million degrees Celsius. The estimated temperature of the Universe 3 minutes after the Big Bang is about 1 billion degrees Celsius, and the estimated temperature of the Universe at the moment of the Big Bang could theoretically have been as high as 142 nonillion degrees Celsius, or 142 followed by thirty zeros, and following the logic that after a billion comes a trillion, quadrillion, quintillion, sextillion, septillion, and octillion, then nontillion. This theoretical temperature is also known as "Absolute Hot". So I guess this a roundabout way of saying that I guess Mother Earth isn't that hot. But don't tell her I said that.

This is all a result of the size and total mass of the Earth compared to something huge like the Sun, or something that contained everything in the Universe, like the Big Bang singularity. Certainly there was enough heat in the early Earth to wreak havoc with its structure, and to form the differentiated structure necessary for more complexity to arise. For clarity, the number of possible chemical combinations that occurred in the Early Earth increased from 250 at the start of planetary formation, to over 1500 by the time that differentiation had occurred.

We took Mother Earth's measurements in the late 19th and early 20th centuries. It goes without saying that it would be impossible to simply dig that deep. Never mind the technical challenge of digging through kilometres of the Earth's crust, once you sank a mineshaft as deep as the upper mantle, you couldn't exactly dig much further with your equipment. Presuming, of course, that the temperatures didn't kill you, or that the mantle didn't just immediately come rushing up the shaft you'd sunk.

Instead, the development of the seismograph was able to monitor earthquakes. By setting up seismographs on different parts of the Earth's surface, geologists were able to measure how long it took for tremors to travel from one part of the world to the other. These measurements allowed them to calculate what sort of substances they were passing through. We supplemented this knowledge with what we calculated would happen in an accretion scenario, how differentiation would operate, and finally how only an iron-nickel core could produce Earth's magnetic field.

When Mother Earth was Young and Mean

The Earth from 4.54 to 4 billion years ago belongs to the "Hadean eon", so called because of the hellish conditions on Earth at the time. This is a bit of a misnomer because the Greek Hades is actually a dull, dark place where the souls of humans swim for all eternity, as opposed to the Christian vision of fire and brimstone that makes up Hell. But scientists like their Greek and their Latin, so who's stopping them? If we consider the Hadean eon to be the very embodiment of the Christian conception of Hell, then indeed the name is quite accurate.

For about 540 million years, the same amount of time that separates us from the Cambrian explosion and the start of multi-celled life like trilobites and jawless fish, the Earth persisted in this phase. The surface of the Earth remained above 100 degrees Celsius, preventing any liquid water from forming, and in places would be as high as 1500 degrees Celsius where Earth was covered in molten seas. Indeed an ocean of lava is a most compelling vision.

Where there was land, it would be paper thin, and would be shooting up jets of steam out of its cracks as the lighter gasses escaped the Earth in the process of differentiation. This job was also done by volcanoes which rose out of the Earth, spewing lava, smoke, and ash. Some of these volcanoes would have been small, given there was not yet much crust in regions of the Earth, would have belched lava up from the ground. As that lava dried into crust and built up, some other volcanoes might have been the size of Mount Everest, towering in the sky at 9 kilometres above sea level, possibly even more.

The sky itself would have been a terrifying red. This was caused by the predominantly carbon dioxide atmosphere (coming in at about 80%). It would be a long time before Earth ever adopted an oxygen atmosphere, which remained at negligible levels for now. Other dominant gasses in the atmosphere were carbon monoxide (highly poisonous) and methane. The combination of these gasses would have captured more of the Sun's energy in a greenhouse effect like Venus does today. But this was moderated in part by the fact that the Sun's luminosity was still growing, and overall it was burning cooler than it is today (in fact over the next 3 billion years the Sun is only going to grow hotter and hotter as it ages, see star lifecycles in chapter 2). This had the other haunting effect of making the sky fairly dark, aside from the redness. If there had been an "eye of Sauron" hovering in the sky like in *Lord of the Rings*, it certainly would not have looked entirely out of place.

When Theia smashed into the Earth approximately 4.51 billion years ago, a lot of the crust was destroyed and flung up into space along with an immense amount of lava. One cannot understate the catastrophic nature of a Mars-sized planet smashing into Earth, and if it were to happen today it would certainly wipe out every trace of life and perhaps even evaporate all the oceans. It would have been roughly 450 times more severe than the asteroid impact that wiped out the dinosaurs.

As the Moon slowly accreted, and appeared in the sky, it was much closer to Earth than it is today (it moves away at about 4 centimetres a year) and would have blocked out much of the sky as it passed overhead. The tidal force exerted by the Moon would have correspondingly been greater. Leveraging massive tsunamis thousands of metres high to wash across the Earth every 12-15 hours. Except these tsunamis were not made of water – they were made of molten lava.

But it gets worse. For 500 million years, the Earth was pelted by asteroids in the Great Bombardment, particularly severe around 4.1 billion years ago in the Late Heavy Bombardment. This is where millions of asteroids struck the Earth, shattering its already thin and fragile crust. As Earth swept up the remaining cosmic debris in its region of the solar system, it suffered continual catastrophic impacts. Some of these would have been as powerful as a nuclear holocaust, some as bad as the Cretaceous impact that killed the dinosaurs, and some of them would have been up to 100 times worse (literally) depending on the size of the asteroid. And unlike the Cretaceous extinction which happened 65 million years ago, these impacts would have been happening *constantly* over roughly a period that separates us from the evolution of the first trilobites.

It goes without saying that any form of life would perish under these brutal conditions. There was no room for higher complexity being the inanimate chemical in any place in the solar system at this point. Something on Earth needed to change for the emergence of life, microscopic and frail, to stand a "snowball's chance in hell" of forming.

Mother Earth Simmers Down a Bit

Despite the destruction, it appeared that roughly 500 million years of hell was quite enough. All that differentiation had belched hydrogen and oxygen into the atmosphere in a process called "outgassing". The bombardment of millions of asteroids had brought tons of ice from outer space. This promptly melted and rose into the atmosphere as well. Over time, the crust had cooled into a black and grey igneous landscape, with no more oceans of lava. And the surface temperature fell below 100 degrees Celsius, and continued falling. Suddenly all that water vapour that had built up in the atmosphere had no choice but to fall to Earth. What followed was something that would resemble the Biblical flood – except it was on steroids. Never mind raining for 40 days and 40 nights, the torrential downpour across the planet continued for millions of years without end. The trenches and low-lying areas of the Earth's crust began to fill up with water. By approximately 4 billion years ago, the Earth was covered with oceans. Only the highest ledges, our continents, managed to keep their heads above water. And even these became pockmarked with lakes and streaked with rivers. Additionally, the water levels varied depending on the average global temperature. For now, glaciation began to occur at the poles.

The Hadean eon was over, and 4 billion years ago the Archean eon had begun. There are a few things to note about the Archean world. First, the Earth below the crust was still much hotter, since it had still recently formed, and emitted a lot of geothermal energy, would be useful for the first forms of life. This compensated for the fact that the Sun's energy (solar thermal energy) was still quite dim, so was a less appealing power source for early life. But even if life had emerged on the surface, the solar radiation blasting down on the surface of an Earth that did not have an ozone layer would have destroyed any life that tried to form. So for now the best bet for life was deep in the oceans where it was warm and safe from radiation.

Archean Earth also had a gigantic Moon which passed overhead, pulling tremendous tides from shore to shore. At least those waves were no longer lava. But the land itself was still dotted with an abundance of volcanoes as eruptions and outgassing continued. These volcanoes pumped out primarily carbon dioxide, which was still the dominant gas in the atmosphere. The land is that it was entirely rocky. All the greenery we would associate with plains and forests did not exist yet. Instead it looked more like the surface of the Moon. But new rocks were forming. We of course still had the "igneous" rocks that spewed out of volcanoes as lava and then dried. We also had sedimentary rocks, which were compressed from tiny loose grains of minerals into larger forms. Finally we had metamorphic rocks which were heated in compressed areas below the surface down to a jelly and contorted in their makeup, becoming neither igneous nor sedimentary, before making their way to the surface.

"I'm Simply Saying that Life, ah, Finds a Way…"

It was in this tranquil smouldering realm, 3.8 billion years ago, that life began. We derive the date 3.8 billion years ago from the chemical signatures in Archean rocks that geologists are confident were created by early microscopic life. The more conclusive evidence is fossil evidence of tiny microbes embedded in rock from about 3.5 billion years ago. Most scientists now use the date of 3.8 billion years, though there are many theories that life may have begun even earlier (around the 4 billion year mark) though there is yet to be evidence for these hypotheses. Still, if it took life 200 million years to get its act together from the start of the Archean, fair enough!

We now come across one of those "blank pages" of history, where we aren't completely sure how the next event happened. There are numerous competing hypotheses for "abiogenesis" (i.e. the emergence of life from non-life) but first we shall go over the version of events that is most within scientific consensus. However, it should be noted that even in this version of events the "how" in some of the details concerning the actual evolution of self-replicating living cells is still a bit fuzzy.

We've discussed how the Archean was able to form oceans due to the Earth cooling down below the boiling point, and having endless rainfall from the water vapour that had amassed in the atmosphere during the Hadean. This is important for the origin of life because all the chemicals needed to form extremely intricate and tangled bonds need an ideal environment in which to do so. Life cannot form if it is encased in solid rock because those chemicals cannot move around. Likewise life cannot form in wispy gas clouds because the necessary chemical arrangements would just flit past each other. Liquid water, however, allows for the ideal environment of movement, but not too much movement.

There is also the consideration that the Sun was the enemy of early life. The surface was barren, dry, and pelted with radiation that would corrupt and destroy the cells of early life as they tried to form. The atmosphere itself was 80% carbon dioxide which created an intense greenhouse effect that added to the deadliness of the surface. The safest bet was to dwell in the bottom of the oceans.

Yet where would life get its energy flows from which higher complexity could be created? The most likely answer is from undersea volcanoes or "vents" also known as "black smokers" which pumped out geothermal energy from cracks in the Earth's crust. Wander too far into those cracks and it was too hot for life to form, and it would have been destroyed. Wander too far away and it was too cold. But for early microbial life, there was a habitable zone just on the edges of these volcanoes to get the energy required for higher complexity. This appears to be the most likely location where life first formed. And in 2017 there was some corroborating evidence from DNA testing that seemed to suggest our earliest ancestors did indeed live in this way. There are other proposals for the location, and we shall discuss these later in the chapter.

But for now we have a plausible location for the start of life – underwater and on the edges of deep sea vents. Now we need the ingredients. We know that the Archean oceans were teeming with a variety of organic chemicals that had come to the surface via differentiation. It is no surprise that most of those organic chemicals, such as carbon (on which all terrestrial life is based), is among the lightest in the periodic table. Carbon is also the most flexible. It forms a vital link in the chain for about 90% of all the chemical combinations that we have discovered.

Besides carbon, equally vital to self-replicating life are hydrogen, oxygen, nitrogen, and phosphorous. But how do you go from a pile of light elements, to organic chemicals, to something remarkable like DNA or a self-replicating cell? This is where things get trickier.

The leading hypothesis is that on the edges of undersea vents, the elements above came together to form amino acids and nucleobases. Amino acids are crucial for fueling life. They are a combination of carbon, hydrogen, oxygen, and nitrogen atoms wrapped up in a chain of about 9 of atoms or so. Amino acids are the building blocks of proteins. Each protein is a tangled strand of about 20 amino acids on average, though some have considerably more. A protein is used to carry out the various commands of a living cell: to burn energy to sustain its complexity, to reproduce, to grow various traits, to react to its environment, and also to simple move things around a cell. Nucleobases, on the other hand, are the building blocks of nucleic acid (the fundamental component of DNA and RNA). In the last chapter we briefly examined four nucleobases: adenine ($C_{10}H_{12}O_5N_5P$), guanine ($C_{10}H_{12}O_6N_5P$), cytosine ($C_9H_{12}O_6N_3P$), and thymine ($C_{10}H_{13}O_7N_2P$).

We know that these organic chemicals could have emerged in the Archean thanks to the theoretical work of biologists Alexander Oparin and J.B.S. Haldane (Russian and British respectively). They observed that life could not begin on Earth today, since an oxygen atmosphere is so reactive it would destroy primitive cells. Currently, Earth's atmosphere is 21% oxygen. If it were 40%, if you rubbed your hands together they might catch fire. A fragile chain of organic chemicals could not long survive in such an environment. So Oparin and Haldane rightly hypothesised that the early Earth's atmosphere would have been almost oxygen-free or "anaerobic". This hypothesis was more or less confirmed by the Urey-Miller experiment in 1952, when scientists Harold Urey and Stanley Miller simulated the conditions of Archean Earth in a laboratory (no oxygen, but with water, and energy flows) and managed to create a handful of amino acids in a brown sludge. Further refined simulations of the conditions on Archean Earth since then have had even more marked success, producing a vast range of amino acids and nucleobases.

But amino acids and nucleobases are a long way from proteins and DNA, which are much more complex and fragile tangles of atoms, and still further away from self-replicating cells. And this is where the enduring scientific and historical mystery lies? How did those building blocks come together and start evolving?

Deoxyribonucleic Acid: The Sexiest Acid of Them All

DNA exists in all living cells and is the database which tells proteins what sort of traits those cells should have and how they should behave. It is the "software" of the organic computer, the disc which contains the program instructions that runs a video game. Alternately, you may consider DNA to be the general which barks orders to the rest of the cell. DNA is what makes the living think look and act like it does. It is why you can tell different people and different species apart by using DNA testing, but all of those things contain DNA.

Deoxyribonucleic acid is made of two strand composed of billions of atoms, twisted around each other in a "double-helix". Each strand is composed of many nucleotides, which in turn are composed of the nucleobases mentioned earlier, which may well have formed in the oceans of Archean Earth. Adenine, guanine, cytosine, and thymine, are the nucleobases that holds the genetic information. They are like the 1s and 0s of the computer. Their combination within a nucleotide determines what information (or what "orders" or "instructions") lie within the nucleotide. And these instructions can yield very diverse results, as you can plainly see from the number of different traits and behaviours a living organism can have.

Correspondingly DNA is extremely complex a structure, which if stretched out would be 2 metres long – and those strands exist in each and every cell in the body. DNA comes together into chromosomes (of which the human body typically has 46) and each section of a chromosome has a gene which gives specific instructions to create a single protein.

Which brings us to the "hardware" of our organic computer. Ribonucleic acid, or RNA, is the buddy of DNA. Made of only one strand rather than two, it has the task of taking the instructions from DNA and delivering them to small parts in a living cell that produce proteins (these protein factories are called ribosomes). RNA does this by unzipping DNA and reading the instructions, or the 1s and 0s of the nucleobases. The RNA then literally moves across the living cell to the ribosome to kick-start protein creation.

The proteins, which are composed of amino acids, then enact all of the instructions of DNA from deciding how the organism will respond to stimuli, to whether it will have muscles and how flexible they will be, to the colour of its eyes or hair (if the organism has them). If the DNA is the "software" with the instructions, then the RNA and proteins are the "hardware", the actual computer with its whirring parts which actually runs the disc. Both RNA and proteins are also extremely complex tangles of chemicals, and the emergent properties of them are correspondingly varied and astounding, being capable of creating the diverse range of animate matter that exists in the biosphere – and all those variations that have long since gone extinct over billions of years.

Do not be worried if all of that seems overly laden with foreign terminology and multiple component parts. That quite simply is testament to how complex chemically a living cell is compared to all the other inanimate forms of complexity we have studied so far in Big History! For our purposes – the purposes of forming a narrative – you won't have to memorise this stuff unless you really, *really* want to. And all the power to you, if you do.

Up to this point 3.8 billion years ago, however, what we are really talking about is just some organic sludge that is enacting some extremely interesting but microscopic chemical reactions. So how does all this complex chemistry translate into a living being?

The important point is that DNA self-replicates or "copies itself" in order to continue giving instructions to the rest of a living cell. When it does so, it splits in two, with nucleobases seeking the same combination that they had in the previous double-helix. Most of the time this copying process is perfect, though occasionally there is a "copying error", or mutation, which slightly modifies DNA's instructions. A mutation happens maybe once every billion copies. Those "copying errors" are the foundation of evolution.

If DNA copied itself flawlessly every single time without a single failure, life would have remained exactly as it was 3.8 billion years ago on the edges of undersea volcanoes. It would not have evolved. Yet if you have a mutation in the instructions for an organism, then how that organism is constructed or behaves will change. Some mutations are deadly to the organism, some don't affect its survival one way or another, and some mutations are useful. Those mutations that are useful are able to copy themselves all over again, and the cycle continues. What results are gradually changing life forms that either succeed or fail due to how well those DNA mutations suit the environment. Thus what evolution actually is: the natural selection of genes based on their evolutionary usefulness, rather than selection of the individual or the entire species.

Thus in this collection of organic sludge we have all the key traits of a living organism: it uses energy flows from geothermal vents and surrounding amino acids (metabolism), it reproduces by copying itself (reproduction), and it gradually changes its traits based on useful mutations (adaptation). These three traits of metabolism, reproduction, adaptation, are the closest things we have when it comes to defining what the heck life is, and how it differs from the inanimate cosmos.

A Blank Spot in the Pages of History

This is where we approach the biggest question mark surrounding the origin of life. It is one thing to simulate the conditions of early Earth and come away with an organic sludge of amino-acids and nucleobases. It is entirely another to wind up with long intricate strands of thousands and thousands of amino-acids and nucleobases in DNA, RNA, and a living cell. What happy accident would have brought about these chains of organic chemicals and kick-started their self-replication?

To answer this question, there are a number of hypotheses.

Location, Location, Location

The one most within scientific consensus is that life formed, as discussed, in undersea vents, safe from solar radiation. This would make sense since fossil evidence does indicate that life evolved first in the ocean before moving on to land. There's also a lot of DNA that our Last Universal Common Ancestor (LUCA), which is the hypothetical organism from which all other organisms are descended, might have shared in common with microbes that currently live on the edges of undersea vents. But let us be under no illusions, life next to an underwater volcano would be an extremely precarious existence. LUCA would have been in constant danger of being burned up if it ventured to close, or if the heat of the volcano momentarily increased. Or it could have gotten very cold if that particular vent died down.

Another proposed location is a "warm little pond" (to use Darwin's phrase) nearer to the surface, on a coastal area, where the right organic chemicals may have coalesced in a puddle without the nearby danger of an underwater volcano. Perhaps the heat source then was not geothermal, but was in fact solar. This location has been deemed unlikely given the immense amounts of solar radiation that would have bombarded and destroyed primitive organisms near to the surface.

Yet another proposed location is in outer space itself and LUCA travelled to Earth aboard one of the many asteroids that crashed into Earth during the Late Heavy Bombardment. This is known as "Panspermia". While it may seem less likely than the previous two locations, this hypothesis still has a number of supporters among scientists. If it was too harsh on Earth, then perhaps the initial catalyst of organic material happened in space. Indeed there are a number of microscopic organisms called "extremophiles" that are capable of surviving in space. And any such microscopic organism could have been buried deep within an asteroid's rocky crags. The hypothesis does throw up a number of problems though, since it just pushes the question of what series of events caused replication back beyond Earth, and no proponent of

Panspermia has been able to explain how self-replication happened in the cold irradiated regions of space. Much less how organic material could survive smashing into Earth in an asteroid, or how it would have survived the last phases of Earth's formation only to wind up in the oceans anyway.

The Method of the Madness

Naturally, none of those locations are confirmed, and we have yet to describe what environmental conditions in any of those locations triggered self-replication. Indeed if scientists knew how to do that then simulated laboratory experiments wouldn't just yield brown sludge, but the newspapers would be heralding that scientists had just managed to create life in a laboratory. This was a misapprehension that the media circulated in 1952 after the news of the Urey-Miller experiment, but creating a few amino acids is not the same thing. Regardless of the location being undersea vent, warm pond, or asteroid, we need to answer how organic chemicals went from a few amino acids and nucleobases to self-replicating DNA and complex proteins.

The frontrunner hypothesis without question is "RNA World". This model postulates a simpler mode of self-replication and protein production evolved first, before the current system which involves DNA, RNA, ribosomes, and proteins. Evolutionarily speaking, it makes sense that this the DNA-RNA system may have been a result of evolution, so that self-replication and transmitting genetic information became more efficient. Why have a strand of chemicals that must contain all the genetic information, *and* carry out its own orders? Yet the first version may well have been just RNA that was both "software" and "hardware". No double-helix. Just a single strand that self-replicated all on its own.

Generally speaking, it would make sense for the earliest versions of this process to have fewer component parts, since that means that there would have to been fewer "happy accidents" for such complex structures to come together. Instead the current DNA-RNA system would have simply evolved as the result of mutation and natural selection. Indeed it is likely at some point, this did happen since neither DNA, nor RNA, can fulfill their functions without each other. The alternative is both forms of nucleic acid formed at the same time and just happened to be complementary to each other.

As a result, the RNA World Hypothesis suggests that a single strand of nucleotides began copying itself and was also capable of producing its own primitive proteins to carry out its own instructions. Mutations from copying errors then spawned DNA as a more efficient way of reproducing. The problem with this hypothesis arises in that no scientist has yet been able to come up with a model of nucleic acid that is capable of both storing information and transmitting it. While it very much is the most feasible hypothesis at present, it is still a hypothesis until proven. Yet RNA World falls into line with the more generalised notion of "chemical evolution" where inanimate organic chemicals came together in complex strands, and the ones that could exist in their environments survived, and then continued to grow more complex, while ones that fell prey to harsh conditions disappeared. The first form of self-replication may have been very primitive and sloppy indeed, and only gradually did it evolve more complex chemical combinations.

Inanimate Complexity to Biological Complexity

Apologies, dear reader, but this brings us to yet another discussion of complexity. Kind of inevitable in a story where rising complexity is the unifying theme. Most pertinently, biological complexity is many times more complex than anything seen in the inanimate cosmos. This may indeed be why the small glimpse of biochemistry in the above pages might have been more difficult to digest than the pages previous to it. Indeed this is a running theme in Big History, as things grow more complex, the historical events require more detail to explain. It is why we are only three chapters in and we have moved from 13.8 to 3.8 billion years ago, and we are already at the start of life, with many more chapters to go to detail evolution and human history.

So far, we've been building complexity from hydrogen and helium at the start of the Universe, to heavier chemical elements formed in stars, to molecules with many different combinations formed in solar systems, to those organic chemicals that are able to trigger self-replication and produce life. In terms of either energy flows, structural intricacy, or emergent properties, the biological realm is miles and yonks ahead in terms of complexity.

Energy Flows

This allows us the most straightforward way to demonstrate the increase of complexity. Remember that in order to create, sustain, or increase complexity, you need energy flows from where there is more energy to where there is less. That is the essence of all historical change in history from the start of the Universe. Without energy flow from fusion, a star dies, and likewise without energy flow from food, geothermal, or solar energy, an organism starves and dies. But the interesting thing is for an organism to sustain its own complexity and stave off death, it requires a lot more energy flow for its size than something in the inanimate realm.

In order to sustain its own complexity, the following system require the corresponding average density of energy flows:

- The Sun: 2 erg/g/s (a unit of free energy per gram per second – see chapter 1)
- A Supergiant Nearing Supernova: 120 erg/g/s
- A Typical Microscopic Organism: 900 erg/g/s
- A Tree: 10,000 erg/g/s
- A Dog: 20,000 erg/g/s

As you can see, the density of energy flow increases from the inanimate realm to the biological realm. Even an organism as simple as LUCA would have required many times denser energy flow to sustain its complexity than the Sun. And this corresponds with the immense structural intricacy of a cell versus a lump of a bunch of disconnected elements gathered together in the Sun.

The difference in complexity between LUCA and the Sun would be on the order of several hundred times. While LUCA would not have been as imposing as a star (it is microscopic and extremely fragile after all) it requires a great deal more energy for a single cell to maintain all its working parts. Increase the complexity of the organism from single-celled and microscopic to multi-celled like a tree or a dog and the difference from a star is exponential.

From the first inequalities in matter and energy that emerged after Guthian Cosmic Inflation, to stars, to planets, and now to organisms, tiny pockets of complexity are growing brighter and brighter in terms of their energy density. This trend will continue for the rest of our story.

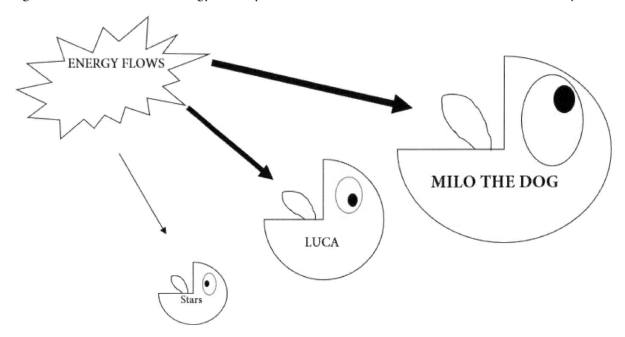

Yet how is life to meet the increased demand for energy flows? Simple, it must go out and actively find them. While a star is content to float in space and simply burn up its fuel, a living being must actively seek out new energy flows in order to sustain its own survival. It does this by chemosynthesising, photosynthesising, munching on plants, hunting, or making a trip down to Maccas at 2am after way too many beers. You don't see stars floating round the cosmos, hungrily chasing after fleeing clouds of helium. But you do see that sort of behaviour in living things.

This difference is so profound that, despite the difficulty scientists and philosophers have encountered in coming up with a definition for life, the act of actively seeking out energy flows to sustain their own complexity is one of the clearest things that divides life from non-life. The corresponding energy flows are denser, and the corresponding behaviour is more complex.

Structural Intricacy

Quarks which emerged at the start of the Universe are the key building blocks of protons, and protons are the key building blocks of atoms. Throughout the process of star formation, we've seen new atoms be created. From these inanimate building blocks, we get the first complex systems: stars, planets, asteroids, comets, interstellar dust, nebulas, and galaxies.

Galaxies themselves are not structurally intricate. Billions of stars of only a few different types are held together by only gravity, and separated by light years. The spaces between them are filled with clouds of gas and dust. Stars themselves are big disorderly lumps of chemical elements. Compared to a living cell, they have no fragile structure. They only need a lot of matter to fuse in their cores in order to continue surviving. Move the atoms of a star around a little, and it will keep burning. Contrast that to DNA, where one slight change in coding will result in a different organism. Anything from a bacterium, to a daffodil, to a dog, to a human, to a T-Rex.

When elements are released from a star, they can form molecules, each with their own unique properties. From these molecules you get planets of a diverse range of about 100 million different known types. Everything from an Earth with thousands of different kinds of minerals, and oceans of liquid water, to the chaotic and terrifying weather patterns of a gas giant like Jupiter, with its metallic hydrogen core.

Then things go a bit nuts in terms of structural intricacy. Each strand of DNA contains billions of atoms, for instance, and those atoms are arranged in so many different combinations that they function as 1s and 0s for an organic cell. And the living cell itself is even more structurally complex. Each cell contains DNA, RNA, cell walls that protect the DNA and RNA from being damaged, plasma through which they can float, ribosomes that create proteins, all of which move busily around the cell keeping the thing alive. Outside the cell walls is often a tail, called a flagellum, or even multiple flagella, that helps the cell move and collect any chemical energy it may need to keep producing proteins. All that structure is vastly more complex than a star.

Emergent Properties

With each layer of building blocks in Big History, comes an emergent phenomenon that is unlike anything we see before it.

In terms of energy flows, we've already discussed how the emergent phenomenon is for life to actively seek out greater energy flows in order to sustain its own survival long enough for it to reproduce. This activity comes in a variety of evolutionary forms, whether it be a microbe munching down on some tiny undersea chemicals, a tree absorbing water and sunlight, or a human waking up hungover and nibbling on cold fries for breakfast (does it count as a potato salad?).

In terms of structural intricacy, we have the cooperation of DNA, RNA, and proteins in order to produce self-replication. Gone are the days of only 100 million or so known chemicals. We now have an organic computer system that by a myriad of different combinations of adenine, guanine, cytosine, and thymine (our 1s and 0s) is able to produce trillions of different species, and quadrillions of differing individuals within those species. And with each mutation in DNA, comes a new trait or instinct, all of which count as unique emergent properties.

In short, the number of emergent properties in the Universe is growing, and their diversity and impact all the more profound. On all three counts – energy flows, structural intricacy, and emergent properties – complexity has increased by leaps and bounds in the transition between the animate and inanimate realm.

A Note on Longevity

There is one more thing that is worth considering. A star lives on for billions of years without need to actively seek out more energy flows. An organism has to seek out new energy flows constantly. For instance, humans ideally subsist on three square meals a day, and certainly can't go more than a few weeks without food, and only an average of 3 days without water. Yet despite all that constant biological activity, an organism does not live for billions of years. It lives on for only a few years, decades, or at most (like with some extremely hardy trees) a few centuries. It would appear as a general rule that the more complex something is, the sooner it dies.

Harkening back to chapter 1, this is not out of keeping with what we know of the nature of energy flows in the Universe. The more energy flows something uses, the more brightly the flame burns, the sooner it flickers out. This is because by using more energy flows, higher complexity actually speeds up the increase of entropy (i.e. the dissipation of energy) in the Universe.

Yet the story of life didn't end with microbial organisms guzzling energy and then dying out. They self-replicated, organic material passed to future generations. You personally are descended from LUCA, and you represent an unbroken chain of constantly evolving biological material on Earth. With one extinction of one single species in your direct line over 3.8 billion years, and you would not be here. At each stage, genetic material was copied and recycled. And this process has been going on for 3.8 billion years, fed by a mere fraction of the energy flows of the Earth and Sun. Yet do not forget this came as a result of 99% of all species that ever existed going extinct. The Earth left a crack open for life to emerge, but it is still trying to kill us. So far, Earth has been fairly (but not completely) successful.

Trying not to Bore Ourselves Completely by Discussing Plate Tectonics

Let us leave aside our earliest ancestors 3.8 billion years ago, chomping down geothermal energy and tiny specks of organic chemicals at the bottom of the ocean. They would shelter there for many hundreds of millions of years. Longer than the amount of time that multi-celled organisms like humans, dogs, dinosaurs, trilobites, and jawless fish have existed. For sake of chronology, something else began in the Archean 3.2 billion years ago. It would prove just as crucial to the geological history of Earth as it would prove to the preservation and evolution of life on Earth. Plate tectonics is the core paradigm of geology, and an essential puzzle piece of Big History.

Plate tectonics is the idea that the Earth's crust is not an unbroken layer on top of a molten Earth. The crust may be as thin as an eggshell, relatively speaking, but it is not as united like an eggshell. Instead, the Earth's crust is shattered into plates that are buffeted about by the flows of lava and squishy rock in the mantle below it. They call the movements of the mantle "convection flows". These push the plates about and constantly change the face of the Earth by moving continents, creating mountains, new oceans, and a friendly deluge of earthquakes and volcanic eruptions.

Prior to 3.2 billion years ago, the convection flows of the mantle were not stable enough to establish a regular system of plate tectonics. Instead geological changes were created by flashpoints where volcanism exploded through the crust in separate points across the globe. These volcanic plumes may have been what triggered the cracks in the crust's eggshell in the first place. Then by 3.2 billion years ago, the Earth's interior had cooled to the point that regular convection flows occurred, moving entire continents at a time in a fairly predictable system. Consider them just like the tides, except molten lava and underground. Because of differentiation, the lightest of rocks had floated to the top to form the Earth's crust. This meant the plates floated atop the squishy molten sea.

The best metaphor for plate tectonics is image a small pot of soup on the stove. If it is a thick milky soup, like clam or corn chowder, it gains a skin on top as the cool air interacts with the soup's surface. The skin is the crust. But below the majority of the soup continues to bubble away and push the skin about. Crack the skin and the individual pieces will flow around. That is plate tectonics in a nutshell. Or in a saucepan, at any rate.

sagaPlate tectonics is the key paradigm of geology in the same way that evolution is the key paradigm of biology, because in both cases they explain how things got to be the way they are. Evolution explains how we got from dinosaurs to cockatoos. Plate tectonics explains why we aren't still living on Pangaea, why mountains exist, why the Pacific Rim gets hit by everything from earthquakes to volcanoes to Godzilla, why the age of rock layers correspond on different continents across the world, and why seemingly disparate species spread across the world's continents should have similarities and a common ancestor. It is a way of chronicling historical change.

The Significance of Plate Tectonics

For one thing, plate tectonics is why we have not drowned in a sea of corpses and literal shit. Because plate tectonics has the habit of pulling one plate under another, from time to time, it takes a lot of the dead bodies of living creatures and their waste products beneath the ground. In some cases this organic material even transforms into coal or oil or gas, which we've used to fuel the industrial transformation of the last few centuries (another rise of complexity). If it wasn't for plate tectonics, the accumulation of organic waste would have long since flooded the surface of the Earth and probably have made life extinct.

In terms of inanimate complexity, plate tectonics has another role to play. It is a key player in the creation of new mineral elements. Planets without plate tectonics do not have as much diversity of minerals because they do not have those same forces which pull rocks underground and fuse them into new chemical combinations. In terms of numbers of minerals it makes the difference of a thousand different types.

In terms of biological evolution, the contribution of plate tectonics is obvious. By constantly moving continents around the globe, and also creating geological barriers like mountains, a species gets separated from different groups, and then millions of years pass and that species evolves into completely different ones. One need only look at the difference between marsupials and mammals in Americas versus the Americas to understand this. In the former you've got woolly mammoths and sabre toothed tigers filling ecological niches, in the latter you've got hippo sized wombats and three metre tall carnivorous kangaroos. I think the latter are the most interesting.

Catastrophism

Prior to the theory of plate tectonics, scientists tried to explain the phenomena caused by continental drift by referring to a hypothetical catastrophic event. For instance, Europeans were puzzled by the presence of fossilised sea shells at the top of the Alps. They were also uncovering fossils everywhere of creatures that were now extinct. French paleontologist, Georges Curvier, introduced the theory that extinction events were caused by periodic catastrophic floods that washed the remains of ancient creatures to various locations around the globe. This was the school "catastrophism" in geology.

Another example was why South America and Africa seemed to fit together like puzzle pieces. In 1804, Alexander von Humboldt observed that the rocks on either continent were also similar. For centuries from Abraham Orelius in 1596, to Francis Bacon in 1620, to George de

Buffon in 1750, to Antonio Pellegrini in 1858, they all hypothesised that the Americas had be separated from Africa by a catastrophic series of floods and earthquakes.

Charles Lyell, wrote the *Principles of Geology* (1830) to dispute the school of catastrophism and prove that the world was indeed much older than 6,000 years old. Lyell's book popularised the notion of "uniformitarianism". This was the idea that physical forces currently at play in the present had always been that way in the past. And so the changes of the past must have been made by slow churning geological change, rather than swift catastrophes that would make the history of all those fossils fit within the past 6,000 years.

Instead Lyell posited that the Earth was shaped by new land and mountains being created by volcanoes. And that old land could be destroyed by erosion, eventually sweeping it into the sea. Both of these could be seen in operation in the modern day. The Earth therefore was shaped by these opposing forces. One to build the land up, the other to tear it down. While the idea of plate tectonics was unheard of for another 100 years, these arguments were at least partly true and held a lot of convincing weight.

The implication of Lyell's assertions was the Earth had existed for millions of years, not just a few thousand. Volcanism and erosion in his own day took a very long time to have an effect. In order to effect change on the scale that Lyell observed, it would require many millions of years. Yet the mechanism could not fully explain why the Americas appeared to have once been united to Europe and Africa.

Continental Drift

In the late 19th and early 20th centuries, geologists became theorizing that the continents actually moved. Edward Seuss, Frank Taylor, and Howard Baker all independently pout forward the idea that the continents had moved across the face of the Earth. But none of them could offer much evidence for their hypotheses, nor a fully satisfying explanation for the mechanisms that would make this happen.

Enter Alfred Wegener (1880-1930 AD) who at least provided evidence for plate tectonics. He was a German meteorologist, rather than a geologist. In fact at the time of his death in 1930, Alfred's reputation was for meteorology and climatology. His legendary contribution to geology was yet to be fully recognised. Alfred Wegener wasn't the first person to notice that South America seemed to fit together, but Alfred Wegener pointed out that they were an even better fit if you match the continental shelves of South America and Africa, rather than their modern day water lines. As was then known, sea levels fluctuated on Earth.

This led Wegener to develop his hypothesis of "continental drift" wherein all the continents of the world were at one time "joined together". Today we know of this super-continent as Pangea which formed 300 million years ago and started to break apart 175 million years ago. In fact we know of an even earlier supercontinent, Rodinia, which existed 1 billion to 750 million years ago.

From 1912-1915, Alfred Wegener gathered evidence for his hypothesis. He demonstrated that Gondwana rock sequences appeared in North Africa, West Africa, South America, Antarctica, and Australia. In 1915, Alfred Wegener published *The Origin of Continents and Oceans* which laid out his evidence. He asserted his hypothesis of a super-continent existing many millions of years in the past. This turned out to be correct. But Wegener estimated that the continents were drifting apart at roughly 2 meters a year, which would have placed Pangea 3 million years ago. But this was not supported by the observable spread of continents.

Furthermore, like Seuss, Taylor, and Baker, Wegener could not explain what caused continents to drift. Wegener speculated that the continents might be moving as a result of the force of the Earth's rotation jostling them about. But there was no evidence for this. Wegener did speculate that the Atlantic ridge might be creating more seafloor, but did not chase this up. Wegener continued to promote his hypothesis in the 1920s alongside pursuing his meteorological work. But continental drift was rejected by most contemporary geologists. Meanwhile, Wegener was making expeditions to Greenland. And in 1930 Wegener was killed by the extreme cold, starvation, and the stress of physical exertions there on his heart.

During the Second World War, the British and then later Americans, were working on submarine detection technology. Sonar came into its own and began mapping the floor of the Atlantic Ocean as never before. The mid-Atlantic ridge was revealed to be a line of underwater volcanoes spewing out lava which created more seafloor. This was confirmed by American Rear Admiral Harry Hess in his 1950 report on the subject. He asserted that the Earth's crust was being wedged further apart from the spreading of new seafloor. Was the Earth expanding?

Furthermore, measurements of magnetic fields in the Atlantic showed that the ridges had the normal magnetic orientation of the Earth. But bands of rock further away from the ridge had the opposite magnetic orientation. This was because the poles reverse themselves every few hundred thousand years. Magnetic north and magnetic south interchange in the Earth's magnetic field. So the further rocks had "reverse polarity". What clinched the issue was that seafloor even further away had the "normal polarity" again.

With this knowledge, geologists were able to calculate the Atlantic was expanding by a few centimeters per year. They were able to figure out the Atlantic Ocean was 150 million years old. Later it was determined that the crust of the Pacific Ocean was subducting under the South American plate, and it became clear that the Earth was not expanding. Slowly, but surely, pieces of the Earth were being recycled. It also explained why the ocean floors seemed so much younger than the lighter continental crust, which floated to the top in these exchanges and could be as old as 3.5 billion years. In short, plate tectonics implied there had been billions of years of dynamic change of the hulking geological structures of the Earth. In short, that the Earth had a history.

Essay Writing Exercise

While some essays ask for you to make fairly empirical, evidence-based, and objective thesis statements, like with the question on the Big Bang, other questions are more subjective and interpretative, but nevertheless require strong arguments. To experiment with a basic example of this sort of essay, our exercise question is:

What do you regard as the most important turning point in the geological history of our Earth?

Choose literally any major geological event to happen in the past 4.54 billion years. The geological event can be chosen from those events discussed in this chapter. Or it can be something a little further along the chronology beyond 3.8 billion years. Perhaps you wish to choose a geological event that happened 65 million or 100 years ago. As with all essays on a subjective and interpretative question, *be creative.* Just remember that you'll need to be able to convincingly argue in favour of your choice. In this case, you'll need to convincingly argue that this event of all events is the most significant turning point in billions of years. So don't choose the time you played in the sandbox when you were five.

Once you've chosen your event, write a thesis statement that directly answers the question. It is not enough for the thesis statement to simply name the event you are arguing for. All good thesis statements have a "because clause" that allows you to encapsulate the main force of your argument. As in, "The most important geological turning point is X, because X, Y, and Z".

Once you have written your thesis statement, come up with a point form list of the arguments you are going to use. Then transform those arguments into full sentences and place them one after another behind the thesis statement. End the sequence with a smart phrase that once again drives home your central thesis.

Congratulations, you've written yet another strong introduction!

Further Reading

Chambers, John, and Jacqueline Morton. From Dust to Life: The Origin and Evolution of Our Solar System. Princeton: Princeton University Press, 2014.

Cloud, Preston. Oasis in Space: Earth History from the Beginning. New York: W.W. Norton, 1988.

Fortey, R. Earth: An Intimate History. New York: Knopf, 2004.

Frankel, Henry. The Continental Drift Controversy: Wegener and the Early Debate. Cambridge: Cambridge University Press, 2012.

Hazen, Robert. The Story of Earth: The First 4.5 Billion Years from Stardust to Living Planet. New York: Viking 2012.

Knoll, Andrew. Life on a Young Planet: The First Three Billion Years of Evolution on Earth. Princeton: Princeton University Press, 2003.

Lunine, J. Earth: Evolution of a Habitable World. Cambridge: Cambridge University Press, 1999.

Maynard Smith, John, and Eors Szathmary. The Origins of Life: From the Birth of Life to the Origins of Language. Oxford: Oxford University Press, 1999.

Macdougall, Doug. Why Geology Matters: Decoding the Past, Anticipating the Future. Berkeley: University of California Press, 2011.

Nicastro, Nicholas. Circumference: Eratosthenes and the Ancient Quest to Measure the Globe. New York: St. Martin's Press, 2008.

Roller, Duane. Ancient Geography: The Discovery of the World in Classical Greece and Rome. London: I.B. Tauris, 2015.

Rudwick, Martin. Earth's Deep History: How it was discovered and why it matters. Chicago: University of Chicago Press, 2014.

Tarbuck, E. and F. Lutgens. Earth: An Introduction to Physical Geology. New Jersey: Pearson Prentice Hall, 2005.

Wegener, Alfred. The Origin of Continents and Oceans. trans. John Biram. New York: Dover Publications, 1966.

CHAPTER 4

LIFE AND EVOLUTION

Or,

IF YOU THOUGHT YOUR ANCESTORS

200 YEARS AGO WERE SHORT,

MOST OF YOUR ANCESTORS LIVED

3.8 BILLION TO 600 MILLION YEARS AGO

AND THEY WERE MICROSCOPIC

DON'T PANIC!

If you were wondering why we haven't had a Threshold Flashcard since the start of Chapter 3, please don't panic, pull at your hair, and rend your clothes to pieces. The next threshold of rising complexity only comes with the emergence of "collective learning" many billions of years from now. Collective learning enabled a form of cultural evolution that sped up the rise of complexity by leaps and bounds. The evolutionary epic of the next couple chapters is a story of biological evolution, wherein changes in species could only happen once every generation at most, or more likely once every few thousand or million years.

This is important to bear in mind because without a further rise of complexity, life's history would have remained within the confines of evolution by natural selection. And without further leaps forward in complexity, this contest of extinction, predation, and fighting tooth and claw would have continued for billions of years until a catastrophic asteroid impact, terrible volcanic super-eruption, deadly super-virus, or the bloating of the Sun finally wiped all life out. Threshold 5 would be as far as we would have got. The following few chapters are a description of the startling history of diverse and remarkable species, and plotting a course to how a gang of microscopic automatons evolved into species capable of consciousness, compassion, and collective learning.

Timeline

- **The First Photosynthesizers (3.4 billion years ago):** Our Last Universal Common Ancestor (LUCA) likely formed on the edges of undersea vents at the bottom of the ocean. It collected energy flows from geothermal energy and chemicals lying on the ocean floor in a process called "chemosynthesis". Approximately 400 million years later, increasing numbers of organisms drifted to the top of the ocean and began to use solar radiation and carbon dioxide to produce energy in what is called "photosynthesis". Over the next few million years, single-celled organisms multiplied spread across the surface of the ocean (of which there is a lot) filling the seas with photosynthesizing bacteria.

- **The Great Oxygenation Event (3 to 2.4 billion years ago):** The waste product of photosynthesis is oxygen, with photosynthesizers utilising only the carbon in carbon dioxide and ejecting the rest. An abundance of photosynthesizers and an abundance of carbon dioxide in the Archean atmosphere thus had the effect of producing a lot of oxygen as the years went by. Over the course of 500 million years, the oxygen levels of the atmosphere increased from nigh-nothing to roughly 2.5%. While still a small percentage, this was enough oxygen in the atmosphere to kill off a huge number of single-celled species, because none of them respired oxygen, and because it is highly reactive and harmful to fragile biota. As a result, waves of species died off in the world's first mass extinction event.

- **The First Eukaryotes (2 billion years ago):** The first organisms on Earth were prokaryotic, which are pretty basic and simpler organisms primarily defined by having no nucleus protecting their DNA, having fewer organelles, and being generally smaller and less hardy. Eukaryotes, on the other hand, are single-celled organisms that have a nucleus to protect their DNA from damage and are more capable. It is likely that during one of the Snowball Earth phases that environmental pressure prompted the evolution of prokaryotes into eukaryotes. The significance of this is that all multi-celled life on Earth, including you, is a collection of eukaryotic cells (though these eukaryotes were still single-celled and many eukaryotes on Earth are still single-celled).

- **The Evolution of Sex (1.5 billion years ago):** During another period of ecological strain, eukaryotes were prompted, possibly by cannibalism, to begin exchanging genetic material. Instead of simply cloning themselves every time they reproduced, they had to exchange genes with a mate. The increase of genetic diversity was a boon for evolution because it allowed for many more positive traits to evolve more quickly, and for negative traits to more quickly be weeded out. This was so effective that evolutionary pressure made sexual reproduction one of our most primary drives, which in turn affected the selection of physical traits and instincts. Hence the reason why you may spend so much time on Tinder or pissed off about a recent ex.

- **The Last Snowball Earth (650 million years ago):** Throughout geological history, there have been recurrent phases where the polar ice caps have extended from the poles to the equator, encasing the entire Earth in ice. When there is too much oxygen in the atmosphere, it reflects sunlight back into space and cools the Earth. White snow and ice also reflect the Sun's light and the process intensifies. There were Snowball Earth phases that occurred 2.2 billion years ago (shortly after the Great Oxygenation), 750 to 700 million years ago, and a final one 650 million years ago, which ended 635 million years ago. It is likely that the last period of strain contributed to the evolution of multi-celled species, which we first see emerge in the Ediacaran era.

The Single-Celled Saga (Featuring Microbes in Viking Helmets!)

Archean Beginnings

It seems fairly clear that life began in the oceans approximately 3.8 billion years ago, imbibing energy flows from the geothermal energy of the still warm Earth. This was because there was no ozone layer in the atmosphere yet, so migrating toward the top of the oceans to absorb solar energy would have pelted this vulnerable early form of life with radiation and destroyed it. The first organisms were, of course, microscopic and quite simple.

These were the "prokaryotes" which are the most basic cellular structure. The DNA and RNA just float openly around the cell, making them more at risk of being damaged. There are ribosomes that produce proteins which allow the cell's walls to form. The prokaryote does not have sex, it just clones itself as it splits into copies. Because there is less genetic diversity in cloning, evolution moved more slowly. Changes in the prokaryotic organism took millions of years. That said, cloning was quite rapid, with cells splitting every few minutes. Some cells could split in mere seconds.

It terms of energy flows, these cells did not require much. Perhaps 450 to 900 erg/g/s which is much less than more complex life, but still a couple orders of magnitude greater than the Sun. As the story of life moves forward, we shall see an increase in the structural intricacy and energy density of living things. Life continues the pattern of rising complexity in the inanimate Universe.

The earliest forms of life split into two distinct "domains" of life, *Archaea* and *Bacteria*, which we shall discuss in greater detail in the following section. The *Archaea* prokaryotes which take their name from the geological eon in which they emerged were likely the first such structures to evolve. These were the "extremophiles" that could live in harsh environments – such as the edges of underwater volcanoes and could eat inorganic chemicals (stuff without carbon) in order to sustain their own complexity. The Bacteria prokaryotes soon evolved to take advantage of the presence of many organic chemicals that pervaded the Earth's oceans, and gained an appetite for all sorts of chemicals that were carbon-based.

The Great Oxygenation or Oxygen "Holocaust"

The bacterial appetite for carbon moved toward one of the most plentiful abundances on Earth: the carbon dioxide that formed 80% of the atmosphere. As the seas filled with chemosynthesizers, there was an evolutionary incentive for more prokaryotes to move toward the surface and seek solar energy rather than geothermal energy. By 3.4 billion years ago, cyanobacteria were using water, sunlight, and carbon dioxide to produce energy to maintain all their complexity. These were the first photosynthesizers. They would eat the hydrogen from the water, and the carbon from the air, and use solar energy to fuel the process. The oxygen would be discarded as a "waste product".

Bear in mind it took approximately 400 million years for this first major stride in evolution to take place. That is roughly the same amount of time that separates us from the Devonian period and the first vertebrates to colonise the land. Yet the Sun was a much more plentiful energy resource than the geothermal energy flows from cracks in the Earth. Once photosynthesizers were adapted enough to take a bit of radiation, more and more prokaryotes started lining the top of the ocean to capitalise on this energy revolution. Some photosynthesizers even began to form large colonies of single cells, big mounts that could stand 50 to 100 cm in height, called stromatolites. The fossilised remains of these colonies can still be found at Shark Bay in Western Australia, and are one of the earliest tangible remnants of early life from over 3 billion years ago.

But what about the waste product of all this activity? The oxygen that was discarded by photosynthesis using carbon dioxide left a molecule O_2 (the dioxide part). For the photosynthesizers this was basically harmful "poop" that they did not need. It was also unhealthy for them. O_2 is highly "reactive" in the sense that it lets off a fairly violent chemical reaction when it combines with other molecules. In large quantities O_2 could kill the prokaryotes. Fortunately 3.4 billion years ago, the amount of dioxygen in the atmosphere was next to nothing. But the more numerous and successful photosynthesizers became, the more this changed.

It takes quite a long time for tiny microscopic beings to exhale enough oxygen to change an entire atmosphere. The first amounts of oxygen 3 billion years ago were reabsorbed into the seabed rocks of the ocean and into the rocks of Earth's barren surface. The effect on these rocks can be seen in their bands of iron. For the first time, the oxygen was making the iron *rust* and turn a reddish colour which can still be seen in rock formations today.

After the 3 billion year mark, gradually the Earth's atmosphere began to change from negligible levels of oxygen to some trace amounts. The difference was still tiny, however. But by approximately 2.5 billion years ago, the rocks of the Earth had absorbed all the oxygen that they could possibly take. These "oxygen sinks" were full. And in the space of just 100 million years, the oxygen share of the atmosphere leapt up to 2.5%.

This had a catastrophic effect on the environment and the organisms that dwelt within it. Most single-celled organisms were not evolved to process oxygen. They were "anaerobic". But the increased dose of oxygen in the atmosphere and the oceans proved deadly. Scores and scores of prokaryotic species (all potential ancestors) died off. Only a few anaerobic species remained. It would not be the last time that the waste products of a successful species would let off a mass extinction event…

The Ozone Layer and the First Snowball Earth

The increase of oxygen in the atmosphere didn't stop 2.4 billion years ago. It accelerated. Levels of O_2 continued to rise as it gassed out of the oceans. This was still a highly noxious gas for early life. The photosynthesizers were messing things up for everything anaerobic. Yet as we shall often see in Big History, devastation provided a catalyst for the rise of further complexity.

As O_2 became more plentiful 2.2 billion years ago, it started to enter the upper atmosphere, where it interacted with the increased radiation of the Sun. The heat from the Sun began to transform the O_2 into O_3 in a process called "photolysis". This is where the Sun knocks two oxygen atoms apart, and then those single oxygen atoms combine with other molecules of O_2 to form O_3. A layer of O_3 began to blanket the Earth. This was the ozone layer. It reflected much of the Sun's rays which had previously scorched the surface back into space.

While today we regard the ozone layer as an extremely vital component of the continuing survival of life on this planet, 2 billion years ago it had a deadly effect. With little to counteract it, the blanket of ozone just got thicker and thicker. With less of the Sun's heat reaching the surface of the Earth, the whole planet started to cool.

The oceans started to freeze at the Earth's poles. A thick layer of ice began to form. But it didn't stop there. The ice sheet began to descend from the poles of the Earth toward the equator. With each movement forward, the snow-covered white ice began to reflect even more of the Sun's rays back into space. This intensified and sped up the process of plummeting temperatures and the Earth's freezing. The average global temperature would have been around -50 degrees Celsius. Eventually two massive ice sheets, many metres tall, met at the equator and joined together, encasing the Earth in a tomb of ice.

The Rise of the Eukaryotes

This whole process should have doomed all life on Earth, including the photosynthesizers that could no longer just drift at the top of the ocean and absorb the Sun's rays. Indeed their numbers must have been culled. A few cyanobacteria likely survived in shallow melted pools nearer to the equator. But the next leap forward in evolution was left to a much more ancestral species.

We have not discussed the *Archaea* prokaryotes much in the last couple pages. They were still doing their "extremophile" thing, munching down inorganic chemicals near the cracks in the Earth. These *Archaea* were much better equipped to survive the catastrophe recently brought upon the Earth by photosynthesizers. And as such they had an opportunity for genetic mutation and evolution to capitalise on the increased levels of oxygen in the atmosphere.

A segment of the *Archaea* evolved the ability to use oxygen for energy. This process is called "respiration". Instead of converting water and carbon dioxide into energy and giving off oxygen as a waste product like photosynthesizers do, a respiring or "aerobic" cell takes O_2 and gives off water and CO_2 as a waste product. It is still in that sense that humans and plants "feed" each other today. The abundance of oxygen in the atmosphere thus became a positive boon for aerobic species.

Yet these were still constrained circumstances. The Earth was encased in ice. The emerging aerobic species had to be made of some pretty stern stuff to survive. And so 2 billion years ago, the "eukaryotes" evolved from a branch of the *Archaea*. This was a dramatically different kind of cell structure from a prokaryote, so much so that these cells are classified under their own domain, the *Eukaryota* (on which more will be said in the next section). O_2 actually affords a cell much more energy once it evolves to digest it, so there was plenty of increased energy flows to fuel this evolution of a "beefier" cell.

The eukaryotes were larger by about 10 to 1000 times (still microscopic though the largest once can almost be seen with the naked eye). Unlike in prokaryotes, the DNA was protected by a nucleus. The structure of the cell had a "cytoskeleton" holding it up. The eukaryotes were a damn tough domain of various species. They also represented a slight increase in structural and energy complexity. This allowed them to survive the Snowball Earth period.

Eventually volcanoes broke through the sheets of ice covering the Earth, and began pumping carbon dioxide back into the atmosphere. This had the effect of warming the Earth. As the ice sheets receded, the carbon dioxide that had been trapped in the rocks of the surface and seabed also began to outgas CO_2 into the atmosphere. The cycle was reversing itself. The Snowball Earth phase was over – for now – and both aerobic and anaerobic species were able to flourish.

Let's Talk about Sex Bay-bee, Let's Talk about "Eu"(karyotes)-and-Me!

After the retreat of Snowball Earth, life in the Archean world had a new lease on life. *Bacteria, Archaea,* and *Eukaryota* all evolved and diversified. The Eukaryotes, especially, found a thousand new niches opening up for them. Some Eukaryotes continued to respire oxygen, using a new organelle, the "mitochondria". Other eukaryotes evolved to become photosynthesizers, and instead of mitochondria had an organelle called the "chloroplast". The former was the ancestor of animals, the latter was the ancestor of plants.

But things could not last this way forever. The environment is treacherous and Mother Earth is always trying to kill us. Approximately 1.5 billion years ago, some catastrophe and period of ecological strain (the cause of which is unclear) led to a shortage of food for eukaryotes. Perhaps it was a regional crisis, perhaps it was global. But the lack of food began to cause eukaryotes to eat one another, surviving via cannibalism.

This act of cannibalism in a few cases must have resulted in the accidental exchange of DNA. In short, this was the world's first sex act, however "Hannibal Lecter-esque" it may have been. Up until roughly 1.5 billion years ago, all eukaryotes simply cloned themselves like prokaryotes do. But the evolutionary advantages of sexual reproduction are profound. The exchange of DNA adds a greater amount of genetic diversity. The mutations of DNA are doubled in frequency, and the mixture of genes between two parent cells can also yield advantageous results. Evolution thus can move at a faster pace.

The first "sexy eukaryotes" still divided like cells normally did. But instead of reproducing all their DNA in an exact copy, they would only reproduce half. The cell would then be tasked with finding a "mate" in order to combine and complete the number of chromosomes required to create a new organism. Those single-celled organisms that did not find a "mate" died off.

So advantageous was this process to evolution, that it spawned a whole new range of tactics and behaviours and, eventually, instincts. Once organisms became multicellular, they began to compete for mates in ways that would influence the evolution of an entire species behaviour (we shall see that in a later chapter in primates). The drive to have sex and reproduce became so engrained in organisms instinctually, that it formed one of the primary motives for living: to survive long enough to attract a mate and reproduce. Much of the emotional life of species even became strongly attached to finding and keeping a mate. The sometimes overpowering desire to have sex would override other instincts and sometimes result in risk-taking behaviours. Sexual selection favoured traits among species that would prove advantageous to rearing young (like good health, strength, or resourcefulness) or simply attracting attention from the opposite sex (like gigantic and otherwise impractical antlers on certain species of deer, elk, and moose).

So powerful and pervasive is sex in evolution that it shaped an overwhelming majority of the traits of complex species, the overwhelming majority of their instincts (making organisms rather Freudian as a result), and in the case of humans, bleeding into how we acted, rationalised, prioritised goals, and even how we shaped our cultures and societies.

The Last Snowball Earth (we hope)

The trend of photosynthesizers pumping too much oxygen into the atmosphere repeated itself in the last billion years. This grew particularly severe when there was not as much volcanic activity to counter-balance the oxygen by pumping carbon dioxide into the atmosphere. As a result, the last billion years experienced two other phases of Snowball Earth. Not just an Ice Age, but the full encasement of the Earth in a layer of ice. There was one case of it approximately 700 million years ago, and another that began 650 million years ago and ended 635 million years ago. The result of that period of strain was multicellularism, which we shall explore further in the next chapter.

The Family Tree

Life is made from strings of hydrogen, carbon, nitrogen, and phosphorus arranged in nucleobases that are in turn strung into nucleotides that form the codes for determining what the organism is. Each nucleotides are grouped into genes, and each gene determines a trait. The proteins that build the organism are similarly built upon strings of amino acids that are made from the same organic chemical elements. In short, all life comes from non-life. Once we arrive (by whatever cause) at DNA (deoxyribonucleic acid) this chemical is programmed to actively seek out energy flows from its environment (metabolism), it copies itself in a form of self-replication (reproduction), and every billion copies there is a mutation which may help the chemical survive in its environment (adaptation). Metabolism, reproduction, and adaptation are three key characteristics of life.

And this is what evolution by natural selection boils down to. Life needs metabolism to maintain its energy flows to keep its complexity from breaking down long enough for it to reproduce. Mutations occur during reproduction, and if helpful they allow life to adapt to its environment so it can survive long enough to reproduce again. And so the cycle continues. From single-celled sludge to slack-jawed *sapiens*. It is from this chemical process that the evolutionary tree grew from our humble microscopic LUCA, cowering at the bottom of the oceans.

Don't lose sight of the fact that ultimately evolution is simply the prohibition of organic chemicals that can no longer exist in the environment (in the same way a bottle of Pepsi cannot exist on the surface of the Sun). The unit of selection is the gene. "Naturally selected" DNA itself is just a sequence of chemicals that got put in the "right" order to survive. Life is simply a chemical undergoing a reaction like any other, it is only that its reactions are decidedly more complex and interesting than pouring vinegar into a papier-mâché volcano full of baking soda. Life is a reddish brown sludge whose reactions have bubbled forth and spawned stegosauruses, mammoths, scorpions, and golden retrievers, instead of simply making a mess of the kitchen.

Over the last 3.8 billion years, a startlingly diverse family tree has emerged from this chemical process. LUCA is the ancestor of everyone, and shares DNA in common with all living things. Similarly, all living things are relatives, and share DNA in common with each other. How much DNA you hold in common determines the closeness of your relationship. Humans share about 40% of their DNA with a daffodil. They share about 98.4% of their DNA with a chimpanzee. And humans themselves share about 99.9% of their DNA with each other. That doesn't mean we are inbred, but we are all closely related. At any rate, I doubt the incestuous feeling you may briefly get will prevent you from giving each other the glad-eye and flirting clumsily at the bar after four beers.

The family tree can roughly be divided into the following simplified set of levels. Though taxonomists love to introduce intermediate categories like sub-phyla, sub-orders, super-families, sub-families, tribes, inside of which species can belong in multiple classifications at once and over which biologists can debate for the course of their entire careers and perpetuate their paychecks. With the one necessary exception of super-classes, we shall try to cut out most of the fat here:

DOMAIN

KINGDOM

PHYLUM

SUPER-CLASS

CLASS

ORDER

FAMILY

GENUS

SPECIES

For example, our species, *Homo sapiens*, belongs to the domain of *Eukaryota*, the kingdom of *Animalia*, the phylum of *Chordata*, the super-class of *Tetrapoda*, the class of *Mammalia*, the order of *Primates*, the family of *Hominidae*, the genus *Homo*, and the species *sapiens*.

And so we don't lose sight of the chronology in this section, our domain of eukaryotes evolved roughly 2 billion years ago. Our kingdom of animals evolved approximately 600 million years ago. The phylum of chordates evolved around 540 million years ago. Our super-class of tetrapods evolved 390 million years ago. Our class of mammals evolved 225 million years ago. Our order of primates evolved 60 million years ago. Our family of *Hominidae* evolved 20 million years ago. Our genus *Homo* evolved 2.5 to 3 million years ago. And our species evolved a currently estimated 300,000 to 350,000 years ago.

We delve more into the evolutionary story of each of these stages in this chapter and the following two. So don't panic about memorising these dates or thinking that is all the historical detail you are going to get! But these classifications and dates are here as a quick point of reference should you need them for the writing of any essays.

The Grand Domains of the Family Tree

Across the evolutionary family tree, there are three major "domains" of organisms: *Archaea, Bacteria,* and *Eukaryota* (the eukaryotes mentioned in the timeline) to which we belong.

Let's start with *Archaea* and *Bacteria*. Both of these domains are "prokaryotic" single-celled organisms. Prokaryotes are the forerunner to eukaryotes. They are a simplified cell (or as simple as a cell can be compared to the much tamer simplicity of the inanimate Universe) that has the most basic functions to ensure survival. A prokaryote is a tiny ball of organic goodness. Hundreds of thousands of them could fit into a single dot made by a pencil. They have a rigid cell wall made from proteins which contains a bunch of goopy cytoplasm. Within the goop are the ribosomes, which create the proteins. Floating around the sea of cytoplasm is a bunch of DNA and RNA, which are unprotected and can be damaged amidst the chaotic traffic whizzing through the cell.

The difference between *Archaea* and *Bacteria* is simple. *Archaea* are genetically distant to *Bacteria*. It is also likely that *Archaea* are the most similar to LUCA in our family tree. This is because many of them are "extremophiles" that live on the edges of volcanoes and hot springs, but others have since spread across the Earth, including into human guts. Due to the Archaean propensity for "risky living" it isn't surprising they should have retained more traits of LUCA than the domain of *Bacteria* which went off in a thousand wild directions starting 3.5 billion years ago.

Bacteria are more distant genetically, and make up huge variety of microbes, some of which inhabit and help the human body, some of which try to kill the human body, and some of which still inhabit the surface of the oceans. The first photosynthesizers 3.4 billion years ago, for instance, belong to the domain *Bacteria*, called "cyanobacteria". It appears that from a very early stage in the family tree, *Bacteria* split off and has been doing its own thing in its little microscopic world evolving to be quite genetically and functionally diverse from the other two realms.

The more extremophile *Archaea*, however, appears to share a closer relationship to *Eukaryota* (which is what we are). This makes sense given that eukaryotes likely evolved from strained circumstances 2 billion years ago, and the best ancestor that would have survived and evolved in a time of strain would have been the extremophile Archaea. More on the precise details of that change 2 billion years ago will follow soon.

The final domain are the *Eukaryota*. We are the youngest, emerging from *Archaea* about 2 billion years ago. We merit a separate domain because eukaryotes are a radically different structure from the prokaryotic *Bacteria* and *Archaea*. Eukaryotes are slightly more robust single-celled organisms, and *some* of them evolved 650 million years ago to become multi-celled organisms like us.

Single-celled eukaryotes are much larger than prokaryotes, though still microscopic. Their DNA is protected by a nucleus which reduces the chances it will get demanded. The goopy cytoplasm of prokaryotes evolved and hardened into a skeleton which made eukaryotes more mobile. Eukaryotes also contain new organelles which aid with either breathing oxygen or photosynthesis. They often have a much thicker tail (called a flagellum) which allows them to zip about. In short, eukaryotes are more adaptable to different environments without having to evolve as much first, and structurally they are more complex.

The Illustrious Kingdoms of the Eukaryotes

Below the domains are the kingdoms of the evolutionary tree. We won't go into the mounds of microbes that infest the *Archaea* and *Bacteria* (known collectively in the Australian taxonomy system as *Monera*), as this would blow out the length of the chapter and be astoundingly boring to everyone except a few aspiring microbiologists (sorry, guys). There is also the justification that from this point forward we will be zeroing in increasingly on "rising complexity" given that is the unifying theme of Big History.

Within the domain of *Eukaryota* (remember you really put the YOU in eukaryotes, get it?) there are four kingdoms, depending on what classification system you are using. But in Australia, there are four eukaryotic kingdoms. Australians are always correct as a nation, being the best nation on Earth, so crack open a can of VB, light up a durry, crank up some Akka Dakka or Waltzing Matilda, ride your kangaroo to work, and let's get to it.

The *four* eukaryotic kingdoms (Aussie, Aussie, Aussie!) are *Animalia, Plantae, Fungi,* and *Protista. Animalia* are animals. Dogs, cats, bats, fish, birds, dinosaurs, frogs, scorpions, trilobites, wasps, squids, slugs, and humans. You know what animals are. They are multi-celled and usually breathe oxygen. But to be clear the kingdom includes vertebrates which have a spine (like dogs), and invertebrates which have an exo-skeleton (like scorpions) which is worn over top the muscle of the animal, and those who have neither.

Plantae are plants. And here we go again. Trees, bushes, grasses, mosses. They are multi-celled and they generally use photosynthesis. They are separated from the first photosynthesizing bacteria that evolved in the oceans 3.4 billion years ago, which are cyanobacteria. Plants on the other hand must have evolved the ability to use photosynthesis sometime after the first eukaryotes evolved 2 billion years ago. For perspective, you share roughly 35-40% of your DNA with most plants.

Fungi are good conversation at a party, who crack a lot of jokes and make the evening interesting. Or they might be single-celled or multi-celled, and do not use photosynthesis, but absorb chemicals from their surrounding environments. Mostly dead stuff. They behave a lot like plants in the sense that they don't move, but simply grow. Fungi include mushrooms but also yeasts and some molds.

Protista are single-celled eukaryotes that are neither animals, plants, nor fungi. Protists are the precursors to those other three kingdoms before they evolved their distinct traits. In a sense, *Protista* are a one size fits all kingdom to which are relegated those eukaryotes that have not evolved distinct traits to merit more precise classification at the kingdom level. The protist kingdom includes amoebas, algae, and slime molds. If it does not look like a dog, sunflower, or mushroom, it might well belong here.

The Fabulous Phyla of the Animal Kingdom

Below the level of kingdom, is phylum (plural: phyla). And here things begin to multiply, given there is such a vast diversity of animal species. There are over 30 phyla in the animal kingdom. A surprising number of them just refer to different types of worm. Including the hilarious *Priapulida* worms (look it up). Others come in the form of jellies or sponges. Another minor phylum of interest is the *Tardigrada*, or water bears, which are only a few millimetres long, but can survive in extreme conditions. Whether cold, or hot, or outer space. They are also capable of switching off their metabolism and entering a sort of coma to survive long periods without food.

The most diverse and complex phyla of the animal kingdom are the *Arthropoda*, *Chordata*, and *Mollusca*. The last of these, the mollusks, include snails, slugs, squids, oysters, and octopuses. They are distinguished by how soft their actual bodies are, possessing neither a spine nor a fully fitted exoskeleton. The shell possessed by a snail or an oyster is not exactly the same thing. The shell is secreted by the part of the body called the mantle, which squirts out calcium carbonate that forms the shell. Mollusks have a radula "tongue" they use for feeding, and the fact their bodies are one open circulatory system full of blood. You share roughly 60% of your DNA with mollusks.

The *Arthropoda*, on the other hand, have armour that truly deserves to be called an exo-skeleton. The armour is closely adhered to their bodies, and has double-joints along the limbs and bodies to allow for movement. Arthropods include insects (like ants), arachnids (like spiders), centipedes, and also crabs and lobsters. Essentially all the creepy stuff that gives some people phobias, and also some of the most expensive stuff on the menu. Extremely numerous and diverse, arthropods were some of the most successful creatures in the early oceans and the first to move on to dry land.

The *Chordata* are anything with a "spine" or "notochord". This essentially is a stick of cartilage or bone that runs inside the meat of the animal to facilitate movement. This includes fish, amphibians, reptiles, and mammals. All of the above mentioned are vertebrate chordates, but the phylum also includes various kinds of sea cucumbers, primitive fish, and worms with primitive spines. Chordates are also distinguished by a nervous system (which usually runs along the spine), and a feeding tube that runs from mouth to stomach. As you may have predicted, it was this variety eventually evolved to become the most complex, largely due to the evolution of their brains.

The Sensational Super-Classes of the Chordates

As mentioned, the chordates are largely comprised of the vertebrates (which is a sub-phylum, just because taxonomists wanted to be extra conveniently confusing) along with other sub-phyla which contain sea cucumbers (tunicates) and small primitive fish (cephalocordates). But the primary super-classes of chordate are: *Agnatha, Gnathostomata, Tetrapoda,* and *Osteichthyes.*

The *Agnatha* are a type of jawless fish that essentially have an open mouth to chomp down food in the oceans. It is likely these are the most primitive kinds of fish that existed in the Cambrian. There are also existing jawless fish like lampreys, which never found the evolutionary need to evolve away from that system of feeding.

The *Gnathostomata* include all the jawed fishes, sharks, and stingrays that first began to evolve in the late-Cambrian and Ordovician periods. Think "gnashing of teeth". They are not only able to capture food by closing their mouths, but they also have teeth which, in the case of sharks especially, allows them to wound and kill prey for consumption. This class was highly successful in the oceans for hundreds of millions of years, and even today still constitutes the majority of chordate marine life. Their skeletal structure is predominantly made from cartilage rather than bone, and the difference there is the same as between the bone of your skull and the softer material of the cartilage of your nose. It is why it is easier to break your nose with a swift punch than your skull, and why ancient skulls don't have a nose any more.

The *Osteichthyes* are fish whose skeletal structure is made primarily from bones. It is harder material and sturdier but less flexible and heavier in water than cartilage is. And it is highly likely that these bony fish share an ancestor with the first tetrapods that crawled out onto land.

The *Tetrapoda* are highly significant in that they are the first vertebrate species to move out on to the land. They did so probably as a type of lungfish in the Devonian period, eventually evolving limbs and digits to help with terrestrial locomotion. The tetrapods are distinguished by possessing four limbs (hence the name) and from the first admittedly very "fishy" ancestors of tetrapods that crawled out of the oceans 400 million years ago have evolved all amphibians, reptiles, birds, and mammals. This includes even snakes, who lost their limbs in subsequent evolution but still hold vestigial traces of them. These are all the "classes" of the "super-class" of tetrapods.

The Classy and Charismatic Classes of Tetrapoda

Not much need be said about the amphibians, reptiles, birds, and mammals, since these are increasingly familiar creatures. We shall also be discussing their evolutionary journey later in this chapter. But for comprehensiveness and brevity, the amphibians are distinguished by their porous skin and need to lay their eggs in water, hence their closeness to the oceans, lakes, and rivers. This is the earliest class of tetrapod once we climbed out of the sea, and it is from amphibians that the other classes of tetrapod evolved. Reptiles meanwhile evolved less porous skin and hard-shelled eggs, which allowed them to move further inland. Birds evolved from dinosaurs 120 million years ago, and retained many reptilian characteristics, but with the addition of feathers and the rather obvious trait of flight. And finally mammals are distinguished by feeding their young from mammary glands.

The Opulent Orders of Mammalia

In case you haven't noticed at this point, taxonomy is quite a messy subject. In fact it is giving the author a whopping headache just trying to clean this up a bit for you. This is largely due to the fact that evolution itself is a chemical reaction of DNA that does not divide itself neatly into categories, and that different species are categorised (sometimes quite subjectively) by humans based on the extent of their variation, and perhaps a couple of key traits.

Once we arrive at the orders of mammals, we arrive at a fairly whopping mess. There are approximately 18 to 30 different orders of mammal, and many biologists are divided on the precise system of classification. That being said, here are some of the major ones for your consideration.

- *Artiodactyla* are even-toed hoofed animals that include everything from sheep, to cows, to deer, to giraffes.
- The *Carnivora* include dogs, cats, lions, wolves, hyenas, mongooses, and bears.
- The *Chiroptera* are bats that are mammals which evolved the power of flight, after being tree-climbing species that evolved flaps of skin that allowed them to glide from tree to tree, eventually forming fully capable wings.
- The *Marsupialia* are mammals with pouches that include possums in the Americas, but in Australia which was separated geographically for much longer, marsupials spread rapidly, evolving into wombats, kangaroos, wallabies, koalas, etc.
- The *Perissodactyla* are odd-toed hoof animals include horses, zebras, and rhinos.
- The *Rodentia* are smaller mammals that stayed closest to the original evolutionary forms that survived the K-T extinction event 65 million years ago. This order includes mice, rats, gophers, hamsters, gerbils, gophers, squirrels, and marmots.
- The *Primates* which is our ancestral line on the level of biological orders. The primates include monkeys and apes, but also shrews, lemurs, and tarsiers. The family of apes (Hominidae) include chimpanzees, gorillas, bonobos, orangutans, and humans.

Below the order is the family, and within the family are different kinds of genus. From there we get closer to the genus *Homo*, and the species *Homo sapiens*. But that evolutionary story awaits us in the following two chapters. For now, some history of science! All you students love that, right?!

So How Did I Evolve From a Microbe, Anyway?

For the majority of human history, the different species of the Earth seemed to us vastly different from each other, and were presumed to be immutable. That is to say, unchanging, since their creation by some kind of deity or supernatural event. There was also, until modern times, no clear explanatory mechanism for how species might change over eons of time. However, in the past three centuries, the picture has become clearer. Today, instead of species that remain static and eternal (much like the Earth was thought to be before plate tectonics, or the Universe was thought to be before Big Bang cosmology), the story of species is a historically dynamic and fluid one.

Lamarck's Remarkable Extending Giraffe Necks

Jean-Baptiste Lamarck (1744-1829) was a pioneer of evolutionary biology. His theory of "soft-inheritance" or "Lamarckism" proposes that living things can acquire new traits during their lifetime and pass them on to their descendants. This means that if you were a giraffe and were constantly straining for leaves in high trees, your neck might get longer, and then your offspring would be born with these longer necks. Or if you were born a fairly thin person but then weight-trained your whole life, you'd pass on your more muscular physique to your children. Lamarck's theory turned out to be wrong because acquired traits are generally not passed on to offspring, but it was an important attempt to explain the immense diversity of species in nature. Lamarck's attempt happened in a world that largely thought species were created already adapted to their environments, and did not change over time.

Lamarck was born in Old Regime France into an aristocratic family that had fallen on hard times. He was educated at a Jesuit school. When he was 16, Lamarck entered the French army where he served with distinction and was promoted to an officer on account of his bravery and competence. Lamarck was still living in poor conditions and began studying to be a doctor. During his studies, Lamarck developed an interest in botany – the study of plants. He soon declared his interest in pursuing botany as a profession.

By the late 1781, Lamarck had become a famous French botanist in the service of the Royal Garden in Paris. From 1781-83 he travelled extensively observing and collecting rare species of plants. Lamarck earned a good living as a botanist in service of the royal family until the French Revolution in 1789. Despite his aristocratic background, Lamarck avoided the purges of the Revolution and continued his work at the Royal Garden, which he renamed the Jardin des plantes. During this time, Lamarck lived a relatively comfortable life where he was able to pursue his studies.

In 1800, Lamarck delivered his first lecture on Lamarckian evolution and subsequently expanded on this theory in three written works. The most famous of these was the *Philosophie Zoologique* published in 1809. According to Lamarck, if a species used a certain trait or body part, it would grow over several generations. If the species did not use that trait or body part, it would shrink and gradually disappear. One of the key examples he gave in *Philosophie Zoologique* was the mole, which had eyes but since it had spent so many generations underground, it gradually lost its sight from disuse. Interestingly, Lamarck also hypothesized that there was a force that promoted increasing complexity in species.

Lamarck's theory laid out that environmental factors determined what traits got used and discarded. If environmental factors changed or a species moved into a new environment, the species would become better and better adapted. Then intermediate species that did not have the same strength of those traits would go extinct. Here was a first stab at an evolutionary explanation for the "origin of species".

Lamarck did not actively promote his theory at the time and it went largely criticised or ignored in a world where most biologists and geologists thought species were "immutable" or unchanging. When Lamarck died of old age in 1829, his theory had not gained popular success.

We now know that species generally do not pass on acquired traits to their offspring in evolution. Instead new traits occur from mutations at the DNA level where there is a copying error (about 1 in a billion copies). In standard evolution, DNA does not change from a person's life experiences to allow them to acquire new or stronger traits and pass them on to their offspring. A creature is born with the DNA and the traits they've got. The traits are either successful enough to allow the creature to survive and reproduce, or the traits are not good enough to permit the creature to have offspring. The experiences a living organism has during its lifetime generally tends not to impact the traits of their offspring. As a result, the process of gene mutation and natural selection is a lot slower, involving a lot more deaths and extinctions than Lamarck's model.

It was this general absence of acquired traits being passed on to offspring that meant Lamarck's theory failed where Darwin's theory eventually succeeded.

However, there is an epilogue to the tale. In the new field of epigenetics ("epi" meaning "outside" of standard genetics), there are signs that environmental factors in a single organism's lifetime can change the actions performed by a gene without changing or mutating the string of DNA inside the gene. As such the same gene is built of the same DNA but starts to act differently. So the fundamentals of Darwinism remain true. But if the function of the gene can change, this means slight changes and acquired traits can occur at the tiny microscopic level and potentially be passed on to offspring.

While much less powerful than natural selection, it does cause some interesting changes in bacteria. And even slight changes in the health of lab rats, or the colours of insects, and or the growth of plants. While less powerful a force and less directly geared toward adaptation and survival in an environment than Lamarck would have liked, it appears that acquired traits can cause slight changes without it needing to change an organism's DNA. So while Darwin was more correct, perhaps Lamarck has had the last laugh.

Darwin's Loquacious "Abstract"

Charles Darwin (1809-1882) was born in Shropshire, England, to a well-to-do family in the gentry. His father, Robert Darwin, was a doctor who married Susannah Wedgewood, the daughter of an early industrialist. Like many children who get into biology, he spent much of his time wandering outside examining and collecting all sorts of creatures.

Robert Darwin wanted Charles to follow in his footsteps and enter the medical profession. He was sent to the University of Edinburgh. Darwin had absolutely no interest in medicine, but his time at university gave him the opportunity to pursue his lifelong love of biology. He learned taxidermy. He joined study groups devoted to biology. He devoured the works of Jean-Baptiste Lamarck, William Paley, and Alexander von Humboldt.

The medical career obviously not working out, Robert Darwin sent his son to Cambridge so he could study to enter the clergy. Charles Darwin was pretty fine with this plan at first, because it meant he could live a fairly comfortable life as a country priest, and spend the rest of his time exploring nature as a hobby.

In December 1831, Darwin joined the crew of the HMS Beagle as the ship's naturalist. The two-year voyage was to take him to South America. In wound up as a five-year journey that took him around the world.

The voyage on the Beagle took Darwin to the Azores, Brazil, Uruguay, the Falkland Islands, Argentina, up the Pacific coast to Chile and Peru, landing again in the Galapagos Islands. The Beagle then darted across the Pacific to Australia, across the Indian Ocean, to Cape Town, before tracing its route home. All the way along, Darwin compiled voluminous notes and scores and scores of specimens. Darwin later published a series of books on his journey that made him a household name.

It is important to remember that, at the time, species were considered "immutable". Even by most prevailing natural philosophers of the day. That is, all species were specifically designed for the environments in a way that could not be coincidental. If a species changed at all over time at all, the changes would only be slight but there was a line between species that a living thing could not cross. One could breed pigeons or dogs to look slightly different, but at the end of the day they were still pigeons or dogs.

Darwin spent much of his time wrestling with the arguments of William Palely and Charles Lyell in this respect. Something just didn't add up.

The journey on the Beagle drove home for Darwin how different species were across the world. There must be some mechanism behind it! One thing all scientists were wrestling at the time was: if species are perfectly designed for their environments, why do we have all these fossils of extinct species, and why would new species replace them? The idea of design and immutable species didn't seem to fit.

What clinched it for Darwin was the well-known story of the Galapagos finches. A finch is a type of bird. On each of the 21 islands in the archipelago, the finches had different traits. An expert on bird, John Gould, told him that these were unique species that had never been seen anywhere else in the world. Why would different species be found on each island?

Shortly afterward, Darwin read the work of Thomas Malthus who studied human population dynamics. Essentially, Malthus asserted that humans will breed until a region is overpopulated then strain the resources before there was a die-off from famine and other complications. Which was certainly true in the agrarian era before 200 years ago. Darwin "at last had an idea with which to work."

If applied to species in nature, a population would breed until there was a shortage of resources for everything to survive. Then there would be competition for limited resources. Only those that survived and reproduced would be able to pass on their traits. Ultimately, over time, certain traits would be favoured over others, and a new species would be created. Darwin now had a framework that explained the diversity of nature, why species seemed so well-adapted to their environments, and why the fossil record showed scores of extinct and replaced species.

Here was the beginnings of natural selection and biological evolution. The core principles of what drives DNA replication and permits certain random traits to be non-randomly selected by the environment.

Even though Charles had devised the theory of natural selection in the 1830s, he did not publish on it until 1859. He wanted to wait until he had compiled a huge amount of evidence to back up his case.

Darwin wasn't even going to publish in 1859, but similar theories from fellow naturalist, Alfred Russel Wallace in 1858, forced his hand. Darwin then modestly published the "abstract" that was the *Origin of Species.*

This book is arguably one of the most revolutionary books ever published in the history of humanity. It sent shockwaves through the contemporary world. Within 20 years, it changed the outlook of modern biology. What is more, it changed how humanity at large viewed nature and grappled with the idea of life on Earth and even human ancestry. Even for people that were not convinced by Darwin's theory, here was a potent idea that at the very least had to be contended with and answered.

While some big questions remained – which Darwin freely admitted – about the age of the Earth being old enough to permit evolution, and about the mechanism for inheritance and mutation of traits, the theory of natural selection grew in scientific consensus. Slowly in the 20th century these questions were answered. The Earth was 4.5 billion years old, giving evolution enough time. And DNA was responsible for the traits an organism possessed and copying errors were responsible for their mutation. Then Darwin's principle of natural selection comes in, with the environment determining which creatures with useful traits are able to survive long enough in order to reproduce.

The vast biodiversity of the Earth, and the 3.8 billion year old story of life, is the result of that process.

Figuring out DNA and Bickering about Intellectual Property

In 1869, Swiss doctor Friedrich Miescher, discovered DNA. Putting it under the microscope, he saw the substance was in the nucleus of human eukaryotic cells. Fifteen years later, German biochemist Albrecht Kossel figured out that this nucleic acid was made of the organic chemicals adenine, thymine, guanine, cytosine, and uracil. In 1889, German pathologist Richard Altmann coined the term "nucleic acid". The "N" and "A" in deoxyribonucleic acid (DNA). In 1919, American scientist Phoebus Levene figured out that phosphorus was used to hold those chemicals together in a strand. And most notably, in 1943, biochemists Oswald Avery, Colin MacLeod and Maclyn McCarty confirmed that indeed DNA was the vessel that encoded the programming of the individual traits of an organism. The software commands of the living machine, which gives organisms their heritable traits.

At last, the mechanism that had alluded Darwin as to how exactly traits were transmitted from parents to offspring in evolution was being made clear. The question was: just how did DNA work? By the 1950s, the great task for biochemists was to create a fully functional model of this highly complex structure.

Francis Crick and James Watson began working on their model at Cambridge in 1951, building prototypes out of steel or paper. Meanwhile at King's College London, Maurice Wilkins, Rosalind Franklin, and her PhD student Raymond Gosling were working on X-ray diffractions to get a better idea of the shape and structure of DNA. The latter group relied heavily on finding solid proof for which model of DNA was the best fit. Francis Crick and James Watson's work tended to be more theoretical, coming up with a model that functioned the best.

Francis Crick and James Watson spent the next year and a half coming up with a thorough but flawed set of models of DNA. Working with blurry X-ray photos taken by William Astbury in the 1930s, along with a few slightly better photos, they eventually they tried the double-helix model. But even this had flaws.

By 1953, Francis Crick and James Watson had been working on their model for nearly 2 years. They realised that they might be outdone by American biochemist Linus Pauling, who had recently put out his own flawed version of DNA's structure. And so Watson went on a trip to King's College London to convince Wilkins, Franklin, and Gosling that they should join forces to beat Pauling to the punch.

During Watson's visit, Maurice Wilkins committed the professional faux pas of showing Watson "Photo 51" without asking his colleagues for permission. This was an X-ray diffraction of DNA that showed the structure more clearly, taken by student Raymond Gosling under the direction of his PhD supervisor Rosalind Franklin. Rosalind also provided much direct input on Crick and Watson's model, personally telling them that their idea of putting the phosphate backbone on the inside was incorrect.

Gosling and Franklin's "Photo 51" was of such high quality that it enabled Crick and Watson to modify the model they had been working on since 1951. The research culminated in an April 1953 issue of the science journal Nature where Watson and Crick published their model for DNA, alongside other papers published by the King's College team, including paper by Franklin and Gosling, and also by Wilkins, Stokes, and Wilson. Originally, Crick and Watson invited Maurice Wilkins to co-author their DNA paper, but he refused. Nevertheless Crick and Watson's paper made direct reference to Wilkins' and Franklin and Gosling's papers citing the contribution of their work to the theoretical model.

This was only the beginning, however. Crick and Watson continued to fine tune and improve their model of DNA over the next several years. It was Francis Crick who first made a splash in the public during his pivotal lecture on the central principles of DNA replication in 1957. But at this point, Crick and Watson's model simply remained theoretical. It needed further evidence to back it up. There were still other contending models at play.

The accuracy of Francis Crick and James Watson's model was confirmed in 1958 during an experiment by American molecular biologists Matthew Meselson and Frank Stahl. They deliberately bred a bacterial species until they could clearly see the DNA process in action.

Meanwhile in the same year, Rosalind Franklin passed away from cancer, possibly brought on by her exposure to X-ray radiation.

Ultimately, the work of the Cambridge and King's College teams culminated in the 1962 Nobel Prize for Physiology or Medicine. It was awarded to Francis Crick, James Watson, and Maurice Wilkins. Nobel prizes are not given posthumously, so Rosalind Franklin did not share in the prize. Nor did Raymond Gosling, Alex Stokes, and Robert Wilson, who were still alive and had also made contributions to the 1953 papers on the subject. Not even Gosling, who had taken the all-important "Photo 51" that is still the subject of much controversy to this day. It might be fairest to say that the decoding of DNA was a team effort by many scientists over many generations in a key example of collective learning.

Around the same period of time in the mid-20th century, three breakthroughs had revolutionized science. The discovery of Cosmic Background Radiation gave us the Big Bang. The vindication of Alfred Wegener's theory gave us plate tectonics. And the development of an accurate model of DNA gave us a microscopic look at the origin of species. All these breakthroughs painted a picture of an ever-changing Universe, rather than one that is static and eternal, where species are immutable. It was breakthroughs like these that make narratives like Big History today possible. And it is breakthroughs like these that continue to update and improve that narrative with every year that passes.

Essay Writing Exercise

This chapter's exercise involves practice with thesis statements on different topics. It also ideally should involve a bit of practice with revision. What you're going to do is, first, compose thesis statements for the following essay questions:

Why is the Big Bang theory the most widely accepted explanation for the origin of the Universe?

What do you regard as the most important turning point in the geological history of our Earth?

Which theory for the origins of life is most convincing?

What do you regard as the most important turning point in the history of life?

Good thesis statements should directly answer the question being asked and encapsulate the central arguments of the subsequent paper without being too vague or general. Once you have completed the thesis statements pass them along to a fellow classmate (or if you don't have any classmates to a friend) and ask if this one sentence answer convincingly answers the essay question. Ask them to give feedback. You can also do the same for a classmate in return.

Then revise your thesis statements to reflect all useful feedback. If you are doing the exercise with a group of classmates, you can even select which thesis statements did the best job.

Finally, for the keeners and over-achievers amongst you, feel free to extend with topic sentences and zingers to make full introductions. But don't feel obligated on this last step.

Further Reading

Barnett, S.A. The Science of Life: From Cells to Survival. Sydney: Allen and Unwin, 1998.

Bowler, Peter. Evolution: The History of an Idea. 3rd edition. Berkeley: University of California Press, 2003.

Browne, Janet. Charles Darwin: Voyaging. Princeton: Princeton University Press, 1996.

Collins, Francis. The Language of Life: DNA and the Revolution in Personalised Medicine. London: Profile Books, 2010.

Darwin, Charles. The Autobiography of Charles Darwin 1809-1882. ed. Nora Barlow. London: Collins, 1958.

Darwin, Charles. The Origin of Species by Means of Natural Selection. 1st edition, reprint. Cambridge, Mass: Harvard University Press, 2003.

Darwin, Charles. The Voyage of the Beagle. New York: Cosimo Classics, 2008.

Davies, Kevin. Cracking the Genome: Inside the Race to Unlock DNA. Baltimore: Johns Hopkins University Press, 2001.

Dyson, Freeman. Origins of Life. 2nd ed. Cambridge: Cambridge University Press, 1999.

Gosling, Raymond (interview). "Due Credit" Nature vol. 496 (2013) Available from https://www.nature.com/news/due-credit-1.12806

Jordanova, Ludmilla. Lamarck. Oxford: Oxford University Press, 1984.

Lamarck, Jean Baptiste Pierre Antoine de Monet. Philosophie zoologique: ou exposition des considerations relatives a l'histoire naturelle des animaux. Cambridge: Cambridge University Press, 2011.

Maddox, Brenda. "The Double Helix and the 'Wronged Heroine'" Nature vol. 421 (2003) pg. 407-408.

Maynard Smith, John, and Eors Szathmary. The Origins of Life: From the Birth of Life to the Origins of Language. Oxford: Oxford University Press, 1999.

Nutman, Allen, et al. "Rapid Emergence of Life Shown by Discovery of 3,700 million year old Microbial Structures" Nature vol. 537 (Sept 2016) pg. 535-538.

Sayre, A. Rosalind Franklin and DNA. New York: W.W. Norton, 1975.

Venter, J. Craig. A Life Decoded: My Genome, My Life. London: Penguin, 2007.

Watson, James. The Double Helix: A Personal Account of the Discovery of the Structure of DNA. London: Atheneum Press, 1968.

Wilkins, Maurice. The Third Man of the Double Helix: An Autobiography. Oxford: Oxford University Press, 2005.

CHAPTER 5

EXPLOSIONS AND EXTINCTIONS

Or,

WHY YOUR GRANDPAPPIES WERE FISH, FROGS, LIZARDS AND HOW THE UNIVERSE WAS CONSTANTLY TRYING (AND FAILING) TO MURDER THEM

"Nature, Red in Tooth and Claw"

We now arrive at a point in Big History that, years ago, I dubbed the Evolutionary Epic. While some people refer to all of cosmic evolution as the epic, it is more appropriate to reserve the title specifically for the period 650 to 65 million years ago. Not only because all 13.8 billion years already have the titles "cosmic evolution" and "Big History" to describe them. The Evolutionary Epic, on the other hand, was a dynamic time of many unique forms and dramatic environmental changes, with the central historical driver being evolution by natural selection above all else. Other periods of Big History might count gravity, or nuclear fusion, or collective learning, among their main drivers of events, but only in the Evolutionary Epic do we see evolution in the classical Darwinian sense forming the overwhelming majority of the shape of the story. Each major phase, each new character, was born out of the basic principles Darwin laid down over 160 years ago.

The period is characterised by blind evolution, and individuals of different species aspiring to no more than surviving long enough to reproduce. In fact the overwhelming majority of players were physically, mentally, and instinctually incapable of conceiving of reality in any other way. It is also characterised by the gradual rise of complexity: but in a blind process with many accidents and backsliding along the way. But for the arrival of species with a highly unlikely and dubious set of traits, it could well have been that the fifth threshold of complexity was as far as we ever got. Let us be under no illusion that the Darwinian world is a decidedly cruel one. A world would have existed for a few billion years of starvation, fear, cruelty, predation, environmental catastrophe, and a torrent of death that claimed 99.9% of all species. Yet great destruction seems to accompany most thresholds of complexity...

(A Rather Extensive) Timeline

- **The Last Snowball Earth (650 million years ago):** The final Snowball Earth begins with an excess of oxygen in the atmosphere, starting the growth of ice and the feedback cycle which reflected more and more of the Sun's rays back into space. The Snowball phase is likely to have impacted life that required sunlight and/or the open unfrozen sea to survive. Not to mention, organic chemicals became scarcer for *Bacteria* and *Eukaryota*. Those organisms that could not survive deeper in the ocean were forced into an ever-contracting appendix of uncovered sea. When the Earth was encased in ice, single-celled organisms had to survive in what slushy waters and surface pools they could find. After 15 million years, vulcanism freed the Earth once again, bursting through the ice and pumping carbon dioxide back into the atmosphere, warming the planet.

- **The Multicellular Revolution (635 million years ago):** Once the ice receded, it was clear something remarkable had been happening. One way single-celled organisms can increase their chances of survival is living in colonies and getting some cells to perform certain functions while others perform other functions in a "diversification of labour". This is a relationship called "symbiosis". Eventually single-celled eukaryotes grew so dependent on each other, the extent of symbiosis grew so strong, that they could not survive without each other. Colonies transformed into multicellular organisms, conglomerates of billions and trillions of cells that lived and died together. All for one, and one for all!

- **The Cambrian Explosion (541 million years ago):** While there were a number of multi-celled species in the Ediacaran, the evolutionary momentum picked up in the Cambrian. Multicellular organisms are able to exploit a lot more "niches" for energy flows and resources than a single microscopic cell. They are bigger, stronger, and more mobile. As such, an explosion of multicellular eukaryotic species spread across the Earth's oceans, filling ecological niches that single-celled organisms could not exploit. The "explosion" is so called because it appears so suddenly on the fossil record, though in reality this evolution would have taken hundreds of thousands to a million years. But even in terms of geological time that is still quite sudden.

- **Plants Colonise the Land (488-444 million years ago):** The first photosynthesizing, eukaryotic, and multi-celled species began moving out of the oceans and colonising coastlines and riverbeds in the Ordovician. Many of them were mosses, shrubs, and ferns and stayed fairly close to the waterways. But groundwater facilitated in many areas the spread of their seeds and spores further inland.

- **The Ordovician Extinction (443 million years ago):** Most species still existed in the oceans. A period of rapid global warming preceded the extinction, which strained the adaptive abilities of many marine species, then CO_2 rapidly decreased in the atmosphere (possibly from the proliferation of plants on land) causing such a sudden cooling that in the shock approximately 60-70% of marine species were killed off.

- **Arthropods Colonise the Land (443-420 million years ago):** In reaction to the environmental pressures imposed on marine environments by the Ordovician extinction, many arthropods (species with exo-skeletons) migrated onto land and continued to evolve there. Their less porous skin, due to their armour, allowed them to adapt quickly. The high levels of oxygen in the atmosphere that followed the Ordovician extinction also permitted the aerobic arthropods to grow to terrifying sizes. Essentially the period that followed was a world ruled by giant bugs.

- **Tetrapods Colonise the Land (420-359 million years ago):** Lagging behind the arthropods were the tetrapods, who were vertebrates descended from fish, with much more porous skin. Moving on to land took much more evolutionary legwork. Though it is possible that the first evolutionary steps toward colonising the land were taken at the same time as arthropods. The first tetrapods were essentially "lungfish" that could breath for a short time out of the water, and could gather resources from the coastlines. Eventually the tetrapods evolved their signature four limbs for locomotion, though they were still reliant on the water due to their porous skin and method of laying eggs. These were the first amphibians from which all other tetrapods (including us) are descended.

- **The Devonian Extinction (358 million years ago):** From a period of rapid global cooling, the Earth rapidly dried out, emptying waterways, draining the waters of oxygen used by aerobic species, and killing off about 50% of species. This extinction event was particularly severe on the amphibious tetrapods, who lost 97% of all species. The ancestors of all land-based eukaryotic life was nearly wiped out except the smallest of them. The pressure to abandon reliance on water likely precipitated the evolution of reptiles, with less porous skin and hard eggs that could live further inland and not have to lay their eggs in water.

- **The Permian Extinction (252 million years ago):** Also known as the "Great Dying" a total of 70% of land-based species and 96% of marine species were wiped out, and an average of 90% of species overall. This is likely to have started with a catastrophic super-eruption in Siberia where an area 7 million km² of the Earth's crust cracked and blew up. Eruptions continued for 500,000 years. This clogged up the Earth's atmosphere with ash, blocking out the Sun and killing many photosynthesizing species. Sulfur dioxide caused acid rain to fall in torrential downpours that burned species alive. The oceans heated up and lost oxygen, killing off nearly everything. Excess CO_2 heated up the Earth transforming the land into a vast desert killing off many plants and amphibians. The surviving reptiles (approximately 30%) were able to thrive in these dry conditions and fill ecological niches over the course of the Triassic, kicking off the age of giant reptiles that would prevail for 190 million years.

- **The Triassic Extinction (201 million years ago):** Yet another extinction event that wiped out approximately 50% of all life on Earth. It is vigorously debated over whether this event was caused by climate change, an asteroid impact, or another volcanic super-eruption. At any rate, another drying out of the world wiped out many of the more aquatic giant reptiles like phytosaurs and most crocodilians. From this point forward dinosaurs and pterosaurs (the flying kind) became dominant over the Earth, with the ancestors of mammals retreating into small, timid forms.

- **The Cretaceous Extinction (65 million years ago)**: What is confirmed to be an asteroid impact of a rock 10 kilometres across smashing into what is now the Yucatan peninsula, created continent wide forest fires, acid rain, a global heating followed by a global cooling, which wiped out approximately 70% of all life on Earth. Particularly hard hit were land-based reptiles. The ecological niches were wiped clean once again, allowing mammals to evolve and fill the many openings left by the extinct dinosaurs.

The Last Snowball Earth & Multicellularism

The final Snowball Earth commenced approximately 650 million years ago, and imposed yet another period of strain on single-celled life on Earth. Symbiosis was used by single cells for hundreds of millions of years by this point. A single cell can only fill so many functions, so colonies of *Archaea, Bacteria,* or *Eukaryota,* would be well served by having a "division of labour". But what the final Snowball Earth appears to have done is send symbiosis into overdrive.

Symbiosis is where two different organisms have a mutual relationship. While some symbiosis can be parasitic (where one organism profits at the other's expense) many forms of symbiosis are mutually beneficial. One of the most basic examples of this is the relationship between flowers and bees. Flowering plants evolved only 125 million years ago, bees evolved around roughly the same time between 100 and 130 million years ago. The relationship was quickly reinforcing. Some species of bee collect pollen to sustain their own complexity, and the flowers benefit by having bees spread their pollen for their reproduction. While evolution is very frequently about competition, sometimes a mutually beneficial form of symbiosis can be equally effective.

When the last Snowball Earth happened 650 million years ago, it was already a world of highly diverse and evolved single-celled organisms, who had been changing and adapting for 3 billion years (the majority of life's history). Archaea were able to ride out this Snowball period because they were extremophiles. Bacteria likely were harder hit, but had already existed through multiple Snowball phases, the last one being only a few million years before. *Eukaryota,* on the other hand, had evolved to sexually reproduce and had the advantage of a much faster pace of evolution. What this allowed was beneficial symbiosis in a time of strain could *rapidly* accelerate in closeness.

A multicellular organism could, in some sense, be defined by such a great extent of symbiosis that the cells of the body can only exist in tandem, i.e. your liver cannot just crawl along the ground without the rest of you. The community of cells are engineered to exist at once, and if one part of the body fails to fulfill its functions, the rest of the cells could die.

Multicellularism is so far beyond just a colony of microbes interacting with each other. A multicellular organism is a collection of multiple *trillions* of cells, each of which is shaped by DNA to act differently, fill a function, and be coalesced with similar cells to form an organ. The organs themselves are built up into a patchwork of intricate networks, like the circulatory system, the respiratory system, and the digestive system. To give you an idea of the scale of difference, there are 37 trillion cells in a single human body. There are only roughly 400 billion stars in the Milky Way. Thus there are roughly 92.5 galaxies of single cells in one human body. Complexity in terms of building blocks and intricate structures are way beyond anything that had been seen before in Big History to this point.

In terms of energy flows, we also see a marked increase of complexity. Remember, a more complex system requires denser energy flows to sustain its complexity. To keep it away from a state of "Heat Death" where all complexity breaks down. The Sun channels 2 erg/g/s of free energy, a typical single-celled organism between 450 to 900 erg/g/s. Cold-blooded fish, amphibians, and reptiles channel an average of 3000-4000 erg/g/s, warm-blooded mammals 20,000 erg/g/s, multi-celled plants 5000 erg/g/s, certain tropical plants 10,000 to 20,000 erg/g/s, and humans foragers generally use 40,000 erg/g/s in order to sustain their nutrition and power their unusually large brains. Whether we are talking structural intricacy or energy flows, all multicellular organisms are miles beyond anything else we've seen in the Universe (thus far).

That said, there is not always an evolutionary incentive for living things to grow more complex. With greater complexity can come greater fragility. A multicellular organism has a lot more moving parts that could break down. And in terms of energy flows if you can get through the day using less energy, evolution will favour that because having to go out and find more energy to survive takes time and imposes possible risks. It is why the majority of life on Earth is still single-celled. They are able to survive without becoming extremely interdependent fuel-hungry species. It is only in evolutionary niches where organisms were *forced* to evolve to become multicellular that more complexity arises. As a wider rule, the same energy logic is why the majority of the Universe is fairly simple and most atomic matter is hydrogen. Only in cases where nature forces complexity to rise and burn up energy more quickly, will it do so.

One final thing to note is that even though a multicellular organism is more complex, it does not relinquish its dependency on single cells. Each multicellular organism typically has a "microbiome" around them without which they could not survive. A microbiome is a community of single-celled organisms that live on/in the multicelled organism that also enjoy a mutually beneficial relationship. In the human body, for instance, these organisms are Archaea, Bacteria, and *Eukaryota*. And there are indications that this microbiome is made up of almost three times as many single-cells as the multicelled body itself.

When we consider just how chemically complex a single strand of DNA is compared to the wider Universe, to speak nothing of the machinery of a single cell, these wider biological conglomerates and communities are small, fragile, short lived, but *immensely complex*. And most of their functions are so automatic and evolutionarily engrained that the human consciousness is largely unaware of them, and can only begin to conceive the magnitude of the community that keeps them living, breathing, eating junk food, drinking beer, vaping dodgy chemicals, and generally abusing their health.

On Explosions and Extinctions

We are now about to launch into the Evolutionary Epic that began at the end of the Last Snowball Earth 635 million years ago, when the ice receded to reveal an assortment of highly complex life. As mentioned the primary historical driver of all the events which occurred in this tale is evolution by natural selection. The major phase shifts of the evolutionary process can also be distilled into two unique components: explosions and extinctions.

An extinction is a necessary component of evolution. In order for the useful traits of an organism to be "selected for" a thousand other competing organisms must cease to exist. There are only so many niches in an environment. Death is thus the engine of evolution, where 99.9% of all species that ever existed have gone extinct. Really "natural selection" is a bit of a misnomer in the sense that "good traits" aren't actively selected for by nature – they are just the ones that aren't wiped from the gene pool. Instead "natural elimination" might be closer to the mark, since all the traits that are negative, deleterious, or simply not good enough, are blasted from existence by starvation, predation, disease, or environmental disaster.

The typical process of evolution by natural selection happens incrementally over long periods of time, as environments gradually change, organisms compete, and gene pools shift gradually to catch up. Occasionally a genetic mutation that lends a fantastic advantage will rapidly move through an ecosystem. But when it comes to "mass extinctions" where millions of species are wiped out by an asteroid, supervolcanic eruption, or rapid change in climate, then the process of evolution for the survivors likewise accelerates. Rapid evolution is referred to as an "adaptive radiation", where species radiate out into empty (or recently emptied) ecological niches. It can also be referred to as an "explosion", as in the case of the Cambrian Explosion 541 million years ago, where a profusion of new multicelled species just appeared on the fossil record. An adaptive radiation typically can occur: 1) after a mass extinction event has swept many species from ecological niches, leaving the resources open to exploitation to other species to evolve and exploit them instead, and 2) when a revolutionary new set of traits completely change the game and those species rapidly breed and populate new areas.

In the case of multicellular organisms, they are much more capable of exploiting niches in ways very different from a tiny microscopic organism. They have fins, gills, wings, legs, teeth, claws, leaves, roots, and so forth, all of which open up avenues for energy flows that are not open to a single-celled bacterium. The entire tale of 635 million to 65 million years ago is shaped by this alternation between an explosion of new species, cut short by a mass extinction, which then prompts another rapid acceleration of speciation, as the biosphere recovers.

The Ediacaran (635-541 million years ago)

The name "Ediacaran" draws its name from the Ediacara Hills, which are in South Australia. It is the region where the first scientifically confirmed multicelled organisms that predate the Cambrian were found. The find was made by Reg Sprigg, whose claims were at first rejected since at the time the start of multicelled life was dated to the Cambrian explosion nearly 100 million years later.

The Ediacaran was typified by a dramatic and sudden climate change at the end of the last Snowball Earth phase. Oxygen levels in the atmosphere were lowered by vulcanism, the Earth warmed, and more CO_2 was pumped into the atmosphere. A dramatic warming and increase in CO_2 was good for photosynthesizers, but there was still enough oxygen floating around that the aerobic eukaryotes could also start to form multicellular organisms.

The first multicellular life formed in the oceans, to which life had so far been confined. Fossils from the Ediacaran are difficult to find, because most organisms were soft and squishy, without growing the carbonate shells or bones that would typify species after the Cambrian. The first multicelled species were somewhat modest, and even clumsy, attempts at forming a new kind of life. This makes sense given natural selection had never had to work on such structures before. As a result, they look very outlandish and bear little resemblance to the life that followed them. Many of them do however bear strong resemblance to microbial mats, which are colonies of single-celled organisms that have not yet made the leap to multicellularism.

Imprints left by Ediacaran life left in sand allow us to gain some idea of what existed back then. In the kingdom of Animalia we have *Ediacara*, which were strange gelatinous structures that look halfway between a coral and a jellyfish. We have *Arkarua*, *Dickinsonia*, *Marywadea*, *Cephalonega*, and *Yorgia*, which were strange multicelled disks that looked like quilts and sat on the ocean floor that, given the apparent absence of a mouth or anus, likely absorbed food through their skin and then excreted waste back out again in the same way. We have *Pteridinium* and *Spriggina*, which look like primitive worms or slugs. And we also have *Charnia*, which looked like a long underwater fern, but it did not photosynthesize but was in fact aerobic and lived in deep waters where the Sun could not reach. Almost all Ediacaran animals didn't have a means of locomotion, though some may have drifted across the ocean floor "grazing" on what food they could find.

In terms of complexity, these organisms were far and beyond any single-celled organism both in structure and energy flows. It is difficult to tell precisely how structurally intricate or energy dense these organisms were given the lack of data from the period. Certainly the lack of different component parts implies they pale in comparison from what came later, but these tightly bound behaviours certainly lent a survival advantage, given that a common ancestor of them would have survived Snowball Earth.

The Cambrian (541-485 million years ago)

The name of the Cambrian is derived from the Latin name for Wales, where the Cambrian layer of rocks were first studied by Adam Sedgwick in the 19th century. The Cambrian world was similar to the Ediacaran in the sense that it was still quite warm. There was little or no ice at the poles during this period, what ice there was would have been definitely receding. The water levels were thus higher due to the melt, and this created a number of shallow seas. The water itself was quite temperate, and oxygen levels were low but sufficient enough to sustain aerobic life. In short, it was a warmer, gentler world than today. What distinguishes the Cambrian from the Ediacaran is underneath the waves, things were getting a lot busier.

The Cambrian Explosion was an adaptive radiation of multicelled species, rapidly entering new ecological niches. This process began 541 million years ago and lasted for roughly 15 million years. We have abundant fossils from this time due to the evolution of hard exo-skeletons and shells. These were the Arthropods, the ancestors of crabs, lobsters, insects, arachnids, etc. As I've already mentioned, either the creepy things or the most expensive thing on the menu. As an aside, the reason why humans are creeped out by many Arthropods is a useful survival instinct, some Arthropods are highly poisonous, and so a deep-rooted instinct that led human to be afraid of most or *all* of them enhanced our chances of survival. Sometimes phobias can be useful.

A notable change that struck across all animals at the start of the Cambrian Explosion, whether arthropod, chordate, or mollusk, was the evolution of the eye. These were primitive sensory tools that animals used to detect changes in light and movement. The innovation stuck, which is why we see eyes across *Animalia*, even when new species might have a declining use for them, like bats, badgers, or deep water fish. Very primitive and experimental, eyes did not evolve in the same direction. For instance, many mollusks have eyes along their bodies rather than centrally located in what we would identify as a "head". Naturally, eyes became dramatically diverse as their usages differed vastly over the following 541 million years. Even species as closely related as humans and dogs have different aptitudes for their eyes, to speak nothing of the difference of the tool between us and, say, reptiles, ants, or spiders.

The most recognisable set of Arthropods were the many different species of *Trilobites*. How to put this – they look midway between a crab, cockroach, and beetle. They may have evolved from *Spriggina* into a more hardened form. Trilobites had evolved a reliable form of locomotion which allowed them to travel around the oceans, finding more energy flows. As a result of trilobites finding a number of new niches, they began to diversify incredibly. They also spread to pretty much every oceanic environment in the world, becoming a truly global species.

During the Cambrian, trilobite species ranged between 5cm and 35cm in size, and fed on a variety of things from bacteria to vegetation to other animals. They were highly successful and sometimes swarmed in hundreds or thousands. Trilobites would continue to diversify, and would manage to hang on to existence until the Permian Extinction 252 million years ago. Over that period, trilobite shapes, sizes, and abilities went off in a thousand different directions. Here was a truly successful evolutionary lineage that lasted longer than most other multicelled life, and it took the near destruction of all life on Earth to finally finish them off.

The chordates (our ancestors) had a somewhat humbler start. Approximately 530 million years ago, the first one evolved. This was *Pikaia,* which resembled a worm and swam like an eel. It was only a few centimetres long and made up only a tiny fraction of the biodiversity of the Cambrian. What is notable about it is that it had a single rod made from cartilage running along its body. This was the ancestor of vertebrates. Due to its mode of swimming, one end of the species was always facing front, to encounter food or danger. This led to the process of "cephalisation", the process by which sensory organs move increasingly to one part of the body. As such nerves began to make their way along the cartilage to what we would now consider a "head".

Nerves collect stimuli from the surrounding environment, whether good news or bad news, and send signals to the rest of the body so it can react accordingly. *Pikaia* had a very primitive system of nerves where there was a fairly even distribution of them throughout its body, with only just a little bit more at the part that faced front as it swam. But very rapidly over the space of just 5 million years, more and more nerves became clustered inside what we would consider the "head", which was also equipped with eyes and a mouth. The tiny knot of nerves became primitive brains. Yet even 525 million years ago, this structure of tangled nerves designed to process information from the outside world had become one of the most complex structures in the Universe. So it was with the evolution of *Haikouichthys* one of the first identifiable Cambrian jawless "fish". Unlike *Pikaia,* it had a distinct head and tail, and a more developed rod (notochord or primitive spine). Its brain would have been quite small and limited. But here is the likely ancestor of Cambrian fish and all vertebrates everywhere, whether in the sea or on land.

Another innovation of the Cambrian was the first true "predation". That brings us to the evolution *Anomalocaris,* roughly 515 to 520 million years ago. It was a vicious Arthropod that is approximately 1 metre in length (dwarfing most other Cambrian life in size). It too had a distinct head and tail with the latter of which it could swim rapidly, an armoured exo-skeleton, and at the front it had two massive grasping spiked "claws". With these claws *Anomalocaris* would scoop up unwitting prey in the oceans, impale it on the spikes, and then bring it up toward its downward facing mouth to be devoured. The name, *Anomalocaris*, hilariously comes from the roughly translated Latin for "weird shrimp" or "weird sea crab".

Predation is a revolutionary innovation in some ways. In others it is business as usual. The key to all forms of complexity are energy flows. Organic life is no exception. In order to gain energy flows, single-celled organisms chomp down on chemicals, or occasionally on each other in a rather inoffensive fashion. From a human perspective, it is difficult to see the viciousness in something microscopic. Similarly when a multicellular organism chomps down on bacteria or plant life, it is regarded by humans as something fairly benign and harmless, since neither bacteria nor plants have the sensory apparatus to perceive something like fear or pain. This is just the movement of energy flows across the ecosystem from one organism to another. Fungi, similarly, just feast on the remains of dead things.

In many ways predation is just an inevitable evolutionary extension of this transference of energy flows. If you can eat chemicals, eat microbes, eat plants, eat dead things, why can you not eat the multicelled creatures that eat all those things? You gain all the energy flows that they had gathered. It is a brilliant and highly effective evolutionary innovation. This is where *Anomalocaris* comes in. Rather than compete with other species for plant and animal resources, they simply absorb the energy of those more peaceful species. The reason why the impaling and devouring of *Anomalocaris* looks much more heinous to humans is because we are instinctually driven to avoid being eaten ourselves. We do manifest impulses like pain and fear in order to avoid being eaten long enough to reproduce. But the violence of the act of energy exchange is a mere matter of human perception. Energy flows are moving like they always do. But as complexity rises in animal nervous systems, comes the increase of awareness of one's environment and oneself, i.e. consciousness. And with consciousness comes the perception of the violence and destruction, and in some cases suffering, which often accompany energy flows and the rise of complexity. Yet the processes of increasing complexity that we choose to dub either harmless or heinous are made subjectively, shaped entirely by our evolutionary instincts. This somewhat complicates moral discussions between human omnivores and herbivores.

Where predation is a game-changer is the evolutionary reaction to predators. It sets off an evolutionary arms race. In response to predators like *Anomalocaris*, certain species of trilobites began to develop spikes on their exo-skeletons in order to discourage being eaten, other trilobites learned to roll up into balls to protect themselves. Or they developed camouflage and faster locomotion to avoid detection and danger. Other trilobites began to eat worms, jellies, and other unprotected animals becoming predators themselves. From this point in the Cambrian onward, the evolutionary arms race between predator and prey would continue to shape and reshape a myriad of species. They would need to develop increasing amounts of instincts and component parts, thus enhancing their complexity.

The Ordovician (485-444 million years ago)

The Ordovician gets its name from the *Ordovices*, a Celtic tribe in pre-Roman Wales where much of the geological work was being done in the 19th century. At the start of the Ordovician the Earth continued its warming trend which had begun at the end of the Snowball Earth phase 635 million years ago. The atmosphere was glutted with CO_2 ten times the amount we have today. In the early Ordovician, the average temperature of the ocean was actually quite warm, being somewhere between bath temperature and a hot tub (35 and 40 degrees Celsius respectively). But by 460 million the warming trend stopped and the seas cooled to an average temperature of 25-30 degrees Celsius, which is still warm, about the temperature of tropical waters.

Meanwhile, plate tectonics had begun to pull the land together into massive continents which continued to inch closer together (at about the same rate your nails grow) into an eventual super-continent 100 million years later. Due to the warmth of the Earth, water levels were as high as they had ever been, and many of these continental puzzle pieces were covered with shallow seas. In short, it was a good time evolutionarily if you were a marine organism.

Marine life continued to diversify, with trilobites taking on a great many new forms as the "arms race" against predators continued. Some trilobites grew up to 70cm. The first ancestors of octopuses and starfish emerged. Coral reefs beginning to form in the warm waters. The ancestors of oysters, clams, sea snails, all multiplied in a diversity of forms. Arthropod predators also kept up the pace, producing the first sea scorpions, some the size of modern scorpions, some the length of your shin, and by the Devonian one species, *Jaekelopterus*, had grown to an astounding 2.5 metres long. Our ancestors, the fish, also diversified into a variety of forms. But still they remained jawless, simply ingesting material via an open mouth. All told the amount of marine species multiplied by four times in the Ordovician compared to the Cambrian.

Meanwhile the first multicelled life began to venture on to the land. These were the plants. Starting as very simple algae on coastlines and rivers, the greening of the Earth had begun. Eventually some of this algae evolved into little weed-like structures that were no more than 10cm in height. The plant transition to land was aided by the fact the plants required sunlight so rested at the top of the water, and were never far from a direct water source. The plants also acted in symbiosis with fungi, which furnished plants with minerals, and became closely attached to their roots.

The spread of plants on the land in the Ordovician was an expansion of the photosynthesizing niche on a titanic scale. As a result, the levels of oxygen on Earth began to increase again, causing a cooling period that killed off warm-water species, but it was short lived. CO_2 rapidly reached its old levels in the atmosphere heating the world and killing off the species that had evolved to adapt to the cooler conditions. All told 70% of marine organisms were annihilated.

The Silurian (444-420 million years ago)

The Silurian period is also named after a pre-Roman Celtic tribe in Wales. The significance of the Ordovician Extinction event cannot be denied. The Silurian world opened with the world sliding back into warmer temperatures, but the massive die-off had prompted life to swerve off in different evolutionary directions. With many ecological niches swept clean, and the seas forming temperature conditions yet again, the Silurian was an ideal time for a great deal of rapid evolution.

On land, plants continued their march inland. But these were still early days and most plants clung to the coastlines and riverbeds. Much of the plant life were tiny shrubs and mosses. They were getting used to dry land, however, and some had evolved a vascular system which allowed plants to suck water up and direct them around the entire plant, making them slightly less dependent on water. The majority of the Earth was still rocky, however, with just a smattering of pygmy forests near water sources.

The kingdom that had a massive spurt of growth in this period were actually the fungi. While most plants remained only a few centimetres tall, some fungi towered over them at the height of several metres. This was because plants could not break through the rocky interior of the Earth in order to plant their roots. Fungi on the other hand had the advantage of being able to eat any sort of chemical. They literally ate into rocks, which gradually over millions of years, created the first soft soils for plants in the Devonian.

In the seas, some fish evolved jaws which opened up a wider range of organisms on which they could feed. Their spines also became more articulated, some hard bony fish evolved, and their nervous systems became more complex, with the tangle of nerves in the brain becoming a little bit larger and responsive to external stimuli. This was necessary given that jawed fish soon led to the evolution of the first sharks and the evolutionary arms race continued. Meanwhile the ever-larger sea scorpions continued the same trend.

The most notable change of the Silurian has to be the colonisation of the land by some arthropods. These were the first animals on land. Possibly driven out of the seas by the pressures of the Ordovician extinction event, the first terrestrial arthropods discovered a food resource in both dead and living plants, which was good for a variety of *Myriapoda*. For instance, *Pneumodesmus* lived 428 million years ago and was an ancient millipede about 1cm in length that fed off of dead plant material. Not long behind these vegetarian bugs were arthropod predators, most notably the first spider-like arachnids. Some of the myriapods also turned predatory.

The oxygen levels of the Silurian remained quite low, however, averaging at about 15%, so these predators remained quite small, only a few centimetres themselves. The Silurian was a world of tiny bugs, tiny plants, in a realm increasingly dominated by fungus. Perhaps you'll agree this is a disgusting mental image.

The Devonian (420-358 million years ago)

The name of the period is derived from Devonshire, a county in England where the rock layers were first studied (but at least we are finally out of Wales). The Devonian period is one of intensely dramatic change both on land and at sea.

The Devonian world was bursting with life. The oxygen levels in the atmosphere had remained stable since the Silurian, and there was still a hefty helping of CO_2 in the atmosphere, keeping up the Earth's greenhouse climate. Though more plants on land were reducing the CO_2 gradually throughout the period as they became larger and more numerous. The world was temperate, probably contained little to no polar ice, and was lush and tropical over most of its surface, with the exception of large deserts forming at the equator. The continents continued to creep together, but had not yet formed Pangea, meaning that precipitation could reach much of the land area. Sea levels were high, which also facilitated territory for the abundance of new marine life.

At first in the Devonian, plant life remained in the same pygmy proportions as the Silurian. The fungi remained dominant and started forming towers and mounds that were up to 10 metres high. But the fungus also created increasing amounts of soft soils. By the mid-Devonian plants had evolved to put down primitive roots, from which they could drain water and nutrients from this newly created soil. Ferns and mosses spread into abundance and the Earth finally became green. By 410 million years ago some plants managed to grow up to 14 metres high, and by 380 million years ago, some plant species had evolved wood to strengthen their stems so they could maintain these massive heights or grow even higher as they competed for sunlight.

The Devonian is also known as the "age of fish", where we see a tremendous diversification of fish and shark species in the oceans. Fish began to grow larger and sturdier, with some reaching between 3 and 7 metres in length. They developed ray and lobe fins, and more intricate body structures. The profusion of different genera and species is beyond counting.

Arthropods continued their evolution on land, though oxygen levels remained quite low so they were not able to grow to very large sizes yet, though their range of sizes began to approach modern standards. Spiders began to develop their ability to cast silk webs in order to catch prey. Flying arthropods appeared during this time and began exploiting the advantages of such mobility. Ancient millipedes grew slightly larger as a result of the great abundance of dead plant life on land.

But as the reader may have predicted the most profound change in the Devonian was the advent of tetrapods on the land. The process involved the evolution of fish to be able to breathe air and spend some time out of the water without immediately drying out. This was easier said than done. Tetrapods had porous skin and were not able to transition as quickly as arthropods had.

Approximately 380 million years ago, we see the first "lungfish" emerge. These fish swam in shallow pools, they still had gills. But they also had a hole in the top of their head that was so angled that air could flow into primitive lungs. Previously lungs would have been used as air sacks to retain buoyancy while swimming near the surface, but gradually these sacks were repurposed to respire from the air. The first lungfish had strong front fins that it could use to drag itself along the bottom of shallow waters in pursuit of food. This impulse gradually transitioned to dragging itself along beaches on the coast. By 375 million years ago, *Tiktaalik* was breathing air, and had strong front and back fins and also primitive hips that would aid with locomotion.

By 370 million years ago, we had transitioned to the stem-tetrapods with *Ichthyostega*. About 1 to 1.5 metres in length, this was the first proto-amphibian, swimming in shallow swamps. The skull hole of its ancestors had evolved into nostrils. It had the signature four-limbs and five digits of the earliest tetrapods. These were the ancestors of all terrestrial vertebrates. The same number of limbs and digits are present or "vestigial" to all terrestrial vertebrates. This includes you, frogs, dogs, cats, horses, lizards, bears, and even snakes. Some species indeed lost their requirement for quite as many digits, and so the bones receded into the body but can still be detected in their skeletons. In the extreme case of snakes, even there vestigial limbs can still be found having shrunk to be almost imperceptible. Over the next 12 million years, the first true amphibious tetrapods would emerge, ranging in size from a few centimetres to under two metres.

By the end of the Devonian, the sheer amount of plants inhabiting the land kicked into overdrive. We now had the first true forests. This had the negative side-effect of sucking a lot of the CO_2 from the atmosphere and pumping out more oxygen at unprecedented levels. The result was a slight cooling and drying out of the planet. This was particularly bad news for the recently terrestrial tetrapods, of whom roughly 95-97% of them were wiped out. What remained of them were species that were only a few centimetres long. It is astounding to think that the diversity of tetrapod life on Earth today, from salamanders to owls to humans, are descended from a 3-5% bottleneck of tetrapods 358 million years ago. Meanwhile, a great deal of oxygen was stripped from the oceans, killing off about 50% of aquatic life, including most genera of trilobite, except for a few which remained until wiped out in the Permian extinction.

The Carboniferous (358-298 million years ago)

The Carboniferous means "coal-bearing" and gets its name from the layer of rock where coal is most commonly found. This is the result of the massive forests that died and formed part of the layer, eventually being pressurized into coal (hence the term "carbon" in the name).

The Carboniferous was in many ways a world different from the Cambrian, Ordovician, Silurian, and Devonian. The oxygen levels of the atmosphere went through the roof, reaching 35% (today's oxygen levels are 21%). This came as a result of Carboniferous forests pumping out a great deal of oxygen as a waste product. As such, the Carboniferous is characterised by a gradual cooling from the beginning to the end of the period, when the climate gradually grew more arid and glaciers and icy poles slowly reappeared.

It cannot be understated how absolutely covered the Earth was with Carboniferous forests. Some of the trees grew to 50 metres in height. The trees continued to pump oxygen into the atmosphere, and when they died they didn't break down as quickly because the microbe that makes trees rot today hadn't evolved yet. So much of the carbon dioxide remained trapped inside of them. As a result the Carboniferous trees were the cause of their own demise, because as the Earth dried out, it provoked the Carboniferous Rainforest Collapse, creating much of the thick layer of coal from which humans derived their industrial energy flows.

Due to the high levels of oxygen in the atmosphere, the most astounding characteristic of the age were the giant terrestrial arthropods. The increased oxygen pumped up the arthropod metabolism, sustaining larger sizes. We're talking giant dragonflies with a metre long wingspan, giant land scorpions nearly two metres long, giant ground-spiders, giant cockroaches, and giant millipedes two metres long and half a metre wide.

The tetrapods also made a recovery in the first half of the Carboniferous. The temnospondyls were giant amphibians that evolved 350 million years ago. They still had porous skin, and still needed to lay their eggs in the water. Reptiles evolved between 350 and 310 million years ago, and their evolution was intensified after the Carboniferous Rainforest Collapse. Reptiles had tough skin that did not lose as much water. This meant they could head further inland, away from abundant water sources. Some could even survive in desert climates, which were slowly becoming more abundant. They also started laying hard shell eggs, which meant they did not need to return to the water to reproduce. As the climate continued to dry out at the end of the Carboniferous, the genetic diversity of reptiles went into overdrive, spawning a wide variety of forms that are ancestral to both mammals and the dinosaurs.

The Permian (298-252 million years ago)

Usually the preoccupation with the Permian is how it ended, nearly killing off life on Earth. But it was also a period where much of the foundations for life on Earth in the age of dinosaurs and the age of mammals. The Permian gets its name from a region in Russia where the rock layer was first identified.

The Permian world was almost equivalent in oxygen levels to the Earth today, just a little over our oxygen levels at 23% rather than 21%. This led to a shrinking in the size of arthropods (thank goodness, though they still freak me out). The bad news was that the most successful arthropods in the Permian were the ancestors of cockroaches, who formed the overwhelming majority of insect biota in the period. As a resident of Sydney who has grown to hate cockroaches with an abiding passion, you have no idea how unappealing this makes the Permian.

The oxygen levels created some glaciation that made the world quite cold at first, but gradually during the Permian the world warmed largely due to increases in carbon dioxide from volcanism, and huge deserts began to appear. Pangea was now fully formed, and precipitation could not reach the interior of the supercontinent, but was largely confined to the coasts. This was astoundingly good news for reptile evolution.

The evolutionary history of both mammals and dinosaurs are wrapped up in the evolution of reptiles in the Permian. The ancestors of mammals and dinosaurs in the Permian were *Synapsids* and *Sauropsids*. The *Synapsids* were actually the dominant terrestrial vertebrates during the Permian. These were proto-mammals, or stem-mammals, which still looked very reptilian. They were characterised by their varied teeth (unlike previous species which had uniform teeth), their straight legs used for fast movements in hunting, and, of course, the use of mammary glands to rear their young. Both *Synapsids* and *Sauropsids* laid eggs in reproduction at this time, though proto-mammals would later give birth to their young. Some *Synapsids* were huge and hunted large creatures, and others were small and ate insects (possibly cockroaches – disgusting!).

But as the Permian continued to dry out, a sub-branch of their lineage emerged 272 million years ago – the *Therapsids*. These are even closer to us in the family tree. They were energetic and fast-moving, and as a result of all that they had a higher body temperature. In other words, they were warm-blooded. And in order to maintain this temperature, many of them began to develop fur. In the final years of the Permian (roughly 260 million years ago) a smaller group evolved from the *Therapsids*, the *Cynodonts*, which were small timid creatures, many of whom were capable of burrowing, which allowed them to escape the devastation of the Permian extinction.

On the other side of the family tree, *Sauropsids* retained what we would describe as much more reptilian characteristics. These creatures were the ancestors of everything from turtles, to crocodiles, to archosaurs, pterosaurs, dinosaurs, and the birds (avian dinosaurs). These reptiles took a back seat to the *Synapsids* during the Permian but those fortunes were soon reversed.

The Permian Extinction or "Great Dying" 252 million years ago is theorised to have been caused by a volcanic super-eruption in what is today Siberia. It was a catastrophe that lasted for about a million years. Ash was thrown into the atmosphere, blocking out the sun and killing off vegetation. Acid rain hurtled down from the skies. Oxygen was stripped from the oceans. It was the one mass extinction event which nearly ended all complex life on Earth. This had such a traumatic effect on the planet that roughly 90-95% of all species, and 70-75% of terrestrial species, died out. Gone were the last of the trilobites. The land-based reptiles were also fairly hard hit. The *Synapsids* and *Therapsids* went into sharp decline. The *Cynodonts* managed to survive because they were small and burrowed, and they continued to stay in such a humble position in the periods to come. Because the surviving *Sauropsids* were soon to rule the Earth.

The Triassic (252-201 million years ago)

The Triassic gets its name from the way German geologists who studied the layer divided the various strata of rocks into three. The Triassic is one of those bizarre periods sandwiched between two massive extinction events. And it took halfway through the Triassic for the biosphere to simply recover from the devastation of the "Great Dying". This resulted in some very odd evolutionary twists and turns.

The Triassic was generally quite dry, with massive deserts forming in the interior of Pangea, more arid than even the Permian era. Rain simply could not reach the interior of the super-continent. Even at the poles of the planet, there was no ice, just some more humid landscapes with some rare forests for species that required greater moisture. The atmosphere had been somewhat stripped of oxygen, and levels sat at 16%, which is below what it is today. Carbon dioxide levels were about 4 times what they are today.

At the start of the Triassic, amphibians and *Therapsids* (particularly *Cynodonts*) were abundant. The *Sauropsid* line had spawned the archosaurs, who were also abundant, and from whom all dinosaurs, pterosaurs, and crocodilians. The archosaurs had an advantage over other reptiles in that they had multiple lungs that allowed them to breath in an atmosphere with only 16% oxygen. Dinosaurs at the start of the Triassic were only a minority part of the family tree, representing only 5% of all tetrapods.

Then approximately 234 million years ago, volcanism increased the climate and humidity of Earth. While rainfall could rarely reach the interior of Pangea in the previous period, now rain was everywhere. In this "pluvial episode" rain belted down across the Earth for 2 million years straight. This had a devastating effect on tetrapods that liked the arid desert climates. Dinosaurs, meanwhile thrived in the more humid environments that briefly emerged. They evolved and diversified while other archosaurs, therapsids, and amphibians (particularly giant ones) declined in abundance.

In the late Triassic, the first pterosaurs began to take flight. The hypotheses surrounding their evolution usually involve archosaurs scampering up trees and gliding with flaps of skin at first, in a form of evolution similar to the bat. We also have the first evidence of fuzzy proto-feathers growing on the first few species of dinosaurs, but their evolution toward the skies would take considerably longer. It should be noted, however, that flight is an extremely complex activity for any species, whether arthropod, pterosaur, or avian dinosaur. The energy flows required to stay airborne, and the precise physical structure required to do so, are quite profound.

The Triassic extinction event 201 million years ago (its cause still being unclear) wiped out a great many amphibians, *Therapsids*, and most archosaur species other than dinosaurs and pterosaurs. As a result dinosaurs grew to be 90% of all tetrapods on Earth.

The Jurassic (201-145 million years ago)

The Jurassic gets its name from the Jura mountain range on the Franco-Swiss border where the rock layers were first investigated. The Jurassic opened with Pangea cracking into pieces and the climate becoming increasingly humid. The modern continents began to take form, with North America and Europe still together and South America and Africa still connecting their perfect "puzzle pieces". The gulf was increasing between these two continental couples. As a result, there was no longer a huge desert interior. Rain was more easily able to reach the coast, which increased the amount of forest and heavy vegetation. The oxygen levels increased to approximately 25%.

Since the Triassic extinction had wiped out the majority of large tetrapods that weren't dinosaurs, the latter began to fill a vast range of empty niches. The humid rainforests afforded herbivores a great deal of food, and the dinosaurs evolved to eat increasing quantities of vegetation. As a result herbivorous dinosaurs got larger and larger. Thus we see the evolution of various species of *Ceratopsia*, and *Stegosauria*, and the long necked *Diplodocidae*, like *Supersaurus* which was 35m long. As the prey got larger, so did the predators, with theropods like *Allosaurus* (10m in length and a classical-looking dino predator) dominating the top of the food chain. The long duration of the rule of dinosaurs is commonly illustrated by the fact that 88 million years separate stegosaurus from *Tyrannosaurus rex* in the Cretaceous and only 65 million years separate T-Rex from humans.

In the meantime, the proto-mammals (*Cynodonts*) kept out of the way. Their average size was not much bigger than a mouse. They burrowed or hid up trees, many ate insects, and many only came out at night. By 165 million years ago, they did begin to show some diversity, but only insofar as they did not try to fill evolutionary niches dominated by the dinosaurs. A few of them became tree-bound, developed gliding abilities, and a few returned to the coastlines and habitats closely attached to the water.

By the Late Jurassic, we begin to see the first avian dinosaurs (the ancestors of birds) take flight. What had begun with a sort of fuzz appearing on just a few Triassic dinosaurs for warmth had spawned other evolutionary advantages. Some dinosaurs remained coated with primitive feathers (T-Rex in the Cretaceous may even have had fuzz), some dinosaurs had no feathers at all, but in some species, feathers were growing more sophisticated and were leading to evolutionarily to flight. Flapping one's wings, even while not being a flying species, allowed some dinosaurs to aid their grip on prey, trees while climbing, or the ground while running. By the end of the period dozens of dinosaurs had taken to the air.

The Cretaceous (145-65 million years ago)

The Cretaceous period's name comes from the Latin for chalk (*creta*) which filled many Cretaceous rock layers as remains from single-celled marine plankton that were abundant at the time. The Earth's climate had cooled slightly from the Jurassic period, oxygen levels rose to 30%, and, and temperatures were slightly warmer than they are today. The break-up of Pangea was complete and the various continents we are familiar with today continued to drift apart, with the Atlantic ocean getting wider, North and South America drifting slowly toward each other, and Australia, Antarctica, and India breaking off from Africa. The last of these was set on a collision course with the belly of Eurasia.

Even though we are talking 145 to 65 million years ago, on an Earth still dominated by dinosaurs, certain corners of the biosphere were beginning to look decidedly more "modern". Not just in terms of the shapes of continents, or the fact that glaciers were reappearing. Grasses evolved for the first time. It is odd to visualise considering how much of the Earth is covered with the stuff, but they had not existed in the masses of vegetation in the greenest phases of the Earth before, whether Carboniferous or Jurassic. Around 140 million years ago, some early species of ants emerged. Additionally, 125 million years ago, flowering plants (which had not existed before) evolved and spread across the Earth, largely thanks to their concurrent evolution with bees. The avian dinosaurs (the ancestors of modern birds) proliferated in a variety of forms, and the first birds of prey began to appear, rivalling the smaller pterosaurs. Finally, also 125 million years ago, the first proto-placental and proto-marsupial mammals appeared on the fossil record. Both gave birth rather than laid eggs, with the former species gestating the offspring for longer in the womb and the latter giving birth and nurturing the offspring in a pouch or pocket. While still quite small and skittish, the placentals would become prominent in the Americas, Eurasia, and Africa, and the marsupials would predominate in Australia. And the ancestors of the platypus would still lay eggs, confusing the hell out of everyone. While "modern" might be overstating the case in a world where you could still see a T-Rex and triceratops duking it out, in small niches which weren't clogged by the dinosaurs, you did indeed see the first glimmers of the Cenozoic Era (the period that runs from 65 million years ago to today) emerging.

The dinosaurs meanwhile continued to reign supreme, with most niches being filled by them. As such this glut of dinos stiffened competition between species. Particularly in terms of the balance between herbivores and the predatory carnivores that hunted them. As a result you get some of the most astounding forms on both sides in this period. Whether that be the emergence of apex predators like *Tyrannosaurus rex* and *Albertosaurus*, or the increasingly diverse defensive tusks used by ceratopsia like *Triceratops*, or the long spines that sauropods grew on their necks to ward of predators, like with *Amargasaurus*, or the heavy armoured plating worn by *Ankylosaurus*.

At the beginning of Chapter 4, we mentioned that if it weren't for the appearance of "collective learning" the game of natural selection and the Evolutionary Epic would be as far as complexity would get in the Universe. And in the event the evolution of collective learning required the appearance of mammalian primate species with sufficiently large brains, social instincts, and a capacity for language. If it were not for the extinction of the dinosaurs, it is impossible that primates would have evolved. But that does raise an interesting question: if the Earth had remained dominated by dinosaurs like it had for the past 140 million years, would any of them possibly have evolved collective learning?

It is impossible to know for sure, since evolution is a blind process with many contingencies. Also, there aren't any candidates that even remotely resemble the sort of species that could have made the transition, to the same extent early primates did. However, it may be of interest of you to consider the *Troodontids* which lived from roughly 150 million to 65 million years ago, getting wiped out in the Cretaceous extinction. They were carnivorous dinosaurs, with fuzz on their bodies and some primitive feathers on their arms. Their teeth and their feet claws were razor sharp. They stood a little taller than an average human. In many ways they resemble a lot of predators of that size. With notable difference that they had forward facing eyes like primates, giving them greater depth perception, and large brains to process all that 3D information. As we shall see in the next chapter, these were the same key traits that eventually spawned collective learning in primates. There is never a single path in evolution toward a certain trait. Niches can be filled by all sorts of organisms with vastly different ancestries. While it is a huge stretch of the imagination, it is curious to consider that if primates had not evolved, that given enough time a dinosaur might have evolved collective learning. This is of particular relevance when considering the probability of other intelligent life elsewhere in the Universe.

At any rate, the Cretaceous extinction event obliterated the *Troodontids* along with 70% of the rest of life on Earth. As Luis and Walter Alvarez (the latter of whom does Big History) discovered, an asteroid approximately 10km in diameter struck the Yucatan peninsula, setting off a slew of earthquakes, tsunamis, continent-wide forest fires, and huge torrents of acid rain killed off plenty of life. Then all the dust flung into the air blocked out solar energy and killed off plenty of plant life, causing the surviving herbivores to starve, followed by the carnivores. The Earth became littered with rotting plants and animals, fed upon by flies, maggots, and other corpse-feeders. Those birds and mammals that could eat insects and survive on what little plant life remained, got out of the catastrophe where non-avian dinosaurs perished. The niches had been swept clean once again, and this time it would be the mammals that would fill them. And so they did, setting off the cycle of extinction and explosions once again, until only a few million years ago, when the Universe began to see the first glimmers of something new, the sixth threshold of complexity.

Essay Writing Exercise

For this chapter's essay writing exercise, pick one of the following essay questions we have examined thus far:

Why is the Big Bang theory the most widely accepted explanation for the origin of the Universe?

What do you regard as the most important turning point in the geological history of our Earth?

Which theory for the origins of life is most convincing?

What do you regard as the most important turning point in the history of life?

You should already have a thesis statement/introduction for at least one of them, derived from the previous exercises. This time, however, don't worry too much about structure or organisation. This time we will engage with a "free-writing exercise". It is fairly simple, just write the body of your essay for 15 minutes straight without worrying about the order of your arguments, or format, or even a cohesive list of everything you could say to support your thesis statement. Just write for 15 to 30 minutes straight (possibly taking a 5 minute break somewhere in the middle) and see what you come up with.

Once you have completed some free-writing, make a list of the key arguments and evidence you brought up during the process. Consider which arguments and evidence are the strongest. If there were any new arguments that dawned on you during the writing process, modify your introduction accordingly. If the free-writing process made you revise your thesis statement, modify the thesis statement accordingly. This may frequently happen when drafting a paper and digging into arguments and evidence – often the core argument begins to appear more nuanced than you may have first thought.

While you would not want to turn in an essay that has a body composed entirely of free-writing, or even try to format and edit on the basis of that writing (could be a massive headache depending on how disorderly your ideas came onto the page) it is a way to develop your arguments to full fruition in a way that an essay outline simply cannot achieve.

Further Reading

Alvarez, Walter. T. rex and the Crater of Doom. Princeton: Princeton University Press, 1997.

Darwin, Charles. The Origin of Species by Means of Natural Selection. 1st edition, reprint. Cambridge, Mass: Harvard University Press, 2003.

Erwin, Douglas. Extinction: How Life on Earth Nearly Ended 250 million Years ago. Princeton: Princeton University Press, 2006.

Fortey, R. Earth: An Intimate History. New York: Knopf, 2004.

Hazen, Robert. The Story of Earth: The First 4.5 Billion Years from Stardust to Living Planet. New York: Viking 2012.

Knoll, Andrew. Life on a Young Planet: The First Three Billion Years of Evolution on Earth. Princeton: Princeton University Press, 2003.

Leakey, R. The Sixth Extinction: Patterns of Life and the Future of Humankind. New York: Doubleday, 1995.

Maynard Smith, John, and Eors Szathmary. The Origins of Life: From the Birth of Life to the Origins of Language. Oxford: Oxford University Press, 1999.

McGowan, Christopher. The Dragon Seekers: How an extraordinary circle of fossilists discovered the dinosaurs and paved the way for Darwin. London: Basic Books, 2009.

CHAPTER 6

PRIMATE EVOLUTION

Or,

WHY YOU LOOK LIKE

A MONKEY

AND

(OCCASIONALLY)

SMELL LIKE ONE TOO

In the Ruins of the World

The Cretaceous extinction event killed off 70% of the world's species, including 90% of terrestrial species and 50% of plant species. Large species were particularly heavy hit because of the collapse of the food chain. Aside from turtles and crocodiles, the rest of the world was populated by tiny creatures like birds and mammals, less than one third of the size of the average human today. In many cases much less. The Paleogene opened 65 million years ago as a wasteland, its climate chilly and dry. The landscape was littered with dead plants and animals, rotting away in the Sun and being gradually covered by dirt and dust.

The ecological niches of the world had been swept clean, presenting an opportunity for the survivors to fill them via rapid evolution. The mammalian radiation that resulted saw small mammalian species, resembling squirrels or rats, diversify into a variety of forms, both large and small. One branch of the mammalian tree began to live in increasingly complex social hierarchies. Their brain sizes increased. Their ability to communicate became sophisticated. And slowly but surely over tens of millions of years, the first glimmers of collective learning emerged. This was to be something new under the Sun, where a species could rapidly adapt faster than evolution could carry it. The complexity this process generated over thousands, rather than millions, of years began to drive things to new heights. It also opened up a portal to many more thresholds of complexity to come in an avalanche to which there is still no end in sight.

Timeline

- **The Cretaceous Extinction (65.5 million years ago):** Struck by an asteroid on the Yucatan peninsula, the Earth lost roughly 70% of all its species. The non-avian dinosaurs were wiped out freeing ecological niches for the mammalian radiation which saw tiny species which had remained on the periphery of the environment for 100 million years to supplant the dinosaurs as the primary organism of the biosphere.
- **The Last Common Ancestor of New and Old World Monkeys (40 million years ago):** As the last remnants of Pangea split apart, the ancestor of all primates found itself divided by the Atlantic Ocean. This split between the New and Old World Monkeys marked a diversification into world zones that profoundly affected the evolutionary traits of each group.
- **The Last Common Ancestor of Old World Monkeys and Great Apes (25-30 million years ago):** The emergence of the Great Apes marks the evolution of larger body sizes, brain sizes, and increasingly complex social groups, hierarchies, and rituals. The increase of social and group complexity in the Great Apes fuelled the evolution of a

variety of new instincts, and the capacity for innovation unavailable to most other species on Earth.

- **The Last Common Ancestor of Humans and Gorillas (10-12 million years ago):** The division of the last common ancestor of humans and gorillas marks a change in social complexity where gorillas maintained groups composed mostly of females, with one male at the forefront, and the evolution of the ancestors of humans where multiple males and females would inhabit the same group.

- **The Last Common Ancestor of Humans and Chimpanzees (5-7 million years ago):** This species would have been remarkably socially complex, with the rudiments of innovation and language, and a wide range of emotions and memory. Social hierarchies became so complex that strength alone was not enough to guarantee dominance, but the ability to keep track of and maintain alliances was also crucial. Alphas could be overthrown by a coalition of other males, or by the rebellion of the females. Competition was so fierce for dominance, food, and mates, that intelligence correspondingly advanced. Territoriality and aggression took on new and vicious heights. While the LCA of humans and chimpanzees would have likely existed in male-led hierarchies, the ancestors of bonobos split off from chimpanzees 2 million years ago and evolved a female-led hierarchy.

- **The First Bipedal Apes (4 million years ago):** Environmental changes in East Africa 4 million years ago dried out many of the forests to woodlands and savannahs. Quadrupedal primates best suited to climbing trees fled further into the receding forests, while those primates which still very much looked like chimpanzees struck out over increasingly longer distances to forage for food on the open plains. As such a new evolutionary invention was required for our ancestors to cover more ground to find food and to be able to carry resources as they moved.

- **Evolution of Homo habilis (2.5 million years ago):** While brain sizes had not dramatically increased in 5-7 million years, and while many primates used tools, *Homo habilis* represented a new level of tool-making and adaptability that increased their odds of survival in a rapidly changing and often hostile East African environment.

- **Evolution of Homo ergaster-erectus (1.9 million years ago):** Dramatic increases in brain size, group size, and presumably social complexity accompanied the evolution of *Homo ergaster-erectus*. The species is notable for being the first to radiate out of Africa and spread across the Old World, indicating they were capable of quickly adapting to a myriad of new environments from Europe to India to East Asia. *Homo ergaster-erectus* may have also been the first species to develop collective learning.

- First Possible Collective Learning (1.5 million years ago): While the tool designs of *Homo habilis* and other primates remained fairly unchanged over the course of millions of years, slight tinkering and improvement of certain handaxes by *Homo ergaster-erectus* in East Africa seem to imply some slow accumulation and refinement of knowledge over the course of a few hundred thousand years. Possibly an incipient version of collective learning.

- The Evolution of Homo antecessor, Homo heidelbergensis, and Neanderthals (1.2 million to 400,000 years ago): The successors to *Homo ergaster-erectus* also spread throughout the Old World, and have clear signs of tinkering, invention, and improvement of new tools. It is highly likely these species all had collective learning. The one aspect which seems to be lacking is the capacity for abstract thought, for which we usually look for body paints or cave paintings as a clear indicator. There is only scanty evidence that Neanderthals may have used paints in this way, but the evidence is inconclusive.

- The First Homo sapiens (at least 315,000 years ago): There is evidence of an anatomically similar member of *Homo sapiens* is from East Africa and dated to approximately 198,000 years ago. There is less copious but fairly conclusive evidence for anatomically similar *Homo sapiens* in West Africa roughly 315,000 years ago. Current estimates for anatomically similar *Homo sapiens* run up to 350,000 years ago. These people would likely have had much the same instincts, intellectual capacity, and talent for collective learning that we do, while some scientists hypothesize that we experienced another revolution in human intelligence around 40-70,000 years ago, but the evidence is still scanty. Either way, these humans would have co-existed alongside many other hominine species until an estimated 40,000 years ago when *Homo sapiens* became the last of our genus on Earth.

The Mammalian Radiation (i.e. when boobs took over the world)

A mammal is defined by the unique structure of its jaws and, more conspicuously, the use of mammary glands to suckle its offspring. The mammal belongs to the domain of *Eukaryota*, the kingdom of Animalia, the phylum of chordates, and the super-class of tetrapods. The first proto-mammals evolved roughly 225 million years ago. For much of the age of dinosaurs we remained on the periphery of the evolutionary tree, and remained quite small. At the time of the Cretaceous extinction event 65 million years ago, mammals were usually under 50cm long and weighing under a kilogram. A few mammals were the size of cats and weighed over 10kg. Smaller mammals at this time were insectivores and herbivores, the rare larger mammals were herbivores, omnivores, and carnivores – the last of these hunting either fish or small infant dinosaurs. Mammals had a tendency to burrow, or to climb trees, and a few might have developed gliding abilities.

Then the asteroid struck the Earth. The smallest mammals survived the collapse of the food chain because they relied on such small amounts of food in the first place. The mammalian radiation took hold. The climate warmed again and by 60 million years ago, North America and Europe were tropical, the majority of the Earth became covered in forests, with huge deserts around the equator. At the poles there was little or no ice.

Many mammals remained the size of shrews or rats. But the absence of larger tetrapods following the dinosaurs allowed mammals to grow and diversify impressively. For example, the ancestor of all elephants had evolved 60 million years ago, at this point no bigger than a dog, but it would gradually evolve to become the world's largest land mammal.

Also 60 million years ago, similarly sized animals with razor sharp teeth used for tearing flesh from their prey evolved. By 42 million years ago, these predators had split into two suborders with either canine or feline characteristics. The caniforms contained ancestors of wolves, foxes and bears. The feliforms constitute ancestors of the lions, tigers, and jaguars. They ranged in size from the very small, to the gigantic.

About 55 million years ago, a small mammal about the size of a cat evolved to be able to escape from being eaten by diving into the water and under the surface until danger passed. These were the ancestors of hippos and whales. Eventually one branch of the family began to spend more and more time in the oceans, first inhabiting shallow waters, later being able to brave the deep and evolving to eat scores and scores of fish. By 40 million years ago, they had come to resemble whales.

In the forests about 55 million years ago, there was the ancestor of the horse. Multi-toed and also the size of a dog. It crept quietly and nimbly among the trees and the brush on the forest floor. Once the climate cooled and dried, they began running increasingly on the dominant third toe. Over time, the other toes receded significantly.

You can still see them, much shrunken, on a horse's skeleton. By the time humans domesticated them, they were taller, possessed hooves, and could run over vast distances. Horse domestication was a great leap forward for human civilizations in Eurasia. And it was an opportunity lost in the Americas, since we hunted those indigenous horses to extinction.

And 55 million years ago, on the same part of the family tree containing rodents and rabbits, remaining quite small for the time being, emerged the primates. Small tree-dwelling mammals with grasping hands and front-facing eyes. These traits were particularly useful to avoid tumbling from the trees. The front-facing eyes, for instance, permitted primates stereoscopic vision and depth-perception. Something which is particularly crucial when judging a leap from one branch to another. And in order to process all that 3D information, primates required increasingly larger brains, something which would have corollary benefits later.

From 55 million to 40 million years ago, primates began to form the facial features familiar to all monkeys and apes today. They lived in complex social groups where the chance to pass on their DNA was determined by social hierarchy, sexual politics, and access to food. The slow waltz of plate tectonics continued to pull Eurasia and the Americas apart, expanding the Atlantic Ocean. Primates colonized the Americas, and, separated by the vast Atlantic 40 million years ago, they continued their separate evolution into the New World monkeys. New World monkeys had flatter noses and side facing nostrils, longer tails useful for grasping things, and most species do not have opposable thumbs. New World monkeys were also more likely to observe monogamous relationships. In the Old World monkeys, from which we are descended, monogamy is a much rarer evolutionary invention which varies from species to species. In Old World monkeys, females stay with their mothers for life, while the males grow up and find their own "harem" of females, chasing off all other males in extremely aggressive displays.

In the majority of Old World monkeys and Great Apes, this show of bravado and tendency toward violence is mitigated to a power hierarchy where alpha and beta males exist in the same group, with the alphas getting priority access to mates and food. Females meanwhile invested a heck of a lot more time and energy in sex, since it could easily result in months of gestation and child-rearing, and were much more choosey about their mates. Not all male primates get to reproduce, while most female primates mate with a smaller section of "worthy" males. It results in female primates being more highly valued on average than males, and in the majority of primate groups it is left for males to compete as disposable candidates. Such are the "economics of gametes" in natural and sexual selection. Thus some of the most distant and rudimentary elements of human sexuality were being laid. This irrational evolutionary wiring still causes much confusion, romantic anguish, and distress to this day.

Gorilla "Warfare"

Meanwhile, in Africa, primates continued to evolve, and 25-30 million years ago the line of the Great Apes diverged from the Old World Monkeys. The ancestral species of chimpanzees, bonobos, gorillas, orangutans, and us. We split off from the evolutionary ancestors of gorillas about 10-12 million years ago. Gorillas dwell quietly in lowlands in the mountains in patches around the many tributaries of the Congo River. They eat plants, fruits, and occasionally bugs. The food they eat is so common that different groups of gorillas don't really need to compete over it, unlike a number of other primate species. This removes the impulse to evolve more intense tribalism and inter-group conflict. While gorillas may look threatening, most gorilla aggression comes in the form of intimidation and displays, though they can make a very good job of defending themselves if the mere threat doesn't cover it. By and large it is warfare by bravado.

Gorilla social/sexual hierarchies are structured in the following way. Typically female gorillas stay with the same group for life, while male gorillas are driven out by the alpha leader of the group, the silverback, when they come of age to wander as bachelors until they can construct female-populated groups of their own or supplant an existing silverback of another group. Male competition led to a high degree of sexual dimorphism, with male gorillas being significantly larger than the females. Much more so than the sexual dimorphism in humans. This definitely plays a role in the sexual politics that result. There are, however, rare cases where multi-male groups exist and beta gorillas submit to the silverback, and perhaps rise to replace him when he dies. If a group loses its silverback without a replacement, external males are liable to kill the group's young in order to favour the passing on of their own DNA. Female gorillas make sure to form relationships with males to gain protection from these predators, not to mention the protection of their young from infanticide. Females who are kith and kin tend to stick together in sisterhood, being very supportive of each other's interests and safety. Female gorillas who are not related tend to compete aggressively in cliques. They also tend to get jealous and aggressive when another female has achieved a relationship with an alpha.

Male gorillas tend to be hostile to each other, even when related. This prohibits the male equivalent of the gorilla "sisterhood". In the evolutionary contest, the male is more disposable, more likely to kill or be killed. All in service of finding food, resources, a mate, and offspring. With one notable exception. When male gorillas have been booted by an alpha from a female populated group, they sometimes band together rather than roaming around solo, and when in exile they are much friendlier to one another, even engaging in mutual grooming, and friendly wrestling. And some gorillas even eschew the harem completely and engage in the occasional bout of gay sex.

Our Closest Cousins

Chimpanzees are our closest surviving evolutionary cousins. We share 98.4% of our DNA. We split off from chimps through a last common ancestor about 5-7 million years ago. This does not mean we evolved from chimps, who simply went down a different evolutionary track, with different pressures and different favoured traits. They are our cousins, not uncles and aunts. After 5-7 million years ago, the chimp ancestors went on to be separated into different ecosystems. Chimpanzees, like most Great Apes, are physically better suited to stick by the trees. Their arms are longer than their legs, and while they have moments where they walk bipedally, it is ungainly and awkward. The evolutionary benefit is the ability to scamper up a tree when danger is near.

Chimps are smaller than humans, about 100 to 120 cm in height. Chimpanzees are typically much, much stronger than we are. It does not take much for a chimp to overpower the average human and do a great deal of physical damage, the most notable being cases where chimps have torn off people's faces. Chimps have a brain that is three times smaller than a human's. Nevertheless we can see a lot of similar instincts and behaviours in them. Not to mention a capacity for inventiveness, genius, and group politics. Chimps eat plants and insects, and not infrequently they are sighted hunting colobus monkeys. Males go round in packs to gain access to this food.

Unlike gorillas, it is entirely common practice for chimp troops to be composed of a collection of beta males led by a male alpha and a corresponding group of female alphas and betas. The chimp "tribe" accordingly has an extremely complex social hierarchy. The male alpha functions as "tribal chief" and dominates a large number of other males and females all vying for alliances and position. The chief *can* be the strongest, the most aggressive, but not always. The chief must also be the most manipulative and savvy at maintaining alliances to support his rule. As a result, it is sometimes the case that the alpha is not the biggest bruiser per se, but a leaner, weaker politician who has managed to incorporate some muscle to do his bidding. Beta males have been known to team up and launch a violent revolution that overthrows and replaces the alpha.

Females have their own firm pecking order of females who either dominate or submit to other females. A lower caste beta male better not try to harass a female protected by alpha males and females who are higher up. The female dominance hierarchy also extends to offspring. A dominant chimpanzee mother will have a daughter. Aggression toward that daughter, even while she is weak and young, is punished by the dominant mother and lesser females with whom she is allied. The daughter is thus protected until she reaches the point where she can start forming dominance alliances of her own. Chimp male dominance is entirely dependent on acceptance by the hierarchy of females. If they don't like you, you cannot be the alpha. If you are already the alpha and they turn against you, they will overthrow you and put a new alpha in your place.

The ultimate result of this entire hierarchy is priority access to food and mates. The two most valuable resources of the species. Or any species, really. What is noticeable about this hierarchy is that it is so complex relative to other primates that a larger brain was definitely required by evolution to cope with all the social interactions necessary to maintain the alliances which underpin the entire tribal hierarchy. While three times smaller than a human brain, it is still significantly larger compared to body size and energy requirements than most mammalian species.

Chimps are smart. Really smart. In all likelihood, our last common ancestor 5-7 million years ago possessed this trait as well. Like many primates, chimps use tools. They fashion sticks to fish termites out of the ground for food. They use rocks as hammers. They leaves as sponges to soak up water. They use branches as levers. They even fashion banana leaf umbrellas. There is also indication that these innovations aren't just sporadic, but are taught from adult to child. This counts as a form of social learning. Even a form of culture. In groups that do not have an innovation, it does not sporadically come into existence. In groups that have the innovation, it is passed on, rather than rediscovered every generation. However, chimps do not seem to accumulate that knowledge, adding more innovations to their culture generation after generation. Hence why wild chimpanzees still inhabit similar environments and lead similar lifestyles as they would thousands of years ago. The lack of accumulation is a clear difference with humans, who have gone from stone tools to skyscrapers in a few thousand years.

Chimps have language, just like gorillas and humans, which implies so did our common ancestors. While most chimp communication is done by gesture (arguably humans still do much, if not most, by gesture as well) they do have a limited range of vocalizations. The limit is imposed by the chimp's physiology restricting the range of noises they can make and also their brain capacity. In captivity, chimps have shown a remarkable aptitude for memorizing a wide range of written symbols. Which means the evolutionary trait that sparked off cave painting and writing must have been buried deep 7 million years ago.

Chimpanzees are highly capable of kindness and compassion. All animals can be altruistic. Particularly where there kin are concerned. Self-sacrifice is entirely common in the case of someone endangering themselves for children, brothers, sisters, and so forth. Evolution permits this because it keeps relatively close DNA replicating. Altruism also occurs in chimps when it is reciprocal. This can come in the form of small kindnesses like sharing, to the tit-for-tat of alliance building. If a primate gains an evolutionary benefit (real or imagined) from self-sacrifice, like possible access to mating opportunities in the future or the construction of a valuable alliance in a group, it will throw itself into the breach. In chimps, it is either through "kin selection" or "reciprocal altruism" that you see them doing something heart-warming like tending to their newborns, hugging a friend, sharing food, or grooming a neighbour.

Chimpanzees can also be highly violent. Male chimpanzees band together, roam their "territory", and see if they can find a lone chimp to beat up. Once they find their quarry, they set about kicking and hitting him without the lone chimp having much of a chance of defending himself. Soon the victim is overwhelmed. It is common practice for chimps to start tearing off bits of flesh. Particularly the ears, bits of the face, and, most shockingly, the genitalia. Once the assault has finished, the lone male is left in the woods to die of his wounds. And it would appear that the chimps go out with precisely this intention in mind, not because they sensed the presence of the stranger in the first place. Warfare in chimpanzees is not a thing. They don't have the numbers or the coordination. But they are perfectly happy to patrol their territory and brutalize strangers.

Make Love Not War

The chimpanzee tendency toward violence can also be contrasted with bonobos, who are also close relatives of ours. Approximately 2 million years ago, the Congo River began with a trickle and in time created a massive river with many tributaries. It separated a group of ancestral chimpanzees. To the north, the chimps continued to display more aggressive traits and lived in male-led societies. Separated to the south, the chimps evolved into a more slender species with radically different habits. Bonobos live in a female-led hierarchy where sexuality is rife. Males are oftentimes physically stronger, but on the very rare occasion where a male shows aggression toward a female, a sisterhood of bonobos gang up on him and put a stop to it. Sometimes they scare him off with hoots and shouting. Sometimes they break his fingers.

There is no way to tell the paternity of the child, in most cases, because bonobo females are extremely promiscuous. Accordingly, males do not have the opportunity to compete for mates or to commit infanticide against offspring that are not theirs. Bonobos don't exactly have DNA testing. As a result males settle for a general indifference to children, one way or another. Not hostile, often friendly to kids in general, but not doting parents to a child in particular either. Access to mates is one of the biggest evolutionary drivers, along with access to food, which keeps the organism alive long enough to obtain the aforesaid sex and reproduction. Demand for sex remains high like in most primates, but in bonobos, females do not put a chokehold on supply. Females are decidedly less choosey over whom they have sex with. This eliminates the need for competition and male aggression. We see a significant decrease in tension.

Bonobos make a jolly good go of it. They have sex in doggie-style but also intimate face-to-face sex (a rarity in most primates). Bonobos are also notable for engaging frequently in fellatio and cunnilingus. Bonobos have also been noted to perform the "French kiss", also a rarity in many primates. It goes without saying bonobos also perform gay sex, like many species do. They also engage in masturbation every few hours, the frequency being slightly higher than other primates. When greeting each other, bonobos have a tendency to touch each other's engorged genitals in what is referred to as a "bonobo handshake" in order to reduce initial tensions.

The after-glow of sex also becomes a prime way to prevent and resolve inter-group conflicts. When two groups of bonobos meet in the woods, the males in the group might get a little tense at first, but then the females from the two groups cross over and start having sex with the strange males. This frequently diffuses the tension and prevents the outbreak of violence.

It is therefore perhaps unfortunate that humans are more closely related to chimpanzees than bonobos. The tendency to restrict access to sex and to indulge in competition and mate selection breeds much of the violence and inter-group conflict in humans that we see in chimpanzees. But then, would we have taken the same evolutionary course, or would we still be roaming the forests of sub-Saharan Africa?

The Bipedal Apes

As the Great Apes toiled for millions of years in the forests of Africa, mostly keeping safe in trees deep in forests, and walking clumsily on the ground with bowed legs and using our arms and fists for balance, the climate of the world continued to oscillate and change from hot to cold, from damp to dry. Between 4 and 5 million years ago, the climate entered one of its dry phases. The forest in which our ancestors dwelt melted away from the landscape. They shrank back leaving woodlands and eventually wide open savannah. This affected evolution.

Those primates that ventured away from the trees found themselves unable to quickly scamper up high to safety when danger was near. They had to range farther and farther to find resources to keep themselves alive. For a species that evolved from tree dwellers this change of habitat involved an increasing degree of difficulty. During the environmental change there were ancestors killed by predators or by starvation. Slowly but surely this non-random elimination shifted our line away from the bowed-leg stance reminiscent of chimpanzees and developed "bipedalism". Our locomotion came from legs that were straight and forward-facing.

Around 4 million years ago, the Australopithecines, were walking on two feet across long distances of East Africa, foraging for food. Australopithecines were not very tall, standing only about a meter or just above three-and-a-half feet. They looked a lot like chimpanzees, aside from being bipedal. Australopithecines were largely herbivores, with teeth adapted for grinding tough fruits, leaves, and other plants. They may have communicated through gestures and limited sounds like chimpanzees. Except now they were bipedal, this freed up the hands for regular use of an even wider range of gestures. And you can communicate a lot via gesture. As such it is likely that Australopithecine social groups were as complex, if not way more complex, than chimpanzees. The most famous skeleton is of "Lucy" a female of the species Australopithecus afarensis. She lived about 3.2 million years ago. She would have wandered the woodlands and savannah on foot. Potentially taking refuge in the trees from time to time, but with a physique that was growing less and less used to such activities. By and large, species like Lucy seem well adapted to their environment in East Africa and survived and thrived there for hundreds of thousands of years.

Bipedalism opened up another evolutionary advantage. Their hands were free not just for gestures, but to carry tools and transport them from place to place. By and large Australopithecines retained the genius of chimps. They used sticks. They used rocks as hammers to beat open tough materials like nuts and bones to scavenge their marrow. But in the wide open savannah being able to carry a tool for later use allows for some important survival advantages.

Homo habilis

By 2.8 million years ago, *Homo habilis* split from a common ancestor with Australopithecus. In the subsequent several hundred thousand years they became increasingly distinct, emerging as a species 2.5 million years ago. *Homo habilis* did not stand much taller than Australopithecines, and their brains were only slightly bigger. But there seems to have been an increase in intelligence and inventiveness. *Homo habilis* not only used tools but modified them. They were known to have hit flakes off stones to use them for cutting. It may seem a minor adjustment to us, but having a ready cutting tool has a myriad of potential uses when it comes to gaining access to food. A cutting tool can come in handy when faced with rough plants, or when hungry and scavenging raw meet off a corpse in the savannah. If you have just a little bit of a survival edge like that, your species can do very well indeed. And such was the case with *Homo habilis*, who survived and thrived for approximately a million years. The other thing is that making stone flakes is kind of difficult. Even archaeologists have tried to re-enact it, and it is tricky with a lot of trial and error. This requires some pretty beefy intellect, intentionality, and the patience of a craftsman.

But there were limits. As important a breakthrough like stone-working is, we see very little sign of technological improvement over the hundreds of thousands of years that *Homo habilis* existed. We see invention. But we don't see the accumulation of invention generation after generation.

As for the social complexity of *Homo habilis*, their success as a species likely led to a growth in their population in East Africa. Their family groups would have remained quite small. But the frequency of *Homo habilis* running into other family groups would have increased by about 2 million years ago. This may have started an evolutionary pressure for more and more complex social interaction. Firstly, between groups, this may have required some alliance building, so that violence would not break out every time they met. Instead of the bonobo method of reducing tension with sex, the practice of gift-giving would have allowed *Homo habilis* to occasionally avoid violence by sharing their stuff.

Another form of diplomacy is inter-group "marriage". It helps with genetic diversity. But it also extends kin selection to two families, since two familial groups now have a vested interest in seeing the successful passage of their DNA through their joint offspring. This sort of behaviour would not have been well-facilitated through the polygamy common in chimps, and so behaviours more closely akin to monogamy would have evolved to keep two people together. This would have been reinforced by the trait of having two adults invested in each other for a longer time, to better rear, raise, and protect a child.

Within groups and between groups, there is a need for alliance building between individuals. Usually this is done by bonding moments between two individuals. The most common way of doing this in a lot of primates is grooming. The simple act of closeness that comes from picking the bugs and dirt out of someone's hair. But if numbers grow there may simply not be enough time to groom everyone required for their complex social alliances. So what else do we do at the beauty salon besides groom each other? We gossip.

Another way of forming a social bond is by conveying certain emotions and ideas. *Homo habilis* would still have had a very restricted range of sounds that was able to form speech. But gesture did its usual magic, added to which they would have used pleasing sounds like hums, and grunts and yells to convey displeasure. Brain growth would be required to further interpret the subtleties of those signals. This may have been reinforced by sexual selection. Females may have chosen males who were able to express themselves in convincing ways. Essentially have "game". There also would have been sexual preference given to males who were able to competently maintain alliances and rise in the social hierarchy. The better you do that, the better your access to food and potential mates.

Then there's the added benefit having a greater capacity for communication, collaboration, and the first stirrings of abstract thought would have on survival in East Africa. This would have formed a positive feedback cycle. One thing is clear. Around 2 million years ago there was an immense evolutionary pressure placed on brain growth in all the offshoots of the genus *Homo* living in East Africa. And evolution got to work very, very quickly.

Homo ergaster-erectus

This brings us to *Homo ergaster-erectus* 1.9 million years ago. There is some debate about the nomenclature and the evolutionary relationship between *ergaster* and *erectus* due to the huge similarities between them, so for shorthand I will henceforth refer to "*erectus*" simply because it is more in common parlance. It also makes more immature people giggle.

Homo erectus was taller than *Homo habilis*. It had perfected the art of bipedal locomotion. In fact it had such robust legs that it would challenge even the most talented Olympic runners. This signals a full transition to the practice of covering large areas to forage for food. The facial structure was looking more and more human. We can also be fairly confident that body hair had receded significantly, leaving only dark melanin of the skin protecting them from the harsh Sun's rays.

But the most notable aspect about *Homo erectus* is that it had a decidedly bigger brain, about 70% that of a humans but roughly twice that of *Homo habilis, Australopithecus afarensis*, or modern chimpanzees. We know they were successful in Africa because there is evidence of a huge demographic boom. And this led to migration. *Homo erectus* was bright enough to adapt to new environments, because the species headed out of Africa in several waves of mass migration on a trek that would take it across the Old World. They adapted to deserts, forests, coastal, and mountain regions. Long before *Homo sapiens* ever existed, our ancestors were now gaining the power to travel the world.

Homo erectus was the first to migrate in this way on such a massive scale. Subsequent species in our line did the same. And by now it is fairly safe to assume that after *Homo erectus* it was becoming more and more common for our ancestors to leave Africa. At the very least they would have the run of most places in Africa from the south all the way to Morocco, though in Africa much of the work discovering new skeletons is still in its infancy.

So *Homo erectus* had a bigger brain and was unquestionably brighter. But when *Homo erectus* first arrived on the scene 1.9 million years ago, they were making tools that were not significantly different from *Homo habilis*. And again we see very little technological improvement in the toolkit of *Homo erectus* over long stretches of time. About 120,000 years after Homo erectus evolved, we see rare and crude new forms of teardrop hand-axes emerge in East Africa. A new invention. Great. But between 1.78 and 1.5 million years ago (almost as long as *Homo sapiens* has even existed) we see no major widespread improvements. In the migratory regions in Asia, in areas where the *Homo erectus* population would have been lower and more spread out, this remained the case. The tools were functional. The object was to get a flake edge. No aesthetics were involved.

But in Africa 1.5 million years ago, where *Homo erectus* populations were at their densest, and thus had a greater chance of somebody innovating and spreading their ideas across familial groups, we see something curious. The hand-axes first made 1.78 million years ago became rapidly more common. What is more, they improved in quality, shaped with a flat edge into multipurpose picks, cleavers, and other kinds of implements.

Why does this matter? Not only did an innovation spread. It was improved upon. It is the first clear sign of tinkering, accumulation of innovation, and the improvement of technology generation after generation. This is the first possible glimmer of collective learning. If a species can not only retain their knowledge from parents to offspring, but have each generation improve on that knowledge, you are no longer as dependent on the slow process of natural selection to help you adapt to new environments. You can adapt by learning.

Until now the products of evolution by natural selection were the peak of complexity in the Universe. We are now entering an era where complexity would be produced not by the random mutation of genes and their selection over millions of years. Complexity would henceforth be produced by invention, tinkering, and improvement. A transition to collective learning, which may well have begun with *Homo erectus*. And from so simple a beginning, endless new cultural forms of complexity have been, and are being, evolved.

Rise of the "Planet of the Apes"

> **Threshold 6: The First Collective Learning – 1.9 million to 315,000 years ago**
>
> - *Wherein a species accumulates more innovation each generation than is lost by the next.*
> - *The trait of collective learning becomes a major survival advantage.*
> - *Collective learning intensifies via evolution by the time we reach Homo sapiens.*
> - *Humans start on the course of simultaneously raising complexity and ruining the Earth.*

Timeline

- **Possible Collective Learning in Homo ergaster-erectus (1.9 to 1.5 million years ago):** The first tinkering and improvement of tear-drop handaxes by *Homo ergaster-erectus* over the course of several hundred thousand years may well be the first slow, incipient signs of collective learning in the genus *Homo*.

- **Clearer Presence of Collective Learning in the Genus Homo (1.5 million to 350,000 years ago):** Numerous tools, implements, clothes and shelters are developed by *Homo antecessor, Homo heidelbergensis, and Homo neanderthalensis* allowing them to quickly adapt to new environments and spread across various parts of the Old World, even surviving in extremely cold climates and harnessing control of fire in hearths.

- **The Appearance of Homo sapiens with Collective Learning (at least 315,000 years ago):** Anatomically and probably intellectually similar *Homo sapiens* emerge in East Africa and manage to rapidly spread across the world, starting at least 100,000 years ago, intensifying 64,000 years ago, winding up in Australia 60,000 years ago, entering Europe 40,000 years ago, and ending with *Homo sapiens* being the first of the genus to enter into the Americas 12,000 years ago. All the while human toolkits became increasingly sophisticated.

- **The Invention of Agriculture (12,000 years ago):** Humans learn to harness and domesticate crops and livestock to increase the number of people who could live in a region, causing the population to skyrocket, which in turn gave human communities more potential thinkers and inventors to contribute to collective learning.

- **The Modern Revolution (250 years ago to Present):** The harnessing of fossil fuels allows production to skyrocket, and the concurrent advancements in science, technology, and agriculture increase the world population into the billions, all of whom are growing increasingly educated and more closely connected, accelerating collective learning still further. Humans become the dominant (and most destructive) species in the biosphere.

Collective Learning

Accumulation. That one, single word, more than any other, sums up what makes humans different. *Homo erectus* showed the first sign of tinkering and improvement of simple stone hand-axes. Sure it took them hundreds of thousands of years, but this is a significant milestone. Once a species starts *accumulating more innovation with one generation than is lost by the next*, innovations begin to stack up. It sets off the snowball effect of collective learning and complexity begins to rise much more quickly.

Humans didn't get to where we are because we are super-geniuses. Look to your own social circle or to the antics of politicians or celebrities to find proof of that. And you can only invent so much stuff in a single lifetime – when you're not just trying to survive, that is. *Homo sapiens* has gone from stone-tools to skyscrapers in only 315,000 years because we slowly tinker away at the ideas of the past.

Take the old creationist metaphor of strolling on the beach and finding a pocket-watch. You presume there was a watchmaker. In biological evolution, you don't need a watchmaker. Organic design is blind via natural selection. And this pocket-watch isn't the product of millions of years of gene mutation. It is a cultural artifact. It is the product of collective learning.

Even then there wasn't just a single watchmaker. There were several hundred people refining their trade, stretching across centuries to bring that watch into existence. For that watch to wind up there, you need several generations of watchmakers, each toiling away with precision tools and gears, experimenting in designs to make an accurate timepiece that could fit inside your pocket.

Moreover, the idea of clockwork itself evolved from a long line of inventors who tried to find ingenious ways of telling the time, all the way back to the first sun dials. Moreover the materials the watch is made of required generation after generation of people refining the craft of metallurgy. And you needed an economy, a division of labour, thus city-states, thus agriculture for any of that to arise in the first place.

Isaac Newton said he stood on the shoulders of giants, when it came to his own brilliant work on gravity. In reality, the "giants" are actually composed thousands and millions of inventors throughout human history. That is why the ability to accumulate innovation is what makes humans so unique. More so than just our raw brain power or capacity for language and abstract thought. We are so different because we have an unparalleled talent at remembering details of the past. Remembering our history.

Biologically, organisms are built with certain genes that are selected or eliminated by the environment. This form of adaptation is effective but painfully slow. Collective learning on the other hand is dependent on the ideas that spring from your brain, not the genes you were born with. You can change your ideas in an instant. You aren't stuck for life with bad ideas like you are with bad genes.

Thus collective learning enables adaptation and improvement thousands of times within a single lifetime, instead of waiting for hundreds of lifetimes for the slightest evolutionary change to take hold. Sure, there will be a lot of people who won't come up with an innovative idea in their lifetimes. They might be too busy just trying to survive. And there may also be a downpour of bad ideas. But over thousands of years, the good ideas do occur and they tend to stack up. This accelerates our ability to adapt and to increase the complexity around us.

Collective learning has two main drivers:

- *Population Numbers*: The number of potential innovators in a population. Not all of them will come up with an improvement in technology, doctrine, or philosophy in their lifetimes. But the more people you have, the more rolls at the dice you have to increase the probability that one of those people will come up with either a minor or major innovation.
- *Connectivity*: In order to build upon the ideas of the past, humans need access to them. This means either access to repositories of oral or written knowledge, or communication with other humans who possess that knowledge. Perhaps even collaboration with them. While today, with instantaneous communication via the internet and the wealth of knowledge of the Great Library of Alexandria being available on your phone, it is difficult to imagine what limitations in connectivity might have imposed on innovation. But for the majority of human history, one of the biggest things holding innovation back was access to the pool of wider human knowledge.

As we shall see, much of the story of human history is the intensification of both population numbers and connectivity, and the resulting acceleration of collective learning and increasing human complexity. Like a highway overpass, looming over older roads, collective learning can blaze along at a much faster rate of speed than biological evolution. Look at how little humans have changed biologically over the past 10,000 or even 100,000 years. But look how vastly our lifestyles have changed in the same space of time. Everything is accelerating.

From Homo erectus to Homo sapiens

If we look at our ancestral species, we can see we had this ability for accumulation long before we had the same capacity for language or symbolic thinking that *Homo sapiens* does. Possibly, there was painfully slow and weak collective learning in *Homo erectus*. Nevertheless this was enough for them to leave Africa and colonize large parts of the Old World. Over the next 2 million years things intensified as collective learning enhanced survival and became selected for.

Homo antecessor evolved 1.2 million years ago and moved into Europe in large numbers, again requiring innovation to deal with the frigid and foreign environments there. *Homo antecessor* were about the same size in terms of height and body weight as *Homo sapiens*, though they had slightly smaller brains and a much more limited form of language. But they also tinkered, innovated, and got better at living in their new environments, the evidence being the many new tools and innovations they left behind.

Homo heidelbergensis evolved about 700,000 years ago in Africa and slowly spread over Europe and West Asia. They had even larger brains that could arguably fall roughly on the low end of the human average. It is likely they had a fairly acute sense of being able to distinguish sounds in speech, like modern humans, and likely had a pretty intricate form of communication. Something which is very useful for the communication of ideas. But no clear evidence for abstract thought.

Closely related to *Homo heidelbergensis* were the Neanderthals (*Homo neanderthalensis* or even, as some have argued, *Homo sapiens neanderthalensis*) appearing approximately 400,000 years ago, who had brain sizes that reached even larger than modern humans. Yet they too do not seem to show a capacity for abstract thought. Would Neanderthals have been as adept at abstract thought? Probably not. But did they have collective learning? In all probability, yes.

Homo antecessor, Homo heidelbergensis, and the Neanderthals presided over the first systematised and regular use of fire in hearths, the first blade tools, the earliest wooden spears, the earliest use of composite tools where stone was fastened to wood, all before *Homo sapiens* were ever heard of. *Homo heidelbergensis* became the first hominine to colonise all of Eurasia. Neanderthals even adapted to climes that made clothing and other cultural innovations necessary for insulation and warmth. They used complex tool manufacture, with prepared stone cores, producing a variety of implements, sharp points, scrapers, hand-axes, wood handles, with deliberate use of good stone materials, and a countless supply of variations and improvements over time. Since it was first used by *Homo erectus* 1.5 million years ago, collective learning had gradually evolved in intensity. And it was that evolution that was the secret to the success of *Homo sapiens.*

Three other species of our genus have been discovered in the last two decades. *Homo floresiensis* was found on the island of Java in 2003, and appears to have shrunk back to a smaller stature, possibly because of their island habitat. They lived concurrent with humans on Earth from 190,000 to 50,000 years ago. *Homo denisova* was discovered in the Altai Mountains in 2010 and appear to be a sister-species of the Neanderthals, and were around for just as long until 40,000 years ago, though there is some evidence to suggest they lasted until 15,000 years ago. *Homo naledi* was discovered in South Africa in 2015 and appears to have branched off between the Australopithecines and *Homo habilis*, because they have a mixture of human and chimp-like traits. They are dated round 300,000 years ago, though it is not yet known when they went extinct. It is as yet unclear whether any these species had collective learning, or to what extent if they did.

Why is it that *Homo antecessor, Homo heidelbergensis, Homo floresiensis, Homo denisova, Homo naledi,* and the Neanderthals are all extinct while we are not? Simply because *Homo sapiens* is the most talented at collective learning. It should be noted, however, that DNA testing has shown that humans outside of Africa actually interbred with Neanderthals and possibly the Denisovans. So there is some overlap. Enough to make connections – biological, sexual, and perhaps even romantic. Once *Homo sapiens* got numerous enough in a region, however, it is likely they outcompeted others of our genus for resources. There may also have been intertribal fighting and even genocide. By one or a mixture of both, *Homo sapiens* are the last of our genus on Earth.

By 350,000 years ago, there was a clear survival advantage bestowed by collective learning. And also by possessing physical traits that made collective learning work better. Bigger brains. A greater capacity for language. A greater capacity for abstract thought. And most of all, the ability to remember our history. It became quite clear that natural selection favoured individuals with a talent for collective learning. Those who were able to adapt to a greater variety of environments. Those who could invent and exploit an environment for more resources, ensuring the survival of higher and higher population numbers. A sort of primate "overachiever" of the biosphere.

From this point forward, collective learning allowed change to occur faster than at geological or biological timescales. Suddenly "events" of great weight and import happened much more rapidly, and changes started to pour into the historical narrative with ever-mounting speed. Even from the lens of Big History, the great thresholds of complexity would occur within a few hundred thousand years, and the most complex systems in the Universe would emerge in just a fraction of that time. Primarily in the last 12,000 years, when human numbers swelled from 6-8 million to 7.5 billion. It is too soon to tell whether this acceleration of complexity is just beginning or whether it will soon disappear as rapidly as it appeared, due to the self-destruction and extinction of our species.

Essay Writing Exercise

For this chapter's essay writing exercise, pick one of the following essay questions that you have not yet done a free-writing exercise on:

Why is the Big Bang theory the most widely accepted explanation for the origin of the Universe?

What do you regard as the most important turning point in the geological history of our Earth?

Which theory for the origins of life is most convincing?

What do you regard as the most important turning point in the history of life?

What is the most important turning point in human evolution?

Engage in another free-writing exercise for 15 minutes. Again, don't pay attention too much to the formalities of academic writing or essay structure. Just get all your thoughts and arguments down on paper.

Then prepare an essay outline for the question. Every outline should include: i) a thesis statement that directly answers the essay question, ii) a list of main arguments with each supported by a list of evidence you will use, and iii) a topic sentence composed for each main argument.

If you like, you can try this exercise on the other essay questions.

Further Reading

Baker, David. "Collective Learning: A Potential Unifying Theme of Human History" Journal of World History vol. 26, no. 1 (2015) pg. 77-104.

Cheney, Dorothy, and Robert Seyfarth. Baboon Metaphysics: The Evolution of a Social Mind. Chicago: University of Chicago Press, 2014.

De Waal, Frans. Chimpanzee Politics: Power and Sex Among Apes. Johns Hopkins University Press, 2007.

De Waal, Frans. Tree of Origin: What Primate Behaviour Can Tell Us about Human Social Evolution. Cambridge: Harvard University Press, 2001.

Dunbar, Robin. A New History of Mankind's Evolution. London: Faber & Faber, 2004.

Goodall, Jane. The Chimpanzees of Gombe: Patterns of Behaviour. Cambridge: Harvard University Press, 1986.

Goodall, Jane. Through a Window: My Thirty Years with the Chimpanzees of Gombe. Boston: Houghton Mifflin, 1990.

Green, R. et al. "A Draft Sequence of the Neanderthal Genome" Science vol. 328, no. 5979 (May 2010): 710-722.

Johanson, Donald, and Maitland Edey. Lucy: The Beginnings of Humankind. New York: Simon and Schuster, 1981.

Ristvet, Lauren. In the Beginning: World History from Human Evolution to the First States. New York: McGraw-Hill, 2007.

Stringer, Chris. The Origin of Our Species. London: Allen Lane, 2011.

Tattersall, Ian. Masters of the Planet: The Search for Human Origins. New York: Palgrave Macmillan, 2012.

Tattersall, Ian. Becoming Human: Evolution and Human Uniqueness. New York: Harcourt Brace, 1998.

Wrangham, Richard. "The evolution of sexuality in chimpanzees and bonobos" Human Nature vol. 4 (1993) pg. 47-79.

Wrangham, Richard and Dale Peterson. Demonic Males: Apes and the Origins of Human Violence. Boston: Mariner Books, 1996.

CHAPTER 7

HUMAN FORAGERS

Or,

HOW WE ENJOYED

THE 6.5 HOUR WORKDAY

BEFORE COLLECTIVE LEARNING

SCREWED IT ALL UP

Getting Our Fill of Foragers

We now enter the realm of human history. Even then, this history may look different from conventional histories involving countries, monarchs, and farmers. For the majority of human history – an estimated 95-98.5% of our entire existence – we dwelled in small groups of foragers, ranging across the Earth hunting and gathering food. Yet it was in this time that many of the foundations for human complexity were laid, including many of our societal structures and our migration into several different "world zones" where the "human experiment" would be run simultaneously in several places, with different outcomes. The historical actors in this part of the story were anatomically similar to modern humans, with the same range of emotions and capacity for invention that we possess today. As such, we can achieve rates of empathy with this part of Big History more than ever before. These people were us. If we had been born in that era we would have behaved the same way. Yet human foragers lived very different lifestyles in a world hit with ice ages and populated by a terrifying range of megafauna, from sabre-toothed tigers to carnivorous 3m tall kangaroos. The past is indeed "another country", if not another planet.

Timeline

- **The First Homo sapiens (at least 315,000 years ago):** There is evidence of an anatomically similar member of *Homo sapiens* is from East Africa and dated to approximately 198,000 years ago. There is less copious but fairly conclusive evidence for anatomically similar *Homo sapiens* in West Africa roughly 315,000 years ago. Current estimates for anatomically similar *Homo sapiens* run up to 350,000 years ago.

- **The First Great Migration (100,000 years ago):** Humans leave Africa in large numbers for the first time, drifting into the Middle East and perhaps as far as India. It is also possible that the groups from this first migration were the ones that made their way to Australia, or otherwise they came as part of the second migration later. At this time, humans did not cross the Caucasus into Russia or Siberia, nor did they make their way to Europe.

- **Human Genetic Bottleneck (between 100,000 and 50,000 years ago):** Human DNA shows a contraction in diversity, perhaps in a disaster shrinking to somewhere between 3000 to 10,000 *Homo sapiens* in the entire world. A people alive today are descendants of those few thousand individuals. There is a hypothesis this genetic bottleneck was caused by a volcanic super-eruption at Mount Toba that occurred the same time, but the hypothesis is disputed in terms of the severity of the nuclear winter and flora and fauna losses that resulted. If not Toba, then there would have to be another explanation for the bottleneck.

- **The Second Great Migration (64,000 years ago):** The largest and furthest reaching mass migration out of Africa occurred in this time, into the Middle East, India, Indochina, Indonesia, and Australia all within approximately 4000 years. The last location was reached via a land bridge and rafting due to lower sea levels at the time. By 40,000 years ago, humans had crossed the Caucasus Mountains and entered Europe, Russia, and Siberia over the next few thousand years.

- **Humans Arrive in the Americas (12-15,000 years ago):** Either by crossing the Bering Strait, which was a land bridge, and then bypassing receding glaciers in Alaska, or by rafting down the coast to the south, or a mixture of both, humans were the first of our genus to enter the Americas. They rapidly spread across the two continents. Every large landmass then had humans on it. The Pacific islands (including New Zealand) were inhabited between 4000 and 1000 years ago and Antarctica was sparsely inhabited in modern times.

- **World Population Reaches 6-8 million (12,000 years ago):** By the eve of the dawn of agriculture, the world had reached the limit to the number of foragers that the surface of the Earth could support.

How to Date a Human (without lying about your age, job, or measurements)

How do we date the start of *Homo sapiens*? When it comes to our evolutionary lineage over the past 4 million years, we have pieced it together by compiling fossil and archaeological evidence and by arranging the different species into possible lines of descent. Each species forms a "missing link" in the evolution of hominines, with the gaps getting smaller and smaller by the decade. That said, there are probably many fossils of many new species out there that could further close the gaps in our knowledge. One such example is the new discovery of *Homo denisova* which like the Neanderthals appears to be a branch of the family tree that is very closely related to our own.

With all that uncertainty in our family tree how can we be sure that *Homo sapiens* evolved where and when they did? In terms of evidence, we have the Omo remains, which were discovered in East Africa between 1967 and 1974. The Omo remains are pieces of skulls, limbs, and teeth which allowed us to establish they were anatomically similar to modern humans (rather than Neanderthals or another species). Radiometric dating puts the first of these fossils at around 195,000 to 200,000 years old. For the past few decades, *Homo sapiens* accordingly have been given the start date of roughly 200,000 to 250,000 years ago. That was correspondingly the date given in this course for years, and may be the date you find in older Big History readings!

Then, in 2017, we discovered pieces of skulls, jaws, and teeth in Morocco that have been dated to approximately 315,000 years ago. These have also been identified as anatomically similar to modern humans, much more so than other species. This find is significant in several ways. First, it pushes the date of the first *Homo sapiens* back to at least 315,000 years ago, and several scholars round this up to 350,000 years ago. But it goes beyond mere dates in a book. The location of the find implies that *Homo sapiens* ranged across Africa from the inception of the species, rather than just being confined to East Africa. This makes sense considering humans had the capacity for collective learning and adaptation to new environments unparalleled by any other hominine species. It also holds open the door for the possibility that humans may have migrated outside Africa beyond the earliest known date of 100,000 years ago, though at present there is no fossil or archaeological evidence of this.

Fossil evidence combined with DNA testing on modern populations find that humans evolved in Africa, which is not unthinkable given our place in the primate family tree. DNA is particularly compelling given that genetic diversity outside Africa is way lower than those populations in Africa itself, implying that the rest of the world was inhabited by a much smaller migrant population. This close blood relationship supports the "Out of Africa" hypothesis, which states there was one place of origin for humans, rather than the "Multiregional" hypothesis which posited that different *Homo sapiens* groups evolved in to their modern forms separately across Afro-Eurasia. In the case of the latter, we would see a great deal more genetic diversity in the human race.

There remains the question whether humans continued to develop mentally, even if they did not change much anatomically after 315,000 years ago. The reason for this question is that many of the more advanced aspects of human behaviour and the more sophisticated parts of our toolkits did not arrive on the fossil record until much later. The most crucial of these is that we do not have much evidence of cave painting until 50,000 years ago, because cave painting is a clear sign that a species has abstract thought. Bear in mind that there is not yet *conclusive* evidence for abstract thought in prior species, even the Neanderthals. For our purposes, this is important because it would imply human collective learning only really intensified 50,000 years ago, rather than being potent 315,000 years ago. The ability to think and communicate about things that aren't really there in the moment (abstract thought) is a crucial element to conveying complex information.

There is a problem with the hypothesis that there was some sort of revolution in human mental capacity 50,000 years ago. Most of the cave paintings were found outside of Africa, and they occur 14,000 years after the Second Great Migration out of Africa was already underway. Yet it is outside Africa where the majority of archaeological work has so far been conducted. Due to political and financial constraints, very little archaeology on this period has been conducted in Africa. In fact there are signs of complex behaviour, innovation, and abstract thought in Africa prior to 50,000 years ago. Humans were using decorative beads in Africa prior to the Second Great Migration 64,000 years ago, they were mining for new materials 100,000 years ago, they were fishing 120,000 years ago and using body paints around 300,000 years ago (also an indicator of abstract thought). This would imply a more gradual cultural evolution via collective learning than a more sudden biological one. Furthermore, the crucial FOXP2 gene which gives humans control over complex syntax and grammar has been in our family tree for at least 200-300,000 years. It did not suddenly appear 50,000 years ago. With further archaeological and genetic work, the debate over the so-called "Upper Paleolithic Revolution" might be cleared up.

It is also worth bearing in mind that 315,000 years is a pretty short amount of time in terms of evolution. It would be highly unusual for a revolution in abstract thinking to occur suddenly 50,000 years ago, given the slow increase in the capacity for tool use and collective learning we have seen in our family tree over the past 2.5 million years. Furthermore, such a profound evolutionary change would leave a trace in our DNA 50,000 years ago, yet humans are the most genetically homogenous (i.e. closely related) of all primate species on Earth. As such the preponderance of evidence places *Homo sapiens*, likely both anatomically and mentally, with their start at approximately 315,000 to 350,000 years ago. Though this is a dynamic field, so watch this space, I may have to update these dates yet again in coming years!

The Getting Stoned and Rocking Out in the Old Stone Age

The majority of human history took place in what is known as the "Paleolithic" which is Greek for "Old Stone Age". The reference to stone in the name and (more obnoxiously) in this section's title is toward the stone tools that humans used at the time. It would be many millennia before we started using bronze or iron tools, long after we invented agriculture The "Neolithic" begins roughly 12,000 years ago, or "New Stone Age", where we invented agriculture but were still digging in the dirt with stone tools. Thus for the overwhelming majority of human history (everything but the past 5000 years), increasingly complex stone tools, in addition to bone tools, composite tools mixing stone or bone with wood, were the backbone of human technology. As Paleolithic humans, we sure did love to rock! (I am so sorry. Really. That dad joke was below the already low standards for humour of even a university textbook).

The Paleolithic constitutes 95-98.5% of human history (depending on where you place the start of *Homo sapiens*) but is seldom what we consider "conventional history", which usually covers the last 5000 years, and usually a lot less. The Paleolithic is extremely important to understand because it depicts societies and obstacles that humans were actually evolved to exist in. The change of the past 12,000 years has been such a blur that our instincts have been unable to catch up. In many ways, the current human animal is an obsolete design for its surroundings. Yet most historians are neglectful of this period, at best maybe a survey textbook or course will devote a bit of preamble to the Paleolithic era in any given region. Why?

There may be a few good reasons. First, the obvious one from Big History if you have been paying attention so far: the rise of complexity. There is no question that societies that came later were more complex in structural intricacy, energy flows, and emergent properties, with a blizzard of changes that simply take more time (and more pages) to describe. This should be qualified by the fact that Paleolithic humans are one of the most complex things we have described *so far* in our story. Second, while the Paleolithic constitutes the majority of human history, it does not constitute the majority of humans who have ever lived. Taking the 315,000 year date for our start, then approximately 100 billion humans have lived and died on the surface of the Earth since the origin of our species. 16-20 billion of those have lived since the start of the Industrial Revolution, with 7.7 approaching 8 billion alive today, at time of writing. An additional 55 billion are estimated to have lived between the start of the Neolithic 12,000 years ago and the Industrial Revolution. That's 71-75 billion people out of 100 billion right there.

That leaves approximately 25-29 billion people who lived between 12,000 and 315,000 years ago, or 303,000 years of foragers. For the majority of that time, most humans lived in Africa, and only in the past 64,000 to 100,000 years has a substantial number of humans lived in the rest of the world. And we know that the carrying capacity of the entire Earth can only support about 6-8 million foragers living at any given time, due to the fact foragers generally hunt and gather food, then move to another region while the previous one regenerates naturally. And for the overwhelming majority of the Paleolithic our numbers were a lot less. So don't be too angry with conventional history because they devote more pages to what came later. The period 12,000 years ago to present constitutes the majority of human "biographies" as well as more complexity.

All that said, the Paleolithic is important because these were the societies to which our instincts were the most attuned. They were also societies which held the seeds of what was later exaggerated by the dawn of agriculture. Finally, although we officially recognise a shift from foraging to farming 12,000 years ago, the majority of the world still foraged until approximately 8000 to 5000 years ago. And the majority of the Earth's surface contained nothing but foragers for much longer than that. Foraging societies represent a huge part of our heritage, a significant part of conventional history, and still hold a great deal of cultural importance in the present.

The Ice Ages

The past 2.5 million years have seen numerous ice ages occurring in waves of cooling and heating, with long "glacial periods" (aka ice ages) interspersed with "interglacial periods" (like the one we are in now) of varying length. More broadly, the trend of having a swing between cold and warm actually goes back about 33 million years. This means humans evolved over a long period of shifts back in forth in climate. There have been as many as nine glacial periods in the last 800,000 years, where the rapid shifts in climate may have affected hominine evolution, perhaps favouring greater adaptability via collective learning. There have been at two or three glacial periods since *Homo sapiens* evolved in Africa 315,000 years ago. The effect of an ice age is the covering of large parts of North America, Europe, and Asia with ice sheets, a drop in the average global temperature, the drying out of previously lush climates in other regions of the world like Africa, and the drop in sea levels. While these changes happened over several thousand years at a time, *Homo sapiens* certainly had an advantage over other species in being extremely adaptable to changing conditions. Though many other species in the genus *Homo* were certainly no slouches in that department either, as shown, for example, by the Neanderthals inhabiting very cold climates indeed.

The "Penultimate Glacial Period" (i.e. second to last) started 195,000 years ago, when anatomically similar *Homo sapiens* were alive and well in Africa. It continued for a further 60,000 years until an interglacial period began 135,000 years ago. The interglacial then lasted for just 20,000 years until approximately 115,000 years ago (interglacial periods are generally shorter than glacial ones – a worthy perspective when considering our interglacial has already lasted 12,000 years). During all this time, the evidence indicates that Homo sapiens remained in Africa, along with a number of other hominine species. During the penultimate interglacial period, they did not invent agriculture like humans did at the beginning of this glacial period 12,000 years ago, so obviously it took more than climate for that change to be brought about – the region, the population levels, and the state of human collective learning would all have been additional factors. The "Last Glacial Period" began 115,000 years ago and it was a particularly long one, lasting just over 100,000 years. It was in this world that humans migrated out of Africa and across the Earth.

Glaciation and the start of a new Ice Age tends to happen quite quickly, over the course of a few hundred years. Ice sheets start to cover more of the Earth, in the North, but also from mountain ranges that contain glaciers like in South America or Central Asia. All told, at the height of the last Ice Age, about 30% of the Earth's terrestrial surface was covered with ice. But do not confuse this with something even more catastrophic like a Snowball Earth, where the entire world is encased in an icy tomb. Where ice sheets do not spread, colder temperatures make forests turn to woodland or even deserts. Winters lasted longer than they do today. While most humans 115,000 years ago lived in Africa, these were much more frigid conditions than experienced by Africa today.

Human Population Numbers and the Genetic Bottleneck

Humans had collective learning, and were well equipped to deal with the pressures of an icy world. They had controlled use of fire in hearths and they were able to sew warm clothing and build shelters draped in animal pelts. The foraging method of finding food remained the same for thousands of years: roam a territory hunting and gathering until the flora and fauna of the region become depleted, then move onto another region while the previous one naturally replenishes itself. There is also some evidence that some foragers were able to husband the resources of the land to some extent to delay the exhaustion of a region. It is this method by which the entire surface of the Earth can support only 6-8 million foragers, though 115,000 years ago inhabiting *just Africa* the numbers would have been considerably less, perhaps 500,000 to a million as the high watermark of the population of which Africa would have been *capable* of supporting and perhaps as little as a few tens of thousands for the majority of the period.

As human populations in Africa grew, there was a need to find more food to support them. The answer to this problem was not to "intensify" the amount of food produced in Africa – these were foragers who did not farm – but to "extensify" by foraging further and further afield for the necessary resources. This may have prompted the First Great Migration of humans out of Africa 100,000 years ago into the Middle East, with some indications that they reached as far as India. These regions were still out of reach of the ice sheets and may have provided humans with more "energy flows" (i.e. food) in order to "maintain their complexity" (i.e. stay alive). Despite this "extensification" the vast majority of humans, meanwhile, remained in Africa.

We have indications in our DNA histories that human genetic diversity shrunk dramatically somewhere between 100,000 and 50,000 years ago. One possible explanation is the supervolcanic eruption that occurred during this period at Mount Toba 74,000 years ago. On the island of Sumatra in present day Indonesia, in the middle of the island, there was a volcano. Where this volcano once stood there is now a lake. Or rather, a crater that transformed into a lake when Mount Toba blew up in an extremely dramatic geological event.

Mount Toba exploded with the force of 1.5 million Hiroshima-sized nuclear bombs and with the force of the nuclear arsenals of every single country in the world today. Multiplied by at least three. The eruption threw an unprecedented amount of rock into the atmosphere, scattering rubble and magma far and wide on a continental scale. A layer of volcanic ash, an average of 15 cm thick settled over everything in South and East Asia, but also in India, Arabia, and getting as far as East Africa. Much more ash was flung up into the atmosphere, darkening the skies, and obstructing sunlight in an era already beset by an Ice Age. What followed may have been a decade of perpetual winter for the entire globe. It may well have reduced the population to 3000 to 10,000 people.

However, in the past decade the Toba hypothesis has been disputed by several scientists. Studies of soil cores from Lake Malawi may indicate that the Toba explosion was not enough for perpetual winter to occur. While no critic of the Toba hypothesis would seriously claim that Mount Toba had *no* atmospheric effect, they dispute whether it would have killed off so many humans. Furthermore, there are some indications that flora and fauna in Africa may not have been too adversely affected by the event, which would not have collapsed the food chain on which humans relied. If so, then there must be another explanation for the Genetic Bottleneck that occurred between 100,000 and 50,000 years ago. It is possible the lack of genetic diversity is due to a small number of people heading out of Africa to found the ancestors of the human race in Europe, Asia, the Americas, Australia, and the Pacific. Certainly there is way more genetic diversity between humans in sub-Saharan Africa today than there is between any population in the rest of the world. That is one possible alternative. If the reduction in genetic diversity was due to a catastrophic event other than Toba, there is still no indication as to what that alternative disaster was.

By 64,000 years ago, we have evidence of the Second Great Migration. This was by far the largest and farthest reaching of the two. Humans spread out of Africa via the Middle East, down into India and Indochina within just a few thousand years. By approximately 60,000 years ago humans had figured out how to use the land bridge that existed in Indonesia at the time (due to lower sea levels from the Ice Age) to make their way by foot and by rafting into Australia. In terms of relative complexity, seafaring is no easy task. The entry of humans into Australia is the foraging equivalent of landing on the Moon. Humans gradually spread across Australia over the next 20,000 years, and headed into Tasmania by 40,000 years ago via another land bridge. Also around 40,000 years ago, humans went north into colder climates, crossed the Caucasus Mountains and entered Russia, quickly making their way into Europe from the east. Most impressively, humans continued to spread into increasingly colder climates, are were found in Ice Age Siberia by at least 20,000 years ago. Consider the survival skills necessary to survive in such an environment.

The entry of humans into the Americas requires a more searching statement, since the date of the human arrival remains a matter of debate. It seems clear that humans would have crossed the Bering Strait (which was then yet another land bridge) between Siberia and Alaska between 20,000 and 15,000 years ago, perhaps following herds of animals that they hunted. But during the Ice Age there were huge ice sheets that would have prevented humans from travelling beyond Alaska. Then between 15,000 and 12,000 years ago as ice sheets retreated a passage may have opened up for foragers to travel through, moving south through the Americas. Other hypotheses state that humans may have bypassed the ice sheets by slowly rafting down the Pacific Coast. Or it may have been a mixture of the two. Either way, *Homo sapiens* became the first and only species of our genus to inhabit the Americas.

Humans "As Nature Intended"

The title of this section does not imply that living "as nature intended" is good or bad, but as with all periods of human history there was a mixture of both. Same goes for the existence of any species in nature. Most species are well adapted to their surroundings, but still have to cope with the harsh realities of Darwinian evolution. Humans were extremely well attuned to life as foragers, having existed in that state for 300,000 years and having evolved from previous hominines that also foraged for their existence. But we also had to cope with the potentially damaging situations that would end our genetic line there and then. Our instincts evolved accordingly.

In many ways, human instincts are designed to exist in small foraging communities. The example I am most fond of is "butterflies in your stomach" when talking in front of a crowd or to a prospective sexual partner. In modernity, there isn't really any good reason to have anxiety prior to giving a talk to a crowd of strangers or being nervous before a first date. There are millions of people out there in Sydney alone. You can humiliate yourself in front of hundreds of audience members or potential mates, and still go out the next day and try again with a different group. This was not the case for foragers in the Paleolithic. A group of humans might be a few dozen in number with whom you would spend your entire life. Occasionally your group would come across another group of humans with whom they were not skirmishing over territory and with whom your group might be able to intermarry. Your enter circle of social contacts might be a few hundred at most, but probably a lot less. Many in your immediate group would be family. The rest of them would be potential allies or potential mates – the latter being an even smaller number when reducing the total by gender, age, and physical fitness. If you made a fool of yourself in front of a large crowd of people, you might be socially ostracised which would reduce your access to food and mates, or you might be thrown out of the group altogether if they disliked you enough. If you made a fool of yourself in front of a prospective mate, they might tell all the others, and your DNA would be rudely ejected from the gene pool forever. In that context, it makes very good evolutionary sense to have an instinct that agitates humans in social situations and produces "butterflies".

Other examples include the tendency to get addicted to fatty or sugary foods, which were both a rarity in the Paleolithic but a good source of energy when you could find them. Or the irrational fear of spiders and other creepy crawlies, since a knee-jerk reaction of fear to a potentially dangerous creature is a good evolutionary strategy, whether they are actually poisonous/dangerous or not. Or the tendency to gossip, make friends, and compete in social hierarchies for dominance, rank, and access to food and mates. Or the tendency to develop strong emotional/romantic attachments to people, that last an average of 12 years, just long enough to properly raise and rear a child. Or the tendency to be wary of outsiders, to be territorial about land which provided your food, and the skirmishing behaviour that humans share in common with chimpanzees.

Life as a Forager

The primary human mode of seeking energy flows to sustain or increase their complexity for over 300,000 years was foraging. This came in the form of either hunting or gathering. By and large, due to sexual dimorphism (differences in average body size and strength) male humans hunted, and female humans gathered. But there was an obvious overlap, as we know from studying modern foraging groups over the past two centuries. Some females possessed the athleticism or specialised knowledge to be hunters, some males possessed either the knowledge of plants or else were too old or infirm to hunt and so were gatherers. To speak nothing of an individual being personally predisposed to one activity or another, just like today different people prefer different jobs. It is only in the realm of overall averages in a population of humans that we derive the traditional distinction between hunters and gatherers.

When it comes to hunting, humans were not the strongest nor the fastest animals. But they had two advantages. One was in the area of stamina. While humans were not able to outrun much of their prey, they could stalk and follow animals for long stretches of distance, and when the prey ran out of steam, the human hunters would strike. The second advantage was the ability to communicate and work as a team of hunters, fostered by speech, intelligence and collective learning. When it comes to gathering, humans had to keep constantly on the move across vast stretches of territory to gather enough vegetation to feed everyone, with one region running out and moving on to another, and also to keep pace with the seasonal nature of many foods that grew in the wild. Humans gathered herbs, leaves, root vegetables, nuts, berries, seeds, and fruits. As such, it required specialised knowledge of what grew where and what was good to eat and what was poisonous. Additionally, humans also collected and ate shellfish, caught and ate real fish, and occasionally ate insects. In terms of land area required to feed everybody, it took an average of 6 square kilometres to feed just one person. Hence why the total carrying capacity of foragers was quite low compared to agrarian or modern ones.

All told, however, the collection of food only took part of a forager's day. The average work day was 6.5 hours for foragers, compared to 9.5 hours on average for agrarian peoples, and the standard 9 hours for modern cubicle jockeys, etc. The surplus time was used in socialisation rituals of various kinds, including feasting by the campfire, dancing, and the all-important politics of mating. And as a result of all these different sources of food, the diverse diets of humans (when times were good) actually left them quite healthy. The nomadic life also meant that there was little opportunity for as many viruses and contagious diseases to grow, meaning humans were much healthier than in the subsequent agrarian period.

"Nasty, Brutish, and Short"

Injury or sickness when it did occur would frequently be a death sentence, and when foragers entered a region where food was scarce, they would constantly be at risk of starving. Simple things like a broken bone, infected wound, or an infected tooth, could kill you. Infant mortality was high, with 50% dying before the age of 5. Furthermore, the fact that foragers constantly had to be on the move to find enough food for everyone meant that infanticide rates were quite high, on the order of about 25% of newborns. Similarly those who suffered injury, or grew too old to keep up, or who otherwise were socially ostracised might be killed outright or abandoned to die in the wild.

When it came to violence, interpersonal conflicts formed the majority of fatalities with deaths from inter-group skirmishes forming a smaller but significant portion. Violence arising interpersonally might be the result of a contest between individuals for dominance in the hierarchy (whether male or female) or out of personal disagreements about something (remember these people were similar in range of temperament to modern humans) or out of sexual jealousy in the contest to find mates. Surveys of various Paleolithic skeletons that show signs of dying from deliberately inflicted violence establishes for us a "murder-rate" of approximately 10%. It goes without saying that modern murder-rates are significantly lower, in Australia with it being between 1-2 individuals per 100,000 people. Skirmishes between groups are inaccurately termed "warfare" because foragers did not have the resources, coordination, or population numbers to field large numbers of fighters in pitched battles. Instead skirmishes between a handful of people occurred over foraging territory, raids for food or to kidnap women, or avenge a previous wrongdoing or insult. Intergroup violence could also be ameliorated by ritual gift exchanges, or even inter-group marriages.

When it came to the sexual politics of foraging groups, men valued signs of fertility in women just like in most other primates. Women meanwhile looked for either strength, intelligence, or political adeptness in forging alliances, or any other personal trait which amounted to "utility" concerning the protection and providing for her and her offspring. In terms of gametes (male and female reproductive cells, or more bluntly sperm and eggs), the female investment in offspring is way higher than the male's, because they must bear and wean the offspring for several months. As such, it was women who were typically the gatekeepers to sex and attachment, for which men competed by displaying their "utility" (strength, intelligence, charisma, etc).

By and large, many foragers maintained monogamous relationships (particularly in ritualised marriages) but a few high-ranking men might practice polygyny (having more than one wife) due to their social status. Emotionally, these humans were similar to modern ones, and thus probably experienced the same degree of emotions, from strong infatuations, to tumultuous break-ups, to jealousies and infidelities, all of which are likely to have contributed to interpersonal violence.

Megafauna

If the cold or your fellow humans didn't kill you, there was always the large terrifying animals that inhabited the Paleolithic! It is also worth noting that human foragers spread out across the world and for thousands of years existed in a world of "megafauna" or animals that were significantly larger than their modern counterparts. These megafauna included woolly mammoths that towered at 4 metres and could weigh 15 tons, and were great for meat and hides if you managed to kill them with stone spears, but rather deadly if they gored or trampled you. There were giant bears that could weigh up to 1000 kg, completely dwarfing a modern 250 kg grizzly bear. Across Eurasia and the Americas there roamed giant sabre-toothed cats admittedly about the size of the modern lion, with the difference that their front fangs were literally the size of sabres. Additionally, there were dire wolves that were 2 metres long. There were giant meat-eating birds with a five metre wingspan. In Australia, there were 3 metre tall carnivorous kangaroos and wombats the size of hippos, and marsupial lions and tigers. While less deadly, there were also giant porcupines, giant deer, giant elk, and bear-sized sloths, and two metre long armadillos. All of which could be extremely deadly to humans if they messed with them in the wrong way.

Yet these large animals also meant plentiful game for human hunters. And on the long timescale of 315,000 years, humans appeared to be quite successful at hunting them thanks to collective learning. With the arrival of humans into new regions of the world (Eurasia, Australia, the Americas, etc), the amount of megafauna in each region was reduced by between 75 and 90%. The proportion of surviving megafauna is only higher in Africa, where they evolved alongside humans and were better adapted to evade our collective learning-inspired hunting methods. But in the rest of the world, this was an extinction rate so high, that if aliens came to Earth a billion years from now and excavated for fossils in the Paleolithic layer of rock, even if they saw no sign of human existence, they would notice a large extinction of megafauna in the geological record long before humans developed cars, airplanes, and smoke-belching factories. In that sense, the extinction of the megafauna thanks to our skill as hunters was a harbinger of what was to come…

One notable megafauna that is often overlooked from this category are the other primates themselves. There is another primate a bit more distant in our evolutionary line, which split off from ours shortly after we became bipedal. This was *Gigantopithecus* a 3 metre, 600 kg biped that would have dwarfed gorillas in size. They lived alongside humans until approximately 100,000 years ago, with one branch of bipeds choosing size and might as their evolutionary strategy, and with the genus *Homo* choosing collective learning and brains over brawn. Unfortunately for *Gigantopithecus*, brains were the trait that won out.

Paleolithic Collective Learning and the "World Zones"

In terms of collective learning, humans do demonstrate an increased sophistication of toolkits over the past 315,000 years. The use of sharp cutting points from rocks existed throughout human history, but their refinement into multi-purpose blades occurred over many generations. Humans developed the knack for gathering shellfish and even practicing aquaculture, where they foster the regeneration of such food sources. Humans also fashioned primitive fishing equipment in the form of nets and spear-fishing. Humans also used bone tools, composite tools, barbed points, and even mined for precious stones and metals used for decorations. In Australia, foragers made strategic use of fire by burning down forests in order to clear paths, kill and cook game, remove deadly predators and poisonous animals, expose edible roots and tubers otherwise obscured by brush, and foster even greater regeneration after the area had recovered.

Because humans are a fairly intelligent, observant, and information processing species, we started to look for patterns in nature. Something that would explain natural phenomena like thunderstorms, droughts, tidal waves, blizzards, and even earthquakes and volcanic eruptions, or why different animals behaved the way they did. And because humans had the capacity for abstract thought, we started to attribute many of these phenomena to supernatural causes. This led to the rise of the first religions, where aspects of nature were imbued having a soul or some kind of spiritual power in a concept known as "animism". Experts in understanding animals or the effects of various plants might become religious shaman. Great creation myths were devised by different cultures to explain the origin of the world, which would then be passed down via oral tradition for generations until these stores became a core part of their identity. It was thus through the process of collective learning that even the first "big histories" were born.

Yet because humans moved in groups of a few dozen people, and from their group interactions only encountered a maximum of a few hundred people, collective learning was quite slow compared to later periods. The two main drivers of collective learning are population numbers (potential innovators) and connectivity. Both of which were rather low in a time when a few dozen people were required to innovate for the group, where intergroup encounters were limited, and where oral transmission (talking) was the only mode of passing on information generation after generation. If you skipped a generation in orally passing along knowledge it would be lost forever. In fact, it is in this period that innovations seem to have most frequently disappeared, in what archaeologists have termed a "Tasmanian Effect" after one of the most notable disappearances of technology from a toolkit in Tasmania between 8000 and 4000 years ago, probably due low populations of a few thousand and the disappearance of the land bridge connection with foragers in Australia, where toolkits did not shrink. Despite its localised name, the phenomena is known to have occurred in several places across the world, most notably in Paleolithic South Africa.

And in a world before the internet, collective learning fluctuated greatly across different regions and would have profound future historical effects. After the two Great Migrations came to a close 12,000 years ago, the Ice Age ended, the seas rose, and the land bridges that had facilitated travel between continents disappeared. From that point forward, the world was split up into large areas into which humans had moved, but now had no communication with each other. These are known as the "world zones": Afro-Eurasia, the Americas, Australasia, and the Pacific.

Within each zone, there was the potential for humans to build networks of information transfer via collective learning. But between the world zones, for many millennia all such contact was cut off. Afro-Eurasia counts as one world zone because it was at least physically possible for a forager or agrarian person to travel across it, or more accurately, for systems of contact and trade to proliferate collective learning between peoples. The Americas (north and south) also count as a world zone for much the same reason. But contact between the two did not exist until approximately 1000 years ago. In similar vein, contact between Afro-Eurasia and Australasia did not exist in any known form, and so Australasians developed on a historically different trajectory as well. Only the connection between Australasia and the Pacific remained, as people set out from Australasia between 4000 and 1000 years ago to inhabit the many islands of the Pacific. But communication between these world zones faltered as the islanders headed out into the vast ocean beyond. As such, the human experiment was being run independently in four major world zones, separate petri dishes, where historical trajectories bear many similarities and differences. And these were determined by environmental conditions and also the two main drivers of collective learning: population and connectivity.

Essay Writing Exercise

This chapter's exercise is all about evidence and argumentation. You should be familiar with our current cache of essay questions:

Why is the Big Bang theory the most widely accepted explanation for the origin of the Universe?

What do you regard as the most important turning point in the geological history of our Earth?

Which theory for the origins of life is most convincing?

What do you regard as the most important turning point in the history of life?

What is the most important turning point in human evolution?

Choose one for which you have at least a thesis statement. Write out a point-form list of all the main arguments you have to support that thesis statement. Then jot down a list of evidence that backs up each main argument. Then write explanations for why each piece of evidence is useful. The resulting outline should look like this:

Main argument 1

- Evidence A
    o Explanation of significance
- Evidence B
    o Explanation of significance

Main argument 2

- Evidence A
    o Explanation of significance
- Evidence B
    o Explanation of significance

You may then wish to take that list you have compiled and transform it into full written paragraphs. Congratulations, you have just produced a well-structured body to an essay!

Further Reading

Baker, David. "Collective Learning: A Potential Unifying Theme of Human History" Journal of World History vol. 26, no. 1 (2015) pg. 77-104.

Barfield, Thomas. The Nomadic Alternative. Englewood Cliffs: Prentice-Hall, 1993.

Biraben, J. R. "Essai sur l'évolution du nombre des homes" Population vol. 34 (1979) pg. 13–25.

Brantingham, P.J., et al. The Early Paleolithic beyond Western Europe. Berkeley: University of California Press, 2004.

Cavalli-Sforza, Luigi Luca, and Francesco Cavalli-Sforza. The Great Human Diasporas. trans. Sarah Thorne. Reading: Addison-Wesley, 1995.

Johnson, A., and T. Earle. The Evolution of Human Societies: From Foraging Group to Agrarian State. 2nd ed. Stanford: Stanford University Press, 2000.

Klein, Richard. The Dawn of Human Culture. New York: Wiley, 2002.

Livi-Bacci, Massimo. A Concise History of World Population. trans. Carl Ipsen. Oxford: Blackwell, 1992.

McBrearty, Sally and Alison Brooks. "The Revolution that Wasn't: A New Interpretation of the Origin of Modern Human Behaviour" Journal of Human Evolution 39 (2000): 453-563.

McNeill, J.R. and William H. McNeill. The Human Web: A Bird's-Eye View of World History. New York: W.W. Norton, 2003.

Pinker, Steven. The Blank State: The Modern Denial of Human Nature. New York: Penguin, 2003.

Rampino, Michael and Stanley Ambrose, "Volcanic Winter in the Garden of Eden: The Toba Super-eruption and the Late Pleistocene Population Crash," in Volcanic Hazards and Disasters in Human Antiquity. ed. F. McCoy and W. Heiken. Boulder, Colo.: Geological Society of America, 2000, pg. 78–80.

Sahlins, Marshall. "The Original Affluent Society" in Stone Age Economics. London: Tavistock, 1972, pg. 1-39.

Scarre, Chris, ed. The Human Past: World Prehistory and the Development of Human Societies. London: Thames & Hudson, 2005.

CHAPTER 8

THE DAWN OF AGRICULTURE

Or,

HOW WE INVENTED BOOZE, BACON, AND TERRIFYING EPIDEMIC DISEASES

That Time Humans Played "Farmville" for 12,000 Years

Threshold 7: Agriculture – 12,000 years ago

- *Wherein humans grab more energy flows from the Sun via photosynthesis of crops.*
- *The crops support more people over a smaller land area.*
- *More potential innovators living at close quarters accelerate Collective Learning.*
- *Complexity goes absolutely nuts in the past 12,000 years.*

Timeline

- **World Population Hits 6-8 Million Foragers (12,000 years ago):** After several tens of thousands of years of "extensification" humans had spread into every major world zone on Earth, except the Pacific. Thanks to the greening of the world following the end of the last ice age, the world foraging population reached its zenith. The largest population was in Afro-Eurasia, with an estimated range of 3 to 5 million people, followed by the Americas with an estimated 2 to 3 million people, and Australasia with 500,000 to 1 million people.

- **Agriculture Invented in the Middle East (12,000 to 10,000 years ago):** Due to the end of the last ice age, the Fertile Crescent in the Middle East experienced a greening and abundance of food so that generations of foragers did not have to migrate in order to find food. Such territories that saw a blossoming of an abundance of food for foragers are called "Gardens of Eden". As a result foragers switched semi-sedentary lives collecting surrounding vegetation and hunting animals, while reducing the amount of distance they travelled over the course of a generation. Then as populations boomed and food became scarcer, these foragers were forced into the "trap of sedentism" and were compelled to domesticate plants and animals in order to prevent themselves from starving. This was the start of farming, where deliberate cultivation of food resources supported larger populations and a greater population density. The practice of agriculture spread into Egypt (or was independently conceived there), across the Middle East, and gradually into Europe.

- **Agriculture Invented in China (9500 years ago):** A similar "Garden of Eden" situation occurred almost simultaneously in the valleys of the Yellow River in the north and Yangzi River in the south. The end result was also similar, with the inhabitants of East Asia beginning to cultivate plants and animals in order to support larger population numbers. Agriculture correspondingly spread into Indochina and Japan. With agriculture now in the Middle East and East Asia, a combination of these practices gradually converged and met in South Asia and the Indus valley in particular.

- **Agriculture Invented in Mesoamerica, West Africa, and New Guinea (5500 to 5000 years ago):** While agriculture had been invented independently in the Middle East and East Asia thousands of years earlier, the barriers of the Sahara desert and the world's oceans prevented the practice from spreading into certain regions of the globe. In West Africa, we see a similar "trap of sedentism" happening independently in the river valleys of the Niger and Benue around 5000 years ago, subsequently spreading across West Africa, and the same region holds Africa's largest population densities to this day. Meanwhile the trap of sedentism occurred in Mesoamerica 5000 years ago, and gradually spreading south into Peru and north into the Pueblo societies of the Southwest United States. Most intriguingly, an independent invention of agriculture also occurred in New Guinea, with populations remaining quite small. Foraging remained the primary mode of life in Australia, with the notable exception of fire-stick "farming", which was quite productive and also instances of aquaculture that sustained a few sedentary populations of several thousand people.

- **The First Agrarian States Emerge in Mesopotamia (5500 to 5200 years ago):** After several thousand years of farming, technologies had advanced to the point that there was a large agrarian "surplus" of food which could support larger settlements of people, many of whom did not farm for a living. The subsequent diversification of labour and rise of complex ruling hierarchies created the very first recognisable city-states in human history.

- **The World Population Hits 50 Million Farmers & Foragers (c.5000 years ago):** With agriculture gradually spreading across the world, and being improved slowly by collective learning, by the rise of the first states, the world population had hit 50 million people of whom most were farmers. The largest clusters of populations containing the most people were in Egypt, Mesopotamia, Greece, Iran, India, China, Mesoamerica, and Nigeria, while large tracts of Europe, Africa, Asia, Australia, and the Americas remained inhabited exclusively by foragers who lived healthier lives but were smaller in number.

The Astonishing Complexity of Merely Planting a Seed

By several different metrics, the start of agriculture marks a new threshold of complexity in Big History. For starters, the amount of energy flows humanity could capture to sustain their own complexity more than doubled from about 40,000 erg/g/s to an average of 100,000 erg/g/s. Both foragers and farmers capture the overwhelming majority of those energy flows from the Sun, as do most organisms on Earth. Foragers will wander across a region and pick vegetation (which gets its energy from photosynthesis) and kill animals (which also eat those plants). But farmers would not rely merely on what grew naturally in the uncultivated wilderness. Some of those things were not fit for human consumption, yet took up valuable soil. So farmers cleared forests, nurtured soil, irrigated fields, and planted rows and rows of high-energy consumable plants, with which they fed themselves and herds of hundreds of tame domesticated animals, which the humans in turn used for their wool, milk, and meat instead of picking off a few wild animals in hunting parties. Humans started selectively breeding both plants and animals to become even more energy efficient, such as fatter animals for meat or grain plants with higher yields.

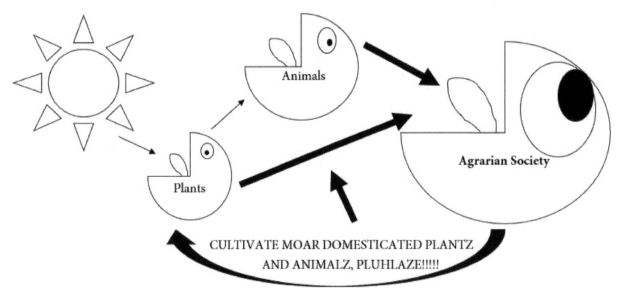

This marks a shift in Big History where a species is no longer adapting to the environment but adapting the environment to *them*. Ultimately, this change in lifeways supported more people. Agriculture drastically increased the amount of people the land could support by 1000 to 10,000% per square kilometre from the foraging era. Suddenly the carrying capacity of the entire surface of the Earth wasn't 8 million foragers, but 80 to 800 million farmers. Of course agriculture did not spread rapidly and it would be many years before such population levels were achieved, but that was the profound revolution that was kicked off in the Fertile Crescent 12,000 years ago.

The impact of increased energy flows and ultimately more people had a positive feedback loop on collective learning. With agriculture, you had more people (potential innovators) who increased the probability that a few of them each generation would come up with innovations. Some of these innovations would raise the carrying capacity of the population still further, whether it be a new mode of farming, a new crop, or a new tool or technology. As a result, you'd get more people, which led to more innovation, which kept the process accelerating.

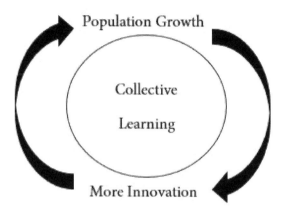

Not only did innovations speed up in agrarian societies compared to foraging ones, but farming regions quickly became the most populous regions on Earth. Instead of dwelling in nomadic groups of a few dozen people, humans began to live on farms with populations that large, and congregating in villages that had hundreds of people. Foragers would not only find it difficult to keep pace with the technological evolution of agrarian societies, but would quickly find themselves outnumbered as well, as the land they had freely used to hunt and gather was gradually whittled away by sedentary farms. This reduced the amount of land foragers had to keep themselves fed, and forced many of them to move further away or else take up farming themselves. Starvation and the disappearance of foraging lifeways, or else enacting raids and violence on farming communities (with probable danger of retaliation) was the upshot. For the next 12,000 years, wherever agrarian societies appeared this tragedy played itself out on the borderlands with foragers.

That Cozy Domestic Lifestyle

Agriculture is the process by which crops in a field and the livestock that feed of them are domesticated and cultivated for human consumption. The key word is *domestication*, which makes a difference between true agriculturalists and those foragers who may be sedentary but still just gather wild foods, or so-called fire-stick "farmers" whose methods are productive but nevertheless just collect wild species after burning down a forest rather than domesticating them. It also differs from aquaculture, which humans had practiced for several tens of thousands of years before agriculture, where sedentary foragers like the Gunditjmara of South Australia would manipulate coastal environments to produce more eels for their consumption. The act of agriculture invariably involves the deliberate planting of seeds of specific plants in terraformed environments, and the deliberate breeding and feeding of animals, for human consumption.

In this sense domestication is no different from other forms of symbiosis, whereby different organisms enter a relationship of cooperation in order for all of them to thrive. Indeed when it comes to domesticated plants and animals, they support humans by feeding them, but also due to selective breeding domesticated plants and animals become variants of species that probably couldn't survive on their own in the wild.

For example, consider how long a domestic sheep would last in the Fertile Crescent or East Asia without human intervention. Similarly, the first grains (whether the direct ancestor of wheat, rice, or maize) all come from the same Cretaceous ancestor of grass. The first wild grains didn't exactly yield much food for foragers and early farmers, but through selective breeding their yields grew larger, even when the ability of these grains to reproduce suddenly became dependent on humans sowing seeds. Even human evolution has been affected, in the sense that early humans were fairly lactose intolerant but with the introduction of cow and goat milk, agrarian populations developed the ability to consume more of the stuff without becoming ill. The disappearance of humans agriculturalists would likely result in the extinction of millions of individual organisms of our domesticates. And certainly the disappearance of our domesticates would leave humans in pretty bad shape! It would leave us starving to death, in fact.

And never mind food sources, what would we do without our doggos? As a side note, the dog appears to be an exception and one of the first animals that humans ever domesticated roughly 20,000 to 30,000 years ago (but not for farming). When we were still foragers, humans began to share food with large dire wolves and cave wolves, who then helped to hunt and ward off other predators. From that point forward, a subsection of wolves were selectively bred to be more friendly and affectionate with humans, and other traits like size and colour were gradually introduced over many generations until 12,000 years ago the transition from *Canis lupus* to *Canis familiaris* was made, the domestic dog was born, and he was a very, *very* good boy indeed.

The Multiple Origins of Agriculture

The practice of agriculture did not emerge once in one region and spread across the world. The four world zones were separated by unrealistic distances for foragers or early farmers to cross and spread their knowledge. Even within one world zone it took many centuries for agricultural practices to spread to different populations. Nor were foragers always inclined to adopt agriculture, especially since early agrarian lives were decidedly harder work and less healthy than foraging. A farmer had to work an average of 9.5 hours a day, instead of the foraging 6.5 hours. And the back breaking labour of producing enough to eat with Neolithic stone tools left its mark on the skeletons of farmers, which show signs of repetitive stress injuries. These early agrarian skeletons also show signs of malnutrition from the relative lack of dietary diversity, and also signs of new contagious diseases which arise from early farmers living in close quarters with their animals and each other, and all of the above peeing and pooping in local water sources. Why would a forager want to buy into that? Instead agriculture was picked up multiple times in several places across the world (the Fertile Crescent, China, Mesoamerica, West Africa, New Guinea) over a timespan of several thousand years in a process that historians call the "trap of sedentism".

The first ingredient to the trap of sedentism is a humid climate. Ice age climates are simply either too cold in northern regions or too dry in southern regions to produce natural abundance of wild plants in any particular area inhabited by foragers. Already, 20,000 years ago, in the Fertile Crescent human foragers had been gathering wild grains like ancestral strains of wheat and barley, and there is even evidence that they smashed the seeds to bake the grains into bread. But there was not yet sign of domestication or the selective breeding of these wild grains. But 12,000 years ago the Ice Age was coming to an end. The average global temperature was increasing, the ice sheets were receding. Rainfall increased in the Fertile Crescent and in river valleys around the world. Places that had been dry and open grasslands became forests and woodlands. The inhabitants of the Fertile Crescent could no longer hunt large grassland animals like mammoths, but began to hunt wild forest game like deer, wild goats, and wild pigs. They supplemented the decrease in their meat intake with an increase in consumption of grains. And thanks to the increased rainfall, wild grains had become increasingly abundant.

As a result of the end of the Ice Age, the Fertile Crescent "greened" for a time and became what historians call a "Garden of Eden" (in an obvious biblical reference) where plant and animal material was so abundant that human foragers no longer need to travel in order to find enough food. The bonanza of food was right there. So the foragers became sedentary. And stayed sedentary for several generations. Since the human community was no longer nomadic, there was less need to exercise birth control to keep populations low, and to not have too many infants at once. Infanticides deliberately declined, although infant mortality remained high due to natural causes.

The important thing to note about these "Gardens of Eden" is that there was more than just one in the Earth's revivified interglacial climate. This "Humid Period" of the Holocene ran until 5000 years ago. Even regions that are somewhat dry today were 12,000 years ago lush with vegetation and animal life. The Fertile Crescent was much greener at the end of the last ice age than it is today, the same applies to much of Northern Africa, where the Sahara was actually green with grassland, lakes, and animal life, instead of the huge desert of today. The inhabitants of the Niger delta and the Nile delta in Africa also enjoyed certain degree of abundance. As did the inhabitants of the Yellow and Yangzi river valleys in East Asia, and the inhabitants of the Gulf Coast in Central America. The abundance of greenery also seems to have been supplemented by ocean and freshwater fishing. These were all regions where humans could have remained sedentary for generations, centuries, if not millennia, without domesticating a darn thing.

The Fertile Crescent was, however, the first region of the world to truly adopt agriculture. This is likely because of the readiness with which the wild grains which grew in the Fertile Crescent could be converted into domesticated crops. The wild wheats and barleys that grew in southern Anatolia did not require too much modification to become reasonably productive grain products. Contrast this to the ancestral versions of rice (for East Asia) and maize (for Mesoamerica) both of which required much more genetic modification and cultivation before they became good agricultural sources of energy (though once they were the yields of rice and maize actually surpassed wheat). As a result, the sedentary inhabitants of the Fertile Crescent who had existed there for thousands of years had a clear option when the next phase of the trap of sedentism kicked in.

The second ingredient to the trap of sedentism is overpopulation. Eventually a sedentary population uses up all the resources of the Garden of Eden. In the Fertile Crescent, the Natufian foragers of the region had existed there 20,000 years ago, and by 12,000 years ago had a huge part of their diet composed of grain. We know this from the rotten teeth of their skeletons, which often results from overconsumption of bread at the expense of other food resources. Meanwhile, the lack of infanticide in the sedentary population meant that families could have half a dozen or a dozen children, rather than just a couple children widely spaced apart in terms of upbringing. Even allowing for high infant mortality, the population would have ballooned in the Fertile Crescent. And here is a problem. Collective learning is at this point only transmitted by oral teaching from adults to young. A lot of foraging skills that had become unnecessary in the Fertile Crescent were lost. Nor was it easy for a large sedentary population to suddenly become nomadic again. The choice was between agriculture and starvation.

The Natufians chose agriculture. Instead of letting wild grains just grow where they may, and hoping there would be enough to sustain the population, Natufians deliberately took the grain seeds and started growing them in the soil themselves. They also cleared forests in order to have more room for grain crops. The Natufians also domesticated the goat, which grazed in newly cleared land, in order to provide a source of milk and meat. By 11,000 years ago, the inhabitants of the Fertile Crescent had domesticated wild aurochs (cattle), wild boars (pigs), and wild caprines (sheep) for use of their meet, milk, and hides. Agriculture likely spread during the same time from the Fertile Crescent to the Nile river delta. And that is how a foraging culture transitions to agriculture, despite the fact farming is unbelievably harder work, the risk of famine and starvation is higher, malnutrition is rampant, and living conditions are generally less sanitary and disease-ridden.

Within a few thousand years, the same trap of sedentism had occurred on the other side of Asia in the Yellow and Yangzi river valleys. The foragers of prehistoric China hunted herds of bison, aurochs, and caprines, and collected wild grains, including millets and rice. The "Humid Period" flooded the two river valleys, creating the idea environment for the further growth of wild rice, and we see sedentary foraging activity in China as far back as 12,000 years ago. Then the trap of sedentism intervened and 9500 years ago we see the deliberate cultivation of dry and wet rice farming in China, along with the cultivation of millet and various ancestral forms of livestock. It is also likely that agricultural knowledge (particularly use of rice) from China gradually spread into India. It so happens that well-cultivated rice can actually support an even higher population density than wheat. And so the largest population densities of the world blossomed in South and East Asia.

The Fertile Crescent and China are our first two independent centres of agriculture. Much of the rest of the world did not adopt agriculture until many millennia later. In Mesoamerica, populations did not hit the trap of sedentism until 5500 years ago, when see sedentary fishing villages spring up along the Mexico coast of the Gulf and the Pacific Ocean. The delay in the adoption of agriculture is likely to have occurred in the Americas because of the shorter amount of time foragers were in the region (they only arrived 12-15,000 years ago) and the subsequent time required to move south and populate the area. Nevertheless it is not surprising that the more lush equatorial regions should spring the trap of sedentism. Around 5500 years ago, Mexicans began to cultivate beans, squashes, and capsicums showing that they too had fallen into the trap. A little farther south around 5000 years ago, the inhabitants of

Peru began to farm potatoes and gourds. It was not until 2200 years ago that the inhabitants of Mesoamerica began to cultivate more productive forms of wild maize, which sent the population densities soaring. Within 1000 years these practices had spread into New Mexico in the southwest USA.

In West Africa, it is likely that sedentary and semi-sedentary foragers had existed on the coastline and on the Niger delta for many centuries. However, the end of the "Humid Period" and drying up of the Earth's climate 5000 years ago started to gradually transform the once lush Sahara desert. What had once been a grassland, began to transform into a wasteland. This drying has continued to the present day, shrinking the amount of fertile land in the Sahel and pushing human habitation further south toward the coast, where things are still reasonably lush. Through a mixture of overpopulation in the Niger delta, and the streaming in of foragers from the north, the critical levels were reached and farming began in West Africa. Over the next several thousand years, this knowledge was spread throughout sub-Saharan Africa by the migratory Bantu peoples, until they had reached South Africa by 2500 years ago. However, many peoples in sub-Saharan Africa resisted the adoption of agriculture until the past few centuries, because of attachment to their traditional lifeways, to the many landscapes that were hostile to pre-modern agriculture, and the many aforementioned disadvantages of making the transition from foraging to farming.

A final note should be made about another region which independently devised agriculture. In New Guinea, the lush environment produced a trap of sedentism roughly 5000 years ago, though there is evidence it happened as early as 8000 years ago. Either way, there is evidence that the inhabitants of New Guinea began to farm taro, bananas, and yams. None of these are particularly high yield crops compared to say, maize or rice, and so population numbers never reached the point where cities and states could be supported. What is more, it appears that despite the proximity of New Guinea to Australia, the transmission of agricultural knowledge either never happened or it simply was not adopted in Australia.

It would appear in Australia that foraging was reasonably sufficient for the population there, with the notable exceptions of aquaculture that prevailed for the past 2000 to 5000 years along the coasts and permitted a certain degree of semi-sedentism and full on sedentism. And so the original inhabitants of Australia were spared the trap of sedentism, and the majority of the world zone of Australasia (with the exception of New Guinea) did not have agriculture until modern times. The same goes for the Pacific, where the human arrival was only in the last 4000 to 1000 years, though limited forms of agriculture were eventually tried there. It was in the world zones of Afro-Eurasia and the Americas that we initially see the threshold of agriculture being firmly crossed. And in the long term, we shall see that the historical and geopolitical ramifications for world history would be immense.

On Dating, Booze, Diseases, and Excrement

From approximately 12,000 to 5000 years ago, agrarian society (where there was agrarian society and not foragers and wilderness) was composed of farms and villages only. No cities, no states, no armies, no writing, no royal dynasties. None of the trappings of conventional history. Just a world of farms and villages that prevailed for 7000 years, or a period longer than what separates us from the foundation of Ancient Egypt. Or rather, the period of time that separates us from the foundation of Ancient Egypt plus an additional period of time that separates us from the reign of Augustus in Ancient Rome. For such a long stretch of time, increasing numbers of humans tried their hand at farming, with all the maladies that accompany it. This period is known in Big History as the "Early Agrarian Era", otherwise known as the Neolithic, and it follows the foraging Paleolithic and precedes the "Era of Agrarian Civilisations".

A further word should be said about dating in Big History (and, no, I'm not talking about my Tinder profile. HA. HA. HA. HA??? I'm starting to doubt I was ever funny). So far we've gotten through 13.8 billion years by simply saying "X number of years ago". Now we are on the cusp of transitioning to the realm of traditional history, we may well start using traditional historical dating systems more and more frequently. So here's a quick rundown. When I say 12,000 years ago, I am talking about 10,000 BC or BCE. When I say 5000 years ago, I am talking 3000 BC or BCE. Essentially subtract roughly 2000 years of the entirety of AD or CE, and you've got your BC/BCE date, and add 2000 years for the opposite effect. The "years ago" thing works well for approximate dates. Obviously it makes more sense to say "Magna Carta was signed in 1215 AD/CE" than to say it was signed "approximately 800 years ago". As for the BC/BCE and AD/CE thing you may just have noticed, these are two ways of expressing the same system. BC and AD are from the old Christian mode of dating in Western countries, BC meaning Before Christ and AD meaning Anno Domini (Year of Our Lord) and is modelled around the medieval estimate for the year of Christ's birth. The calendar of months within the years actually predates Christianity and "year one" used to be from the estimated date for the founding of Rome. The newer BCE/CE formulation stands for "Before Common Era" and "Common Era" and is an attempt to secularise the dating system while not stopping the calendar revolving around the birth of a religious figure, which one would think would be the bigger issue. It is rather ironic for a practitioner of Big History, since there is nothing "common" about what happened in the last 2000 years of rising complexity.

With that minor digression we can move on. The Early Agrarian Era is generally characterised by a poor standard of living compared to the Paleolithic or the Era of Agrarian Civilisations (though the latter certainly varies by circumstances). For the entirety of the Early Agrarian Era farmers used stone tools. And while the implements were inventive and testament to the power of collective learning, they weren't very efficient. Nor did early farmers have very good fertilizers or irrigation.

As a result, the carrying capacities of the Early Agrarian Era were generally low. This meant after the initial burst of plenty that the first farmers may have enjoyed, there were numerous periods of overpopulation, malnutrition, starvation and famine. Animal power was not adequately harnessed (no pun intended) in this period and so most of the planting and tilling was conducted by humans with the aforementioned primitive stone tools. It was down to adult and child labour (another advantage of having more kids compared to foraging) to cut down forests with stone axes, break open rough soils with stone hoes, and cut down the crops for harvest with hand-held scythes made of stone or bone. Nor were the fertilizing benefits of animal poop fully realised at the time, meaning that soil would rapidly lose nutrients and render cropland useless for several years. Early agriculture was also highly dependent on natural water sources (rivers) since there was neither the technology nor the manpower to conduct sophisticated irrigating techniques to make wider stretches of land suitable for growing crops, meaning the amount of land that could be effectively farmed was also limited.

Even without famine, the conditions of the Early Agrarian Era were fairly disgusting compared to the Paleolithic. Foragers had a fairly diverse diet, there is every indication that in normal circumstances they cleaned themselves regularly, and because they lived constantly on the move in small communities without domestic animals there was a notable lack of communicable diseases. In the Early Agrarian Era, on the other hand, humans were sedentary and remained within the same few square miles for their entire lives.

For a start this meant that the waste from their food products (rotten vegetables, carrion and offal of dead animals) and the improperly disposed of results of digestion (human and animal excrement) stuck around whipped up unsanitary conditions from which they could fall ill if discarded too close to the domicile. Typhus and cholera, as a result, became huge problems and were quite deadly and contagious. Typhus was caused a virulent bacteria that could be transferred from person to person via mutual contact with food and could also spread through a water source. Once infected a person was highly contagious and suffered from fatigue, swelling, pain, fever, delirium, hallucinations, heart problems, ulcers, and intestinal bleeding. Cholera meanwhile is caused by a bacteria that infests the lower intestine and causes extreme bouts of diarrhea and vomiting, so dehydrating the victim that the skin retracts, the eyes sink, the skin turns blue, and the person eventually dies. This speaks nothing of the various viruses and poxes that were whipped up within larger populations living in close contact and spread by contact and by coughing and sneezing, and which disfigure the skin, cause swelling in the brain, seizures, fevers, and death.

It also did not help that humans frequently bathed and defecated in their own water supplies, as did their neighbours, as did many of their domesticated animals. In such instances, bathing did not necessarily get one clean and one could fall ill from the regular practice, so, depending on the region (because some agrarian communities still bathed regularly by custom), personal hygiene might fall out of fashion with regular bathing actually being considered unhealthy. This further exacerbated health problems. And there would not be reliable soaps or antibacterial agents for thousands of years. On the bright side, one would get used to the smell of body odour and (as a result of diet and lack of dental hygiene) the smell of bad breath and the sight of rotten teeth.

There was also the problem of contaminated drinking water from these same causes, which actually made drinking of pure water quite unhealthy. The happy result of this (or unhappy result depending on your perspective) was the invention of alcohol, which via its fermentation process actually made watered down meads, beers, and wines, safer to drink than pure water. That is not to say that humanity went the next several thousand years of history drunk off their heads (though that would be an amusing explanation for some decisions) because most beverages were not as potent as the ones that began to be distilled, commercialised, and sold for recreational drug use purposes in the 19th and 20th centuries. For instance, the average alcohol content of pre-modern beer was around 2%. That said, one could still get drunk off of the right stuff, or the right amounts, and so moral codes involving moderation and artistic flights of virtuosity involving alcoholic lubrication manifested themselves within religion and the arts. The addictive qualities of the substance that blight 10-25% of the population arise from the dependency on the massive release of dopamine and serotonin that comes from ingesting the mind-altering drug, along with a more primitive impulse to ingest the large amounts of sugar and calories that come from the ingestion of fermented fruits and grains when they were rare, which we actually share with our shrew-like mammalian ancestors from 65 million years ago.

Early farmers also lived at close quarters with domesticated animals, sometimes even within the same dwelling, and the transference of viruses and bacteria between humans and their domesticates bred avian and swine flu that could rapidly sweep through and ravage a human population. This speaks nothing of the pestilence that human sedentism nearby various food sources and waste products brought. Rats, fleas, and cockroaches became commonplace. The regular denizens of filth kindly shared a new range of diseases, including various forms of infection, dysentery, and dreaded variants of the plague.

Does all this sound good? Now is the time, I think, for anyone who wishes to try and state that the rise of complexity is always synonymous with "historical progress".

It Takes a Village…

Placing all the famines, pestilence, and diseases that could make you poop yourself to death aside, even these early farming societies were able to support way more people per square kilometre than the foraging cultures from which they emerged. The result was an acceleration of collective learning and a resulting rise of complexity. In the foraging era, the centre of gravity for a society was the family. Kinship was the primary mode of maintaining governance, and alliances between groups were maintained by ritualised intermarriage. The rise of agriculture added another layer to this societal complexity. The farm would still consist of the family, with each member engaged in daily duties for subsistence, and with intermarriage occurring between families on neighbouring farms. But the social life of the agrarian society would converge at the village, a place populated by a few hundred people who would gather to exchange things (agricultural goods, tools, and information) and engage in the governance of affairs that affected the wider community (crop yields, problems arising from the weather, possible threat of raiders, and the resolution of disputes between families). Villages would also be places for the stockpiling of grains in the event that the wider community was struck by famine. There even appears to have been the development of religion in the Early Agrarian Era, with villages partaking in increasingly elaborate burial traditions for their dead. These same burials also yield an array of jewellery and other decorative items, which may well have denoted status, and thus the increasing sophistication of hierarchies.

In terms of violence, the majority of it doubtless remained interpersonal, much like in the foraging era. But with sedentism and the introduction of land claims, crop yields per farm, and possession of livestock by a family came the conflict over property. This may have manifested itself in either thievery by neighbours or legal land disputes between them that were arbitrated by the wider community. There was also the new problem of raiders, neighbouring cultures (that may have been sedentary farmers too, or else may have been non-sedentary foragers) who would rampage across a farming region taking crops, livestock, tools, and perhaps even kidnapping women and children. As such the earliest agrarian settlements don't show much sign of defensive apparatuses, like the village at Abu Hureya in Mesopotamia which housed sedentary farmers 10,000 years ago (8000 BC). But as the agrarian era dragged on, farming communities begin to show signs of walls, ditches, and watch-towers to surround a local village. One of the most impressive examples of this is the village of Banpo in China, which lasted from 7000 to 5000 years ago (5000 to 3000 BC), and has all dwellings clustered in a group behind a wall which was surrounded by a ditch. An even older example is the settlement of Jericho in the Fertile Crescent, which was converted into a farming village 11,500 years ago by the Natufians who had occupied the region for thousands of years. The original settlement had no structural defenses, but had a cluster of houses built upon a freshwater spring, that was directed via primitive irrigation ditches toward the surrounding 10 square kilometres of farmland. By 10,000 years ago, however, a wall was erected around the village.

The purpose in both of these cases seems clear. In a village where trade was conducted between farmers, where some grains may have been stockpiled, and thus there would occasionally have been a cluster of resources, defenses were required in order to prevent large raiding parties from coming along and "redistributing" the community's wealth. Please note, however, that these defensive structures in a village do not necessarily denote the existence of large-scale warfare – that would still be beyond the resources of Early Agrarian societies. Instead these would have been opportunistic raiding parties who would skirmish with defensive militias formed by local farmers on the frontier.

In order to organise this extra layer of society, and cope with the many legal and defensive needs of a denser agrarian community, we see the microcosm of "entrenched hierarchy", which is any dominance hierarchy that is established on more than personalities, physical traits, or kinship. Bear in mind that during the Early Agrarian Era that the overwhelming majority of the population were engaged in subsistence farming to stay alive. Yet a very small minority of people would have taken on positions of authority to arbitrate disputes and organise infrastructure projects that could not be executed by a single individual or family.

The appointment of such authorities within a farming community would have come about in one of two ways (or both). The first, and most likely the earliest, occurring was "bottom up power". When we discuss power, we are talking about an individual or council of people possessing the authority to issue commands and have reasonable expectation that those commands would be carried out. If you wanted to translate this into Big History terms, it would be the direction of energy flows in the form of food or human effort toward a certain goal laid out by an individual in authority. In the "bottom up" scenario, the farming community would appoint an experienced or sensible individual, usually an elder or council of elders (in Latin this is translated as maiores, from which we get the term "mayor") to arbitrate disputes and make decisions for the community. These decisions would have bearing on the entire community (the system of energy flows). And in order to afford the time to make these decisions and shoulder these duties, the elders might be afforded food they did not farm themselves, so they would spend less time at subsistence living. At first, these positions would be appointed on basis of merit, and decisions would have to be obeyed by the community without a great deal of coercion beyond the interpersonal and the social browbeating of an individual or minority faction that did not want to play ball.

In this sense, the hierarchies of Early Agrarian societies were not that much different from foraging ones, or even most primate ones. All primates have a dominance hierarchy of some sort. The difference is that once an agrarian population extends into the hundreds or thousands, it is difficult for an elder or group of elders to maintain dominance from merely being the strongest or maintaining the strongest interpersonal alliances. There are only so many people within an agrarian community with whom the reigning authority could form a personal relationship. Instead, a power structure might involve formalised procedures of bestowing power, by vote, inheritance, or by religious ritual. And in order for the commands of such an authority to be obeyed, the elder might quickly require a voluntary or paid group of enforcers.

Which brings us to the second method of establishing power, the "top down" method. This is where consent from a community is not necessary, because the authority of an individual or council is backed by the threat of violence. It is quite clear that by the time that agrarian settlements begin constructing defenses, that there will be some militia or group of men capable of violence in numbers. These groups would not just be used against outsiders, but would be used against members of the community who did not obey commands or accept the judgement of arbitration in a community dispute. These enforcers would also need extra energy flows as payment for their efforts, so they too did not have to spend their entire time at farming. In order to maintain this cycle of energy flows, the elder could always use the enforcers to collect further tribute from the surrounding population. All this would have been done gradually with the veneer or legality and consent within the village. And it is the coalescing of extra resources in the hands of the authority that pays these men that sows the seed for the entrenched hierarchies of Agrarian Civilisations, with their pharaohs, kings, and emperors that we shall explore in the next chapter. But for now, Early Agrarian societies remain in the gray area between the personal relationships of alphas and betas in foragers and the entrenched authority of elites in the subsequent period.

Please also bear in mind that Early Agrarian societies did not have the long history of ideological conditioning that predisposes us toward democracy. For instance, inheritance of authority might seem to them the much more natural course of action. The transition from a bottom up, democratic (or at the very least meritocratic), appointment of a reigning authority to a hereditary entrenched aristocratic hierarchy could actually happen quite quickly. The finest modern examples we have of this transition come from the Pacific world zone. In Hawaii, Tonga, Samoa, New Zealand, Marquesas, and Easter Island, all of these societies had a notion that virtue and authority were passed on by blood. This is not such a departure from our instinctual primate past, where chimpanzees also maintain alliances based on inheritance, with the offspring of alphas inheriting the alliances and protection that were once afforded to the parents. As such, the time elapsed between "bottom up" and "top down" approach may not have been equally distributed, though at the end of the day, the exact timing of the development of leadership traditions (democratic, meritocratic, and hereditary) would differ by region and culture.

Essay Writing Exercise

This time we are returning to structured introductions. Consider the questions below.

What is the most important turning point in human evolution?

Why did humans invent agriculture independently in several places around the world?

For each of them, write a succinct answer to the question (your thesis statement). Define all key terms and concepts. List the evidence that supports your answer. Explain how the evidence supports your answer.

Once you have written your first draft introduction for one of the questions, rewrite it so it is no longer than 100 words. And then rewrite it so it is no longer than 50 words. Try to make each word count, and have your choice of phrasing and structure be as concise and incisive as possible. The introduction is the most important part of your essay for establishing your argument, so practice writing punchy, substantive introductions that make good use of space.

At the end of the day, this also makes writing the rest of your essay much easier!

Further Reading

Bellwood, Peter. First Famers: The Origins of Agricultural Societies. Oxford: Blackwell, 2005.

Cohen, Mark. Health and the Rise of Civilization. New Haven: Yale University Press, 1989.

Cowan, C. and P. Watson, eds. The Origins of Agriculture: An International Perspective. Washington: Smithsonian Institution Press, 1992.

Fagan, Brian. People of the Earth: An Introduction to World Prehistory. 10th ed. New Jersey: Prentice Hall, 2001.

Johnson, A., and T. Earle. The Evolution of Human Societies: From Foraging Group to Agrarian State. 2nd ed. Stanford: Stanford University Press, 2000.

McNeill, J.R. and William H. McNeill. The Human Web: A Bird's-Eye View of World History. New York: W.W. Norton, 2003.

Livi-Bacci, Massimo. A Concise History of World Population. trans. Carl Ipsen. Oxford: Blackwell, 1992.

Smil, Vaclav. Energy in World History. Boulder: Westview Press, 1994.

Smith, Bruce. The Emergence of Agriculture. New York: Scientific American Library, 1995.

CHAPTER 9

AGRARIAN CIVILISATIONS

Or,

WHY BEING SLIGHTLY

TOO GOOD

AT FARMING

ULTIMATELY CAUSED

5000 YEARS OF WAR

The Start of Conventional History (nine chapters in)

We have finally arrived at the era of agrarian civilisations, where states began to form from the early farming communities of the Neolithic. Gradually agrarian surplus got so large that farming communities were able to sustain cities – huge settlements that contained thousands of people, most of whom were not engaged in farming. The city is where we get the term "agrarian civilisations", with the root word "civic" referring to a city. Rather than a more abstract notion of being "civilised". As we shall see, the rise of the city-state did not always result in behaviour that to modern eyes would seem as "civilised", with the rise of warfare and slavery. This did, however, represent a major increase in societal complexity.

Timeline

- **The First States in Mesopotamia (5500 years ago, 3500 BC):** While there were a number of sedentary settlements of over 1000 people prior to this date, with villages growing larger and larger, the first city-states arose in Mesopotamia, like Eridu and Uruk, where there was a clear hierarchy, division of labour, and not all people engaged in farming. Notably all of the world's first states emerged where agriculture had first arisen, implying a long stretch of time where collective learning operated until farming was good enough to support cities.

- **The Invention of Writing (5500 to 4500 years ago, 3500 to 2500 BC):** The first writing was made to keep track of increasing amounts of "stuff" in an agrarian civilisation, corresponding to the agrarian surplus that sustained cities. These logistical writings were pictographs in Sumer and hieroglyphs in Egypt, with one symbol representing a thing or concept. Then 5200 years ago this had developed into the first written language in Sumerian text. And 4500 years ago the first actual literature was being written. For collective learning, the ability to transmit information without relying on oral tradition was an enormous help.

- Start of the Bronze Age (5300 years ago, 3300 BC): Previously Near East cultures were able to smelt copper, starting around 8000 years ago (a transitional period between the Neolithic and Bronze Age sometimes called the "chalcolithic"). By mixing copper with tin imported by trade from other places in the world, the cultures were able to produce bronze in their smelting ovens. Bronze was able to produce more durable and effective tools and weapons, and the practice rapidly spread across Afro-Eurasia in the space of a few centuries, with independent discovery of bronze in the Americas a few millennia later.

- **The Origins of the Indus River Valley Civilisation (4600 years ago, 2600 BC):** With agricultural practices spreading from Mesopotamia in the West and China in the East, the agriculture took off in the Indus River Valley, and by 4600 years ago, villages began growing to large cities of several thousand people. This agrarian civilisation lasted for just over a millennium before disappearing for reasons that are still as yet unclear.

- **The First Large Empires in Mesopotamia (4300 years ago, 2300 BC):** The city-states of Mesopotamia were frequently at war with one another and eventually were coalesced into a large territory known as the Akkadian Empire, unifying much of Mesopotamia under one rule. This marks another increase in complexity, from the state that controls a single city and some surrounding territory, to a state that is able of directing the energy flows of multiple cities and a region several hundred miles across and imposes control on cultures that are not its own. It is possible that the first empire actually predates Akkad, depending if you would deem the unification of Upper and Lower Egypt by 5100 years ago as an imperial, rather than a state, system.

- **The First States in China (4100 years ago, 2100 BC):** The emergence of the legendary Xia dynasty may have details that are mythological and may not reflect the real history of the region, however, it is quite clear that by this time cities and kingdoms, with hierarchy and a division of labour did exist at the 4100 year mark. In fact, the first city states may have arisen even earlier, somewhere between 4100 and 5000 years ago.

- **Urgartic and Phoenician Alphabets Invented (3400-3100 years ago, 1400-1100 BC):** This represents a fairly significant leap forward in collective learning because unlike writing that uses a symbol to signify one word or concept, an alphabet is able to use a relatively limited number of symbols to express all words and concepts that one can conceive. This made it easier for written languages to proliferate and represent spoken language, ultimately aiding the rate at which information was able to be transmitted through script.

- **Start of the Iron Age (3200 years ago, 1200 BC):** While the mining of iron ore was possible much earlier than this date, it was only around 3200 years ago that the melting temperatures necessary to forge iron were achieved in Near Eastern kilns. Over the next seven centuries this knowledge spread across Eurasia from west to east, and proliferated more slowly into Sub-Saharan Africa. There was no comparable discovery in the Americas, though there is trace evidence iron may have been used in smelting. Iron resulted in extremely effective weaponry, agricultural tools, and other technological implements.

- **The Beginning of the Silk Roads (3000 years ago, 1000 BC):** Trade spread across Afro-Eurasia shortly after the Iron Age began. The Silk Roads linked east to west, aiding the transference of knowledge and collective learning. Traders would not travel across the entire route, but transport trade goods and information part of the way, and sometimes it took entire lifetimes or generations for some things to travel the full length of the road.

- **First States in Mesoamerica and Sub-Saharan Africa (2000 to 3000 years ago, 1000 BC to 1 AD):** In keeping with the slightly later timing of the rise of agriculture in these regions, agrarian surplus enabled the emergence of ancient city-states, states, and empires, around 2000 to 3000 years ago. However, it would not be until many years later that these states came into direct contact with the states of the other agrarian hubs and so much of their evolution is unique without cross-pollination of ideas and technologies.

- **World Population Reaches 250 million (2000 years ago, 1 AD):** Agriculture had proliferated into enough regions in Afro-Eurasia and the Americas, collective learning had raised the carrying capacity, and enough agrarian surplus had fostered enough cities, that the world population had grown from 50 million people 5000 years ago to 250 million 2000 years ago. The overwhelming majority of these people were engaged in farming, while sizeable portions of them were wrapped up in agrarian civilisations. More potential innovators meant an accelerated pace of collective learning, although only a fraction of this population was literate, and most of them lived in highly traditional societies with their main occupation being to toil in the soil.

Rise of the City

The village was nothing new to the Early Agrarian era. For millennia, farmers had interacted via these settlements in order to trade and conduct themselves in formal social situations. Sometimes these settlements might also be built on locations where there was some sort of religious significance, as we can see from monuments and trinkets that were part of some form of worship. Other times, they were part of a defensive strategy where in times of violence, people could take refuge behind the fortifications of the town. Jericho was a large agrarian settlement in the Levant from 11,500 years ago, and by 9,000 years ago had grown into a town of 2000 or 3000 inhabitants. Many of these were still engaged in farming, with irrigation running right through the town. But there was evidence of increasing levels of hierarchy and the diversification of labour. Another example is Catalhoyuk, an agrarian settlement in Anatolia in modern day Turkey, dating back to approximately 9000 years ago. Here the population engaged in farming activities, what we today would call kitchen gardens, but also in the farming of grain and herding of livestock outside the town. There also seems to be a significant religious component to life in the settlement, symbolised by paintings and statuettes. There the settlement could have contained 3000 to 8000 people.

This is significantly larger than your typical Early Agrarian village which would house a few hundred people, to maybe 1000 or 2000 people at most. These settlements are what you could call "transitional" since they possessed large populations (the first cities proper would have tens of thousands) but still had the majority of the population engaging in agriculture, even though they lived within a built up settlement. You also would have seen the hardening of religious orders and the beginning of either the bottom up or top down approach to power, in order to govern several thousand people and the surrounding regions.

In order to support a city of people, many of whom are not engaged in farming, you need to be quite productive in the countryside. This can come in the form of hardier agricultural tools (as happened at the start of the Bronze Age 5300 years ago) or the discovery of higher yield crops. Irrigation was also growing more efficient in the land of the Euphrates and the Tigris around 6000 years ago. When you introduced water to soils that were normally dry and didn't grow anything, you could unlock a great deal of untapped nutrients. This drastically raised the local carrying capacity. Also the harnessing of livestock for more and more purposes around 7000 years ago contributed to the rise of the city. In Mesopotamia, people were using animals not just for meat, or their hides, or their wool, or even just their milk. They were using animals for their labour power. They were hitching up large ploughs to teams of oxen in order to cut up more of the soil, in a faster rate of time, and cutting deeper into the soil, than any human labour could do. These agricultural innovations, combined with fairly favourable temperatures in the region 6000 years ago, increased the overall production by leaps and bounds.

The first major settlement to emerge in Mesopotamia was Eridu, which had been a farming village in the millennia prior. By 5500 years ago (3500 BC), the settlement had grown to approximately 5000-10,000 people in the city, covering an area of 0.33 kilometres squared or roughly three times the size of Catalhoyuk, making it fairly large by the standards of the Early Agrarian era. And a number of settlements roughly that size sprang up in Mesopotamia 5500 to 5200 years ago. But these were not as large as Uruk, a city to the northwest of Eridu, which attained an even more impressive size. Covering an area 15 times the size of Eridu, Uruk contained at least 10,000 people and at its height was home to a maximum of 80,000 souls. This was a permanent human settlement truly on a scale that was never seen before. The stone buildings and city walls of Uruk were constructed between 5500 and 5200 years ago. It is also at Uruk that we see the first clearest trappings of the Era of Agrarian Civilisations.

The city of Uruk houses two temples, built on top of step pyramids called "ziggurats" that rise 15 metres in the air. While not particularly tall by modern standards, these structures would have been the most impressive sight at the time. "Monumental architecture" is one clear symbol that we are dealing with an agrarian civilisation with a division of labour, and a powerful religious order. The city of Uruk worshipped An, Nammu, and their son Anki, and a pantheon of other gods and spirits that explained the various forces of nature, and who could be appeased in order to have a successful harvest.

It is quite clear that Uruk had a powerful priestly caste, from which eventually evolved a priest-king for whom royal palaces were built. The development of Sumerian writing shows that there were scribes handling logistics. And the presence of such magnificent temples is proof of a large artisanal and construction labouring force, numbering in the thousands of people. There would have been soldiers maintaining law and order amidst the tens of thousands of citizens, and manning the city walls. The city had a burgeoning linen and wool industry that employed thousands. There would have been wealthy aristocrats and merchants. There would have been slaves who were coerced by force to perform work as either household servants or labourers. These changes amount to a massive "diversification of labour", or to put it another way, diverse new component parts in our structure of human societal complexity.

Outside the city were pastures and farms, and these farmers would have constituted roughly 90% of the population under Uruk's control, and a good portion of these, too, would have been slaves. The essence of power in agrarian civilisations is to control enough land, which produces the food that feeds a population, thus vastly enriching you, and to control labour – either by paying people wages to perform tasks or else forcing people to work for you by enslaving them (pretexts for this were they got into debt, or were criminals not heinous enough for execution, or they were enemy captives from a war). And in order to maintain control over all this, you needed to fight for it.

It would appear that the evolution of hereditary monarchy in Uruk was the result of a bottom up process, albeit not with democracy or meritocracy being the starting point, but theocracy. The first "wise councils" would have been chosen from the priestly class as the most "qualified" to rule the city because of their connection with the divine. In order to have the resources to support their rule, the priestly class controlled 30-65% of the farmland around the city. Somewhere between 5200 and 5000 years ago, a leader emerged with not only high authority in the religious order of Uruk, but respect as a leader of warriors. Shortly thereafter this leadership became hereditary, and so the line of Uruk priest-kings was created.

Warfare over land became a common feature because it was so crucial to maintaining the power of the ruling class of any of the Sumerian cities. These priest-kings would provide military leadership in conflicts either within the aristocracy of one city-state, or in the many conflicts over land between city-states. Since the rise of the first city-states 5500 years ago, coordinated warfare between the large cities involved larger and larger armies of thousands of men. For the initial period of 5500 to 5000 years ago, Uruk was able to maintain dominance in the region due to its much larger size, and its trade goods spread across the Middle East from Anatolia to Persia, and into the Indus River Valley. There was increased competition between the city-states after 5000 years ago, as new cities grew larger. We see the trade goods from Uruk gradually taper off in more far flung regions. The biggest rival of Uruk was the nearby city of Ur, which was to the southeast. After many generations of warfare, Uruk was conquered and sacked by Ur approximately 4550 years ago (2550 BC). Much of Uruk's wealth was then carted off to Ur, along with a lot of captives who would then be used as slaves.

Cycles of warfare between Sumerian city-states continued for centuries, with one state conquering and devastating another, conquering farmland and pillaging riches to momentarily place itself in a dominant position. The soldiery were generally foot soldiers, bearing either bronze spears or swords, and proved fairly effective on the flat floodplains of Sumer. Some were paid wages, others were given grants of land, which over a generation or two could transform a humble soldier into a member of the warrior aristocracy. There had always been violence in primate dominance hierarchies, even in human foraging ones, but now the bloodshed occurred on the scale of thousands of dead or enslaved people, with no sign that the cycle would ever stop repeating itself.

Rise of Writing

Uruk has the honour of providing us with the oldest surviving writing, inscribed by sticks into clay tablets dated to 5500 years ago (3500 BC). These writings were predominantly logistical, discussing the transporting of agricultural produce and livestock. This "cuneiform" inscribed on these tablets is pictographic, meaning one symbol represented one thing or concept. All told, over a thousand symbols are required to cover everything necessary in this form of writing. At this point the symbols had no relation to how the word was spoken in ancient Sumerian.

By 5200 years ago (3200 BC), certain symbols began to represent sounds in a spoken word, and combined with pictographs for concepts, one could begin to use the writing as a guide for spoken language. A system of numbering was developed 5100 years ago, allowing scribes to account for things in their dozens, hundreds, or thousands by leaving the appropriate symbol. By 4500 years ago (2500 BC), Sumerian literature included a wealth of syllabic symbols that allowed for songs and poems to be composed and laid down, and for complex prayers and histories to be written. One such example is the Epic of Gilgamesh, the tale of a semi-divine priest king who lived 4700 years ago (2700 BC), and his many adventures and conflicts as he travelled across the region.

In terms of collective learning, the advantages of written records are fairly self-evident. Instead of passing on all knowledge by oral tradition where, if there is a single break in the chain, a generation where it is not shared, it disappears, written records can slumber in an archive for centuries only to be rediscovered. One can also communicate more complex and abstract information that if it were transmitted orally would probably have the details obscured, much like in a game of telephone. This would include details of a history, but also calculations made in mathematics. All told, the written record made it less likely that the knowledge would be forgotten, as frequently happened in the foraging era.

That said, at the time very few subjects of a city-state were literate. It would have been seen as a specialised skill possessed by the scribes and the priestly class. Perhaps some of the aristocracy and merchants would have been literate as well, but these levels would vary depending on need and the cultural emphasis placed upon the skill. The vast bulk of the population would not be literate, nor would they require writing to transmit knowledge in their daily lives. The vast amount of collective learning that was transmitted in an agrarian civilisation (whether agricultural or artisanal techniques) would be done by spoken word and physical mimicry between parents and children, or masters and apprentices.

Rise and Fall of Empires

Uruk had fallen to Ur during one of many wars between city-states in the earliest period of agrarian civilisations. Only a few decades later, another city, Lagash, began to dominate the region. King Eannatum of Lagash lived around 4500 years ago (2500 BC) and managed to conquer all of the city-states of Sumer, including Ur and Uruk. He also expanded into part of the Levant, Assyria, and a good portion of southwest Persia (then known as the kingdom of Elam). It is not known how firm his hold was on these outer regions, however. Arguably Legash is responsible for establishing the world's first "empire", wherein a core kingdom or ethnic group imposes its will on other kingdoms or ethnic groups. Sumer was Eannatum's core empire, if you will, though the ethnic group that lived there largely spoke the same language and observed similar customs. Whether or not we would consider this an empire is really a question of definitions and semantics, since we wouldn't consider the unification of the Anglo-Saxon kingdoms into a united kingdom of England as an "empire" per se. Nevertheless this represents a moment in history where power of a ruler extended beyond one city-state and territory, and controlled the energy flows and building blocks of other cities and territories. The Legash Empire lost many of its lands after Eannatum's death around 4400 years ago (2400 BC), and Legash was eventually conquered by the city of Umma, which ruled Sumer until roughly 4300 years ago (2300 BC).

Somewhere to the north of Sumer (the exact location is not clear) was Akkad, a small city-state (or settlement) of Semitic peoples, of a different ethnic and linguistic group from the Sumerians. This city-state was ruled by Sargon of Akkad, whose origins seem to be clouded both by myth and politics. Sargon overthrew the ruler of the Sumerian city of Kish, and began multiple years of war and conquest. Sargon conquered almost the entire river valleys of the Euphrates and the Tigris, and pushed into the Levant, landed in Crete, and as far north as Anatolia, and east into Elam. There are even indications that he pushed as far south as the far end of the Arabian Peninsula and the territory which is today Oman. Sargon's reign seems to have consisted of almost perpetual warfare and conquest. Either the subjugation of new territories or the crushing of revolts by people he had just conquered. Multiple cultures were incorporated into the Akkadian Empire, and in some cases the Akkadian language was imposed upon subjugated peoples. The Akkadian Empire thus reflects a clear imperium imposed upon territories that were not of the local ethnicity, requiring a system of governors and military force to maintain control of the energy flows of the region. The empire lasted until approximately 4150 years ago (2150 BC), when it collapsed into a dark age that appears to have been caused by ecological strain and constant invasions and warfare. This would not be the first time such an outcome was to occur.

Secular Cycles

This is a phenomenon known as a "Malthusian Cycle", or more accurately a "Secular Cycle" (the modern version of the theory) which drives the rise and fall of empires. Around 4200 years ago (2200 BC), droughts, an exhaustion of the soil from overuse, the increased levels of salt in the soil from short-sighted irrigation techniques, seems to have significantly reduced the carrying capacity of Mesopotamia, particularly in Sumer. Suddenly this region was not the abundant powerhouse it once was, with a high carrying capacity that birthed the first cities composed of tens of thousands of people. This appears to have kicked off a population crisis, where famines were more frequent, where uprisings by various cities and aristocrats became more common, and the Akkadian Empire's control over Mesopotamia weakened as the empire shrank. Then there are accounts of invasion by the Gutian "barbarians" into the weakened empire until it was destroyed.

This story bears some similarities to other historical periods and empires, and indicates there is a pattern. Ultimately, there is a relationship between collective learning, carrying capacity, and the sociopolitical stability of an empire. The key to this is that despite the fact that collective learning was gradually increasing the carrying capacity so that the world population increased from 50 million 5000 years ago (3000 BC) to 954 million 200 years ago (1800 AD), population levels frequently outstripped the carrying capacity. Agrarian people just had too many babies, and their innovations in agriculture simply could not keep pace. So instead you have these cycles of rise and decline every few centuries that had a profound impact on micro-historical events.

The pattern proceeds as follows:

Expansion - when the population is still low and expanding, things are prosperous for the average person because there is more land, more food, and higher wages, the crown has fairly good control over the aristocracy, and the empire is generally stable and able to expand its territory. *Strain* - as the population approaches the carrying capacity, the average person pays more for basic essentials and gets paid less for their work (if they get paid at all), rents go up, peasants sell off their land because it no longer supports them, as such land and wealth coalesces into the hands of the very wealthy and they multiply in number. *Crisis* - when famine or disease or some other disaster reduces the population, the wealthy lose their peasants, their taxpayers, and the source of wealth from rents and payments for agricultural produce. *Depression* - the wealthy begin competing with each other in tremendous civil wars and uprisings, also competing with the government, until i) an invading army takes over, ii) the population of the elite is reduced to the point that peace and stability reigns again for another population recovery, or iii) the empire collapses completely and the region becomes depopulated.

Gradually collective learning raises the carrying capacity, but this does not keep pace with population growth, and so a kingdom or empire is thrown into these cycles of rise and fall every 2-3 centuries. This is how some of the big trends we've been observing have an influence on small scale historical events. It is also how humans differ from other species in nature. Usually when a species hits the carrying capacity of its ecosystem, the population declines and then recovers. But in the human case, there is an extra layer of complexity where large-scale violence and civil war can hold a population low for decades after the population crash.

Phase	Population	Real Wage	Elite #s	Violence Level
Expansion	Growing	High, with good standards of living for common people	Low/Moderate	Low with large amount of state stability
Strain	Slowing	Shrinking, with declining standards of living for common people	Increasing	Rising with mostly popular rebellions without much elite support
Crisis	Dropping	Increasing, with increasing standards of living for common people who survive	Top heavy societal hierarchy, lower orders begin to be impoverished	Substantially increasing with elite factionalism, competition, discontent
Depression	Kept low	Increasing, with standards of living eroded by violence and possible oppression	Gradually declining as sociopolitical strife continues	High, with elites competing with each other and weakening government for what resources there are left
Recovery (aka another Expansion)	Growing	High, with good standards of living for common people	Low/Moderate	Low with large amount of state stability

Aegyptus (Eye-Gip-Toos)

Wherever in the world agrarian civilisations arose, we see similar patterns to the ones we've covered in Mesopotamia. Agriculture had spread to Egypt from the Fertile Crescent not long after its invention 12,000 years ago. It didn't hurt that the temperatures of the Sahara were much more temperate and Egyptian farmers enjoyed a life in grasslands, dotted with lakes. Egyptians domesticated aurochs (cattle), goats and sheep were imported from Mesopotamia, and Egyptians farmed gourds, grains, and fruits. Large agrarian settlements began to develop in the Nile Delta on the Mediterranean coast and on a few places to the south along the Nile. Then 7000 years ago, the climate began to dry and the Sahara was slowly transformed into an inhospitable deserts. Egyptians were driven into increasingly denser populations along the Nile. Like the lands between the Tigris and the Euphrates, the Nile was particularly good at fostering fertile soils for farming. As such there was still a significantly high carrying capacity to produce an agrarian surplus.

Populations of agrarian settlements got larger and larger. By 5200 years ago (3200 BC), at the latest, there were settlements of tens of thousands of people that could be considered cities, most notably Hierakonopolis. Some may have been independent city states and many already have been incorporated into the larger networks of the Upper and Lower Kingdoms of Egypt. It is possible that such populations were reached as early as 5500 years ago (3500 BC), essentially "tying" Egypt with Mesopotamia for the first agrarian civilisations. Then 5100 years ago (3100 BC), this network of cities along the Nile were divided into two major states, the Upper and Lower Kingdoms. Legend then has it that Narmer, the Egyptian pharaoh, unified the Upper and Lower Kingdoms via a war of conquest. There is an abundance of archaeological evidence, like the Narmer palate, but also many seals and pots that such an event occurred.

A fairly similar system of hierarchy to the Mesopotamian city-states emerged. The pharaoh himself was considered a living god. The priesthood worshipped a pantheon of gods that each had control over some aspect of nature, or represented a concept dealing with life and death. There were soldiers for armies, scribes for logistics, artisans for pottery and clothing, blacksmiths for tools and weaponry, and engineers and architects for irrigation and buildings. Egyptians engaged in the practice of "monumental architecture" with elaborate tombs, statues, and buildings. Most notable of all these forms of architecture are the pyramids, with the first step pyramid of Djoser being constructed 4650 years ago (2650 BC), and the pyramids of Giza built between 4550 and 4490 years ago (2550-2490 BC). These later buildings served as tombs for the pharaohs and would have required a massive amount of manpower and collective learning to construct.

The largest pyramid of Khufu took 20 years to build, and would have required nearly 100,000 people to shift 6 million tons of limestone rock. And impressive feats of architecture took place in almost every single dynasty. Even in less than 500 or 1000 years since the rise of the first major Egyptian cities, an immense amount of collective learning, specialist expertise from a division of labour, and the massing and coordination of tens of thousands of labourers, were constructing forms of complexity the like of which the world had never seen.

Collective learning was also aided by the emergence of a pictographic form of writing – the hieroglyphs. Not much is known about the origin of Egyptian hieroglyphs, except we do know that they were in full use by the sculpting of the Narmer palate 5100 years ago. Eventually these pictographs, like in Mesopotamia, lent themselves to syllabic writing, in a system of thousands of symbols. The writing was drawn on walls and chipped into stone. By 4800 years ago, these symbols were used in writing on papyrus, made from the reeds of the Nile. A more easily modified form of writing (than stone) on relatively abundant materials like papyrus reeds was a major boon for the amount of writing produced and the overall impact of collective learning.

The history of Egypt is too long and ponderous to recount here. But we do know that Egypt experienced many periods of stability and instability, of plenty and famine, every few centuries, conforming to what we know of "Secular Cycles". Pharaohs were sometimes overthrown by their armies, aristocrats, or priestly classes. The Old Kingdom lasted until 4180 years ago (2180 BC), when the population declined, the pharaoh had lost most of his powers to aristocrats and regional governors, only for the weakened kingdom to be invaded and cast into a dark age. The Middle Kingdom lasted approximately 350 years from 4050 to 3700 years ago (1700 BC), enjoying renewed prosperity followed by the same pattern of demographic decline, civil war, and invasion by the Hyksos, which cast Egypt into another period of chaos. The New Kingdom that emerged 3550 years ago (1550 BC) inaugurated a period of extreme prosperity and military expansion, which saw Egypt stretch its control down the Nile like never before and into the Levant. Then 3070 years ago (1070 BC), civil infighting took its toll and Egypt collapsed into multiple small states, frequently invaded by foreign conquerors. These invasions continued, with only a brief period of rival, until Egypt was finally conquered by Alexander the Great 2351 years ago (332 BC). After his death, his empire was split between his generals, and the descendants of Ptolemy ruled Egypt. Still, despite foreign rule, Ptolemaic Egypt can still be considered fairly independent until the conquest by the Romans under Octavian (later Augustus) 2049 years ago (30 BC). Like in Akkad and Sumer, we see a link between collective learning, the carrying capacity, periods of population strain, sociopolitical instability, and the collapse of empires. In fact, within these major phases of Egyptian history, there are even more cycles that impacted conventional micro-historical events.

Contiguous and Continuous China

On the other side of the Afro-Eurasian world zone from Mediterranean agrarian civilisations was the embryo of the agrarian civilisation of China. We have seen in the previous chapter how the foragers of the Yellow and Yangzi River valleys independently developed agriculture 9000 years ago. It would fall to the Yellow River Valley in the north to develop the first agrarian civilisations in China. The Yellow River actually flows from Tibet, and bends and weaves its way across much of China toward the north until it flows into the Yellow Sea. While the Yellow River is treacherous because of its tendency to overflow and flood, it does breed some particularly fertile soils in which the inhabitants of Northern China produced a lot of dry grains and fed their domesticated animals. The first agricultural settlements with fortifications and irrigation appear in the region by 4500 years ago (2500 BC), which may indeed be the start of the first cities, though not much is yet known about their population size, or whether the population was still mostly engaged in farming.

By 4100 years ago (2100 BC), the Yellow River Valley produced China's first agrarian civilisation, what had previously been considered the legendary Xia dynasty. The population of the valley had increased dramatically during this time. Cities sprang up at Luoyang, Erlitou, Ao, and Anyang. We know these cities had a diversification of labour. They contained average housing, aristocratic housing, and palaces, making it clear a hierarchy was emerging. We find evidence of artisanal works, metallurgy, and barracks for troops. What is intriguing is this territory was completely landlocked and under the Xia dynasty did not even extend as far as the Yellow Sea. It was also quite far away from any other agrarian civilisations on Earth, the nearest one being the Indus River Valley Civilisation on the other side of the Himalayas. Warfare would have consisted of campaigns between city-states until the Xia dynasty gained control of the entire area, along with the subjugation of farming communities that had not yet fallen under state control.

Not much is known about the Xia dynasty compared to the Shang dynasty that replaced it approximately 3600 years ago. The Shang dominated more of the Yellow River and the regions beyond it, and extended their rule to the sea. Here we see all the trappings of agrarian civilisation coming into full view. The Shang Empire was ruled by a king who claimed to have semi-divine ancestry. He was supported by a warrior aristocracy. These people owned most of the land in the agrarian state (with only a very few smallholders) with peasant serfs working the land, who also formed the foot-soldiery of Shang armies. Slavery was also quite prominent in Ancient China, mostly being captives of war who worked the land, worked as servants, and who were occasionally the victims of human sacrifice. The Shang engaged heavily in trade with surrounding regions. They were already producing silk, they imported chariot technology from Central Asia, they exchanged resources with agrarian peoples of Korea, southern China, Indochina, and Malaysia. But the Shang Empire remained glutted with warfare in northern China, and did not expand beyond the region.

Chinese pictographic writing was well in being by 2600 years ago (1600 BC), though it probably had existed much earlier. Writing is probably as old as China's agrarian civilisation itself, or at least the Shang dynasty which began 3600 years ago (2600 BC). The problem is that unlike the Sumerians, the Xia and Shang did not write on clay tablets, but instead wrote on silk and bamboo, which rotted away. It is inconceivable to think that Chinese agrarian civilisation would have reached such a level of complexity in terms of hierarchy, religion, architecture, and irrigation engineering without some form of written language. It is also telling that the earliest surviving Chinese writing already deals with political matters, rather than logistics required to manage increasing amounts of agrarian surplus. This points toward a gap in our evidence, centered around the earliest dates of writing.

While the first agrarian civilisation in China emerged in the northern Yellow River Valley, another agrarian civilisation emerged in the Yangzi River Valley to the south. It also begins in Tibet, and winds across southern China until it pours out into the East China Sea. Here early farmers domesticated rice farming, which allowed for quite a lot of population growth, since rice can support far more people than dry grains. Agrarian settlements had emerged in South China by 6000 years ago (4000 BC), but we see the first confirmed emergence of a cities with populations of tens of thousands by 3400 years ago (1400 BC). The three dominant ones that would grow in the following centuries were Sanxingdui, Mawangdui, and Echang. Archaeological work is still in its infancy but we know these cities also bore the trappings of hierarchy, artisanal work, and armies, with significant degree of sophistication. While not as unified as Shang China, and living for much of its existence as city states, the agrarian civilisations of South China enjoyed 1000 years of independence from the North, when China was unified under the Qin and the Han.

Meanwhile to the north, the Shang dynasty approximately 3045 years ago (1045 BC) underwent a period of civil strife where the ruling king was overthrown by another claimant (King Wu of the Zhou dynasty, whose ancestry much mythologised and imbued with the divine) after a tremendous series of wars spanning three generations. Much like the later history of China, most of the devastating wars would appear from within, as the country broke down into sparring provinces, rather than from without (with a few notable exceptions like the Mongols). There are some indications that the period of the Shang-Zhou transition was characterised by population strain, the rise of disease, and possible collapse, although archaeological evidence is scanty and mythological histories are unreliable. But notably the same pattern of ecological strain, collapse into warring regions, and overthrow is more certain in the fall of the Zhou dynasty 700 years later. Accordingly, most phases of Chinese history can also be connected to Secular Cycles to some degree, depending on how recent a dynasty we are discussing and the availability of evidence.

Indus River Valley (or how to make your state mysteriously disappear)

A more puzzling case of an early agrarian civilisation is harder to decipher since we know so very little about it. Both in terms of its rise, its hierarchies and culture, and also why it disappeared. But let us start with what we do know. The Indus River Valley was a fertile region primed for agriculture like so many other hub regions of agrarian civilisations. The Indus is an extremely large river with many tributaries, and it nourishes an area larger than Mesopotamia and Egypt combined with fertile soils, potentially supporting a larger population once farming kicks in. Yet as far as we can tell it did not independently devise agriculture like the Fertile Crescent, East Asia, West Africa, or Mesoamerica did. Instead, by 9000 years ago (7000 BC), farming knowledge had transmitted from the Fertile Crescent, across Persia, and into the Indus. One or two millennia later, farming knowledge arrived from East Asia. The Indus River Valley farmers domesticated a wide variety of grains and domestic animals. By 5200 years ago (3200 BC), we see the first major agrarian settlements emerging along the Indus, with populations of a few thousand people along the lines of Catalhoyuk and Jericho, such as the settlement at Mohenjo-Daro and Harappa. By 5000 years ago (3000 BC), the population of these settlements in the river valley increased dramatically because a drying of surrounding regions and a decline of farming there. By 4600 years ago (2600 BC), the first cities of tens of thousands of people were born. Mohenjo-Daro and Harappa, for instance, both had a population of 20,000 to 50,000 people, within the range of the major cities of Mesopotamia. So far the transition from foraging, to early farming, to cities looks pretty standard.

In addition to large populations, we see some trappings of agrarian civilisations, but the absence of others. Key traits like fortifications, large dwellings for the rich, barracks for the soldiery, and a thriving mercantile and artisanal network all existed. The Indus River Valley civilisation at its height even boasted indoor plumbing and public baths. We know that they practiced religion, though we have no knowledge of the names of their gods, what they represented, or whether there is any link to the Hindu gods that would follow them. We do not know much about the hierarchy of the Indus, but we can detect a difference in wealth between subjects. The difference in dwelling size is not, however, excessive though the jewels, adornments, trinkets and decorations do seem to signify differences in wealth. We do not know how they were ruled, whether through monarchy, oligarchy, or any other form of government. Beyond the obvious presence of fortifications, barracks, and the odd bit of weaponry in this civilisation, there isn't much sign of large-scale warfare between 4600 and 3900 years ago (2600-1900 BC). Though the very presence of these things is evidence that violence did indeed exist to some degree. Perhaps the Indus were more peaceful, perhaps they focused more on mercantile pursuits, and naval forces than armies (much like many other agrarian civilisations that followed them), or perhaps absence of evidence isn't evidence of absence. We don't even know if for the majority of its life whether the cities of the Indus were independent city-states or whether they were contained in a larger coalition or empire.

Yet the Indus River Valley Civilisation did fall like the rest of them. Due to climate change, droughts began 4200 years ago brought in a period of population strain, and lasted in waves until 3700 years ago (1700 BC). The fertility of the soil seems to have continued to decrease from overuse and erosion. After 3700 years ago, the region did not appear to have recovered in complexity. Large cities were increasingly abandoned, the plumbing system fell into disuse, and houses fell into disrepair. New dwellings were not of the same quality and seemed to have housed smaller population numbers. There is such a decline in trade and technology between 3700 and 3300 years ago, that it is conceivable that some disaster had been so severe that it caused a Tasmanian Effect (the loss of collective learning). By 3300 years ago (1300 BC), the Indus River Valley Civilisation disappeared without a trace. Yet it is unclear if natural disasters were accompanied by any sort of violence like in other cases where we have more evidence. If there was a breakdown of social order or a devastating invasion from the outside, we have not yet seen conclusive sign of it. As such, the Indus River Valley Civilisation may be the case that makes or breaks the rule.

It will be difficult to determine this, however, since we simply don't know much about them. We know that they had writing, from a few hundred symbols we have discovered on various artifacts. We don't know whether this writing is pictographic or part-syllabic, and both are disputed. And there appears to be little continuity between this writing and what followed in the region later. As such we cannot supplement the dearth of archaeological evidence with written accounts to gain some idea of the history of the region, whether they did fight major wars, and what kind of hierarchies and beliefs they had. Whereas the ability to translate hieroglyphics in Egypt was lost after the Arab invasion of Egypt in the seventh century, we regained the art once the French found and translated the Rosetta Stone (which had inscriptions in hieroglyphs and Greek) in the nineteenth century. We have no such Rosetta Stone for the ancient language of the Indus. It is possible that these people, their history, and their way of life will always remain a mystery to us.

Livin' in America

While agrarian civilisations were the most common in Eurasia, there were notable agrarian civilisations in the Americas and Africa. They arose later than the Eurasian ones simply because agriculture also started in the Americas and Africa later (roughly 5000 years ago). In Mesoamerica, people domesticated maize, squashes, and beans. They notably did not have livestock, with the exception of turkeys. The horse had been hunted to the extinction in the Americas. There were no herds of sheep at this time. The dog remained the only other domesticate, with the process of taming wolves beginning even before humans had crossed into the Americas. The lack of meat from animals was compensated for by fishing, hunting, and the fact that many American crops like maize gradually became high yield. But the Mesoamericans were somewhat disadvantaged by the fact that there were no large domesticates to pull ploughs.

Nevertheless, the population of Mesoamerica grew, with large agrarian settlements of the Olmecs springing up on the coast of the Gulf of Mexico 3200 years ago (1200 BC). Eventually these settlements turned into full blown cities, at San Lorenzo and La Venta. The Olmecs show all the signs of diversification of labour. They had coordinated warfare, and thus they had armies and soldiers. They constructed fortifications. They collected taxation. They had temples where religious rituals were practiced. And, most notably for the Olmecs, they engaged in a great deal of monumental architecture. The Olmecs built pyramids, as did many agrarian civilisations since it is the easiest massive structure to build, and these could get as high as 33 metres. But most famously the Olmecs carved giant stone heads throughout the period of their civilisation, of which seventeen have been found. These heads weighed 10-20 tons. The heads themselves seem to be representatives of chieftains/kings which indicates there was a clear top down hierarchy in place.

The Olmecs collapsed around 2300 years ago (300 BC) with a quite shocking population decline, possibly caused by changing climates that reduced the carrying capacity of the region. There is no available evidence that the drop was followed by a period of civil war as characterises a typical Secular Cycle, but this is not necessarily evidence of absence. What we do know is that shortly after the Olmecs declined, other agrarian settlements began popping up in neighbouring regions, which may imply that after agriculture became increasingly difficult for the Olmecs in their homeland, many people just migrated elsewhere. In the coastal lowlands of the Yucatan peninsula (where the asteroid that wiped out the dinosaurs had struck 65 million years earlier) the Mayans thrived for in cities with a clear division of labour from 500 BC. Their agrarian civilisation peaked with immense cities of 50,000 to 120,000 people from 200 to 950 AD. Thereafter, urbanisation was drastically reduced by a falling population and decades of sociopolitical instability and fighting between Mayan elites.

To the south, on the Pacific coast and in the Andes Mountains beyond, agrarian civilisations also arose in roughly what is modern day Peru. The fact that agriculture and agrarian civilisations arose here is quite remarkable given the forbidding landscape. The Andes squeeze the coast being only 100 kilometres away. They are over 6000 metres tall and Andean peoples formed settlements at around 500-1000 metres. The narrow strip of coastline is was arid, getting very little rain, and was frequently smitten by earthquakes. To the south was the desolate and inhospitable Atacama Desert.

Despite the difficult environment agriculture nevertheless started here 4500 years ago (2500 BC) with the domestication of yams, peanuts, and beans. The Andean diet was supplemented with fish. Due to the small amount of land for habitation, large agrarian settlements sprang up fairly 4000 years ago (2000 BC), just 500 years after agriculture was adopted. Thereafter, people started to colonise the Andes increasingly, living in terraced farming communities, and adding tobacco for rituals and potatoes as a major source of nutrients for the soil, and an easy source of food for people that raised the carrying capacity. Agrarian settlements tended to be quite small because of the landscape, perhaps 2000 or 3000 people being the norm. However, a few places in the Andes grew over 10,000 people and show clear signs of hierarchy and public places for religious ceremonies. The earliest city was Chavin de Huantar that reached its height 3000 years ago, as part of some kind of religious pilgrim movement, but was in many ways the exception at the time. The city declined in 300 AD. But between 300 and 1200 AD, numerous cities like Mochica, Ayachuco, and the Tiwanaku on Lake Titicaca sprang up along the coast between. Yet by the end of this period the arrival of the Spanish was drawing near, threatening to destroy all this slow careful evolution.

Sub-Saharan Africa

West Africa independently developed agriculture around 5000 years ago (3000 BC). Complex agrarian settlements emerged in West Africa around 1500 BC. And by 600 BC, there were some large towns and villages in West Africa where there was enough agrarian surplus. By this time many cultures were also using iron technology, further increasing farming productivity. In 1000 AD, the climate of West Africa was wetter than it is today, with the Sahel (a band of fertile farming and grazing land) forming a larger part of the region. As the climate changed over the next thousand years, people moved south to where the Ghana Empire would eventually emerge. The heartland of Ghana itself was able to support many people, who formed a variety of kingdoms. Around 300 AD, West Africans domesticated the camel. This revolutionized trade across the Sahara, which fed a lot of wealth into West Africa, just as Ghana was getting its start. By 700 AD, a mixture of agrarian surplus and trade revenue had made Ghana the most powerful state in the region. The city of Koumbi Saleh, thought by many archaeologists to be the empire's capital, is estimated to have supported 15,000 to 20,000 people. This may not seem like much compared to other ancient cities. However, this was an astounding feat for a city in the Sahel, where the climate was dry and drinking water was scarce.

Ghana was ruled by a king. The founding myth of Ghana is that a man named Kaya Magar Cissé established a kingdom called Wagadou around 300 AD. The sons and grandsons of his house extended their rule over other kingdoms turning them into vassals so that by 700 AD the Ghana Empire was born. Many of the names of the Ghana rulers are unknown and only a few of their deeds have passed into recorded history. Much of the king's power was dependent on the immense wealth of the trans-Saharan trade which included a great deal of gold and slaves. Ghana was a mixture of farmers, traders, and wealthy nobles. It ran under a feudal system much like other realms of the age. To a certain degree, the nobility gained their power from the land, but the greatest source of the king's power came from gold. Ghana had control over three major gold fields. The king of Ghana had a monopoly on all gold nuggets that were found in the mines. People were allowed to trade in gold dust, but had to turn over any gold nuggets to the government.

Ghana's long period as the dominant agrarian civilization of West Africa came to an end in the 1200s. Scholars have argued that climate change played a role. The wet climate that had once made farming prosperous in the Sahel continued to deteriorate. With dwindling resources and power, along with some political in-fighting, Ghana left a power vacuum that was soon filled. Rivals called the Sosso briefly occupied territories of Ghana, including its capital and built their own short-lived empire. Then the Mali Empire conquered the Sosso, and around 1230 forced the ruler of Ghana to swear fealty to them as a sort of lord paramount, holding a lesser title.

Australasia and the Pacific

While numerous regions of the Americas and Afro-Eurasia were forced into the agrarian transition, and thus had a lower standard of living than foragers, the world zones of Australasia and the Pacific largely escaped this fate. In Australia, it was certainly much more preferable for people to forage, with little incentive to adopt agriculture. Especially because many Aboriginal practices were so productive. For instance, fire-stick "farming" by burning down forests to kill game and expose food sources in dense forests, and to clear paths, turned out to be an extremely productive form of foraging, and the fire-loving eucalyptus forests rapidly recovered so the region did not exhaust itself very quickly. Other Australians were skilled aquaculturalists and managed to support rather sizeable populations with this practice. All told, the Australian continent was able to support between 500,000 and 1 million foragers and aquaculturalists.

In Papua New Guinea, the constraints of the environment prevented them from getting enough agrarian surplus to create cities. So these people went as far as the early farming phase and no further, prior to the modern era. And in the Pacific agriculture was sometimes tried piecemeal, with settlers of new islands bringing sweet potatoes, taro, and fruits with them to grow. But ultimately the lack of land area in Pacific Islands prevented large scale agriculture from being manifested, to speak nothing of the surplus required to support cities.

From a number of perspectives, this was quite fortunate for the inhabitants of the world zones since the many maladies and evils that come with agrarian civilisations did not blight the fate of these peoples. Yet, while enjoying thousands of years of fairly productive and healthy lives, all that would come crashing down once agrarian civilisations from Afro-Eurasia came into contact with them, due to the greater virility of Afro-Eurasian disease that had travelled across the continent for thousands of years, and also due to the fact that Afro-Eurasian collective learning had a wide network and more people to accumulate innovations. But for now the human experiment continued separately on all the world zones.

Essay Writing Exercise

For this exercise, try writing an essay outline for one (or more) of the following essay questions:

What is the most important turning point in human evolution?

What was the greatest change in the human condition caused by the advent of agriculture?

Are there any predictable patterns or 'laws of history' visible across 5,000 years of agrarian civilisations?

Make sure your outline includes i) a clear thesis statement that directly answers the essay question, ii) a list of main arguments with carefully considered topic sentences that support that thesis statement, and iii) a list of evidence that you would use to support these arguments.

A good essay outline should be 1-3 pages, but can be considerably longer depending on the length of the essay or the amount of research performed.

Further Reading

Adshead, S. China in World History. 2nd ed. Basingstoke: Macmillan, 1995.

Coe, Michael. Mexico: From the Olmecs to the Aztecs. 4th ed. New York: Thames and Hudson, 1994.

Crawford, Harriet. Sumer and the Sumerians. Cambridge: Cambridge University Press, 2004.

Earle, Timothy. How Chiefs Come to Power: The Political Economy in Prehistory. Stanford: Stanford University Press, 1997.

Hansen, Valerie. The Open Empire: A History of China to 1600. New York: W.W. Norton, 2000.

Gates, Charles. Ancient Cities: The Archaeology of Urban Life in the Ancient Near East, Egypt, Greece, and Rome. 2nd edition. Abingdon: Routledge, 2011.

Kenyon, Kathleen. Digging up Jericho. London: Ernest Benn, 1957.

Kicza, John. "The Peoples and Civilizations of the Americas before Contact" in Agricultural and Pastoral Societies in Ancient and Classical History. ed. Michael Adas. Philadelphia: Temple University Press, 2001.

Leick, Gwendolyn. Mesopotamia: The Invention of the City. London: Penguin, 2001.

Marcus, Joyce. Mesoamerican Writing Systems: Propaganda, Myth, and History in Four Ancient Civilizations. Princeton: Princeton University Press, 1992.

McNeill, J.R. and William H. McNeill. The Human Web: A Bird's-Eye View of World History. New York: W.W. Norton, 2003.

Rothman, Mitchell. Uruk, Mesopotamia, and its Neighbours: Cross-Cultural Interactions in the Era of State Formation. Santa Fe: School of American Research Press, 2001.

Schamandt-Besserat, Denise. How Writing Came About: Handbook to Life in Ancient Mesopotamia. Austin: University of Texas Press, 1996.

Turchin, Peter and Sergei Nefedov. Secular Cycles. Princeton: Princeton University Press, 2009.

CHAPTER 10

THE EVOLUTION OF AGRARIAN CIVILISATIONS

Or,

YOU NOW GET TO WATCH ME

COVER A MASSIVE AMOUNT

OF CONVENTIONAL HISTORY

THAT COULD FILL 1000 BOOKS

IN ONE CHAPTER

...AND FOR GOOD REASON

Three Major Forms of Human Society

We've now covered the transitions between the three main types of human society in Big History: foraging, early agrarian, and agrarian civilisations. At each new phase, complexity rose in terms of both structure and energy flows, and collective learning accelerated. Foraging societies were the earliest form of society, consisting of a few dozen to perhaps 50 people in a sub-tribe that ran together and perhaps a hundred to a thousand people who identified with the same language and ethnicity. Lifestyles were healthy than anything seen before modernity, society was organised around the family and the subtle shifting of social alliances and interpersonal relationships. In terms of collective learning, progress was slow given how foragers lived in small, relatively disconnected societies, but still manifested a faster rate of adaptation and extensification than any other species in the *Homo* genus.

Early agrarian societies increased the number of humans living in a tightly-knit community to several hundred, with the family still being the source of most of the social order, but with the glimmer of the first sign of bottom up and top down government that didn't rely on interpersonal relations. As agriculture grew more efficient, settlements and villages sprang up, most of them being populated by a few hundred people, but some grew to impressive sizes numbering in the thousands when the landscape and food sources would allow it. But at this point, everybody was still engaged with farming. In terms of collective learning, we can note a slight acceleration of innovation, from the invention of irrigation, many forms of agriculture, and the cultivation of new and effective crops.

Agrarian civilisations on the other hand consisted of cities populated by tens of thousands or more, and these eventually were linked into states numbering in the millions of people. Collective learning went nuts. Bronze and iron were harnessed kicking off entire archaeological eras of production. Literacy set down knowledge on papyrus, paper, or stone, so transmission was not as reliant on oral tradition and more collective learning could survive across the generations. For the first time, a fairly sizeable percentage of the population (10-20%) were not involved in agriculture. There was a diversification of labour, and a wide new range of social roles. Armies fought battles, states gathered tax from the peasantry, scribes jotted down histories and logistical records, and kings and priests claimed a high and mighty authority based on religion. More often than not, kings and aristocrats claimed that this authority was hereditary. And every two to three centuries on average, agrarian civilisations went through secular cycles of expansion, stagnation, crisis, and manmade depression when population growth outstripped the carrying capacity. The key traits of agrarian civilisations are: most people are engaged in farming, but there are cities, there are states, there is a diversification of labour, armies, writing, taxation, and secular cycles.

Yet these transitions between foraging, early agrarian, and agrarian civilisations didn't just replace one form of society with another. After 5500 years ago (3500 BC) these three societies lived alongside each other in the world, and profoundly impacted each other's history. In fact, there are still foraging and early agrarian societies in small slivers of the world today, and certainly some states that have not fully industrialised that could be considered agrarian civilisations, although the number of all of these is shrinking rapidly all the time due to the spread of industrialisation all over the world, and the unification of the world into a single global economy and complex system. It was between 5500 years ago and the 1700s AD that there was still a clear distinction between them. Since then, the borders between them have vanished astonishingly fast, as the world was swept up in the Modern Revolution.

During the period from 3500 BC to 1750 AD, agrarian civilisations grew larger and larger. At the beginning of the period, the city-states of Mesopotamia and the kingdom of Egypt only covered 0.2% of the Earth's terrestrial surface. By the time East Asia, West Africa, and the America produced their first agrarian civilisations that percentage grew to between 2 and 6%. Despite having such a small share of the total land area, these agrarian civilisations now possessed the largest share of the world population of 250 million and the fastest rates of collective learning. By 1000 AD, the land area controlled by agrarian civilisations had only increased to 13%. It was only with the onset of the Age of Explorations that agrarian civilisations increased their control to 33% of the Earth's land area in 1600 AD and the overwhelming majority of the world's 600 million people were contained within them. During the period of 3500 BC to 1600 AD, agrarian civilisations expanded, increased the carrying capacity through collective learning, set up increasingly sophisticated trade routes that spanned entire world zones, and went through dozens of secular cycles that governed the rise and fall of empires in a flurry of rather pointless (in hindsight) factionalism, ethnic and religious hatred, and bloodshed.

Between these ravenous civilisations, were simple agrarian peoples without cities or state control, and beyond them, foragers who were free of both the shackles of the state and sedentary living. But foragers and early farmers would facilitate trade between agrarian civilisations, such as on the Silk Road in Central Asia that united Afro-Eurasia, or on the band of trade that ran between the Andes, Mesoamerica, and North America. And more often than once these foraging and early agrarian societies triggered the collapse of agrarian civilisations, when the latter hit the downward spiral of a secular cycle, whether we are talking about the German role in the fall of the Western Roman Empire, or the startling and devastating Mongol conquest of half the known world which killed approximately 50 million people.

Timeline (we have now transitioned fully to the conventional dating system)

- **The Chinese Develop Woodblock Printing (220 AD):** The invention of writing is a huge leap forward for collective learning, but a further advantage is given to being able to rapidly copy and distribute anything that is written across a population. Instead of painstakingly copying manuscripts out by hand, which is a slow process, wood block printing allowed for an impression of writing to be carved into a block of wood, and then stamped with ink upon paper, allowing for the diffusion of different forms of literature across China. The practice would remain the most common form of printing in China until the 19th century.

- **The Fall of the Western Roman Empire and Tasmanian Effect (400 to 490 AD):** While Tasmanian Effects (the loss of collective learning where technology regresses either wholesale or within specific disciplines) were fairly notable in the Palaeolithic, they became harder to achieve in the agrarian era, particularly with writing. However, the Western Roman Empire fell with such calamity and depopulation that certain technologies and practices actually were lost for several centuries, setting back the development of collective learning in the region, while the states of East Asia continued to tear ahead. This is one of the few confirmed Tasmanian Effects in the era of agrarian civilisations, though there are a few other candidates such as multiple states in the Bronze Age Collapse, the Indus River Valley Civilisation, and the Americas after the arrival of the Spanish.

- **The Great Divergence of China (900 to 1500 AD):** The spread of wet rice farming in China caused the already dense population there to double in just 200 years, increasing the number of potential innovators for collective learning. As a result, China becomes the most advanced and powerful agrarian civilisation in this time period, *almost* achieving the first sparks of the heavy industrialisation that would kick off modernity. This "great divergence" also precipitated the European interest in trading with them, which in turn kicked off the Age of Explorations that initiated modernity.

- **Koreans Invent Moveable Metal Type (1200 AD):** While woodblock printing is efficient for distributing collective learning, each page has to be laboriously carved into a cumbersome block of wood for each new page of literature. Moveable metal type allowed for different symbols to be quickly rearranged according to what was written on the page, increasing the speed at which things could be printed, although woodblocks remained the dominant form of printing in East Asia.

- **Humans Arrive in New Zealand (1280 AD):** The great migrations of humans across the world had begun 100,000 years ago, and had intensified 64,000 years ago. The world zone of the Americas was inhabited by humans roughly 12,000 to 15,000 years ago. But even after all those millennia, it was not until the last 800 years that humans first arrived in New Zealand, nearly 60,000 years after humans had arrived in Australia just across the Tasman. With this date, all regions of the world (with the exception of the fairly uninhabitable Antarctica) were inhabited by humans.

- **Invention of the Gutenberg Press (1450 AD):** The technology of stamps and metal moveable type proliferated into Europe via the Silk Roads, which were combined with European wine press technology to create the Gutenberg Press. This kicked off a flood of literature production that rapidly increased the amount of books being spread across Europe, accelerated collective learning still further, and played a pivotal role in the start of the Scientific Revolution.

Complexity in Agrarian Civilisations

The years covered within this single chapter are full of detail, countless sociopolitical events, and the rise and fall of hundreds of empires, and thousands of ambitious dynasties. Yet it is the pride of Big History that we can view such a complex span of time with our "universal acid" connects conventional history to the broad trends of the Universe: collective learning and complexity. By zooming out, the endless catalogues of conventional history, and even the minutia of world history fade into the background, and we can view human history's overall arch and shape.

Collective learning in this period continued to accelerate as the world population increased from 250 million in 1 AD to 600 million in 1600 AD. The gradual raising of the carrying capacity was the result of the spread of agriculture into new regions of the globe, and the improvement of farming techniques by collective learning. During the incremental rise of the carrying capacity of each region, agrarian civilisations continued to be smitten with the secular cycles that influenced sociopolitical instability and micro-historical events. But overall, from the widest lens, the trend was up. The world was being filled with an increasing number of potential innovators, with 90% of them existing in Afro-Eurasia, which was increasingly being unified into a single network of collective learning by the Silk Roads. With any trade route that is forged between agrarian civilisation, or any form of writing or printing that emerges to save and transport information, comes an increase of connectivity (the second driver of collective learning after population) and we see the connectivity of agrarian civilisations increase throughout this period as well.

In terms of the shorthand for complexity, structural intricacy, or the number and diversity of building blocks, networks, and connections in a system, agrarian civilisations also represent a huge leap forward. Instead of groups of a few dozen foragers, or early farming communities of a few hundred farmers, we now have cities of tens of thousands, with people doing a dramatic range of different jobs other than farming (a greater diversity of building blocks), increasingly connected in states and empires of dozens or hundreds of towns and cities, villages and hamlets, and country farms. And between these states, the nodes and connections of trade routes are also growing stronger and more numerous. In terms of structural intricacy, complexity is increasing in agrarian civilisations. The tools, inventions, and doctrines used by those states also grow more advanced between 1 AD and 1600 AD, increasing the number and diversity of building blocks. Just bear in mind that an overall increase in population in one single state does not necessarily mean an increase in complexity. You can have 40 million in one state and 2 million in another, but in terms of their structural intricacy, they may be just as complex as each other. But more *potential innovators* in a large population increases the probability that a new innovation will be found via collective learning and thereby complexity will be increased.

In terms of energy flows, we can also see complexity increasing. As before in Early Agrarian societies, most of the energy comes from the Sun. Plants absorb this energy via photosynthesis, and these plants are then eaten by humans and animals (which humans also eat or from which humans harness their energy for labour). The food and wealth generated from farming goes to support non-farmers (artisans, scribes, soldiers, merchants, cooks, architects, kings, etc) in the rest of the agrarian civilisation. At the highest level, at the government of the state, much of the energy flows from all this farming and economic activity is taken in the form of rents, tributes, and taxation. Currency itself is representative of the energy flows, because currency represents value, and can be used for goods and services. So in order to conduct the complex business of the state, governments harness a greater *density* of energy flows (FERD) than has been seen before in foraging or early farming societies, or anything else in the Universe.

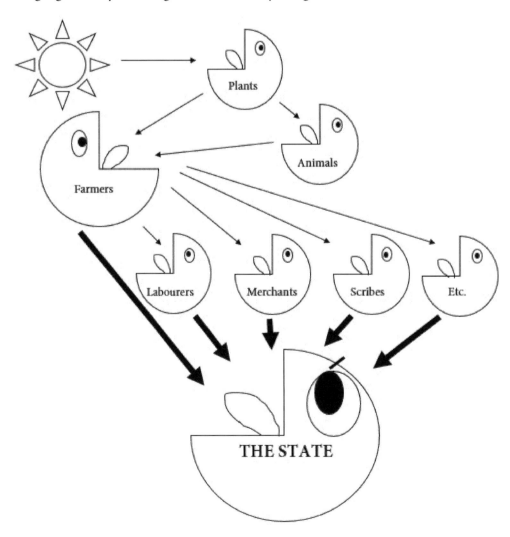

One artifact that displays this complex system of diverse component parts and energy flows is the Standard of Ur, made in 2500 BC in the Mesopotamian city of that name, which displays the social orders functioning in both peacetime and war. Essentially, all the social orders place themselves at the service of the complex system of energy flows that is the agrarian civilisation. They are all united by building blocks and energy flows in the same way as a star or organism.

In fact, the comparison of states to organisms is not without merit. An agrarian civilisation is driven to bring more territory and resources under its control in order sustain or increase its complexity. If the agrarian civilisation runs low on energy flows (is bankrupted or the tax-paying population shrinks) it spirals into the downward stages of a secular cycle of population crisis and manmade depression with civil strife and infighting, which can threaten to reduce that agrarian civilisation's structural complexity, just like an organism can starve, or else destroy the agrarian civilisation completely – for that, one needs just imagine the ruins of Ancient Rome, or the Aztecs, or Persepolis, which resemble the dead skeletons of organisms in more ways than one.

In fact, some agrarian civilisations prey on each other for much the same reason. In warfare, brutal violence is used in competition over resources and energy flows. Sometimes one state succumbs completely to the other, as depicted in the Narmer Palette from approximately 3100 BC, which depicts king Narmer, unifier of Upper and Lower Egypt, about to kill a captive. Much of the symbolism of the palette, from the crown of Narmer to the cartouche at the top is symbolic of this momentous event when one state annexed another, and brought all its energy flows under its government's control.

The Evolution of the State

The course of the past 5000 years of history consists of several trends. First, the average size and power of agrarian civilisations increased. This in turn signifies an increase in complexity as more component parts and energy flows are incorporated into the complex system that is a society. Second, there were numerous inventions throughout this period that enhanced one of the two drivers of collective learning (either population size or connectivity) and the overall global population increased accordingly. Third, despite the overall increase of the carrying capacity agrarian civilisations frequently hit their Malthusian limit and went through periods of rise and decline every few centuries. Fourth, the connections between agrarian civilisations increased as well along trade routes, the massive network of Afro-Eurasian exchange that was the Silk Roads, and eventually the establishing of connections between the world zones. This process gradually transformed individual states and separate world zones in to one global complex system through which collective learning could move faster than ever before.

We last left off with the first agrarian civilisations arising in Mesopotamia and Egypt around roughly 3000 BC. The tendrils of these civilisations gradually expanded down the Nile and out into the Mediterranean world. By 2000 BC agrarian civilisations in China and India had also emerged (though the latter would mysteriously disappear and reappear after a few centuries). By 1000 BC, the Mediterranean and China had become a patchwork of various agrarian civilisations that maintained networks of trade. On the other side of the Sahara, the first city states were stirring in West Africa, and across the world's greatest oceans agrarian civilisations began in Mesoamerican and South America. Only in Australasia and the Pacific were agrarian civilisations yet to arise.

Human societies are some of the most complex systems that we know of in the Universe. It is perhaps no surprise then that the story of agrarian civilisations over the past several thousand years involve many historical events, many peoples, many competing states and dynasties, and mounds of detail. The through-line of all this history is the evolution of the state, in terms of its complexity, its collective learning, and perhaps at a more granular level its interactions with secular cycles. It is from these lenses that we can make sense of the overall picture of conventional history.

So let us launch into the evolution of agrarian civilisations and the mammoth task of trying to summarise several thousand years of complex history. Already much of the detail in this chapter will be too microscopic for a typical Big History course, but you are more than welcome to cite any of the information contained herein for your essays. You may also consider using the world history literature in your recommended readings for more detailed research should any particular region or civilisation pique your interest! Ultimately, however, the difference between Big History and conventional history, and even world history, is that as you zoom out the millions of timeline markings of the past blur together to form long graceful lines signifying broad trends and patterns.

The Afro-Eurasian World Zone

Afro-Eurasia was the first world zone to devise agriculture, and the first to establish agrarian civilisations, so in a sense they had a "head start" in the seventh threshold of complexity. Particularly in Asia, Europe, and North Africa where agrarian civilisations were the earliest and most numerous. Afro-Eurasia is also aided by the fact that it is a massive landmass (to the extent that it could be called a super-continent) inhabited by the majority of the world's population (roughly 90% depending on the time period) who could be realistically connected in a network of collective learning in an age before long trans-oceanic sea voyages were possible. As a result, much of the tale the evolution of agrarian civilisations can be told by the Afro-Eurasian world zone in terms of rising societal complexity, collective learning, and the establishment of a wider global network of trade and information exchange. But not exclusively, as we shall see in later sections. This section is divided by major region, and does not intend to provide an exhaustive world history (which would make for a considerably longer chapter!). Instead the focus is on those key moments when complexity, collective learning, or the global trade network increased.

The Middle East

One of the world's first large empires was the Akkadian Empire in Mesopotamia which collapsed around 2150 BC. Mesopotamia would nevertheless remain a seat for a succession of some of the world's largest and cohesive empires in the ancient period. From the perspective of complexity, this meant a lot of land, energy flows, and different specialist professions, not to mention a network of millions locked in exchange of collective learning.

In the 1700s BC, the ruling seat of Mesopotamia was at the city of Babylon, where the ruler Hammurabi created the first written law code, which was then carved on phallic pillars all around the empire. A written law code was a leap forward in terms of collective learning, since it was a written document, widely dispersed that manipulated and directed the behaviour of millions if subjects. Essentially allowing for more efficient coordination of activities, economies, and ultimately the energy flow through the region. The next millennium saw almost perpetual warfare between states competing for dominance in this region, where the trappings and infrastructures of agrarian civilisations were the oldest and most well-established.

The reign of Cyrus (r. 558-530 BC) saw the unification of Persia under his control and a wave of aggressive military campaigns into Mesopotamia, the Levant, Egypt, and Anatolia (modern Turkey). He also pushed east into Afghanistan. By 480 BC, Achaemenid Empire (the name for the Persian dynasty taken from an ancestor of Cyrus's) was the largest empire so far in history, covering about 9.5% of the Earth's surface and controlling an estimated 50 million people or 40% of the world population at the time. A massive concentration of energy flows in one state.

However, in order to maintain the connectivity of this sprawling territory (both in terms of energy flows and collective learning) the Persians needed to construct roads, and a lot of them. All told they constructed a network of 13,000 kilometres of roadways. Most famously, the Persians tried to invade Greece between 490 and 480 BC, and were thrown back by a coalition of the Greek city states at the battles of Marathon, Thermopylae, and Salamis. A century and a half later, and the Persians would be conquered by Macedonia led by Alexander the Great, with all Persia's power and complexity passing into Macedonian hands.

After Alexander died 323 BC, his generals divided up the empire among themselves. Greek general Seleucus's Persia spread Greek commerce as far as Afghanistan and down into the Indus Valley and facilitated trade between Asia and the Mediterranean as a crucial connection along Afro-Eurasian trade routes. For the next thousand years successive dynasties of Persian Empires from the Seleucids, to the Parthians, to the Sasanians, would continue this role as an important hub of trade along the Silk Roads until the Arab conquest in the seventh century AD.

Thereafter the Middle East became even more deeply embedded within a wider Afro-Eurasian network due to the rapid spread of Islam across the old world. The "House of Islam" spread across the Middle East, North Africa, into Spain, and as far as India between the seventh and ninth centuries in a spate of conquests. Muhammad was born around 570 AD, and as an adult became convinced he had received a mission from Allah to undertake the spread of his religion. Muhammad had to content with the polytheistic beliefs of pre-Islamic Arab culture, and between 622 and 632 AD went on a series of campaigns to overthrow the old religion and established Islamic dominance in the Arab peninsula. Muhammad accumulated all state powers unto himself, as political leader, religious leader, military leader, and head of the judiciary. This concentrated power passed to his successor, Caliph Abu Bakr, upon Muhammad's death in 632. The energy flows of this particular society became immensely concentrated for a time.

This period of Islamic strength coincided with the weakness of the Byzantine and Persian empires who had recently fought themselves to exhaustion, and were also both in the grip of a downward trend of a secular cycle, with much infighting and civil strife. These two empires collapsed spectacularly fast in the face of Islamic invasion, with Mesopotamia, the Levant, Egypt, most of North Africa, and most of Persia by 651 AD. The armies of Islam crossed the Strait of Gibraltar in 711 AD and conquered Spain, and would have conquered France had they not been turned back at the battle of Poitiers in 732 AD. Meanwhile, far to the east, the Islamic invasion of India had begun, with numerous Hindu states falling to Islamic invaders in the eighth and ninth centuries. All these territories now formed an even more tightly unified network of collective learning, with Greek, Roman, and Hindu knowledge from across Eurasia being gathered in the Baghdad library, or "House of Wisdom", where further advancements (particularly in mathematics) were made.

The House of Islam now controlled three-quarters of former Christendom and dominated in Persian and northwest India. The total empire covered 13 million square kilometres. In terms of total energy flows being controlled by the state, this certainly would have been a new level of energy density – if the vast Islamic empire had not fragmented into pieces. The Islamic world had already split into a Sunni majority and Shia minority after the death of Muhammad in 632, in a violent dispute over his succession which resulted in numerous battles over the next few decades. Meanwhile the Umayyad clan had fought several civil wars in the later seventh century to control the rapidly expanding caliphate, as it continued to spread across the world. The Umayyads maintained a limited amount of control over the vast territory of the House of Islam, with Arab provincial governors maintaining a great deal of local control, until the Umayyads were overthrown and obliterated as a dynasty by the Abbasids in 750 AD. Thereafter, the Abbasids retained control over part of North Africa, Egypt, Mesopotamia, Persia, and Northwest India, with the Maghreb in Northwest Africa, and the Islamic holdings in Spain passing beyond their control. The remaining size of their empire fluctuating while numerous Islamic challengers, Orthodox Byzantine emperors, and Catholic crusaders invaded and fought for a slice of their territory.

The Abbasid caliphate lasted from 750 to 1258 AD. But numerous regions within this caliphate were largely autonomous powers. The high point of the Abbasids was the reign of Harun al-Rashid (r. 786-809) who managed to control the caliphate at its largest extent. During his reign, the degree of energy flows concentrated by the state was unsurpassed in world history. As wealth and knowledge filtered into the capital Baghdad, monumental architecture, the pursuit of science, industry, and trade, all advanced. Aside from China to the East, the Abbasid caliphate was one of the wealthiest and most complex agrarian civilisations of the time. After al-Rashid's death, the caliphate fragmented into a collection of local warlords, only nominally under Abbasid control. In the 900s, the Abbasid caliphate was taken over by Persians who claimed the title of caliph, and then in the 1000s the real power of the caliphate was wielded by the Turks who had migrated from Central Asia into the Middle East. Ultimately the Abbasid caliphate, in its much weakened form, was destroyed by the invading Mongols in 1258 AD, with the Siege of Baghdad resulting in the slaughter of 500,000 to 2 million inhabitants of the city. Much of the Middle East then passed into an event wider Eurasian network of the Mongol Empire.

The Mediterranean

To the west, in the Mediterranean, we see the emergence of a fairly effective trade route between agrarian civilisations, thanks to the fact that sailing allows the transportation of goods on average six times faster than a caravan could manage on land. This connected Mesopotamia and Egypt to the newly emerged kingdoms of Israel, the Phoenician colonies, Minoan Crete, and Mycenaean Greece. Facilitating this trade between different Mediterranean groups were the Minoans and the Phoenicians. The Minoans inhabited the island of Crete which between 2700 and 1700 BC served as a trading hub for goods exchanged between states in the Eastern Mediterranean. They were a largely peaceful people, without the military power to become a great empire, but they maintained their useful role as traders until their conquest by the Mycenaean Greeks in 1400 BC.

Then the Phoenicians between 1200 and 800 BC were the Mediterranean's foremost mercantile power. Their reach extended across the Mediterranean and even through the Strait of Gibraltar and as far as the Atlantic coastline of Europe. Across Europe and North Africa, the Phoenicians also set up colonies on the coasts, local hubs toward which inland trade could be directed, in order to access the wider Mediterranean trade network. It was by these means that the Western Mediterranean was opened up to agrarian civilisations. They are also known for their alphabet which was more effective than most pictographic forms of writing due to their being fewer symbols to memorise, which was another boost for literacy, expression, and collective learning.

Between 800 and 500 BC, Greece reorganised itself into powerful city states that thrived on commerce and overseas trade. The Greek cities experimented with multiple systems of government from monarchy, oligarchy, to democracy. The Greeks became quite advanced in terms of art, architecture, natural philosophy, and military tactics, all thanks to increasing collective learning. When united, they were even powerful enough to throw back an invasion by the Persian Empire. But in order to sustain their complexity, each Greek city-state could not rely upon vast tracts of agricultural land. Instead they needed to rely on the Mediterranean network of trade. So they followed the Phoenicians in the practice of overseas trade and creating trade colonies in the Mediterranean and the Black Sea. The downside of Greece being divided into city states is that they were frequently engaged in warfare with each other, with one particularly bad period being the Peloponnesian War (431-404 BC) between Athens and Sparta and their respective coalitions. This infighting left them vulnerable to external conquest by the Macedonians. Phillip II of Macedon (r. 359-336 BC) conquered Greece, and after his assassination Alexander the Great (r. 336-323 BC) conquered the entirety of the Achaemenid Empire.

Upon Alexander's death in 323 BC, his empire was carved up among his generals. But Greek philosophy and culture continued to spread as a form of collective learning. In Greek general Ptolemy's Egypt, a new trade port Alexandria was erected upon the Mediterranean coast (rather than the Nile basin) and became an important hub for commerce. Perhaps more significantly was the creation of the Library of Alexandria, which was compiled over centuries of scholars routinely collecting and copying books for posterity. At its height, the library is estimated to have contained approximately a million different books. As such it acted as an unprecedented repository of collective learning for the ancient world.

Rome first emerged as an agrarian settlement around 2000 BC, and grew to a city-state around 700 BC. They overthrew their monarchy in 509 BC and became a republic with an elected senate. Each year executive power would be possessed by two consuls who were supposed to keep each other in check. This was not a particularly democratic system, rather more oligarchic, since the majority of votes were monopolised by the landholding elite, with very little electoral power being held by the masses of common people (plebeians). Slowly the Roman plebeians began to gain some electoral power for themselves, by representative called tribunes with veto powers and a plebeian assembly that could theoretically pass legislation, but the majority of control still remained in the hands of the patricians and the senate. The fourth century BC saw Rome take to the offensive, fighting with Gallic invaders and conquering the other cities of Italy. The third and second centuries BC saw Rome go to war with Carthage in the three Punic Wars (264-146 BC). Carthage was a mercantile power based in modern day Tunisia that dominated trade in the Western Mediterranean. After several hard fought wars, brutal battles which saw the annihilation of entire Roman armies, the Romans eventually emerged victorious and completely obliterated the city of Carthage and absorbed its empire. Also in the second century BC, Rome conquered Greece.

By the end of the second century BC, Rome had become the foremost agrarian civilisation in the Mediterranean, dominating both land and sea. Only the Parthians controlling Persia to the east were powerful enough a rival to fend off their expansion. In the first century BC, the Republic transitioned to the Empire. Julius Caesar was a radical reformer who at least nominally fought to better the lives of the plebeian classes, and fought a civil war against the patrician class in order to achieve this goal. Caesar quite obviously entertained ambitious designs to permanently dominate Rome as dictator. After Caesar's assassination in 44 BC, another spate of civil infighting continued until Octavian (later Augustus) defeated all potential rivals, ending with the deaths of Marc Antony and Cleopatra and the annexation of Egypt in 30 BC, and became emperor. More precisely, he became "imperator" (commander) and "princeps" (first citizen) which do not have the royal connotations they do today, as Romans had rejected the idea of monarchy since 509 BC, but rather had the trappings of military dictatorship that were later sacralised into something more regal in the third and fourth centuries AD.

Roman emperors controlled a vast territory that at its widest extent in the second century AD covered 6.5 million square kilometres, and an estimated 70-100 million people, or an estimated 25-40% of the world's total population. Roman emperors also wielded extremely concentrated executive power, having reduced the powers of the senate from the days of the Republic. That said, life expectancies for all but the most competent emperors was fairly short. Assassination was a constant danger for emperors in the first and second centuries AD, and thereafter the empire was hit with numerous periods where provincial governors would declare themselves emperors and set off civil war after civil war.

Nevertheless, the immense wealth that came from controlling such a vast territory and the entire trade network of the Mediterranean funnelled immense energy flows into this agrarian civilisation. For as long as the empire lasted, it alone could have rivalled the might and complexity of China at the other end of Afro-Eurasia. These two great powers even interacted with each other via trade along the Silk Roads.

In terms of collective learning, the Romans profited greatly from the previous works by Greek philosophers, but also continued to develop learning of their own at places like Alexandria. Much of Roman innovation was also practical, from mass production of naval vessels to beat the Carthaginians, to opening up new land for farming with new agricultural techniques. The Romans laid down 80,000 km of roads. Ultimately, the pace of Roman collective learning slowed down, largely due to the chaos of the civil strife of the third century AD, from which the Roman Empire never fully recovered. Not even after a century of relative stability thanks to the efforts of powerful emperors like Diocletian and Constantine. Even in the fourth century AD, it was quite clear that the Roman Empire was gravely weakened, and when another depression phase of a secular cycle set in after roughly 350 AD, the Western Empire left itself vulnerable to Germanic invasions.

The period of depopulation in Western Empire in the fifth century that followed seems to have profoundly affected the collective learning of Western Europe, with numerous technologies and doctrines disappearing from the West for nearly a thousand years before their rediscovery or reinvention. This is known as a "Tasmanian Effect" where collective learning is no longer accumulated but is actually lost. Common during the Paleolithic, when oral teaching was the only way to transmit information generation by generation, it is extremely rare in agrarian civilisations that have both denser populations and writing (indeed it was the rediscovery of Roman and Greek writings in monasteries and also the delivery of them from the Islamic world that kicked off the European Renaissance). The Western Roman Empire currently stands as one of the best known candidates for a post-foraging Tasmanian Effect, although there are certainly other candidates. It also acts as a warning to what may happen to even modern societies, if they undergo a period of extreme devastation that collective learning is actually lost.

The Eastern Empire (or Byzantine Empire) centred on Constantinople managed to evade the decline of the fifth century, and actually prospered for a time until the extreme depopulation of the Justinianic Plague in 541-42 AD, the first outbreak of the bubonic plague or "Black Death", which reduced the population of the Byzantine Empire by 30-50%. Intriguingly, Western Europe was already too depopulated for the plague to spread as far as it did in 1347-48 AD. A depression phase followed with decades of elite infighting, accompanied by an exhausting war against Persia, until the Arab invasions laid both empires low. The Byzantines continued to fight off the armies of Islam in Anatolia until Constantinople itself was conquered in 1453 AD.

China

The Chinese meanwhile had transitioned from the Shang to the Zhou dynasty in a secular cycle around 1045 BC. Unlike the Mediterranean world, Zhou China was the largest power in the region and was able to annex or create vassals out of smaller states, which then had to either swear loyalty, pay taxes, provide slave labour, or all of the above. A large state that controlled most of the energy flows of the area and unified them into a single state system certainly allowed China to become one of the most complex agrarian civilisations on Earth – provided the central government could maintain effective control over such a vast territory.

The Zhou dynasty used a religious justification for their dominance of China, via the "mandate of heaven" which asserts that the forces of heaven had assigned rule of the Earth to the Zhou dynasty provided they perpetuated justice and order. If they did not, then the dynasty would lose their mandate. This would be used as a justification for royal authority, as well as the overthrow of royal dynasties for thousands of years. Zhou era philosophy also extended to the establishment of the three core paradigms of Chinese thought until the 20th century: Confucianism, Daoism, and Legalism, which Bill Wurtz concisely described as "having good morals", "go with the flow", and "fuck you, obey the law" respectively. That rather sums it up, but more nuanced definitions would describe Confucianism as the need to educate future leaders in order for them to have good morals and govern effectively, Daoism as living in harmony with the forces of "heaven and earth", and Legalism as the use of the law to an almost extreme degree to keep societal order intact. All three paradigms assisted collective learning in the sense that Confucianism prided education, Daoism allowed for some degree of natural philosophy, contemplation of nature, and proto-science, and Legalism promulgated a sophisticated system of laws that was used to govern human behaviour and thus direct energy flows to sustain that society.

Yet another secular cycle struck the Zhou dynasty in the fifth century BC, and China fragmented into smaller states, as it would for many times in its history. This was followed by the Warring States period (480-256 BC) which was witness to some of the most brutal fighting of the ancient period, and only ended when the Qin dynasty came out of the depression phase and re-established central authority by defeating all other competitors, consolidating their power in 221 BC. The Qin dynasty (221-207 BC) succeeded in being more brutal than their rivals by adopting Legalism, wherein authoritarianism, draconian punishments, and an emphasis on warfare and agriculture over philosophy or commerce were reputed to make the state strong.

The Qin dynasty only had one emperor: Qin Shi Huangdi. He certainly did innovate in military techniques and managed to field larger armies relative to population than previous periods in Chinese history. The Qin were relatively successful in centralising control over the various far flung regions of China, building roads and trade routes, and fortifications like the Great Wall of China. So long as the emperor remained strong and competent, this centralised and militaristic approach seem to keep the vast Chinese empire together. The Qin are also notable for expanding the bureaucracy, allowing for more direct government control over agrarian regions, and making sure they were literate. Chinese literature at the time still remained hand-copied, however, which slowed the pace of distribution.

Once Qin Shi Huangdi died in 210 BC and was buried in a tomb with several thousand terracotta warriors guarding him, the Han dynasty succeeded him, and lasted until 220 AD. The Han benefited greatly from the system that Qin Shi Huangdi had constructed, and managed to triple the territory they controlled by several conquests. In all, the Han gained control of 6.5 million square kilometres, or roughly the same area covered by the Roman Empire at its height. The Han also controlled a population of approximately 60 to 100 million people when their empire reached its furthest extent. In order to adequately govern such an enormous population, the Han had to multiply the number of bureaucrats even more, and to ensure that they were literate and educated administrators. As a result, the Han under

Emperor Wudi established educational institutes based on Confucian philosophy starting in 124 BC, and also instituted a system of rigorous testing for everyone wishing to enter the imperial bureaucracy. This system would continue to thrive into the nineteenth century.

China entered another crisis and depression phase of a secular cycle around 220 AD, wherein the empire broke up into rival factions once again (a common theme in Chinese history) and was not reunified for another 300 years. After centuries of warfare, China was reunited under the short-lived Sui dynasty (598-618 AD) and then the Tang dynasty (618-907 AD). This period of Chinese history saw a tremendous amount of developments in terms of societal complexity. They constructed the Grand Canal which allowed for food to be transported to the north from the more agriculturally fertile south. The network of roads expanded. Literate communications were aided by a system of messengers that extended across the empire. The Chinese also expanded their empire far into the West, increasing the size of the Chinese empire to 11.7 million square kilometres, in a series of conquests that would only be stopped when they fought the Abbasids at Syr Darya in Central Asia in 751 AD. Due to the relative decline of innovations in the Mediterranean, it is really a matter of open debate as to whether the Abbasids or the Tang dynasty was the most advanced and complex agrarian civilisation of the age.

India

As noted in the last chapter, the Indus River Valley Civilisation disappeared around 1300 BC. There followed the Vedic Age (1300-500 BC) which derives its name from the Hindu Vedas, the oldest of that religion's holy texts. This was a period characterised by a mixture of nomadic migrations fighting over territory by the so-called Aryans (there is a debate whether these nomads migrated into the region or were native to it) and communities engaged in early agrarian societies. The period is characterised by northern India being divided into chiefdoms and tiny kingdoms which fought almost perpetually for dominance. Of particular note was the Aryan use of the horse chariot against slower moving bands of foot-soldiers. By the 500s, the smaller kingdoms were coalescing into larger territories, the Mahajanapadas, which attained enough agricultural surplus to sustain growing cities in the valleys of the Indus and Ganges rivers.

In 327 BC, Alexander the Great invaded northwest India. In the subsequent campaigns of 326 and 325, Alexander won a number of battles, but imposed indirect rule (either vassal states or forming new allied kingdoms out of foes) due to the vast distance of India from either Babylon or Macedonia. Local elites would wield authority on his behalf. Shortly thereafter, Alexander's army revolted due to the many endless years of campaigning which had taken them to the furthest reaches of the known world and forced Alexander to turn back toward Babylon. Alexander punished his army by choosing the route home through the harsh deserts of northwest India and Persia, in which a large portion of his army died. Eventually Alexander reached Babylon where he died in 323 BC, at the age of only 33.

In 321 BC, after the departure of Alexander, Chandragupta paid the Greeks to remove what remained of their rule from Indian lands, and conquered large tracts of territory in northern India and established the Mauryan Empire, which lasted approximately 140 years. The Mauryan Empire flourished during that period and textiles, spices, and agriculture expanded by leaps and bounds, with trade being facilitated by a newly constructed road network. The Mauryan Empire collapsed in 185 BC, and suffered from a series of foreign invasions and occupations. Most notable is the Kushan Empire of Scythian descent from Central Europe, which played another vital link in the chain of the Silk Roads until its collapse in 225 AD. A century later, India was united under the Gupta Empire in 320 AD and lasted till 543 AD. The Gupta Empire managed to conquer much of the populous valley of the Ganges River. The first 80 years of the empire was one of immense prosperity and population growth, with many advances in the fields of agriculture, industry, and mathematics, until a secular cycle gradually broke the empire up into smaller feuding regions, a state of chaos that culminated with the assassination of Harsha and final decline of even nominal empire to smaller fiefdoms in 648 AD, and the division would last until the arrival of Islamic invaders in the eighth and ninth centuries.

Sub-Saharan Africa

For much of the ancient period, the Sahara posed an obstacle to most interactions between the agrarian civilisations of Sub-Saharan Africa and those of the Mediterranean and Middle East. Those interactions, when they did occur, were limited. Meanwhile there was bustling activity in Sub-Saharan Africa itself. Agriculture originated in West Africa roughly 5000 years ago. It slowly spread east and south over the next several millennia. There was a huge delay in agriculture's adoption in many regions because Africa is one of the most suited environments to human foraging, and one of the least forgiving in many regions for those who try sedentary farming. Nevertheless, agriculture had spread into Central Africa by 1500 BC and managed to pierce deep into the Congo with some cultures adopting agriculture by 500 BC. The practice of agriculture reached South Africa by 300 AD.

Bear in mind, that the spread of agriculture here is the spread of the lifeways most connected to the Early Agrarian Era, rather than agrarian civilisations with cities and all the key features we have discussed. Nonetheless because the seeds of agrarian civilisations had been planted (no

287

pun intended) we begin to see agrarian civilisations arising across Sub-Saharan Africa over the next several millennia of conventional history.

We have already seen how complex agrarian settlements began popping up in West Africa between 1000 and 500 BC. Around 300 AD a few of these settlements could be deemed towns and cities, and a trade network of agricultural produce, manufactured goods, gold, and slaves sprang up across West Africa. The Ghana Empire lasted from 700 to 1240 AD. They had submitted to the Mali Empire which had adopted Islam as a result of the religion coming filtering down from the caliphates to the north. It is with the entry of Islam onto the scene that West African agrarian civilisations become inextricably tied to the wider system of collective learning that was forming in Afro-Eurasia. West Africans traded extensively in gold and slaves via a newly emerging trans-Sahara trade route, where camels charted their way across the desert. Millions of African slaves made their way across the Sahara Desert toward the Middle East, with many of them dying under appalling conditions, only to face harsh treatment (and frequently castration) at the other end.

Meanwhile the rise and fall of empires in West Africa continued, with the Songhai Empire overthrowing the Mali Empire and lasting until 1591 AD. Numerous other empires like the Oyo, Benin, Ashanti, and Sokoto empires sprang up in West Africa between the fifteenth and nineteenth centuries. Further to the south, a number of other large empires emerged in the same period of time – the Kongo, Luba, Malawi, and so on – but due to the late stages of their rising, they had to deal with increasing European interference as the countries of Western Europe began taking to the seas in the fifteenth century AD. The European influence would become even more pronounced as the Age of Explorations gave way to the Age of Imperialism in the modern era.

The American World Zone

The Americas had been separated from Afro-Eurasia since humans crossed the Bering Strait between 12,000 and 15,000 years ago. People in the Americas independently discovered agriculture in Mesoamerica and the Andes, which then proceeded to spread north and south. And eventually some cultures of Central and South America began to produce agrarian civilisations. All this occurred despite the American world zone having a smaller share of the world population (approximately 8%), and thus a slightly slower pace of collective learning than many parts of Afro-Eurasia. The evolution of agrarian civilisations proceeded for thousands of years with the Atlantic providing a figurative and literal *cordon sanitaire* between the Americas and Afro-Eurasia. As such, the Americas allow us to see a fresh scenario of historical change if the variables and environments were slightly different. Pay close attention to the differences and similarities.

Mesoamerica

Some of the earliest agrarian civilisations, like the Olmecs, sprang up in Mesoamerica. It is no coincidence that this happened not far from where the Americans independently conceived agriculture. As early as 100 AD, two cities in the region had populations over 50,000 people (in what is modern Mexico and Guatemala) and possibly as high as 100,000 people. They had developed long distance exchange of crops, built monumental architecture, had a division of labour, had ruling elites, and systems of writing.

In the Basin of Mexico was the city of Teotihuacan. It began as an agrarian settlement and achieved the size of a city of 10,000 people around 100 AD. Because the region is teeming with rivers, lakes, and plenty of fertile soil, it had a fairly large carrying capacity capable of supporting a massive city of around 200,000 people at Teotihuacan's height in 500 AD. It is unclear whether Teotihuacan was the centre of a Mesoamerican empire or whether it was a city-state. Certainly it is clear that the city had to control large tracts of land in the Basin of Mexico in order to have enough agrarian surplus to sustain such a large population. While the lack of surviving written records make it difficult to know much of the history of this city, ancient murals seem to indicate Teotihuacan was ruled by a theocracy of priests, which is something it has in common with the earliest city-states of Mesopotamia. There was certainly a division of labour, with a temples, monumental architecture, large ornate dwellings for the rich, and signs of various forms of craftsmanship and engineering. We also know that Teotihuacan had trading links with the densely populated regions of Mexico and Central America, making it a massive hub for collective learning. Teotihuacan experienced severe droughts in 535 AD and it appears the city when into significant decline in terms of population, shrinking to about 50,000 people. Then in the 600s or 700s, the city was razed to the ground by a group of unknown invaders. This sequence of events may indicate a secular cycle. But a smaller city remained at the site until modernity, being absorbed by state after state.

To the southeast, the Mayan Empire in the Yucatan and Guatemala was a powerful agrarian civilisation between 200 and 900 AD, and continued in a reduced form until the Spanish arrived. Much of their activities include a triumph of agricultural engineering in a rather infertile landscape hostile to many forms of agriculture. The Mayans drained swamps for more fertile soils and carved nicely terraced fields into the hillsides. Mayan irrigation also was quite advanced for the time. Within the 50 cities of the Mayan Empire, there was a clear division of labour, with a clear king and aristocracy, and caste of priests/shaman. Like in many early agrarian civilisations, there was definitely a blurred line between royalty and the divine. Mayan kings were claimed to be able to speak with the gods, and were even were considered divine themselves. The priestly caste was responsible for communing with nature, often venerating different animals, especially the jaguar, and managing the calendar. The Mayan calendar was particularly important for figuring out the passing of seasons for agriculture, as did the calendars of most agrarian civilisations. But the astronomy of the Mayan calendar is particularly impressive in that they managed to fairly accurately calculate the orbit of the planets and the length of a year on Earth. The reliability of these calculations wasn't surpassed by most agrarian civilisations until modernity.

Mayan collective learning was somewhat limited by the small size of their population (they covered only a small area in Mesoamerica) and the limited trade that occurred north and south at the time. Nevertheless there are clear signs of a great deal of innovation over the centuries of their history. Mayan writing is largely pictographic, with the thousands of symbols occasionally being used for syllabic pronunciation. A more condensed alphabet was not conceived by the collapse of Mayan civilisation. It would appear that the majority of the population aside from the priestly class and most of the bureaucracy were illiterate. But this is not unusual for an agrarian civilisation. It is difficult to gauge the range of subjects covered by Mayan writing, since while 15,000 carvings survive, the overwhelming majority of Mayan books were destroyed by the Spanish. A tremendous loss to the historical record, and arguably a form of Tasmanian Effect.

The Mayan collapse between 750 and 900 AD may have been the result of a secular cycle, possibly exacerbated by environmental exhaustion. The period includes a massive amount of depopulation and the abandonment of cities. A reduced Mayan civilisation continued to persist in the Yucatan peninsula, enjoying another period of expansion and growth from 900 to 1250 AD, until the society fractured into several smaller states between 1250 and 1500 AD. This may represent yet another secular cycle. At this point the Mayans had largely abandoned writing, the cities were considerably smaller, but many of the key traits of agrarian civilisations like a division of labour, agrarian surplus, and monumental architecture remained.

Meanwhile in the Basin of Mexico, the city of Tula succeeded Teotihuacan as the region's predominant state between 750 and 1200 AD. It too appears to have fallen on hard times and was similarly violently destroyed, with its population reduced. Again it is likely this indicates a secular cycle. The region remained in a state of instability and violence, with no city-state managing to restore order until the arrival of the Aztecs.

Which brings us to those lovely people. The Aztecs were foraging/pastoralist nomads from northern Mexico who invaded the Basin of Mexico in 1325 AD. To some degree, the Aztecs mirror the story of the Germans invading and taking over the former provinces of the Roman Empire. The Aztecs established a city which they called Tenochtitlan or "city of cactus fruit" on an island in the middle of Lake Texacoco. The city eventually reached a population of 200,000. In 1428 AD, they allied with two other city-states and began to conquer the surrounding region. By 1519 all of Central Mexico fell under their control, including a population of 5-10 million people.

The Aztecs have all the trappings of an agrarian civilisation. The diversification of labour divided society into merchants who travelled widely into North and South America, and could possibly have set up a massive network of collective learning had they not been interrupted by the Spanish. Within the cities, artisans engaged in the production of clothes, weapons, jewellery, pottery, and a fabulous array of architecture and artwork. The Aztecs had a very firmly established religious system presided over by priests, who were in turn governed by a ruling military elite. The military elite in turn elected two leaders, much like the Roman consuls, to make governing decisions. The warrior elite would grant land to vassals in exchange for services and taxation. The Aztec educational system was divided into training for warriors and training for those who would go on to become literate bureaucrats and scribes. The education system varied in quality depending on the social orders involved, while the larger farming population did not receive much formal instruction by comparison. The Aztecs also ruled over a fairly large cohort of slaves, and like many early agrarian civilisations those slaves were taken from populations conquered in war, though occasionally one could be forced into slavery if one could not repay debts. The religion itself involved heavily ritualised human sacrifices atop pyramids, from which blood would run down to the ground. Human-sacrifice was practically industrialised with the Aztec priests being in almost perpetual operation killing about 10,000 to 20,000 people per year. The Aztec Empire was the first massive empire in

Mesoamerica and was still quite young chronologically when Cortes and the conquistadors arrived in 1519. Thereafter a combination of devastating European diseases and Spanish brutality completely destroyed the Aztec Empire in 1521. It is only a matter of speculation how the agrarian civilisations would have continued to evolve in Mesoamerica had the collision with Afro-Eurasia been forestalled for another few centuries.

The Andes

What is perhaps astounding about the agrarian civilisations of the Andes is that they evolved under pretty unfavourable conditions. Much of the coastline is too dry for reliable agriculture, save the riverbeds. The Andes start very close to the coastline (100 kilometres) and impose massive obstacles not only to agriculture but transportation. Yet agrarian civilisations continued to sprout and grow in size. The Moche were building agrarian settlements and cities between 100 and 700 AD. The Wari dwelt in the highlands between 650 and 1000, and were quite successful at both pastoralism and agriculture. Both cultures left behind impressive architecture and artwork. The Chimu Empire emerged around 870 AD and lasted until their annexation by the Incan Empire in 1470 AD. The Chimu Empire managed to united most of the region in a unitary state. Their capital, Chan Chan, achieved a population of approximately 120,000 people, a similar size to the larger cities of Mesoamerica and many of the notable cities of Afro-Eurasia – a tremendous feat considering the constraints of the environment.

The Incan Empire remains the best known agrarian civilisation of the region by virtue of their being the last and having conquered and absorbed the others in the region. The Incans established their first city at Cuzco in 1200 AD. At the time they were no more remarkable than the other city-states and large agrarian settlements of the period. However, the Incans began a spate of conquests around 1438, and appear to have been largely successful. Much of the region inhabited by agrarian civilisations was subjugated by 1471 AD. Then the Incans went further and conquered a huge stretch of land running down the spine of South America between 1471 and 1493 AD. The empire stretched about 4000 kilometres from modern Ecuador to Chile, or roughly the same distance from Tasmania to Darwin. However, the Andes environment had a low carrying capacity and the entire empire encompassed perhaps 12-20 million people. But this certainly was a large amount of energy flows controlled by one empire compared to the rest of the Americas, and many agrarian civilisations in Afro-Eurasia. Like the Aztecs, it would appear the Incans were just getting started in establishing the region's first large sprawling empires before they were cut short by the Spanish. Perhaps the best equivalent milestone would be the establishment of the Akkadian Empire or Shang China in Afro-Eurasia.

The Incan Empire bears some similarities but also significant differences to other agrarian civilisations, perhaps as a result of the fact it evolved in a rather unusual environment. For the similarities, it was ruled by an emperor who claimed to be descended from the gods (seldom did agrarian civilisations come up with a better reason for someone to wield executive power). The emperor claimed to own, in theory, all lands in the empire in the same way European feudal vassals ultimately gained their lands from the crown. The priestly classes were closely linked with royalty and the aristocracy, usually being derived from those higher orders. They practiced human sacrifices occasionally, but not on the industrial scale of the Aztecs. The Incans constructed monumental architecture, mountain fortifications, and thousands of kilometres of roads to connect the empire. Some of these roadways were 10 metres wide. Like in China, the Incans had a sophisticated transportation and courier service, and it is said that fish could be delivered from the Pacific Ocean to Cuzco within two or three days. Bear in mind that the horse had been hunted to extinction in the Americas 11,000 years ago, and the trip was made by people running on foot.

For the differences, the Incans did not have a sophisticated form of taxation, but instead subjects periodically owed the emperor various forms of indentured servitude: acting as soldiers, farmers on his lands, and working as artisans, architects, craftsmen, and textile workers. The Incans did not have a formal system of currency, per se, and merchants did not arise as a class as they did in most agrarian civilisations. Perhaps as a result of the narrow roadways that ran along the Andes Mountains, the elite were able to maintain a stranglehold on the shipping of agricultural goods. As a result, the elite took a huge helping of all agrarian surplus and then distributed the rest amongst the wider population. One could consider this the agrarian equivalent of a "command economy" though there certainly was no pretense of equal distribution of wealth.

Most intriguingly the biggest difference is in the Incan method of record keeping. The Incans did not use pictographs or an alphabet, nor wrote records on paper, papyrus, or chipped in stone. Instead they used a complex system of strings called a "quipu". Several dozen or hundred strings would hang from a central hanger. Encoded on each string would be a series of knots. A different knot would symbolise a different concept, and its meaning would change depending on how far down the string it was. The colour of the string itself would also change the meaning of the sequence of knots. We know for certain this system was used to record logistical information, just like the earliest writing in other regions, and there is marginal evidence that more complex sequences of knots could encode prose. Quipu was a highly specialised skill and took years of training, meaning that only the most educated scribes and bureaucrats possessed it, while the wider populace remained illiterate. Not only does this make it difficult to learn more about Incan history (the practice of quipu was lost in a Tasmanian Effect after the Spanish conquest) but it undoubtedly impeded certain forms of collective learning. That said, there are a few qualifications to be made. First, most collective learning in most agrarian civilisations happened by oral tradition (like parents teaching children how to farm) and mimicry (when it came to artisanal trades). Most people in most agrarian civilisations were illiterate. Many of the early writing systems were limited and pictographic. Writing was useful for retaining information and expressing more abstract and convoluted ideas. It is likely that the Incans would have needed to develop a more efficient system of writing had their agrarian civilisation continued to evolve in isolation. But for the time being it seemed to function for their needs.

The Americas Beyond

The nature of human habitation and society beyond the lands of the Aztecs and the Incans appear to either be composed of early agrarian societies and foraging societies. In the Amazon, agriculture had taken root (no pun intended again) approximately 4000 years ago after the practice had spread from the Andes and Mesoamerica. However, agriculture was difficult in the Amazon due to poor soil fertility, and they never appeared to have gained the agrarian surplus to create cities. That said, the inhabitants of the Amazon appear to have created reasonably large villages and settlements of a few hundred or even a thousand people. In the deeper regions of the Amazon, people remained foragers. Some cultures practiced cannibalism. Other cultures mixed rudimentary farming with foraging. Further south, toward the Horn of South America, some people remained foragers until the modern era.

A similar pattern plays out in North America, with agrarian civilisations appearing nearest the equator, and with early agrarian and foraging societies appearing the further away from the equator one moves. The Pueblo societies of the (US) American Southwest started farming around 3000 years ago, and managed to create large agrarian settlements by 600 AD. The most impressive of these is at Chaco Canyon, built between 850 and 1150 AD, where approximately 5000 people lived in two to four storey buildings constructed in the side of a cliff. In the (US) American South and Midwest, the so-called "mound builders" adopted agriculture in approximately 500 AD. The mounds are attached to a burial culture that extends over a surprising amount of territory. The mound sites themselves were once inhabited by agrarian villages of a few hundred to few thousand people, with some evidence of monumental architecture and fortification, but little evidence of division of labour or the existence of large cities. Beyond these settlements in the Great Plains, California, the Eastern seaboard, and Canada, were semi-sedentary cultures that mixed farming and foraging, and many cultures that exclusively foraged.

If it were not for the arrival of Europeans in the Age of Explorations, it is likely that agriculture would have continued to spread across North and South America. And certain early agrarian regions would likely have, via collective learning, improved agriculture to the point that they too produced agrarian civilisations. Or perhaps like large parts of Africa, Central Asia, and the world zone of Australasia, the majority of American cultures would have rejected the oppressive nature of agriculture and agrarian civilisations. It is an interesting counter-factual history to run. If the Americas were the only world zone populated by humans, how would history have turned out? But all this is speculative. By 1500 AD, time had run out for the separate experiment. The world had begun to be agonisingly thrust together into a single global system.

Australasia and the Pacific

The past few chapters involving the rise of agriculture unfortunately has produced a neglect of two of the four world zones. That is a product of the fact that the lifeways of these world zones largely remained the same as they had for thousands of years (with the exception of early farmers in New Guinea). Australasia and the Pacific evaded the malnutrition, disease, warfare, and increasing social stratification that came with agrarian civilisations. Foraging lifeways remained unchanged in fundamentals from when humans first entered the Australasian world zone 60,000 years ago, and these lifeways were not much altered when humans entered the Pacific world zone in the last 5000 years (with the exception of the Solomons 40,000 years ago). But they were humans who benefited from generations of collective learning. Their skillsets were immensely attuned to their lifestyle. Instead of filling one's brain with the minutia of farming techniques, or military tactics, or religious dogma, one had a full intellectual view of how to survive in nature. Drop an agrarian or modern person into the Outback, for instance, and they would not have the skillset to survive very long. Yet the skills of a forager, built up over many generations of collective learning, allowed them to survive in even the harshest of environments and prosper in the more bountiful ones.

The difference in lifeways did, however, affect population sizes. While Afro-Eurasia had approximately 90% of the world's population thanks to thousands of years of agriculture and the rise of agrarian civilisations (but not too much thanks since it made the world zone a hotbed of deadly contagious diseases), the Americas contained 8-10% of the world population, the Pacific and Australasia combined held roughly 1-2% of the world's population. Australia, the largest landmass, had a population of oscillating between 500,000 to 800,000 people in a world that agriculture had filled with hundreds of millions. Tasmania had a population of a few thousand, and the small islands of the Pacific were home to a few hundred to thousand people apiece. This did impact collective learning in terms of number of potential innovators, just as the tendency to exist in small disconnected information impacted connectivity and transmission of information. But all that pales in comparison to the lack of immunity to the disgusting cocktail of Afro-Eurasian disease that would devastate Australasia, the Pacific, and also the Americas, as we shall see in the next chapter.

Notably, in Tasmania you see an extreme decline of collective learning. Humans migrated into Tasmania via a land bridge from Australia approximately 34,000 years ago. For millennia there must have been communication between the cultures of Australia and Tasmania because their toolkits remained as sophisticated as each other. Then the land bridge was covered by rising seas approximately 10,000 years ago. The small population that Tasmania's carrying capacity could support were then isolated for millennia. Between 8000 and 3000 years ago, many tools gradually start to disappear from the archaeological record. There quite simply weren't enough people to pass on all knowledge by oral tradition. By 200 years ago, the inhabitants of Tasmania no longer used controlled fire in hearths, bone tools, spears, compound tools, sewing of clothes, or most forms of fishing despite Tasmania being an island. In short, many of the technologies possessed by humans in Africa 100,000 years ago were lost. This is the most pronounced disappearance of collective learning in human history, and resulted from the loss of a large population of potential innovators and any connectivity between groups in mainland Australia.

In Australia itself, we see a diversity of productive techniques. In South Australia, eel aquaculture managed to support large semi-sedentary populations, and perhaps even settlements of thousands. Fire-stick "farming" was also immensely productive in clearing brush, killing poisonous animals, killing and cooking animals for food, and unearthing edible roots and tubers. But in terms of domestication of plants and animals, the results were limited. Large parts of Australia are desert or dense forest, and many regions have rather poor soils for most forms of early agriculture. There also are not many animals that are easily domesticated. That said, why would the Australians want to make a painful transition to sedentism and early agriculture if they did not have to? Remember back to the Natufians, the "trap of sedentism", and the appalling drop of the standard of living from the chapter on early agriculture.

The Pacific world zone meanwhile is tricky to place in a Big History chronology. Humans migrated fully across the Pacific only in the last 5000 years, long after the other world zones had been settled, and around the end of the period that the other world zones were adopting agriculture or even agrarian civilisations. It also requires some qualifications. Humans arrived in the Solomon Islands close to New Guinea roughly 40,000 years ago – not long after humans first arrived in the region. But to spread across the entire Pacific world zone it required much longer sea voyages on rafts and boats with no promise of reaching land out in the fast wide ocean. Then 5000 years ago, the Austronesian language group that inhabited Southeast Asia (most likely Taiwan) spread across the rest of the islands of the Pacific, reaching Vanuatu, Fiji, and Kiribati by 3000 years ago. These peoples had domesticated animals from their host region, including chickens, pigs, and dogs, which they transported with them. Polynesia (a far flung region of islands including Hawaii, Tonga, and Easter Island or Rapa Nui) was settled between 400 and 1200 AD. The settlement of New Zealand was delayed until approximately 1280 AD because of the lack of sailing winds blowing down from the north to make navigation feasible. The most intriguing thing about the Pacific world zone is its diversity. The smaller islands only supported populations of a few hundred, and we see a similar simplification in toolkits as these small populations became isolated and shed unnecessary collective learning that wasn't passed down by oral tradition. But larger island chains like the Hawaiian islands supported up to 30,000 people, and we see a degree of domestication and even irrigation to the point that we could almost call deem it an agrarian society (scholars still debate this point).

The Silk Roads

We see collective learning manifesting itself in a variety of ways across all four world zones, depending on the needs and constraints of the environment. However, it is clear that Afro-Eurasia, with 90% of the world's population had a distinct advantage in collective learning as we approached the modern era. There were many agrarian civilisations spread across the Afro-Eurasian "supercontinent" all of whom could potentially come into contact with each other and exchange (or steal) ideas and innovations. Nevertheless for the majority of the Era of Agrarian Civilisations, these different regions were separated by vast distances, huge deserts, and impenetrable forests, not to mention the possibility of any traveller or trader being murdered along the way. So for the majority of the past 5000 years of agrarian civilisations, the transmission of information was rather slow across Afro-Eurasia. In a sense, the different regions highlighted earlier in this chapter may well have been different disconnected world zones anyway! But all that was to change with the start of the so-called Silk Roads, which sent collective learning in Afro-Eurasia into overdrive.

Collective learning had been transmitted piecemeal across Afro-Eurasia for millennia. The spread of agriculture into different regions from the hubs of Mesopotamia, East Asia, and West Africa, is one such example. Although this gradual adoption took centuries or even thousands of years. Collective learning was also spread by warfare, whether it be with the establishment of massive empires like that of Alexander the Great, or the spread of Islam across Africa, the Middle East, and India. The odd merchant might also stumble across the trade goods of a distant land and circulate them within their own local network, whether it be the Mediterranean or the valleys of the Yangzi and Yellow Rivers. However, the first pan-world zone trade route did not take hold until 50 BC, relatively "recently" in both human history and Big History. It was at this point that trade goods and collective learning first crossed from China to India, to Persia, to the Mediterranean.

Along this complex web of trade routes ran material goods, yes, but also religions, philosophies, inventions, and mathematical ideas. The most famous and straightforward example of the last of these is the invention of the Hindu numerical system which pre-Islamic Arab merchants picked up in the fifth century AD. Thereafter, the Islamic Conquest spread the numerical system across the "House of Islam" and aided their own advances in mathematics (largely piggy-backing off the Greek knowledge contained in the lands they had just conquered). The numerical system often mistakenly called "Arab numerals" then was transmitted by Arab merchants into a backward medieval Europe, still dwelling in the ruins of the Roman Empire, which slowly replaced the clunkier and less functional Roman numeral system. Without the adoption of Hindu-Arab numerals, it is highly unlikely that European science, engineering, and mathematics would have advanced as far or as quickly as they did. The pan-world zone trade route amounted to more than just the sale of silk or spices, but rather the enhancement of collective learning.

The Silk Roads began around 50 BC as the result of nomadic peoples trading more with the rapidly multiplying agrarian civilisations across Afro-Eurasia. The most integral nomadic peoples at the start of the Silk Roads were the Scythians, Wusun, Xiongnu, and Yuezhi. It is perhaps not a surprise that the most densely populated and most complex agrarian civilisation of the age, China, kickstarted the exchange of trade down the Silk Roads (perhaps one could argue that the Romans were equal in complexity at the time, but they were not the most densely populated and as a result had fewer agricultural or manufactured products to sell). In fact, it was China that remained the centre of gravity for trade until the 19th century, whereupon industrialised countries managed to compensate for the imbalance of population by industrial production, until the modern age where the demographic pull of gravity has us heading once again toward Chinese market dominance.

The Chinese engagement with nomadic peoples began a few decades earlier when Emperor Wudi (r.141-87 BC) sent out a trade mission to Central Asia. When the leader of the mission, Zhang Qian, emerged from the western deserts 12 years later emaciated and half dead, he spoke of the economic advantages of trade with the nomads. Naturally, Zhang also advocated military conquest in order to assure their economic cooperation. By 50 BC, Chinese exports flooded Middle Eastern and Mediterranean markets. The primary product was the luxury good of silk, from which the trade route gets its namesake. Silk was highly in demand by the elite in pretty much any region or time period. It is colourful, flashy, fashionable, and feels good on the private parts and nipples. There was also a run of appeal on Chinese iron, which was slightly harder and durable than its Western equivalents but certainly felt less pleasant on the private parts and nipples. Arab and Aksum traders also made a fortune as middlemen of the sale of spices from India and China to the Middle East and Mediterranean. In return, the West gave the East grapes, manufactured products, and horses. But there was no doubt the balance of trade lay with the larger populations of Asia.

The land-based route of the Silk roads was an agonising journey from East Mediterranean ports across the grit of Mesopotamia and Persia, and across numerous mountain ranges and deserts into India and China. These Central Asian routes not only promised a harsh commute but engagement with numerous nomadic and imperial forces which would soon as kill and rob you as let you pass. Otherwise, the sea route took one down the Red Sea to Aksum (which made a fortune allowing its tiny population to become a mercantile superpower in the first millennium BC) and then on to one of the many ports of India, and then onward to Indochina and South China. It was by these sea routes that Islam spread from India to Malaya and Indonesia.

Secular cycles disrupted the Silk Roads for a time in the third century AD as Han China collapsed, Rome entered a period of civil infighting, and the South and Central Asian trade routes fell prey to numerous nomadic invasions. The Silk Roads then passed into the night while human beings engaged in their most common hobby of killing each other. After several centuries of slaughter, the Tang dynasty arose in China in 618 AD and the "House of Islam" forcibly established itself in the Middle East and North Africa by 650 AD. Chinese and Muslim merchants engaged with each other in trade and filtered the results of their economic intercourse piecemeal across the rest of Eurasia. The Chinese and Muslim powers clashed for dominance over Central Asia and came to a standstill a century later.

The two disadvantaged partners of the Silk Roads relationship, Africa and Europe, began to trade increasingly again with the rest of the Silk Roads in the eleventh century AD. The European kingdoms were gradually starting to recover from centuries of decline and chaos, and the Italian mercantile states of Europe began to reinvigorate their seaborne trade routes. The thirst for eastern goods increased as new items began to filter back to Europe via the Crusades. The Sahel kingdoms and empires of West Africa meanwhile adopted Islam and engaged with the gold and slave trade across the Sahara. While West Africa certainly did not possess the spices and many manufactured goods of the East, they did possess gold in abundance, which allowed them "buy-in" and engage with the Afro-Eurasian market. Thus by the eleventh century AD the agrarian civilisations of West Africa entered regular trade and contact with the rest of the Afro-Eurasian world, and the Silk Roads truly included all the super-continent.

The upshot of this is that Afro-Eurasia now had a conduit through which collective learning could flow through hundreds of different agrarian civilisations on a super-continent which in 1000AD was populated by roughly 220 to 300 million people. The overwhelming majority of trade did was not carried by one merchant from one end of the Silk Roads to another, but rather goods were traded piecemeal from one location to another, gradually working their way down the Silk Roads. So the transmission of trade goods and information could take years or even generations to travel across Afro-Eurasia. Nevertheless, the Silk Roads were kicking off a slow, creeping revolution in Afro-Eurasia, which contemporaries would not have noticed at the time but would soon provoke massive changes in human history.

Meanwhile a sharp increase in the Chinese population after the tenth century created the "First Great Divergence" of collective learning, which rapidly advanced numerous technologies and manufacturing practices. Thus the trade goods of China became even more desirable and this intensified the desire for trade in the rest of Afro-Eurasia. In the past thousand years, Europeans began to make increasingly bolder attempts to secure a more regular flow of trade from the east with traders trying to reach China directly. From this perspective, the Silk Roads acted as a direct catalyst for the beginning of European explorations and globalisation. We shall discuss the First Great Divergence of China more in the next chapter. And here we rest as the Silk Roads intensified and the market incentives for the Age of Exploration had begun.

The Evolution of Printing (220 to 1450 AD)

The development of writing is important in that it allowed human knowledge to be written down and stored, without it having to constantly pass through a game of telephone from mouth to mouth, as it did for 315,000 years in the Palaeolithic and early agrarian era. The greatest limitation to written knowledge from the perspective of collective learning is the circulation. The vast amount of collective learning was still done orally in the pre-modern period, with all the slowness and flaws that method produces. Literacy still remained in the hands of the few. It was the province of scribes, bureaucrats, philosophers, and the elite. Written works remained relatively scarce until the printing press. Transmission of the vast bulk of cultural innovations, from farmer to his son, or from artisan to apprentice, still was done by the oral tradition. Printing, however, allowed ideas to circulate among a wider and wider circle of innovators.

In the Han period, the Chinese wrote on bone or bamboo. Original Chinese printing was done with woodblocks, emerging at the end of the Han period in 220 AD. Then with the introduction of woodblock printing, the Han began to make paper out of silk, rice straw, and wooden pulp. The cheaper paper became, the more output of works and documents there was. Each page had to be carved into the blocks, slowing efficiency. Woodblocks were extremely bulky and hard to store and transport. The carver did not necessarily have to be literate, though a certain degree of artisanship was required, with every new copy or variation being started from scratch.

In 1045 AD, Bi Sheng invented movable type, where words were placed onto clay tablets which, while large and cumbersome, could be rearranged to create a new sequence of words and then be imprinted on the page. Until the twentieth century, Chinese printing was still dominated by the woodblock, which took longer to produce new books. The expansion of printing in the Song period in China (960-1279 AD) made literacy and books fairly universal among the elite and bureaucracy of the time. As opposed to the West in the early medieval period, with its largely illiterate kings and nobility, even Charlemagne could not properly read or write. Chinese woodblock printing on paper and silk began in the seventh century AD, with the first surviving specimens from the eighth. By the tenth century numerous philosophical, scientific, and agricultural works were regularly produced. Some books had a circulation of thousands, especially those sanctioned by the government, while frequently woodblock editions had a print run of a few hundred. Bureaucrats and the elite dominated book consumption until the late Ming period. From 1644 AD onward, however, books became available to the middling and lower orders, provided they were literate.

The Koreans in the 1200s AD invented a metal moveable type. The advantage of metal moveable type is it is durable, smaller and easier to rearrange, and ultimately produces books at a faster rate. The first book using it was the 50 volume Code of Etiquette (1234 AD). The Koreans did not use a press of any kind. They laid thin paper over inked type and took the impression by rubbing it with a wooden spatula. This was painfully slow in comparison to a printing press. Nevertheless, with woodblocks or metal moveable type applied by spatulas, the impact of early printing in China and Korea was to reproduce more copies of written knowledge at a faster rate than could be done by hand, increasing the number of books in circulation and the array of knowledge that could reach any one person who was literate.

In the Middle East printing did not catch on until much later, and Muslim states continued to rely on hand copied works until a few centuries ago. In 751 AD, the Arabs acquired paper from the Chinese and by 900 AD, the hand-written book trade in the Middle East grew by leaps and bounds. But the Arabs did not fully adopt printing techniques from the Chinese, and this may have slowed their collective learning comparative to either Europe or East Asia, and may explain part of their technological stagnation in the coming centuries. It is notable, however, that woodblock techniques were used by Arabs to stamp amulets and playing cards, a practice that was later passed to Europeans during the Crusades.

In Europe, Gutenberg's printing press was invented around 1450 AD and combined metal moveable type with a wine press for quick composition of new pages and then relatively fast imprinting upon paper. It utterly revolutionised the transmission of knowledge: both Renaissance translations of antiquity and new ideas of contemporaries. To give you an idea of the scale of the revolution that swept Europe, it is well to look at some numbers. During the sixth century AD Benedictine monasteries made a rule of housing around 50 books. And Benedictine monasteries were more conscientious than most. The monasteries were of course vital to the preservation of knowledge and literature from Antiquity that survived to be handed down to the West. The largest library in the mid-fifteenth century West was that of the Vatican. It contained around 2000 books. That was the largest library in medieval Europe before Gutenberg – a few thousand – while after the printing press a private scholar of middling rank could easily acquire that many in the seventeenth or eighteenth century. There were perhaps half a dozen libraries with 500 books or more in the possession of kings or prominent noblemen in the early fifteenth century. In addition there were libraries of 50-100 books in a few dozen locations, either aristocratic or ecclesiastical.

By contrast, there was an abrupt increase in the number of books after c.1450 AD – an influx of books that was by no means gradual. There were an estimated 8 million copies of books published in the short period 1450-1500 AD. In just the space of 50 years this quite likely exceeds the entire amount of books that were hand-copied in Europe since the year 500 AD. In the 1460s, while printing technology was still its infancy, three men could make 200 copies of a book in 100 days with a Gutenberg-style printing press. The same amount of copies would take 45 scribes two years. And over the next century, printing presses became more efficient and more common. By 1480, there were 380 printing presses in Europe and between 1500 and 1600 AD 140-200 million books were printed. This proffered the Europeans a tremendous advantage in collective learning that aided the spread of the Renaissance and Reformation and would trigger the Scientific Revolution.

In comparison Chinese woodblock printing produced 250,000 separate titles, with half of them being produced between 1644 and 1911. The abysmal pace of woodblock printing was not improved until the twentieth century, seriously hampering diffusion of knowledge compared to Europe, which by the nineteenth century had adopted the even more efficient roller press. Similarly in the Middle East, which did not adopt printing until 300 years after Gutenberg, relatively few handwritten documents survive from the period before 1500. Between 1500 and 1700, at least 600,000 hand-copied manuscripts are known to have been produced. In the case of printing, Gutenberg's designed allowed for millions upon millions of books to be printed and distributed throughout Europe after 1450. This made a major impact on the dissemination of Graeco-Roman knowledge in the Renaissance and ultimately facilitating the spread of the Scientific Revolution and the Enlightenment. Meanwhile, during this production and expansion of connectivity, the Middle East missed out on the Gutenberg revolution completely and the Chinese continued to labour at woodblock printing and inefficient clay tablets. This was a major blow for collective learning in two powerful regions of Eurasia that is not often recognised and goes some way to explain why Europe pulled ahead technologically in the modern period.

Essay Writing Exercise

For this exercise, consider the following essay questions:

What is the most important turning point in human evolution?

What was the greatest change in the human condition caused by the advent of agriculture?

Are there any predictable patterns or 'laws of history' visible across 5,000 years of agrarian civilisations?

What single cause did most to bring about the profound changes encompassed by the 'modern revolution' (1750-present)?

Pick one of the questions. Write up a thesis statement, introduction, and essay outline. Exchange your work with one of your peers and marking according to the course rubric by which your instructors will mark your essays. If you are reading this book independently from a university course, put your work in front of an intelligent friend and ask them to evaluate it on the basis of a standard essay rubric (you will easily be able to find one online).

Further Reading

Adas, Michael. Islamic and European Expansion: The Forging of a Global Order. Philadelphia: Temple University Press, 2001.

Allsen, Thomas. Culture and Conquest in Mongol Eurasia. Cambridge: Cambridge University Press, 2001.

Bairoch, Paul. Cities and Economic Development: From the Dawn of History to the Present. trans. Christopher Brauder. Chicago: University of Chicago Press, 1988.

Bentley, Jerry. Old World Encounters: Cross-Cultural Contacts and Exchanges in Pre-Modern Times. Oxford: Oxford University Press, 1993.

Biraben, J. R. "Essai sur l'évolution du nombre des homes" Population vol. 34 (1979) pg. 13–25.

Christian, David. Maps of Time: An Introduction to Big History. Berkeley: University of California Press, 2004.

Christian, David. "Silk Roads or Steppe Roads? The Silk Roads in World History" Journal of World History vol. 11., no. 1 (2000), pg. 1-26.

D'Altroy, Terence. The Incas. Malden: Blackwell, 2002.

Diamond, Jared. Guns, Germs, and Steel: The Fates of Human Societies. London: Vintage, 1998.

Ehret, Christopher. An African Classical Age: Eastern and Southern Africa in World History, 1000 BC to AD 400. Charlottesville: University Press of Virginia, 1998.

Flannery, Tim. The Future Eaters: An Ecological History of the Australasian Lands and People. Chatswood: Reed, 1995.

Jones, Rhys. "Fire Stick Farming" Australian Natural History, (Sept. 1969), pg. 224-228.

McNeill, J.R. and William H. McNeill. The Human Web: A Bird's-Eye View of World History. New York: W.W. Norton, 2003.

Strayer, Robert. Ways of the World: A Global History. Boston: St. Martin's Press, 2009.

CHAPTER 11

THE AGE OF EXPLORATIONS

Or,

WHY GLOBALISATION

IS MORE THAN JUST

MCDONALDS AND STARBUCKS

BEING ON EVERY EFFING

STREET CORNER

The Unified Global System

We have watched agrarian civilisations evolve in the Afro-Eurasian and American world zones. Agrarian states have grown more technologically complex, they have developed their systems of writing and printing, and they occupied more territory. Collective learning has gradually raised the carrying capacity so that by 1200 AD the world population was approximately 400 million. This was not without the dips and declines of secular cycles, however. After threshold 7, the origins of agriculture, collective learning did not rise fast enough to prevent periods of population strain, famine, and manmade sociopolitical instability ever few centuries. For instance, in 1 AD the world population was roughly 250 million. But after downward spiralling secular cycles in the Roman Empire, Han China, and numerous other agrarian civilisations, the world population had shrunk to 200 million by 600 AD. Yet gradually innovations in agriculture do raise the carrying capacity and by 1200 AD the world had not only recovered it had surpassed the old ancient maximum.

Yet another tremendous breakthrough would be required to end agrarian secular cycles. This breakthrough would have to be as earth-shattering and life-changing as the first transition from foraging to agriculture in the last major surge of complexity. That would come in the form of the Industrial Revolution, which had just as profound an impact on farmers as the introduction of agriculture did to foragers 12,000 years ago. However, one of the prerequisites for such a breakthrough was the unification of the world zones into one single complex system of collective learning. More potential innovators, more connectivity between them. With the events of this chapter, hundreds of millions of people across the globe were tied ever more tightly in a global exchange of goods and information. There certainly was a great incentive for this as the agrarian states of Western Europe sought to increase the amount of wealth, natural resources, and land they controlled (i.e. increase their energy flows). As such it appeared that the growth of mercantile commerce and globalisation from the fifteenth century onward was the key to unleashing the next threshold of complexity.

Yet the unification of the world zones was in many ways destructive and catastrophic. As most of the increases of complexity have been: from the tooth-and-claw nature of biological evolution, to the grueling conditions of early agriculture. The same would be the case with the unification of the world zones and the Industrial Revolution. And the same will probably be the case should humanity ever undergo yet another increase of complexity in the near or remote future. An increase in complexity does not uniformly represent "progress", while at the same time failing to sustain and safeguard our complexity leaves nothing but the Second Law, degeneration, and death. The world seldom exists in gentle equilibrium, and no form of complexity is safe forever.

Timeline

- **The Great Divergence of China (900 to 1500 AD):** The spread of wet rice farming in China caused the already dense population there to double in just 200 years, increasing the number of potential innovators for collective learning. As a result, China becomes the most advanced and powerful agrarian civilisation in this time period, *almost* achieving the first sparks of the heavy industrialisation that would kick off modernity. This "great divergence" also precipitated the European interest in trading with them, which in turn kicked off the Age of Explorations that initiated modernity.

- **Chinese Fleet Explores the Indian Ocean (1403 to 1433 AD):** China commissions the most technologically advanced fleet in the world to go on a series of exploratory, mercantile, and military journeys as a form of power projection in the Indian Ocean. They increase their direct contact with India, Arabia, and East Africa. The journeys are notable in that had they not been discontinued, China may have rounded the Cape of Africa, may have discovered Australia, and crossed the Pacific to the Americas, thus making the unification of the world zones a Chinese rather than a European project.

- **Unification of the World Zones (1492 to 1788 AD):** The Spanish, Portuguese, Dutch, French, English, and other European nations begin to explore and colonise numerous regions across the globe. This creates direct and regular contact with all the other world zones, which continued to intensify as the centuries went on, and increased the overall collective learning of humanity into one world system.

- **The Columbian Holocaust (1520 to 1620 AD):** The period in which European diseases carried by the Spanish spread rapidly across South and Central America, killing an estimated 20 to 100 million people (current consensus 50 million people) or 90% of the population, due to lack of immunity of native populations to European diseases. The imbalance in disease exchange resulted from Afro-Eurasia having much larger agrarian populations that experienced several pandemics and the development of particularly virulent maladies. Peoples of the other world zones would continue to perish in this large numbers from European diseases well into the nineteenth century.

- **Start of the Industrial Revolution in Great Britain (1700 to 1780 AD):** As a result of the unification of the world zones into a single global system and opening up of world markets, key innovations in Britain allow it to begin a new era of mass production and rapidly accelerating complexity that kicks of the eighth threshold and continues to spread across the world to this very day. The West pulls ahead of the world in the "Second Great Divergence". And arguably it is after this period that humans become the most influential and destructive species on the planet. We may be just at the beginning of this threshold.

310

The Medieval Origins of Globalisation

There is a substantial argument to be made that globalisation began in approximately 1000 AD. At this time, the world population had recovered to 250 million people, the same level that it was at in 1 AD. The major regions of agrarian civilisations had recovered from multiple waves of state collapse, civil war, and foreign invasion, and were flourishing again. The Silk Roads were again in full swing and the regions of Africa and Europe, along with the Middle East and Asia, were included as shareholders seeking wealth via international trade.

Populations were growing and merchants were becoming extremely wealthy in what in Roman times had been the backwater of Western Europe. The eleventh century AD saw the outbreak of the Crusades which brought Europeans into closer contact with the Muslim world than ever before – experiencing the lucrative trade goods they possessed and the Classical Greco-Roman knowledge they had imported and preserved. Around the same time, this knowledge also started to filter into France across the Pyrenees from Spain.

The Vikings had established sea routes from Russia to Constantinople to Italy to England, and were beginning explore Iceland, Greenland, and North America. The small Viking colony in Newfoundland at L'Anse aux Meadows contained 50 to 100 people, and although the Vikings did not stay there long, it represents the first connection between the Afro-Eurasian and American world zones since 12,000 years ago.

In 1000 AD the process of globalisation was already underway, albeit in small and halting forms, and global unification became not a question of *if* but *when*. By 1000 AD, it became almost inevitable that the world zones would collide. Just at that point it was still unclear what region or agrarian civilisation would drive the process. But given enough decades and centuries it had become clear that *someone* would do it.

During most of the Era of Agrarian Civilisations the state gained the overwhelming majority of its wealth (i.e. energy flows) from agriculture. Landlords would have a share of the crops produced, or would collect rents, and central governments would collect taxes and tributes. This was enough to sustain the complexity of the state in most cases, and in Afro-Eurasia and the Americas there was still a lot of surrounding land to conquer should a state need to increase their energy flows (provided you could defeat your neighbours). Merchants and their trading pursuits tended to be more peripheral to this endeavour. Merchants were a good source for luxury goods from far off lands, but the income the state received from taxing them was a tiny proportion compared to taxing one's agrarian subjects. But thanks to the Silk Roads that was changing.

Merchants were making more money, and were becoming increasingly influential. The Italian merchant states of Venice, Genoa, and Florence had become the wealthiest in Europe despite their small size, the spice traders and Tamil Kings of Ceylon and South India managed to achieve the same dynamic, and the bustling international spice trade brought increasing wealth and power to the Srivijaya kingdom Indonesia. All were smaller states that wielded tremendous wealth simply by account of commerce, which in many ways outstripped states of a similar size that relied on tax income from the land. The cultural impact of cross-continental exchange created unusual results. In the eleventh century AD, Europe received the first gunpowder by long distance trade with China, and over the next 500 years with the development of the cannon and blunderbuss, the small plodding nature of medieval warfare where a few hundred knights scrapping in a field decided the fate of kingdoms and where castles stood as impenetrable objects began their slow demise at the hands of modernity. In the eleventh century AD, coin currency in either bronze, silver, or gold, became universal to facilitate the increased volume of trade that could not be handled by bartering. In 1270 AD, Persians provided cobalt glazes to the Chinese kicking off a lucrative white and blue porcelain trade that made a fortune for merchants all over Afro-Eurasia. In 1271 AD, Marco Polo travelled across Central Asia on a perilous journey to China, and his subsequent account published in 1300 AD shocked European society at the state of riches in East Asia and intensified the motivation of European merchants to trade there.

And there was a very good reason to be motivated to trade in China. Equal interest did not exist along the Silk Roads. Europe and Africa were eager to access Asian markets in order to obtain what they could not produce themselves – silks, spices, pottery, etc. The successive Muslim caliphates of the Middle East were still making quite a packet of cash playing middlemen for Chinese goods and Indian spices, since they dwelt along the only trade routes to the East (nobody had rounded the Cape of Africa yet). China, however, produced the most desirable goods and in large quantities and thus had a dominant position in the entire network of trade. Already China's large population contributed to it being a "centre of gravity" for international trade, but now collective learning was going nuts there. Thanks to the First Great Divergence, China had rapidly accelerated its collective learning and had become the most advanced empire on Earth by the thirteenth century. Just modern globalisation has been driven by a wealthy and technologically advanced West, the medieval origins of globalisation were driven by a wealthy and technologically advanced China. And it is this imbalance that would lead to the European desire to expand and explore and also Chinese indifference to such ventures and their eventual and disastrous turn inwards.

The First Great Divergence

Much hay has been made in world history of the "Great Divergence" of the eighteenth and nineteenth century where an industrialising West raced ahead of the other regions of the globe in terms of mass production and technology. We shall examine this in its turn. But collective learning had already produced a prior Great Divergence in China which had the potential to set off Threshold 8 several centuries earlier.

Remember that collective learning is in part driven by the number of "potential innovators" who could potentially come up with a new innovation in their lifetimes. The larger the population of humans, the more rolls one has at the dice every generation. In the sixth century BC, the carrying capacity of China was already ahead of ancient Europe. China was already growing crops in rows, paying attention to weeding, and frequently employing iron ploughs. All of these innovations would not be employed in Europe for centuries. The Chinese also used horse harnesses by the third century BC, avoiding the risk of strangulation of the horse and permitting them to carry ploughs and heavy equipment. The seed drill was in use by the second century BC. In the first and second century BC, types of mouldboard ploughs that only became available in Europe after Charlemagne were already in use in China.

At the time, the majority of the Chinese population centred on the north in the Yellow River valley where they farmed millet and wheat – not rice. Even before the explosion of wet rice agriculture in China, these innovations served to create a higher agricultural output and carrying capacity compared with Roman Europe centred on the Mediterranean, both in the East and especially the sparsely populated backwater that was then the Roman West.

Even further divergence happened between 500 and 1000 AD with the spread of wet rice production in China, which has a much higher yield than grain. Per hectare, traditional varieties of rice support around 5.63 people compared to 3.67 people on a hectare of wheat. Dry rice farming came first. However, it has a carrying capacity that is not much higher than wheat. The problem is that dry rice farming requires constant weeding. It was also ill-suited to the climate of northern China. In the north, millet farming in the Yellow River valley began 6000 BC. By 200 BC, the Han north was sustained by the farming of millet and wheat in an inefficient two-crop rotation. The inhospitable soils and temperatures of the Yellow River valley in the north usually permitted only one crop a year. From 1 AD, wheat was immediately planted after millet or soy to increase crop frequency. In order to avoid too much loss of nutrients from repeated planting, the crop was often planted in alternating furrows, with new furrows being planted in between the old ones. The Han plough had limited depth of ploughing. Over-seeding was sometimes used to save labour at the expense of the yield.

Meanwhile in southern China, rice was domesticated in 7000 BC along the Yangtze River and by 3000 BC, large scale wet rice farming was present. For several thousand years, the yield was still relatively low because farmers did not employ terracing and paddy systems. Instead wet rice was grown beside streams and in small irrigated plots. This is the reason why northern China held the bulk of the population despite a long history of wet rice farming in the south.

Nevertheless, wet rice farming even without terracing and paddies was fairly productive. In the second century BC, the Qin Emperor Shi Huangdi constructed a Grand Canal to facilitate transport of wet rice from southern China to the populous north. Slowly but surely the carrying capacity was being raised. Finally, labour intensive methods of terracing and paddies caught on in south China in 200 AD. The employment of a crop with much higher yields than grain and that can sustain higher population densities, might go some way to explaining the higher rate of collective learning and innovation that set these civilisations ahead of other world zones in terms of population and cultural complexity.

At the fall of the Han dynasty, barbarian attacks forced more Chinese south to the Yangtze River basin. Reunification under the Sui in 589 AD made the region more stable, and rice expansion and the migration of the northern population to the south continued in earnest. Gradually, migration between 500 and 1300 AD transformed the agricultural output and population distributions of China, particularly intensifying in the Song dynasty (960-1276 AD). The Song government initiated a set of policies to shift agricultural production from the northern millet and wheat regions to the wet rice producing south.

In 1012, the Song introduced a strain of rice from Vietnam that allowed for multiple harvests per year, or the alternation of rice in the summer and wheat in the winter. The government appointed 'master farmers' from local communities, who were to disseminate new farming techniques and knowledge of new tools, fertilisers, and irrigation methods. The Song also introduced tax breaks on newly reclaimed land and low-interest loans for farmers to invest in new agricultural equipment and crops. The Song encouraged terracing, created fields that were evenly flooded and trapped fertile silts from being washed away. The Chinese government distributed 3000 copies of *Essentials of Agriculture and Sericulture* to landowners in order to improve crop yields. Wet rice farming by this method produced 2-3 crops a year compared to the meagre one-crop harvest of the millet producing north.

The adoption of wet rice farming and the migration of many people to the south had a profound impact on collective learning in Song China. In 1 AD, the population of China was around 50-60 million and did not exceed that number level prior to the tenth century. During the 900s and 1000s under the Song dynasty, migration to the Yangzi river valley to farm rice raised the carrying capacity of China from 50-60 million to 110-120 million (nearly half the world's population), with record high population densities like 5 million people farming an area of 65 by 80 kilometres. By 1100, this constituted 30-40% of the population of the globe, compared to all Europe's 10-12%.

The population was raised in China, so was the density, and so the number and connectivity between potential innovators was increased. So profound was the impact that it really constitutes the First Great Divergence between East and West, 700 years before the Industrial Revolution. Chinese collective learning advanced by leaps and bounds due a much higher carrying capacity. It is no coincidence that the Song dynasty was one of the most technologically advanced and industrially prodigious societies in pre-modern history, almost to the point that the late Song dynasty could conceivably have had an Industrial Revolution of their own.

For instance, the annual minting and use of coin currency was increased greatly under the Song. They introduced paper currency. Farming techniques improved: use of manure became more frequent, new strains of seed were developed, hydraulic and irrigation techniques improved, and farms shifted to crop specialisation. Coal was used to manufacture iron and iron production increased from 19,000 metric tons per year under the Tang (618-907 AD) to 113,000 metric tons under the Song. Similar use of coal to enhance iron production was a key component of the British Industrial Revolution several centuries later. The Song dynasty was the first to invent and harness the power of gunpowder. Textile production showed the first ever signs of mechanisation. Thus the adoption of wet rice farming and the migration of Chinese farmers from the northern grain producing region to the Yangzi River valley triggered a rise in the number of potential innovators and a Great Divergence that placed China as one of the most technologically advanced and culturally complex regions of the globe from 900 to 1500 AD – at the very least.

It is perhaps worthy of speculation what modern history would have looked like if the Industrial Revolution had happened in China. Certainly the sociopolitical history of the world would have looked decidedly different, with Chinese ships arriving off the coasts of America and Australia perhaps with the intent of colonising there (and inadvertently passing on deadly Afro-Eurasian diseases), and the Age of Imperialism happening at the expense, rather than to the profit, of Europe. Yet through the lens of Big History and the rise of complexity, the result would have been much the same: Threshold 8. The most important lesson to derive from this section is that once the world was set on the course of wider international commerce and globalisation, the fate of the world was sealed. By 1000 AD, the next threshold of complexity had become almost inevitable.

The Black Death & Secular Cycles

Despite the advances made after 1000 AD in terms of collective learning, despite the gradual rise of the carrying capacity in most of the agrarian world, and the sharp rise of the carrying capacity in China, the world had not yet escaped the periodic assault of secular cycles. The world population in 1000 AD was 250 million, about the same level it had been in 1 AD. Plagues, invasions, and the collapse of empires had reduced that number to 190-200 million by 500 AD. But between 1000 and 1100 AD the world population reached new and unprecedented heights, adding another 50 million people to a total of 300 million as new lands were opened up for the first time to farming and as new agricultural techniques were employed. The next century was even more impressive. The common population was fairly prosperous with low rents, decent sized wages, ate meat semi-regularly and were in fairly rude health by pre-modern standards. Agrarian civilisations were fairly stable (internally at least) compared to the periods that came before and after. The world population ballooned from 300 million in 1100 AD to 400 million by 1200 AD.

Thereafter, the agrarian world started to approach its carrying capacity. Between 1200 AD and 1300 AD, the population only grew to 432 million. Strain was starting to set in. The standard of living for the agrarian peasantry declined: they ate less meat, their wages shrank, their rents rose, small-holding farmers had to sell their land and elites set up huge estates as the number of elites multiplied by several times. The world in 1300 AD teetered on the brink of the downward spiral of another secular cycle. From 1315-17, for instance, the Great Famine of Europe killed off an estimated 15% of the total population. A famine in China 1333-37 carried off similar numbers. The common population declined, and the elite incomes that depended on them were reduced and some elites even became impoverished. Under normal circumstances, this would be enough to kick off a period of elite infighting, and certainly politics destabilised across the world with an increased number of elite rebellions, assassinations, and palace coups.

But much worse was on the way, courtesy of the Silk Roads criss-crossing Afro-Eurasia that people had been so dutifully expanding. The important thing to remember regarding densely populated agrarian regions with high rates of collective learning that these places are also hotbeds for disease. The stark result of this would become even clearer when Europeans moved into other world zones. However, at this point, it was Afro-Eurasia that suffered greatly as a result of its own human web.

The Black Death is an extremely deadly disease caused by the bacterium *Yersinia pestis* which, if you were paying attention in Chapter 4 and 5, belongs to one of the other three major domains of life. Here the domain of Bacteria returns to our story to wreak havoc on the history of Eukaryota in spectacular fashion. Perhaps you were feeling high and mighty so far in this story as a eukaryotic multi-celled human capable of collective learning! But with complexity comes increased fragility. A star is not particularly complex, but large amounts of its radiation can still kill you.

Yersinia pestis is carried by fleas (another fairly simple organism) which in turn are carried by rats. In the medieval period, rats congregated pretty much wherever humans did, including farms, cities, on trade caravans, and on merchant ships. It takes two weeks for fleas to kill off an average sized rat colony, during which time the fleas can transfer to any nearby mammalian species and infect them as well, whether dogs, cats, pigs, or humans. We did not know at the time what spread the plague and were fairly oblivious to the threat posed by tiny fleas that are only a couple of millimetres long. Once a population of humans becomes infected, any close contact runs the risk of fleas jumping on to the observer and continuing the chain. The greater the population density of the area, the faster the disease is likely to spread. From so simple a set of piggy-backing creatures came the destruction of human society complexity, with the fleas and rats being carried along the trade routes of Afro-Eurasia.

Once bitten a human develops swollen lymph nodes around the groin, which are painful at the touch. These sores are round in shape and were called "bubos" hence the name bubonic plague. Once the bacteria works its way through the human bloodstream, plague victims begin to experience fever, weakness, delirium, headache, bloody vomiting, and the death of flesh and internal organs which can turn black and gangrenous. Death usually occurs within a week to ten days, and death was the outcome of roughly 80% of bubonic plague victims. If the plague turns pneumonic, then fleas are no longer required. The bacteria enters the victim's lungs and can be transferred by the sputum and blood that they emit from coughing. Pneumonic plague tends to spread even faster than bubonic plague, with death rates being 90-95%, and very often people with pneumonic plague die within just two to three hours of catching it.

The bubonic plague reared its ugly head in the sixth century AD Justinianic plague, and returned in waves throughout the so-called "Dark Ages", and then returned in the fourteenth century and continued to cause massive waves of death into the nineteenth century. It is still present in parts of the developing world today, infecting a few hundred people annually. But it is the marked obliteration of large swathes of the human population, in an overcrowded world already undergoing a crisis in the fourteenth century, which is the object of our attention here.

The Black Death of the fourteenth century is hypothesised to have begun in a "plague reservoir" in Central Asia, in the vicinity of the Caspian Sea. A plague reservoir is an area not populated by humans where bacteria can evolve among other mammalian populations, like rodents, until it achieves a particular virulence. Then once the bacteria comes into contact with humans, they have very little resistance to the disease, the body does not know how to react, and it becomes immensely deadly. Trade in Central Asia is likely to have brought the Black Death in contact with agrarian civilisations for the first time. There is also a school of thought that says the disease began within densely populated China, but that is less likely given the timing of the infection of Persia.

The Black Death is reputed to have spread east from Central Asia to more populated areas between 1300 and 1330. It is likely many of the initial infected peoples in Central Asia who were cut down by the disease were illiterate and did not lay down the epidemics to written record so it is difficult to plot the course of the disease's spread. There is some written evidence that illnesses struck Yuan China as early as 1308 and again in the 1310s and 1320s, but it is not clear if these illnesses were plague. The first confirmed recorded outbreak happened in 1331 in Yuan China. A second outbreak occurred in 1334. In both of these cases, the outbreaks were "localised" to Central China. This is not to say the consequences were not severe. Up to 25 million people in those provinces are estimated to have died. These deaths occurred in the same decade that a fast famine swept across the land, so it is difficult to estimate how many people died from starvation and how many died from plague. Sporadic outbreaks occurred in the 1340s and a more severe pandemic swept across all of China between 1353 and 1354. Already Yuan China was experiencing a vast downturn of their secular cycle, which the Black Death exaggerated to an extreme degree. Population loss worsened elite competition and infighting and contributed directly to the overthrow of the Yuan dynasty in favour of the Ming in 1368. The population of China in 1200 was roughly 120-140 million people. A terrible combination of famine, Black Death, and civil war shrank the Chinese population to just 65 million people by 1393. For a time, the number of potential innovators in China was reduced with negative effects on the accelerating pace of Chinese collective learning.

Meanwhile the Black Death also spread to Persia from Central Asia by 1335 AD, killing an estimated 30-50% of the population, including the ruler of the Ilkhanate which had dominated the region since the fragmentation of the Mongol Empire 1256-59 AD. This caused the collapse of the khanate in to several rival kingdoms and several decades of war for dominance in the region. From 1338 to 1344, the Black Death spread across the trade routes of the Golden Horde to the north killing an estimated 30-70% of the population. The reason for the slow spread of the Black Death in the khanates is due to the sparser populations and the difficulty of trade caravans reaching their final destination before the caravan merchants had all died. The Black Death also didn't spread much further north into Russia *at the time* because of the long distances between population centres and the cold weather which slowed the progress of the disease.

It is as yet unclear whether the Black Death spread to India, or when. If it occurred in 1335, then it is likely to have spread from Central Asia around the same time that it arrived in the Ilkhanate. If it occurred in 1346-48, then it likely spread via seaborne trade with Byzantium or the Arabs. There are accounts of terrible diseases striking India in the 1330s and 1340s, but it is not yet clear from written accounts whether the illnesses and deaths were caused by the Black Death or one of a number of other pre-modern epidemic diseases. We also don't have estimates for population loss.

In 1344, an already infected army of the Golden Horde besieged the Genovese-held Crimean trade port of Kaffa. The Golden Horde placed plague corpses onto catapults and flung the bodies over the city walls, in one of the first recorded instances of biological warfare in human history. It is unclear whether the plague corpses managed to spread the disease, or whether rats had simply slipped into Kaffa, but soon enough the inhabitants of the city were dying of the disease. The Mongol siege was ultimately ineffective, since a Genovese relief force arrived and compelled them to withdraw, only for the Mongols to try again the following year. The Black Death continued to ravage the region through 1345 and 1346.

Thereafter, the Black Death managed to get on board Genovese trading ships and began the infection of the Mediterranean. The disease arrived in the port of Constantinople in 1347 and thereafter spread overland across Anatolia reaching Damascus in 1348 where an estimated 2000 people died per day. That same year the Black Death reached Egypt where it killed an estimated 50% of the population of Cairo. In fact, the disease spread right across North Africa, reaching Tunisia and Algeria before the year was out. Due to the Muslim tradition of making a pilgrimage to Mecca in the Haj, the Black Death arrived in their holiest of cities, Mecca, in 1349.

Meanwhile, back in 1347, the Genovese traders had also traveled on to Greece, Sicily, Sardinia, Corsica, and Marseille. All of these places quickly became infected. At the port of Messina in Sicily, the authorities had actually quarantined the ship to avoid the spread of the disease. The entire ship's crew died while docked. Unfortunately, rats from the ship walked across the ropes mooring the ship to the dock, and that is the likely cause of the spread of the disease into the city and subsequently across Sicily. In 1348, the Black Death swept across southeastern Europe from both Greece and the Byzantine Empire, it swept across Italy from Sicily, and across southern France and northern Spain from Marseille. Also in 1348, traders reached England, Ireland, and northern France setting off separate infections there which spread over the next year. In 1349, the Black Death rushed through southern Spain and got as far as Morocco, and infected ships arrived at Bergen in Norway. The plague spread from England to Scotland, Norway to Sweden, and France to the Holy Roman Empire in 1350. Thereafter the plague managed to spread overland via dense Eastern European populations from Poland to Russia, which had evaded infection from the south, between 1351 and 1353. Only the small cold-dwelling population of Finland was spared.

While written evidence is often scarce or non-existent, population studies and DNA evidence indicates that the plague also spread down the valley of the Nile into the Sudan, and may have gone overland as far south as Tanzania. Evidence of significant depopulation in Nigeria also seems to suggest that the Black Death crossed the Sahara aboard trade caravans, a particularly impressive feat for the disease. The Black Death is likely to have travelled the full extent of the Silk Road.

The death rate for a population infected by the Black Death is an average of 50%. Emphasis on the word average, since the rates varied widely due to the peculiar nature of transmission. Some villages and regions experienced death rates of 90%, others had a death rate of 30 or 50% before the disease was somehow contained from spreading, and other small isolated regions escaped the mid-fourteenth century wave of the Black Death completely (though these regions were very few in number). While more deadly, the pneumonic plague tended to kill its victims too quickly for long-term transmission. The Black Death spreads by rats to population areas. At least some of the caravan drivers or ship's crews need to survive the journey. Any region with regular trading links with the outside world is likely to get infected eventually. Once in a human settlement, the fleas prefer a fairly dense population to keep the daisy-chain going. Cities were ideal, but the Black Death could also flourish in the countryside provided there were humans or rats coming into contact with new people. Cold weather tended to slow the spread of the disease, so the outbreaks during these years were seasonal, with a fresh bought of hell occurring in the spring. Once the mid-fourteenth century wave died down, the plague remained embedded across Afro-Eurasia, carried by small flea populations and rat colonies, and recurrent outbreaks continued to occur in subsequent years. While never again would the plague be as devastating as 1331-1353, subsequent pandemic waves would continue to kill of millions into the nineteenth century.

In 1300 AD, the world population had been approximately 450 million. Roughly 90% of that was contained in Afro-Eurasia, due to the jumble of agrarian civilisations there. By 1400 AD, a mixture of famine, plague, and the decades of violent instability that usually followed depopulation, the world population had shrunk to 350 million people. That is a net loss, despite the fact that the survivors continued to have multiple children. For comparison, despite the millions who died in the First and Second World Wars, numerous famines, and the Spanish Influenza, thanks to births the increase of the world population from 1.6 to 2.5 billion between 1900 and 1950 scarcely registers the slightest slowdown on a graph. If one were to zoom into a more detailed example, the population of France in 1300 AD was approximately 20 million people. After a century of famine, plague, civil war, and English invasion, around 1400 AD the population was 10 million.

An intriguing side-effect of population cycles, however, is that once depopulation is over, once all the civil wars and manmade violence have settled down, life becomes quite prosperous again for the common people. A shortage of labour means higher wages, an abundance of land left over by the dead means lower rents and sustainable peasant farms, and food is cheap because there are fewer people buying it. The peasantry might even possess what we would call a "disposable income" for a few modest luxuries. Because the death toll of the fourteenth and early fifteenth century was so profound, around 1450 AD, the common people of Afro-Eurasia had a high standard of living and a larger "real wage" than any period prior to the Industrial Revolution. And it is in this era of Afro-Eurasian recovery that the unification of the world zones truly takes hold.

The Age of Chinese Explorations

After the Black Death, the Ottoman Turks shut down much of the overland trade on the Silk Roads between the Mediterranean and the regions to the east. The disruption of the network of exchange prompted explorers at either end of the Afro-Eurasian supercontinent to find new routes by the sea. This ultimately set off a chain of events that would lead to the unification of the world zones. The question remained whether that unification would be accomplished by Europe or China?

Zheng He was born in Yunnan China in 1371 AD to a Muslim family. Yunnan was then ruled by a Muslim Mongol, and Zheng He claimed ancestry from those conquerors. During his life Zheng mixed his Islamic faith with belief in traditional Chinese spirituality. When Zheng He's was 10, his father was killed during the Chinese Ming dynasty's conquest of Yunnan. Zheng He was placed into the service of Prince Zhu Di, who would one day become the Yongle Emperor. It was traditional in those days to castrate the servants of the court so they could not "interfere" with the royal family's bloodlines by seducing any family members and bringing about an unwanted pregnancy. And so Zheng He was castrated and became a eunuch.

Despite having his balls cut off, for the next 20 years Zheng He faithfully served his prince and became his trusted friend. In 1402 AD, the Prince Zhu Di had overthrown his nephew and now became the Yongle Emperor. He set about an ambitious program of projecting China's power around the world via maritime trade and exploration in order to legitimize his rule. In 1403 AD, the Ming began construction of a gigantic fleet of warships and merchant vessels that dwarfed anything else in the world at the time. At this time, China still enjoyed a significant lead in collective learning over the rest of the world, including other states in Afro-Eurasia. Even despite the technological stagnation of the Mongol Yuan era, and earlier Ming rulers. This allowed them to build a fleet that was unparalleled by any other navy in the world. The Chinese exploration fleet was composed of 317 ships, some of them approximately 120 metres high with three or four decks, carrying a massive army of 28,000 men to, shall we say, add weight to trade negotiations. At the head of the fleet was Zheng He, the emperor's loyal eunuch and most trusted servant.

Starting in 1405, numerous expeditions were launched. The Chinese fleet sailed round Southeast Asia and to India on several occasions. They sailed down and conducted trade in Indonesia. They made landfall in Arabia and East Africa on several occasions. In total seven expeditions were made. In terms of commerce, the goods brought back from these voyages proved lucrative and it appeared these voyages more than paid for themselves. They also opened up trade in various ports which allowed other merchant expeditions to enrich themselves.

The maritime operations of Zheng He were partly commercial and partly military in nature. Thousands of troops were brought along with the flotillas, in order to make a show of force in several regions, and the warships were used to enforce the idea that Ming China was the preeminent naval force of the age. In essence, that they "ruled the waves" of the Indian Ocean. In one notable voyage in 1424, they engaged pirates in the harbour of Palembang, killed 5000 people, and executed the pirate leader.

When Zheng He returned from this voyage, he found out that the Yongle Emperor had died. He was succeeded by his son who stopped Zheng He's voyages for a time and appointed him to work on building some fortifications. This son died in 1425. He was succeeded by the Yongle Emperor's grandson, the Xuande Emperor, whose attitude to Zheng He was sometimes hostile. But he did commission one more voyage from Zheng He in 1430.

The final voyage ended and returned home in 1433. It is highly likely Zheng He died during this voyage and was buried at sea, since his grave in China is empty. If these voyages had continued it is not unreasonable to speculate that the Chinese could have eventually sailed round the southern tip of Africa, perhaps even achieving direct trade with Europe. It is also possible the Chinese could have moved further south from Indonesia to Australia. And perhaps the Chinese could even have navigated the Pacific, taking them to the Americas. The imperial implications of all this are open to question. But it is possible that the unification of the world zones may well have been achieved by China and not Europe.

But global unification under Chinese naval power was not to be. The Xuande Emperor, presided over a fairly peaceful and prosperous reign in China that made such voyages less important. And at the same time the eunuch faction that advocated for a strong naval presence in the Indian Ocean had fallen from government and the voyages were discontinued. Thereafter, China fell back into the isolationism and traditional modes of production that had ended the industrialization and commercialization of the Song dynasty 150 years earlier. So ended the possibility that the Chinese would be the unifiers of the world zones. Yet the 1400s CE were primed for such a unification. It was only a few decades after the end of Zheng He's voyages and the termination of his life that the attempt was made from the other end of the Afro-Eurasia.

European Extensification

The previous centuries had given Europe a taste for the spices, silks, and luxury goods of Asia. Yet after the Ottoman Empire invaded the Balkans at the end of the fourteenth century, devastating Christian armies at the Battle of Nicopolis in 1396, the Turks shut down much of European trade in the Eastern Mediterranean and along the Silk Roads. What trade remained saw goods sold to Europe at hugely inflated prices. As a result, Europe was virtually shut out from the network of collective learning which had once connected it to Africa, the Middle East, India, and China. To beat the Ottoman Empire was an impossibility at the time. The only other course was to find an alternative route to Africa, India, and China. And so the merchants of Genoa and the kingdoms of Europe recoiled west, to head around Africa and gain access to the Indian Ocean.

Several factors made this possible. The first was the Portuguese improvements in ship design and navigation. The second was the increasing thirst of European states for more income in the depopulated fifteenth century. They could not gain as much income from taxing the farming population as they had prior to the Black Death, and so merchants and commercialism began to be looked upon more favourably by Western European states. The third factor was the desire to access West African gold which was now being monopolised by Muslim traders and transported across the Sahara to the Ottoman Empire and beyond. The fourth was the notion that one could "discover" lands that were previously unknown to Europeans. From the 1340s to 1420s, the Portuguese and Spanish had landed in the Canaries, Madeira, and the Azores, and charted a good distance down the seemingly unending African continent. It was theorised that if one could sail to the southern end of Africa, one could access the rich trade networks of India and China beyond.

Throughout his life, Prince Henry "the Navigator" of Portugal commissioned merchant expeditions to the Atlantic islands and various locations along the West African coast. In the 1440s and 1450s, this opened up a great deal of trade with West Africa. He also set up sugar plantations on the Atlantic islands. One of his merchant expeditions headed up the Senegal and Gambia rivers to the Mali Empire, opening trade relations with Portugal and giving the latter access to pepper, ivory, gold, and the African slave trade. Economic relations between Portugal and West Africa intensified in the years after Henry's death in 1462. So much so that the Mali Empire reduced the number of merchant caravans heading on the dangerous journey across the Sahara and redirected the trade toward the West African coast, where Portuguese ships would be waiting. This actually reduced the incomes of Algeria, Tunisia, and the size of the Muslim Mediterranean trade with West Africa. A Portuguese trade fort was constructed in

West Africa in 1482. Bartolomeu Dias reached the Cape of South Africa in 1488. And in 1498, Vasco da Gama rounded Africa and reached India, and brought back a cargo of spices.

Bypassing the hostile Ottoman and the Islamic middlemen of the Eastern Mediterranean, da Gama was able to purchase his cargo for 5% what it would have cost him buying from Eastern Mediterranean sources. The Portuguese then sold the spices in Europe at a huge profit, undercutting all of the competition. By this point the virtues of exploration and sea navigation to Asia had become undeniable. From this point forward it was clear that Europe was going to unify the world zones.

Only a few years after Dias had reached the Cape of South Africa, Europeans were looking for more efficient ways of reaching Asia. The problem with sailing around Africa is that around the equator, one hits a region called the "doldrums". This is a long stretch of ocean where the winds are frequently too weak to propel sail, and where ships could frequently be hit with dangerous storms. As such, the journey was quite risky in the late fifteenth century, and could take an inordinate amount of time. And so, in 1492, Ferdinand of Aragon and Isabella of Castile commissioned an expedition led by Genoese explorer Christopher Columbus. He left Castile in August, sailed west, and reached the Bahamas in October. He went on to visit Cuba and Hispaniola. Upon the native populations, Columbus enacted a regime of enforced slave labour, sexual slavery, and mutilation for disobedience, and all the while the island populations were gradually wiped out by European diseases. Columbus would go on to make four separate voyages that took him all over the Caribbean, including one that saw him stranded on Jamaica for a year. To his dying day, Columbus was certain that he had landed in Asia.

In 1497, Henry VII and several London and Bristol investors commissioned Italian merchant sailor Giovanni Caboto to sail west in search of a passage to China. He landed in Newfoundland, being the first European in nearly 500 years to set foot there. But historical records seem to imply Caboto did not go very far inland and merely spent a while exploring the Newfoundland coast. It is likely he encountered some Native Americans, since on his next expedition he brought with him items intended for trade, but not much is known about the nature or mood of the contact. Very little is known of his third expedition, or whether he died in the attempt. All we know is part of the expedition made it back, with one sailor recorded to be living in London in 1501.

Due to the success of the late fifteenth century expeditions, the number of commissions multiplied in the sixteenth century. Instead of discovering a faster route to Asia, Columbus and Caboto had found another world zone. Nevertheless, in regard to the former, in 1519 the

Spanish monarchy commissioned Portuguese explorer Ferdinand Magellan to take five ships, sail south of the Americas and enter the Pacific, whereupon Magellan crossed the vast ocean and reached the Philippines, where Magellan was killed in 1521. Only one ship managed to return to Spain in 1522, under command of Juan Sebastian del Cano, being the first crew to circumnavigate the globe.

The voyages transformed Europe from being a region on the periphery of the Afro-Eurasian trade network, sitting at the (admittedly poorer) end of the Silk Roads, to a maritime network of global trade in which Europe sat in the centre. While much of the next century or so would involve Europeans redistributing the resources of a much more populous and arguably more advanced China, Europe was beginning to ascend to world dominance. And it was through this global network of trade that the next threshold of complexity would be crossed.

The sixteenth century set off an explosion of European and colonial merchant ventures to Asia and the Americas, with states, private investors, and individuals seeking vast fortunes. Habsburg Spain dominated these trade networks for the hundred years, due to the immense dynastic power of the Habsburg dynasty in Europe, and their acquisition of colonies in some of the most mineral rich parts of South and Central Americas. Other prominent nations that joined the colonial game were Portugal (who controlled what is now Brazil), England, France, the Netherlands, and with even a few attempts to set up colonies by Scotland. The nations of Central and Eastern Europe largely missed out on the Age of Explorations due to their geographic locations, but individuals were frequently commissioned by the Atlantic nations of Western Europe to join expeditions.

During the sixteenth century, the centre of gravity of trade and population in the world remained in Asia. Particularly China, but also India. These vast populations had a number of textiles, spices, silks, pottery, jewellery, and other luxury goods in relative abundance. In exchange, Western Europe possessed very few trade goods that Asians wanted. The exception to this rule was the Chinese hunger for silver, which the Spanish were unearthing in the Americas. Beyond that, the European powers focused their attentions to trade with smaller Asian states in South and Southeast Asia, which they could overawe with small military forces armed with naval cannons and gunpowder weapons. Portugal was the first to gain dominance over the spice trade in the Indian Ocean by military means. A century later, the Dutch and English began to squeeze them out, eventually leading to Dutch dominance in Indonesia, English dominance in India, while the Spanish managed to retain control over the Philippines. The French also made small advances in India, seizing a few lucrative trading posts.

In the Americas, the Spanish led the way. From 1519-1521, Hernan Cortes led a few hundred Spanish conquistadors, armed with gunpowder weapons and a cocktail of diseases against the Aztecs. As a result of the high death rates of Aztecs at the hands of European disease and Cortes allying with various local enemies of the Aztecs, all of Mexico fell into Spanish hands within a few short years. The Spanish started launching expeditions to the north, and claimed North America as far as California and even British Columbia, but Spanish colonial settlement seldom stretched very far beyond Mexico in large numbers.

The Spanish focus was much more prominently directed south. In 1532, Francisco Pizarro led a similar expedition against the Incan Empire, and was also aided by gunpowder weapons and the horrible ravages of European disease. However, the Incan Empire stretched across vast and difficult terrain and the Spanish did not fully conquer the empire until 1572, as the result of a long and gruelling war of annihilation. The motivation for this was not just conquest for conquest's sake. The Spanish realised that one could make a tremendous profit by taking resources from the Americas and transporting them to Europe and Asia.

The biggest part of this exchange network was with China. The Ming dynasty had all the attractive trade goods, and the Spanish had discovered large amounts of gold and silver in Mexico and the Andes. The largest find the Spanish was made in the 1540s at Potosi, in what is now Bolivia, which was a mountain with enormous silver deposits. China's population grew rapidly from 65 million in 1393 to 200 million in 1600 AD. As a result, its economy also rapidly grew in size. And so the Chinese needed more silver for coinage. Spanish silver was taken from the Americas to the Spanish holdings in the Philippines, where the Spanish purchased silk, spices, and manufactured goods from Chinese merchants. The silver thus made its way into the Chinese economy while East Asian luxury goods filtered back to Spain and were sold in Europe at high prices. Even the silver that Spain brought back from the Americas to Europe was used in the Habsburg's many wars for European domination in the sixteenth and seventeenth century, which in turn entered the European economy and was frequently used by merchants to purchase silks and spices in East Asia. Due to China's huge economy, even the majority of this silver ended up there. In either direction, 75% percent of American silver was ultimately funnelled to China.

It should be noted that currency is used in exchange for an entire range of goods and services. These goods and services are produced by agrarian civilisations which are supported by agriculture. And agriculture uses domesticated plants to collect energy via photosynthesis from the Sun. Thus in a very literal sense the movement of Spanish silver from the Americas, to Europe, to China represents one of the first energy flows through a united global complex system. Energy literally flowed from one world zone to another. Human complexity no longer needed to be measured by individual states, but could be measured on a truly globalised scale. And all of this globalisation occurred 400 to 450 years before McDonalds or Starbucks were ever heard of.

Sugar and the Slave Trade

We now turn to a much uglier side of the unification of the world zones. One of many. Because as I have already mentioned several times in this book, complexity usually comes with destruction and, where there is consciousness, suffering. While the Spanish were busy in the sixteenth century obliterating the agrarian civilisations of the Americas, the Spanish-Portuguese treaties of Tordesillas (1494) and Zaragoza (1529) gave the Portuguese the "right" to claim the lands of Brazil. A little later, in the late sixteenth and seventeenth centuries, in North America, England launched exploratory missions to what is now the Eastern seaboard of the United States and the lands surrounding Hudson's Bay, France sent explorers to what is now Quebec and the Canadian maritime provinces, and the Dutch carved out a niche for themselves in what is now New York, New England, New Jersey, Pennsylvania, and Delaware. The Dutch colonies were later appropriated by the English. To these regions, the Europeans sent settlers, but also traders seeking natural resources to sell back in Europe. While they did not have as much luck as the Spanish in regards to mineral wealth (though there was some) fur became a roaring trade with pelts being sent back to Europe. Meanwhile the English, French, and Dutch jostled with the Spanish for control over the various Caribbean islands.

As bountiful as the Americas were, they were not as full of luxury goods as the initial explorers had hoped (that statement goes double for the explorers who thought they had landed in Asia). But there was land. A lot of land. If one could not simply buy goods to sell at high prices back in Europe, perhaps one could grow something in the Americas and sell it back in Europe. The answer was *sugar*.

Prior to 1492, Europeans used honey as a primary source of sugar and a sweetener for various delectables. With the exception of Cyprus, Crete, and Sicily, Europe did not have the climate to grow sugar cane. The Portuguese explorations down the Atlantic coast of Africa in the fifteenth century had yielded the discovery of the Canaries, Azores, and Madeira. Small sugar plantations were duly set up. As an evolutionary aside, because such sugars are rare in nature they are highly addictive to humans, who as foragers were driven to eat up whatever sugar they could find. With the establishment of sugar plantations in the right climate, sugar could be sold in high volume at high prices in Europe, to an almost inexhaustible European hunger for the stuff. That hunger was so inexhaustible that a marked decline in dental quality occurred in Europe between 1500 and 1600. While medieval Europeans actually had surprisingly good teeth considering the pre-modern circumstances, early modern Europeans consumed so much sugar that they rotted their teeth out of their heads and the average set of chompers looked pretty horrific by comparison.

And now in the Caribbean and South America, Europeans had stumbled across a climate that was also ideal for sugar plantations, and there was a *lot more land*. At this point, one could find a market for as much sugar as one could produce. The question was finding enough labour to engage in such gruelling work. Lower class Europeans weren't the answer. Only indentured servants shipped over to the Americas could possibly be forced to do such work. And they soon moved on after their contract was up, and there certainly weren't the numbers of people willing to do it. The Spanish and Portuguese initially tried forcing the native inhabitants of the Americas to do it. But they knew the countryside and frequently escaped back to their people. Those that stayed often died of European diseases. There was not, however, a long period of experimentation with such things. Already in the fifteenth century, the Portuguese had bought into an African market that the Muslim world had interacted with for years – the trade of African slaves.

Slavery had existed since the inception of agrarian states 5500 years ago. It is possible that slavery existed in places even earlier, either in the world of agrarian villages, and in some isolated cases in foraging interactions between groups. But both of those depend on how we are defining slavery. What is clear is ever since humans began existing in ancient states, slavery was an ugly part of that complex societal web. There had been slavery in Europe, in Africa, and in Asia. The Aztecs and the Incans had held slaves. Of the roughly 55 billion people who lived between the start of agriculture 12,000 years ago and the start of the Industrial Revolution 250 years ago, an estimated 3 to 10 billion of them may have been slaves. In that sense, the European expansion of African slavery to the Americas was a continuation of a foul trend that had reigned almost unbroken for millennia.

Europeans themselves had a legacy of enslaving each other in classical antiquity and also in the early medieval period. The Romans enslaved entire nations of people that they had conquered, from Gauls to Greeks. They owned huge plantations across the Mediterranean world operated by millions of slaves. The Middle Ages blurred the lines between slavery and serfdom in Europe. And by the time we arrive at Western Europe in the 1400s, the newly exploring kingdoms were still slowly emerging from a world of serfdom, which wasn't much better. In fact, serfdom was an early medieval perversion of older systems of slavery, even in its name, serf being derived from servus (slave). To the east, Russia did not abolish serfdom till 1861.

The Atlantic slave trade kicked off with the Portuguese. In their explorations of the African coastline in the 1400s, they opened trading relations with African rulers. The kingdoms of West Africa had been engaging in the Arab slave trade for several centuries at this point, with the transport of people in bondage across the Sahara. The Africans themselves derived their slaves from the peoples they conquered in war, then retained them or sold them off across the

Silk Roads. When the Portuguese opened up trading relations with African rulers, they were sold slaves too.

The horrors of transportation killed 10-50% of African slaves, depending on the route. Whether it was being packed in inhumane conditions in the Atlantic crossing by Europeans or the route-march across the Sahara only to potentially perish during castration by the Arabs and Ottomans. For the survivors, in total 11-13 million Africans were taken West across the Atlantic and 15 million Africans were taken East across the Sahara into lives of bondage. Meanwhile in Asia, from India to Vietnam, to China, to Korea, the enslavement of tens of millions carried on as it always had for thousands of years. The Aztecs of Mesoamerica, when not engaging in massive human sacrifices, enslaved individuals for debts, crimes, and being defeated in war. This was not a nice world. Slavery was the rule. Absence of slavery was the exception. And abolition of slavery on moral grounds was practically unheard of. From the perspective of the chained, across the globe, all told it had been a very ugly past 5000 years.

The Portuguese were the first and most overzealous slavers in the Atlantic trade. Despite being such a small country (or perhaps as a result of it) they were responsible for 45% of all slaves taken during the Atlantic slave trade. Their former colony, Brazil, was the destination of 35% of all slaves in the Atlantic trade and also one of the last of these countries to abolish slavery in 1888. It was there that Africans were taken to produce increasing amounts of sugar for Europe.

The Spanish account for roughly 15% of all African slaves, transporting most of them to South America and their Caribbean island holdings. They also made more determined use of Native American slavery, particularly in their mining operations. Thus Spain and Portugal, briefly an Empire of the Iberian Union from 1580-1640, account for 60% of all African slaves transported to the Americas between the 16th and 19th centuries. This is not entirely surprising given their early arrival in the game and their massive territorial holdings in South and Central America.

The French transported 10% of African slaves to their holdings in the Caribbean, mostly plantations. They barely transported any slaves to Canada, as there was no economic need for forced labour. The Dutch brought slaves to their Caribbean holdings, enslaving about 5% of the total number. In the seventeenth and eighteenth century, forced plantation slave labour expanded from sugar to include the production of tobacco (another highly addictive product) and cotton for textiles. This made slave labour desirable for farms in the southern half of the Thirteen Colonies. As such the British imported 15% of the total number of African slaves to their Caribbean plantations and approximately 10% were imported to lives of bondage in the future United States for a total of 25% of the slave trade.

In the 1500s, an estimated 400,000 to 500,000 people were sold in sub-Saharan Africa (primarily West Africa) and transported into hellish lives of servitude. The majority of this was to the Portuguese and Spanish empires. In the 1600s, the other imperial rivals gradually increased their share, and about 1 million to 1.5 million souls were taken to the Americas in this time.

The 1700s were the worst for slavery in the Americas. The power of the Spanish and Portuguese empires had faded on the world stage during this time, but the importations, particularly by the Portuguese, continued. Meanwhile the British and French became rivals for world domination and took the slave trade to all new heights. The plantations of the Caribbean grew to huge scales and the demand for slaves took off in the British Thirteen Colonies. Approximately 5 million to 8 million slaves in this time were bought, bound, packed into appalling conditions in ships, and sent to the Americas.

It was the excesses of this period that sparked the abolitionist movement in Great Britain. A 30 year public and parliamentary campaign led to the British abolition of the slave trade in 1807, making further purchase and transportation illegal. And the British navy became actively engaged stopping the transportation of African slaves by other European powers and the United States as well, even at the frequent risk of ships and personnel. Nevertheless the remaining slave-holding powers of the Atlantic succeeded in transporting an additional 3 to 4 million slaves from Africa in the 1800s, an enormous number from which we are only a few generations removed.

The British Empire abolished slavery itself in 1833, and slowly, either by brutal war, gruesome revolution, or peaceful legislation, the rest of the Atlantic nations followed suit in the subsequent decades. After 5000 years of this cruel and disgusting practice, we had successful and lasting abolition for the first time, and a revolutionary step in world history, and a shift in how different cultural groups view their fellow human beings. Increasing numbers of activists, ideologues, and generally decent people became willing to lay down their lives to the eradication of the practice of slavery.

But the mission of abolitionists was far from over. In Africa itself, slavery continued, particularly in North Africa, where slavery was given a religious and ethnic justification. In the late 19th century, European imperialism and intervention attempted to expunge slavery from Africa itself, but very slowly and often ineffectively. Or, depending on the colonial power, even half-heartedly. Even today, in the post-colonial era, slavery in Africa is still a problem. In modern Nigeria, there are 700,000, in Ethiopia, 650,000, in the Congo 500,000, and in total roughly 5-10 million people leading lives effectively as slaves in Africa. Beyond Africa, there are 12-14 million de-facto slaves in India, 2 million in Pakistan, and 3 million in China.

At any rate, it is through the malformed practice of slavery through which Sub-Saharan Africa primarily engaged with the wider network of the world zones, first in the trans-Sahara trade, then later in the Atlantic slave trade. The latter connected Africa to the American world zone for the first time, further reinforcing the point that one should never view the rise of complexity in Big History through rose-tinted, Whiggish, and linear goggles. History is much more sinister than that.

Ecological Imperialism and the Columbian Exchange

The field of world history is very much indebted to Alfred Crosby in coining two related terms that almost perfectly describe the revolution that swept across the world with the unification of the world zones: ecological imperialism and the Columbian exchange. Not only were different networks of collective learning colliding in the Age of Explorations, but so too were continents that had been separated geologically for the past 100 million years. This had a profound effect on the subsequent evolution of different continental environments. From the 1500s to the 1800s, plants and animals were transported across the globe to where they never had been before in what Crosby called the Columbian exchange. Despite the reference to Columbus, this term equally applies to the transportation of new plants and animals to Australia as well (as well as from Australia – as anyone who has looked at kangaroo farms in Europe or eucalyptus trees in the Middle East and California will tell you). The idea of ecological imperialism comes in when you consider that the exchange fairly lopsided, with Europeans bringing in their stuff to terraform entire continents into something resembling their environments back home.

The simplest example is livestock. Europeans brought to the Americas and Australasia all their domesticated farm animals, a necessary ingredient for settler colonies. This included sheep and cattle, who began grazing in uncharted territory and which were bred so prodigiously that they quickly became some of the most common mammals to be found in either world zone. In the case of Australia, colonial authorities quickly found that a lot of the soil wasn't exactly ideal for agriculture, but was quite good for grazing pasture and British settlers began making a fortune off of beef and lamb. In the Americas, by 1600 AD, there were 10 to 20 million sheep and cattle, though these catered more for the domestic market. Only the American bison/buffalo exceeded them in number as a large mammalian animal, clocking in at an estimated 45 million.

A more dramatic example is the horse. The horse had started to evolve roughly 50 million years ago, though at the time it was a small multi-toed creature about the size of a dog. The ancestral genus of the horse managed to be dispersed across the Americas and Eurasia before the two were completely disconnected from each other. When humans arrived in the Americas 12,000 years ago, however, they hunted American horse species to extinction. As agrarian civilisations arose in the Americas, there were no large mammals that humans could domesticate as draft animals to pull heavy ploughs. As a result, the carrying capacity of the Americas was lower than it otherwise might have been, hence the low share of the overall world population prior to 1500. Once Europeans arrived, they reintroduced the horse. The Spanish conquered the Incan Empire and Mexico in the sixteenth century. Once the Spanish started pushing north into the Great Plains, they attempted to set up colonies there, but ultimately were beaten back by native resistance. But they left their horses behind. These horses were obtained by Native Americans, and others ran off into the wild.

As a result of the spread of domesticated and wild horses across a large swathe of North America, the lifeways of Native Americans in the Great Plains were radically changed. Many cultures switched from the sedentary or semi-sedentary agrarian cultures that had existed in the southern portions of the Great Plains for thousands of years to become nomadic foragers once again. Those Native American cultures that were already foragers suddenly had a powerful weapon to use against their prey. Prior to the horse, Native Americans would camouflage themselves with pelts and crawl along the ground to get close enough to herds of buffalo. When they got near, they'd spear a buffalo before the herd started to stampede away. With the arrival of the horse, Native Americans could now keep pace with the buffalo and spear them as they chased them, or else herd them off the edge of cliffs. From this point forward, many tribes ran with the buffalo and developed new mythologies and a profound respect for their horses. By the time citizens of the United States arrived in the Great Plains in the nineteenth century, the Native Americans there had kept horses as a keystone of their culture for 300 years. A long enough duration of time for an oral culture that some Native American accounts claim that the horse had always been in the Americas and part of their way of life.

Despite the fact that European plants and animals were being transported to the Americas and Australia, and that much of the landscape was being reshaped to resemble European towns and farms, occasionally the Columbian exchange would work in the other direction with profound effects. The best example of this is the impact of New World crops. The agrarian civilisations of the Americas enjoyed some highly productive and/or soil-enriching crops. An example of the former would be maize. In terms of caloric intake, maize bequeaths more than wheat and only falls short of rice, per square kilometre. An example of the latter would be potatoes, which is not only quite good on the caloric front but actually enriches the soil with nutrients as they grow. Maize and potatoes also come with the advantage that they are easier to prepare and cook than something like wheat or rice. Potatoes themselves earned the sobriquet "ready-made bread" due to the fact that one does not need to grind or bake them, but simply drop them in a pot or fry them for a few minutes. The Americas also gave the world tomatoes, yams, and squashes that were similarly high yield per square kilometre. The upshot of all this was that the carrying capacity of both Europe and Asia were increased in the seventeenth century by the importation and adoption of these products. The European carrying capacity, where American crops were adopted increased by 20 to 30%. In China, the population was starting to experience famines in the 1630s (and a downturn of a secular cycle that killed the Ming dynasty in 1644) but adoption of American crops prevented another mass famine from happening until the 19th century, during which time the Chinese population increased from 150 to 330 million people.

But the most brutal aspect of the Columbian exchange, which does not receive nearly enough attention, is the spread of disease. This undoubtedly can be called a form of ecological imperialism, because without European diseases, it is highly unlikely that the extensive colonisations of the Americas and Australia would have been possible. It is more likely that colonialism in the Aztec and Incan Empires would have more resembled the European occupation of India, where Europeans formed a sliver of the population and were eventually turfed out. And in more sparsely populated areas like Australia and North America it might have at worst resembled the European occupation of South Africa, where Europeans would have formed a minority of the population as the indigenous population grew dramatically from the innovations of modernity. Instead, it is difficult to exaggerate the scale of depopulation caused by the ravages of disease.

Remember that for thousands of years, at this point, Afro-Eurasia had been host to 90% of the human population, most of whom were living in densely packed agrarian civilisations where basic hygiene and germ theory were conspicuously absent. The Afro-Eurasian trade network was a six lane highway for every foul and deadly disease. The bright side is that the inhabitants of Afro-Eurasia had developed resistances to these diseases over hundreds and hundreds of generations, but the populations of the Americas and Australia had no such biological experience. European colonists brought over smallpox, typhoid, cholera, measles, tuberculosis, whooping cough, and numerous influenzas to which indigenous peoples had no resistance. While these were still deadly to Europeans, the impact on indigenous populations with no resistance was much worse.

In the Americas, European diseases are estimated to have wiped out 90% of the population between 1500 and 1620. That is a rate even higher than the Black Death in Afro-Eurasia. For instance imagine medieval France being reduced from 20 million to 2 million people (instead of 10 from a mixture of famine, violence, and disease), or China being reduced from 120 million to 12 million people. Or the modern population of the globe being reduced to 700 or 800 million people, lower than the global population in 1750 or 1800. As the Spanish conquistadors made their way across Central and South America in the 16th century, their diseases actually arrived in new areas before they did. Acting as a vanguard, killing off huge population numbers before the locals had even heard of the interlopers. The total death toll on American populations is debated, and is highly dependent on estimates for the total population of the Americas. Estimates range between 20 million (probably too low) and 100 million (probably too high and usually used for political purposes rather than scholarly ones). Most historians estimate the population of the Americas in 1500 was 55 million people, based on the extrapolation of settlement patterns in archaeological sites to a larger area. That means 50 million people were killed in a world populated by 500-580 million. Just from the simple act of Europeans showing up. And that was done in the space of a century. European diseases would continue to wreak havoc on Native American populations throughout the nineteenth and into the twentieth century.

In Australia, the impact of disease has been less well documented and calculated, partly due to a historiographical preoccupation since the 1980s with the role of frontier violence. Yet from initial study and calculation it is nevertheless clear that the cocktail of European diseases (smallpox, tuberculosis, measles, chickenpox, influenza, typhoid, cholera, and infertility caused by venereal diseases) reduced the Aboriginal Australian population by a significant amount 1788-1900. The rate of spread depends on the contagiousness of the disease and how often people came into contact with Europeans. Aboriginal Australians lived in more sparsely distributed populations than the agrarian societies of Mesoamerica and South America, so the spread may not have been quite as rapid. But also one cannot underestimate the impact of diseases on a people with no immunity over the course of 60-100 years, as frequency of European contact increased.

Much of the Australian estimate depends on the estimated total population of Australia prior to 1788. This ranges between 300,000 and 1.5 million people, with an increasing number of scholars placing the figure at around 800,000 people. In 1850, the Aboriginal population was roughly 200,000 people. In 1900, the Aboriginal population of Australia was roughly 90,000. This is a reduction from all causes of 75% by 1850 and 89% by 1900. The mathematical ratio used by historian Henry Reynolds to calculate the average number of Aboriginals killed in frontier violence (he assumes written records underrepresented the casualties) in reprisal for the death of one European (which were much better documented) arrives at an estimate of *at least* 20,000 killed during the Frontier Wars to roughly 2500-3000 Europeans. Furthermore, adjusting for a population of 800,000, Noel Butlin's calculations give us a maximum of 100,000 people who may have starved because good foraging land was gradually acquired for farming. That gives us a remaining figure of 85% of Aboriginal Australians dying of disease between 1788 and 1900, with at least 500,000 of them dying from disease by 1850, rather than starvation or frontier violence, which falls in line with the impact of European diseases in the Americas. Even if we *triple* the estimated number of deaths from frontier violence, that still leaves 80% of Aboriginal Australians dying from disease, 12.5% dying from starvation, and 7.5% dying from frontier violence.

It is with no little sense of tragedy that the Columbian exchange should have been so heinously lopsided. At the same time that American crops were raising the carrying capacities of Europe and Asia, sending their populations soaring, the populations of the Americas and Australia were being reduced at a rate worse than what was experienced during the Black Death, and delivering them to levels below what they had been for several tens of thousands of years when those world zones were first inhabited. Even writing this now, one can barely conceive the devastation and suffering wrought by such biological terror.

On the Verge of Threshold 8

In the study of complexity, we frequently find that new phenomena emerge when building blocks are laid in a specific order. The different component parts of a strand of DNA, the many organic chemicals which form its code, taken individually are no more than a simple sludge on the surface of the Earth. Yet when they come together they create the phenomenon of self-replicating life and the bizarre myriad of forms that have arisen in the past 3.8 billion years. Similarly, at the end of the Age of Explorations, many of the building blocks were in place within a unified global system for another titanic leap forward in complexity. The history of the nineteenth and twentieth century, and the previous two sections of this chapter, entitle me to add the phrase "for better or worse."

The Age of Explorations had opened up a vast reservoir of trade and exchange. The agrarian states of Europe began to think more favourably of mercantilism and commercial ventures. Many of the goods of this network of exchange thus far had been natural resources sold off in another corner of the globe, or luxury goods that were acquired from Asia and transported back to Europe. But the world market of 680 million people by the year 1700 could clearly be supplied with more. And at great profit. What of goods whose value did not strictly rely on their point of origin or delivery, but were valuable by virtue of the fact that you could cheaply construct them anywhere and sell them off to a wide population of upper class, middling, and even poor peoples?

The world in 1700 was very different from the one that had existed 300 years prior. Instead of a world of separate world zones, each evolving via collective learning on different trajectories, explorers had reached every single one of them. Even the Pacific and Australia had started to be explored by Europeans, with the Dutch sighting Australia in the early seventeenth century. Meanwhile the main conduit of collective learning in the world was no longer the Silk Roads. It was the sea. And the locus of trade had drifted from Central Asia to Europe. The British, Portuguese, and French were engaged in trade and local rule over the vast populations of India, as the Mughal Empire crumbled. Even though the economic centre of gravity remained in China, the majority of mercantile activity was now conducted by Europeans. And they had a great deal of motivation to expand these endeavours. Individuals wanted to enrich themselves, yes, but Western European governments were collecting more of their tax revenue (i.e. energy flows) from trade than traditional agrarian taxation. In fact, Britain in the year 1700 got more than 50% of its revenue from taxation on trade.

The impulse toward commercialism had struck deep. All that was required now was the hard machinery to expand these ambitions still further. As different as the world in 1700 was from that in 1400, no one could possibly have foreseen the tremendous transformations that would occur in the same space of time between 1700 and the year 2000.

Essay Writing Exercise

For this exercise, consider the following essay question only:

What is the single most important theme you have discovered in 13.8 billion years of Big History?

Engage in some free-writing. Don't worry about structure or your outline. Just try to answer the question without stopping. Go for about 15 minutes. Then take a break. Then go for another 15 minutes. Then take another break.

Then consider what theme you chose and why you chose it. Now that you have a moment to reflect, is there another less obvious theme that really captures your passions and interest? Also consider in what way this theme connects to all the major periods of Big History. Does it connect to all of them equally, or does it rear its head in specific periods but its impact remains the most important and pivotal? Finally consider whether your chosen theme has been explored before in traditional scholarship and to what extent.

Further Reading

Black, Jeremy. War and the World: Military Power and the Fate of Continents, 1450-2000. New Haven: Yale University Press, 1998.

Bray, Francesca. The Rice Economies: Technology and Development in Asian Societies. Oxford: Basil Blackwell, 1986.

Chi, Z. and H. C. Hung, "The Emergence of Agriculture in South China," Antiquity vol. 84 (2010) pg. 11–25.

Cipolla, Carlo. Before the Industrial Revolution: European Society and Economy, 1000-1700. 2nd ed. London: Methuen, 1981.

Crosby, Alfred. The Columbian Exchange: The Biological Expansion of Europe, 900-1900. Cambridge: Cambridge University Press, 1986.

Diamond, Jared. Guns, Germs, and Steel: The Fates of Human Societies. London: Vintage, 1998.

Dunn, Ross. The Adventures of Ibn Battuta: A Muslim Traveler of the Fourteenth Century. Berkeley: University of California Press, 1986.

Elvin, Mark. The Pattern of the Chinese Past. Stanford, Calif.: Stanford University Press, 1973.

Faser, Evan and Andrew Rimas. Empires of Food: Feast, Famine, and the Rise and Fall of Civilisations. Berkeley, Calif.: Counterpoint, 2010.

Fernandez-Armesto, Felipe. Before Columbus: Exploration and Colonisation from the Mediterranean to the Atlantic, 1229-1492. London: Macmillan, 1987.

Fernandez-Armesto, Felipe. Pathfinders: A Global History of Exploration. New York: W.W. Norton, 2007.

Hansen, Valerie. The Open Empire: A History of China to 1600. New York: W.W. Norton, 2000.

Headrick, Daniel. Technology: A World History. Oxford: Oxford University press, 2009.

Higman, B. How Food Made History. Chichester: Wiley Blackwell, 2012.

Hsu, Cho-yun. Han Agriculture: The Formation of Early Chinese Agrarian Economy, 206 B.C.–220 A.D. ed. Jack Dulled. Seattle: University of Washington Press, 1980.

Korotayev, A., and A. Malkov, and D. Khalturina. Laws of History: Mathematical Modelling of Historical Macroprocesses. Moscow: Komkniga, 2005.

Levathes, Louise. When China Ruled the Seas: The Treasure Fleet of the Dragon Throne, 1405-1433. New York: Simon and Schuster, 1994.

Man, John. Atlas of the Year 1000. Cambridge, Mass.: Harvard University Press, 1999.

McNeill, William. Plagues and People. Oxford: Blackwell, 1977.

Otfinoski, Steven. Marco Polo: to China and Back. New York: Benchmark Books, 2003.

Pacey, Arnold. Technology in World Civilisation. Cambridge, Mass.: MIT Press, 1990.

Polo, Marco. The Travels of Marco Polo. trans. Aldo Ricci. reprint. Abingdon: Routledge Curzon, 2005.

Pomeranz, Kenneth. The Great Divergence: China, Europe, and the Making of the Modern World Economy. Princeton: Princeton University Press, 2000.

Pomeranz, Kenneth, and Steven Topik. The World that Trade Created: Society, Culture, and the World Economy, 1400 to the Present. 2nd ed. Armonk: Sharpe, 2006.

Ponting, Clive. A Green History of the World: The Environment and the Collapse of Great Civilisations. London: Penguin, 1991.

Richards, John. The Unending Frontier: Environmental History of the Early Modern World. Berkeley: University of California Press, 2006.

Russell, Peter. Prince Henry the Navigator: A Life. New Haven: Yale University Press, 2000.

Temple, Robert. The Genius of China: 3000 Years of Science, Discovery, and Invention. New York: Touchstone, 1986.

Woods, Michael and Mary Woods. Ancient Technology: Ancient Agriculture from Foraging to Farming. Minneapolis: Runestone Press, 2000.

Zheng, Y. et al., "Rice Fields and Modes of Rice Cultivation between 5000and 2500 BC in East China," Journal of Archaeological Science vol. 36 (2009) pg. 2609–2616.

CHAPTER 12

THE ANTHROPOCENE

Or,

HUMANS SIMULTANEOUSLY

BECOME ONE OF THE

MOST IMPRESSIVE COMPLEX SYSTEMS

IN THE UNIVERSE

WHILE PROFOUNDLY

BUGGERING UP THE EARTH

How humans love burning 350 million year old trees…

> **Threshold 8: Industrial Revolution – 250 years ago**
>
> - *Wherein the British start burning coal and implementing steam engines in the economy.*
> - *Mass production sets off a blizzard of economic and scientific innovation.*
> - *The rest of the world endeavours to catch up because why let the British have all the fun?*
> - *The world enters a new geological age known as the Anthropocene.*

Timeline

- **Industrialisation Spreads across the West (1820 to 1880 AD):** The Industrial Revolution that began in Great Britain in the eighteenth century gave that country a definite lead and advantage in the nineteenth century. After the Napoleonic Wars, other Western countries began to understand the advantages industrialisation held in terms of tax income and global political and military power. As such, Belgium began to industrialise in the 1820s and 1830s, and it was followed by the larger countries of France, Prussia (later Germany), and the United States. Those that did not industrialise as effectively or at all in the nineteenth century fell behind. By the 1880s even the Russians were making slow initial efforts to industrialise, though this process would not be completed until the following century, and across the world Japan also began industrialising with aplomb. This process would affect the balance of power and geopolitics of the twentieth century.

- **Invention of the Telegraph (c.1845 AD):** The invention of the telegraph allowed for almost instantaneous communication of information in the world for the very first time. This level of connectivity was a major advantage for the pace of collective learning. The level of connectivity via modern communications was only intensified by the laying down of the trans-Atlantic telegraph cable in the 1860s, and the first fruits of the telephone in the 1870s. The radio, television, and internet would follow in the twentieth century. From this point forward, collective learning went into overdrive.

- **Expansion of Car and Airplane Travel (1870s to 1900s AD):** Similar to the transmission of information, the transport of peoples and goods sped up significantly in the nineteenth and twentieth centuries. Railroads were an early example of this, with transport being made rapid along fixed arteries. Cars and airplanes allowed for more flexible transport across vast distances, permitting a level of transport for goods and peoples on a level as efficient on land as previously had been seen on the sea (which also sped up and grew more efficient with the invention of steamships). All told the average distance an average person would travel in their lifetimes increased significantly.

- **The Green Revolution (1930s to 1960s AD):** Innovations in the modification of crops raised the carrying capacity of the globe. In the nineteenth and early twentieth century, the most populous regions of the world, particularly Asia, underwent several waves of famine (some of which being exacerbated by human incompetence or malice) and appeared to be entering into another downward phase of a secular cycle. Yet modification of wheat and rice crops managed to raise the carrying capacity to allow an explosion of growth across the world, causing the world population to double, then triple, and soon to quadruple. The only question now is whether we will hit another human carrying capacity for the globe in either the twenty-first or twenty-second century, with population estimates for 2100 varying between 10 billion and 13 billion people.

- **The Great Acceleration (1945 AD to Present):** As impressive as the changes of the nineteenth century were, most of the growth in terms of population, energy flows, and societal complexity has occurred since the end of the Second World War, as markets recovered and industrialisation continued to spread across the globe. Often represented graphically, the level of growth since 1945 appears as an L-shape or "hockey stick" as increasing numbers of billions of people engage more actively in a unified global system of complexity. This is short enough a period to be within many people's lifetimes. It is also alarmingly short a period considering what strains or difficulties may lie beyond of such a vast rate of expansion.

Measuring Threshold 8

The Industrial Revolution is another remarkable threshold of complexity that leads us into the immense transformations of modernity – whether we are discussing the veritable Cambrian Explosion of new inventions and innovations, the revolutions of thought and doctrine, or the radical alteration of lifeways of every human on this planet. This speaks nothing of how it opened the door to another geological epoch, the "Anthropocene" where humans are impacting the planet more rapidly and drastically than any single species has in the 3.8 billion year history of life. From the first sparks of heavy industry in Great Britain has come an avalanche of change and growing complexity, in just the past 250 to 300 years. This is much more rapid a space of time than even the immense changes wrought to the globe by seventh threshold of agriculture.

In terms of complexity, Threshold 8 marks a great leap forward by either notion of how complexity is measured. In terms of diversity of building blocks, connections, and structural intricacy, the unified global system of modernity contains an unprecedented number of people (7.7 billion at time of writing) who are all potential innovators in a system of collective learning. And these human minds are united by almost instantaneous communication, transportation, unprecedented levels of literacy, and with the modern equivalent of the Great Library of Alexandria available at their fingertips. Sustaining this web of knowledge are immensely intricate networks of trade, supply, laws, and energy production, and a wider diversification of labour than ever before. Even in terms of energy flows, the free energy rate density of society has increased from 100,000 erg/g/s in the Agrarian Era, to 500,000 erg/g/s in the industrial 19th century, to 2 million erg/g/s in today's twenty-first century "technologist" or "post-industrial" societies. Both in terms of the more qualitative "building blocks" and the more quantitative "energy flows" human society today is one of the most complex things we are aware of in the known Universe.

How did this happen? The first key ingredient was the harnessing of fossil fuels for industrial production. Fossil fuels include coal, oil, and gas. They are so called because they are actually the remains of living things that perished between 10 and 600 million years ago. Coal is made from the giant trees that fell to the ground 350 million years ago in the Carboniferous (hence the name) and got compressed by plate tectonics to form hard, thick layers of coal in rock beds. When burned, coal released the aggregated of energy of millennia of thousands upon thousands of plants. Thus fossil fuels far outstripped the energy output of human labour, animal labour, or the burning of wood, when harnessed by industrial machinery. This powered the Industrial Revolution of the eighteenth and nineteenth centuries, and still powers much of the human energy grid today.

Oil similarly forms from single celled creatures, and some multi-celled creatures, that died hundreds of millions of years ago and were compressed by the tectonic pressure into a form of sludge. This powered much of the Great Acceleration of the twentieth and twenty-first centuries. As did gas, which is a by-product of the fossilisation process of oil, when the pressure forces out all the residual gas inside the organisms. Today, in the Anthropocene, we are experiencing a transition to renewables in some sectors and in some countries, like solar or wind or hydro, as well as energy produced by nuclear fission in power plants. But none of these innovations would have been possible without the first rise of machinery spurred on by coal in the Industrial Revolution.

The Industrial Revolution began in Great Britain in the eighteenth century (please note that I do not say the United Kingdom – Ireland was agrarian). In many ways it resulted from the harnessing of several individual innovations of the time. The continued refinement of the steam engine, from Thomas Newcomen in 1712 to James Watt between 1763 and 1775, which then could harness fossil fuels to drive machinery. Coal enabled faster production of textiles in spinning machines compared to hand-weaving, the better refinement of iron in larger quantities, and eventually the rise of the train and the steamship. By 1800, the rate of British manufacturing was already was three times higher than any other agrarian civilisation on Earth. Despite its tiny population, this made Britain the richest nation on the planet. And as the country continued to industrialise, its lead continued to grow until roughly 1880 when it produced 23% of the world's goods, despite it being tiny in terms of population (approximately 2-2.5% of the world's total population in 1880). Thereafter numerous other countries, particularly Germany and the United States, began to catch up. By comparison, in 1880, China represented 30% of the world's population but only produced 12% of the world's manufactured goods, whereas in 1800 it produced about 33% of the world's manufactured goods, roughly proportionate to its population size as an agrarian economy.

The Industrial Revolution had another impact on countries that industrialised – the curse of secular cycles was temporarily lifted. For the first time, despite rapid population growth in the nineteenth century, wages rose continually faster than prices. The inhabitants of Britain between 1800 and 1900 gradually enjoyed more extra income which they spent on luxury goods of which their ancestors could only dream.

The same could not be said of predominantly agrarian economies, who did not see the same increase of the real wage, still suffered during periods of overpopulation, and still lay in danger of recurrent famines. From 1800 to 1950, much of the West was liberated from these fears, and between 1950 and 2000 much of the rest of the world continued to industrialise and enjoy the fruits of the Green Revolution. Overall the carrying capacity continued to grow, from a world population of 670 million in 1700, to 954 million by 1800, 2.5 billion in 1950, and 7.7 billion today. It is only on the timescale of the next century that the potential ballooning of the population to the level of 10 billion or even 13 billion, could start to hit the global carrying capacity once again, and threaten secular cycles.

Why Britain and not China?

We covered the First Great Divergence in China in the last chapter. Due to a vast increase in the Chinese population and an acceleration of collective learning, China under the Song dynasty appeared close to achieving an industrial revolution. The Ming dynasty that succeeded it, while less hospitable to commerce, briefly looked like it could have unified the world zones with their voyages of exploration between 1403 and 1433. Yet the Industrial Revolution happened in Great Britain, and the Second Great Divergence set Europe and North America ahead of much of the rest of the world, an imbalance which still largely remains today.

The reasons for this is still a huge area of debate for modern historians and is likely never to be fully resolved. Perhaps one reason for this is there isn't a single clear and easy answer as to why the Industrial Revolution happened in Britain. Instead it appears to have occurred due to a confluence of factors, and scholars debate over the various weight of their significance. Some of the key factors involve: access to fossil fuels, access to world markets, access to raw materials to be transformed by manufacturing, a potential industrial workforce, the right set of inventions to kick off mass production, and a culture of consumerism that fosters entrepreneurship and capital investment.

By 1750, Great Britain had all of these things. And this was directly the result of the unification of the world zones. Without the unification of the world zones, Britain would not have a culture of consumerism that had grown out of mercantile ventures and colonialism. It would not have access to large quantities of cotton from the Americas or India for textile manufacturing, it obviously would not have access to world markets. In fact, it wouldn't even have had the right inventions in Britain to kick off mass production. The steam engine was refined in eighteenth century Britain to be useful for industrialisation, but it was not invented there. The Ancient Romans had a prototype steam engine, it was written at least in blueprint in Turkey in the sixteenth century (though for rapid cooking of a sheep not for industry), and designs for steam engines and machinery filtered into Britain from seventeenth and eighteenth century France. In fact, without the agricultural innovations of the Dutch and Belgians, Britain would not even have had its agricultural revolution and enclosure movements which freed up a lot of farmers (willingly or unwillingly) to form an industrial workforce in the cities. So in many ways the unification of the world zones was a key prerequisite for Great Britain having the first sparks of Threshold 8.

In contrast, China enjoyed a huge burst of population growth during the Song dynasty, which continued throughout much of the Ming dynasty into the seventeenth century. Then after a brief slowdown, crops from the Americas enhanced the Chinese carrying capacity for another

100 years. But the problem with having a population that is too large and too dense is that, while it may be good for collective learning generally, there is no shortage of labour and thus no need to invest in machinery to do the work of what a bunch of low-wage peasants can do. China even had access to coal, but while Britain's coal was easily accessible in the west of the country (particularly in Wales) the Chinese coal was deposited mostly in sparsely populated northern regions, hundreds of kilometres from the main populous and potentially commercial areas of the centre and south.

Furthermore, after the fall of the Song dynasty, China entered a long period of economic conservatism where traditional modes of production were valued far above any new and innovative ideas. Continued industrialisation was seen as a disturbance to social stability (and they were not wrong given the upheavals the Industrial Revolution brought to the West). Furthermore, the Chinese government relied mostly on old fashioned feudal taxation of the landed gentry and peasantry, with merchants after the 1400s making up a tiny part of government incomes yet again. They had no need for wider world commerce at the time.

Finally, China sat at the end of Afro-Eurasia, separated from world trade by either the vast Pacific Ocean, the slow trudging sea route around Africa, or the dangerous overland routes across long barren tracts of Afro-Eurasia. And given that they held the centre of gravity in terms of world trade for much of the past 1000 years, with Europeans bringing business and silver to them, they were hardly incentivised to transport their goods across the world themselves at the same scale. After China ceased to be a naval and economic force in the Indian Ocean after 1433, this allowed the Portuguese, and later the French, British, and Dutch to enter into intensified trade in South Asia instead. And Europe may sit at the other end of Afro-Eurasia from China, but with the discovery of the Americas, they actually sat as a geographically central hub between the two largest world zones, with plenty of commercial incentive to also explore Australasia and the Pacific.

But why Britain in particular, above all the other countries of Europe? Why not the Spanish, the French, or the Dutch? As early as 1700, Britain was already on the road to industrialisation. It was already refining the steam engine and methods of iron production. By the Seven Years War (1756-1763) Britain had indisputably the most powerful navy in the world, which gave it a massive advantage over its European rivals. By 1763, Britain dominated North America, South Africa, and India both in terms of territory it controlled and in terms of its markets. Even after the American Revolution saw much of North America split away from the British Empire in 1783, the USA's primary trading partner was Great Britain. By that point it was clear, Britain was going to become the first industrial power, and much of the nineteenth century would belong to the British Empire.

By 1750, roughly 50% of the British economy was built on commercial ventures. The introduction into Britain in the sixteenth century of the Dutch method of four-crop rotation, allowed for agricultural land to become more efficient. Instead of letting one third of the soil lay fallow (i.e. unused) as it regained some nutrients, legumes were planted to replenish the soil instead. This became common practice in Britain in the eighteenth century, making agriculture more efficient and freeing up workers for textile production. Then in the nineteenth century, Britain began to mechanise agricultural production, and imported more food from the outside world, freeing up even more people to begin to work in the first factories. Between 1700 and 1850, the number of farmers dropped from 60% of the population to 30% of the population. A huge diversification of labour ensued, with many people becoming factory workers, but also increasing numbers of people becoming lawyers, doctors, scientists, and entrepreneurs. The number and diversity of building blocks in British society increased, aiding the increased growth of the middle class. The diversification of labour also enabled a vast mass of innovations to occur in fields that previously were populated by a small sliver of the population, setting off a flurry of new breakthroughs in engineering, architecture, medicine, and technology.

Mass production had a profound effect. Britain's textile industry drove down the price of cotton textiles by 100% between 1750 and 1800. Britain became the world's leading iron and steel producer by 1820. Coal production increased by 600% between 1750 and 1870. Canned goods production became an enormous industry in the 1840s, with previously perishable products now being able to be transported long distances across the world. The steamship rapidly increased the speed of trade in the 1830s and 1840s, by up to six times. 21,000 kilometres of train tracks were laid down across Britain between 1830 and 1870, improving the nation's connectivity. As mentioned, Britain's share of global trade increased to 23% of the world total by 1880, despite only being 2-2.5% of the world's population. And release from the pressure of secular cycles, and with an increasing real wage and standard of living, and also improvements in medicine, the British population increased from 6 million in 1750 to 32 million by 1880, to speak nothing of the additional millions who emigrated to Britain's colonies around the world.

It is important to note, however, that the improvement of living standards did not happen overnight. The transition from agrarian life to industrial life was extremely painful, casting many people into poverty and fairly unpleasant working conditions, by both the standards of the day and also by modern standards. The painful transition of this rise of complexity mirrors those agonies of previous thresholds, like the transition to agriculture. Nevertheless, by 1900, the British population enjoyed a greater average standard of living than any country prior to 1750, and even the majority of the world population in the early twentieth century. Certainly if one compares it to China in 1900, which had just undergone a century of brutal civil wars and famines claiming tens of millions of lives, and a fairly grim outlook from 1900-1970 as well.

The World Tries to Catch Up

The extremely resilient performance of Britain in the Napoleonic Wars, allowing it to punch above its weight despite its small population, made clear that it had an economic advantage, which translated into a military and geopolitical advantage. During that period, they managed to hold a coalition led by Napoleon at bay and cope with an attack by the United States upon Canada. The advantage was again put to the test in the First Opium War between Britain and China from 1839 to 1842, in which Britain, a much smaller country, managed to defeat and humiliate China, which had been the world's leading economic and military power for much of the past thousand years. As the nineteenth century progressed, Britain's naval and economic power managed to create the largest empire in human history. The advantages of the Industrial Revolution were undeniable, and so it was not much of a surprise when other nations in the world began to play catch-up. Industrialisation takes time, since it involves the reshaping of so many sectors of society, and so Britain enjoyed a lead time of several decades.

Belgium, rebelling against the Netherlands in 1830 and becoming an independent country, began to industrialise first. This was aided by the fact Belgium already had a long history of intensified textile production and had access to nearby coal. In 1834, they also began to lay down railroads. But Belgium's population was too small to bestow it with "great power status". France, arguably Britain's biggest rival prior to the rise of Germany and the United States, began to industrialise in the 1840s, although a somewhat antiquated agricultural system and too many inland tariffs made sure this did not bear fruit until after the Revolution of 1848. Nevertheless, France did not have the same access to coal, did not have as powerful a navy, and did not have as large an overseas empire. Its industrialisation made it only 8% of the world's total manufacturing compared to Britain's 23% in 1880, despite having a roughly comparable population of 39 million. France would not achieve an economy roughly equal in size to Britain's until the late twentieth century.

Germany requires a more searching statement. Prior to 1871, Germany was split into a number of independent states. Prussia began to industrialise in the 1840s, shortly after serfdom was abolished, but things really only kicked in with government intervention in the 1850s, with the King of Prussia investing in railroads. The rest of the German states lagged behind somewhat. After unification in 1871, Germany achieved a larger population than Britain or France. Once it industrialised this would give Germany an important advantage. Meanwhile the Germans invested far more in scientific and industrial education than the British, giving them some advantages in terms of chemistry and means of production. Nevertheless, Germany's share of industrial production in 1880 was only 8.5%. Germany's industrial sector would not equal Britain's until 1914, and would only surpass it thanks to

Germany's larger population in the 1920s and 1930s. This definitely correlates with many of the events of the early twentieth century.

The United States would be the first power to clearly surpass Britain in terms of industrial production. During the American Revolution, the US population was approximately 2.5 million, or less than half that of Britain's. But the Louisiana Purchase of 1803 and the Mexican War of 1846-1848 gave the Americans control of the vast swathes of land that form the continental United States. In 1850, the US population was only 23 million people (still smaller than Britain's 27 million) and the majority of the population still laboured at agriculture rather than industry. Nevertheless, the industrialised northeastern states produced 7% of the world's manufactured goods by 1860 (slightly less than France) and gave the Union a definite advantage over the Confederacy during the Civil War. After the end of the Civil War in 1865, the United States invested in a period of settlement in the west, heavy industrialisation in the north, and let vast numbers of immigrants into the country. In 1865, the US population was 31 million, by 1880 the population had grown to 50 million, outstripping Britain in numbers, and produced 15% of the world's manufacturing goods. By 1900, Britain was fully eclipsed. The US population had grown to 76 million people, and it produced 25-30% of the world's manufacturing. The US lead in both population and industrialisation would continue to grow. Again, these few metrics explain a lot about the transformation of the global balance of power during and after the two World Wars.

Beyond the West were two other early industrialisers eager to even the score and maintain a prominent place on the global stage. The humiliation of Russia at the hands of Britain and France during the Crimean War (1853-56) prompted some early attempts at modernisation. Unlike Western Europe, Russia had remained an agrarian economy that still had serfdom. There was very little incentive for commercialism or industry in such an environment. But between 1861 and 1866, the "Great Emancipation" saw 50 million Russian serfs freed by Alexander II in hopes of kick-starting industrialisation. The government sought to encourage some of these newly liberated workers toward the cities to work in subsidised factories, and in 1892 the government paid for a massive railway network to extend across the Russian Empire. Yet the government-led industrialisation was fairly ineffectual, and both landowners and peasants were incentivised to keep up traditional modes of agrarian production. Very few peasants wanted to leave their farms to engage in hard factory labour in the cities. By 1900, only 5% of the population were industrial workers, and the Russian share of total global production was only 8.9% despite having a population of 136 million people. It would require the First World War, the rise of the Soviet Union, and the bloody excesses of Stalin, to force a greater degree of industrialisation and even then the total Russian world share of manufactured goods increased only marginally.

Japan was somewhat more successful. After Japan was humiliatingly forced to open their country to trade by American warships in 1853, they embarked on a period of rapid modernisation and industrialisation. With British backing, the Japanese Emperor seized power from the warlords in the Meiji Restoration of 1868. Thereafter the central government invited in Western experts, crafted a fairly Western-looking constitution, and heavily subsidised all attempts at factory production. By so doing, Japan transformed from a feudal to a modern society within half a century. The Japanese dominated the market in silk production, since they were able to out-produce and undersell the Chinese, who were not yet industrialising. Japan also had a fairly large population from which they could build a large industrial economy. However, in 1900, Japan made only 2.5% of the world's industrial output, and this share did not grow significantly until after the Second World War. Thereafter, the Japanese "economic miracle" allowed its large industrialised population to become the world's second or third largest economy (depending on the decade) and it still enjoys the position of third place, after the United States and China, today.

"The West and the Rest"

The Second Great Divergence saw the "West" pull ahead of the rest of the world for the nineteenth and twentieth centuries. Indeed, Europe, North America, Australia, and Japan still enjoy a tremendous economic lead over the rest of the world today. It is perhaps more accurate to divide the world into the "Developed" and "Developing" world, since Japan is definitely not Western (though it has adopted a plethora of Western ideas and modes of production) and Australia is definitely south of Asia and east of Africa, not west of them. "Developing" economies generally refer to those countries that are still industrialising, and this includes many of the countries of Asia (including India and China), the countries of Africa, and many of the countries of Central and South America. The former Eastern bloc (the states that fell under communism in the middle of the twentieth century) are not considered "developing", although their economies were severely damaged by their Soviet-style systems and have still not recovered to the same level of other industrialised nations even to this day. That includes Russia, despite its large population and tremendous mineral wealth. But what of the developing world in the story of industrialisation? These countries did not industrialise in the nineteenth or early twentieth centuries, but have been industrialising to varying degrees of success since the Second World War. In that sense, it is clear that Threshold 8 is still proceeding, with most of the world's population still making the agrarian-industrial transition, just as it took thousands of years for agriculture to spread across the globe.

The result of the Second Great Divergence in the nineteenth century was the rise of imperialist industrialised states. Imperialism had been a facet of history since the dawn of agrarian civilisations. However the unification of the world zones, the power of fossil fuels, and the imbalance of trade and scientific advancement, allowed larger empires than ever before to be forged and fast swathes of land and the majority of the world's population being controlled by relatively small armed forces of Europeans, Americans, and the Japanese. By 1914, roughly 85% of the world's surface had fallen under foreign imperialist control. The British had the largest empire, stretching from Canada to Australia, the majority share of Africa, all of densely populated India, and a sizeable share of Southeast Asia. The French built a large empire in Northwest Africa and Indochina. The Dutch, Belgians, Spanish, Portuguese, Italians, and Germans also boasted imperial holdings in Africa, Asia, and numerous islands in the Pacific and Caribbean. Despite American rhetoric against imperialism, the United States expanded their holdings into the West via the claim of "Manifest Destiny", acquired Alaska from the Russians, annexed Hawaii, occupied numerous Pacific islands, took control of the Philippines and Puerto Rico from Spain, built and controlled the Panama Canal, and exerted undue influence over the Caribbean and the states of Central and South America. Even Japan got in on the game, occupying Korea and fragments of China prior to World War I, and expanding their holdings at the end of that war to many islands in the Pacific. All of this is testament to the clear advantage that an industrialised nation had over agrarian ones.

Threshold 8 Warfare

Mass production doesn't just exist for textiles, canned food, and motor cars. Mass production can also be turned toward producing artillery shells, rifles, airplanes, and battleships. By the mid-19th century, the rifled barrel of a gun was making them much more deadly and accurate. By the late 19th century, machine guns were becoming rapidly common in a country's arsenal. Armour was a thing of the past so soldiers in cloth uniforms became immensely vulnerable. Gone were the days of neatly ordered armies marching slowly toward each other in their battle lines. You can't march toward a hail of bullets.

The European powers were slow to catch on to this lesson. The quick defeat of France by Prussia in the 1870-71 Franco-Prussian war gave a lot of military experts the impression that industrial wars would be brief. Many people ignored the example of the United States Civil War fought only a few years earlier. That was a bitter war that quickly turned to stalemate. It was only by a grinding war of attrition that the greater industrial potential of the Northern Union over the Southern Confederacy was finally brought to bear. After use of deadly rifles, huge amounts of artillery and explosives, and even some trench warfare. The US Civil War killed off 620,000 people, or roughly 2% of the population. More than the US population lost in WWI and WWII combined. Military leaders and statesmen should have paid closer attention to this industrial war and what slaughters can happen when hopes of a quick victory have faded.

In the First World War, many military theorists still operated under the illusion that wars could be fast ones of movement. And that the superior "fighting spirit" of your troops was all that was required to win the day. But how does an army of millions of men quickly win a war against another army of millions of men? What is more, rifles were standard. Machine guns were plentiful in every industrialized country. Artillery shells could be launched at enemy lines, so that millions of them could be dropped within a week or so. And new inventions, like poison gas, could strangle enemy lines. In the First World War, the great difficulty was how to win battles when weapons were more deadly than ever before, and soldiers wore nothing but their uniforms. The result was 4 years of slaughter and millions of men dead on the battlefields of Europe. It was only late in that war that the usefulness of armoured tanks combined with air attack was discovered as the key to breaking enemy lines.

However armoured tanks and air forces would not lead to quick wars with low casualties. WWII proved that industrialized wars between powerful nations with modern technology would forevermore be bloody. Worse still, because factories powered the armies, it was considered fair game to target civilian populations. Terror bombing was used in WWI with

German Zeppelin raids on the United Kingdom. But it was escalated by the air forces of WWII. They targeted industrial centres, air fields, and even just civilian populations to try and reduce morale. Industrial warfare meant that any person, at any time, could find themselves on the battlefront.

The costs of modern war became so high, that industrialized nations stopped using war as a form of policy against each other like they did prior to WWI. Increasingly war became an apocalyptic last resort. A trigger nobody at the helm of an industrialized nation wished to pull. That said the late 20th century and 21st century still saw many wars. Largely powerful nations intervening in or targeting regions that did not have the same degree of industrialized firepower. Nevertheless, even cases like the Vietnam War or the Iraq War proved surprisingly costly for powerful industrialized nations. Even though there was a huge imbalance of power between opponents. Such is the world where you don't need a bunch of factories to be deadly. This is the world where the AK-47 machine gun, the grenade, the rocket launcher, and the road-side bomb, are easily acquired by even the most impoverished opponents.

And we haven't even begun to talk about nukes. Since the Second World War, there has been no major conflict between the most powerful nations of the world. If the Cold War had happened between the USA and Soviet Union 50 or 100 years earlier, it would have likely ended in war. But war had simply become far too costly. Nowhere is this better expressed than by the threat of nuclear obliteration for the globe. During WWII, the British, the Germans, and the Americans, all invested scientific resources in the race to develop the atomic bomb. The Americans made the bomb first and destroyed Hiroshima and Nagasaki. In 1949, however, the Soviet Union had managed to steal plans via espionage and build their own bombs. The British and French followed suit in the 1950s. The Chinese got their first bombs in the 1960s. Meanwhile, the even deadlier hydrogen bomb or "H-bomb" was developed.

Throughout the Cold War, the threat of mutually assured destruction loomed over the globe. USA and Russian arsenals were loaded with tens of thousands of bombs. Delivery systems shifted from planes to intercontinental ballistic missiles that are very difficult, if not impossible, to stop. At the end of the Cold War, the threat of nuclear annihilation somewhat faded in people's minds.

Nevertheless, nuclear annihilation remains one of the most likely ways the human story of rising complexity will get cut short. In the 21st century, the USA has roughly 1800 nuclear warheads deployed and ready to go. The Russians have roughly 2000. The United Kingdom, France, and China all have a 200-300 apiece in case they need to retaliate against a nuclear attack. India and Pakistan both have 100-150 warheads pointed at each other in case war erupts. North Korea has been developing nuclear weapons, has a stockpile of at least a few dozen, and has made strides with H-bomb technology and delivery systems. Other countries could develop this technology within a few years, provided they have the right designs and secretly enrich the right nuclear materials. And there may be other countries already out there that are undeclared nuclear powers.

It doesn't even require a country to shoot off its entire stockpile to cause global destruction. All it would take is maybe 50 to 100 nuclear weapons going off in the wrong place, and so much dust and ash could be thrown into the atmosphere that a global winter results and causes the starvation of billions. Never mind asteroids or supervolcanic eruptions which can do the same thing. At any minute, of any day, at the pressing of a few buttons and a few commands shouted down a telephone, humans could be the authors of the great Mass Extinction event in Earth's history.

The Great Acceleration

From 1870 to 1914, the average annual rate of growth of the world's exports was 3.4% and the average annual rate of growth of GDP per capita was 1.3%. These levels are largely dictated by Britain and the entry of the United States and Germany (and other Europeans and the Japanese) as similarly potent industrial giants in this period. The disastrous period of the two World Wars from 1914 to 1945 saw the average annual rate of growth of exports shrink to 0.9% and the average annual rate of growth of GDP per capita to 0.91%. Thereafter, the nuclear bomb made warfare between Great Powers too costly to even begin a direct violent contest with another Great Power (though this has not stopped the industrial giants of the world going to war with less powerful nations when they are sure it would not draw in other industrial giants on the opposite side). As a mildly ironic result of the creation of the most devastating weapons in world history, the period 1945 to present has been one of the most "peaceful" (relatively speaking) than any other period in world history since *at least* 5500 years ago. Possibly far longer when one considers the skirmishes and raids of early agrarian societies, and the so-called 10% "murder-rate" of foraging societies stretching back 315,000 years to the birth of *Homo sapiens*.

As such, the period 1945 to present has been one of unprecedented growth in terms of exports, GDP, population, and complexity. In fact, despite the foundations for Threshold 8 being laid in the eighteenth and nineteenth centuries, most of the "busy-work" has happened in the past seventy years. Still within living memory for some. This period is known as the "Great Acceleration". From 1945 to 2019 the average annual rate of growth of exports has been 6% and the rate of growth of global GDP has been an average of 3%. This outstrips both the late nineteenth century as the world caught up to Britain, and absolutely blows out of the water the World War and inter-war years. As such, you live in one of the most complex and rapidly changing historical periods ever in the history of the Universe. And it is likely that the transformations of Threshold 8 are only just beginning. The only thing that remains to be seen is whether we shall hit a downward trend in Threshold 8, or whether our global complex system will hit Threshold 9 in a few decades, as the rate of complexity's increase continues to accelerate.

In the aftermath of World War II, the United States enjoyed the majority of the astounding rates of growth in terms of economy and collective learning, and as a result is the poster-boy of the Great Acceleration. This was because it possessed the world's largest industrialised population – as it still does today. In 1950, the United States population was 152 million, dwarfing any other fully industrialised (and non-communist) nation and accounted for 30% the world's GDP. The populations of Britain, Canada, Australia, or France, didn't even come close, being roughly 40 million, 12 million, 7 million, and 40 million respectively. The population of the Soviet Union was roughly 160 to 165 million people in 1950, due to the tremendous loss of roughly 27 million people in the war. Its economic potential was hugely exaggerated during the Cold War, but it certainly didn't come close to the rates of growth of the United States. The Soviets compensated for this by investing a disproportionate amount of GDP in their military, nuclear, and space programs.

Today the United States still holds the lead, with a population of approximately 330 million producing roughly 25% of the world's GDP. The slight drop of the share is due to the recovery of nations like France, Britain, Germany, and Japan from the devastation and bankruptcy of the war, and the growth of the economy of China (now 16% of global GDP from a still-industrialising population of approximately 1.4 billion). Of the next largest economies, Japan is 5.8%, and Germany is 4.3%. The Russians, by contrast, constitute only 1.8% of global GDP. The combined GDP of the United Kingdom, Australia, Canada, and New Zealand is 6.8% of global GDP, which may be of interest should they engage in CANZUK-based unification in the wake of Brexit. Like China, India also has a large population of 1.35 billion, but currently produces only 3.3% of the world's GDP as it lags behind the other Asian giant in industrialisation. This may change in the coming years. In regard to China and India, the growth of their GDP is really just the adjustment back into proportion with their share of the world population, finally reversing the Second Great Divergence of the nineteenth century. Provided such enormous populations don't provide an obstacle to further economic growth somewhere in the near future.

Globally, the world population has increased from 2.5 billion in 1945 to 7.7 billion today (although by the time most of you read this book it will probably have reached 8 billion – luckily I shall be updating constantly with further editions as long as I teach this course!). It took 300,000 years for the world population to achieve its first billion people, it took 100 years for the second billion, and further billions were added every few decades. The Green Revolution from the 1930s to the 1960s produced a number of highly effective chemical fertilisers, pesticides and artificially enhanced grain and rice, raising the global carrying capacity. While regions like India and China experienced horrific famines in the early to mid-twentieth centuries, their populations have been able to explode since then, soaring into the billions. Such was the immense increase of the carrying capacity that resulted from Threshold 8.

In terms of global production, the world's GDP output was 2.7 trillion USD in 1914, 33.7 trillion in 1997, 63 trillion in 2008, and is now 87 trillion at the time of writing. In terms of food production, total grain output has increased from 400 million tons in 1900 to over 2 billion tons today. The amount of irrigated land increased from 63 million hectares in 1900, to 94 million hectares in 1950, to 260 million hectares today.

What this all amounts to is that within a very short amount of time the world has more people, producing more stuff, than at any point in the last 315,000 years of human history, working in a global system more complex than anything in the past 13.8 billion years of Big History. We now live in a network of 7.7 billion potential innovators, within an instantaneous communications network of email and the internet. This bodes well for the acceleration of collective learning into the future.

However, these global statistics obscure the unequal distribution of all this growth, these resources, the opportunities for education and collaboration, which paint a more unbalanced picture in terms of collective learning. If you earn over $100,000 USD per year, you are in the world's wealthiest 10% of people. If you earn over $10,000 USD per year, you are in the world's wealthiest 25% of people. If you were to compare the unified global system to a singular agrarian economy, 10-20% of the population would be considered "elite" in terms of earning and societal power. So pretty much any citizen of the developed world forms the world's global aristocracy, alongside any moderately "rich" people living in the developing world. This is particularly important to remember should secular cycles ever rear their ugly faces again in a potential global crisis down the line. We'd be the ones who'd hold the world down in another depression phase that tends to kill an average of 20% of the population. Furthermore, if you are in the world's poorest 75%, the chances are you don't have much access to education, or diverse job opportunities, or perhaps even regular unfettered access to the internet. As such, the rate of collective learning is probably much slower than the simple statement "7.7. billion potential innovators" might imply on the surface. Yet on a long enough timescale without any sort of natural or manmade crisis, the increased access to education and job opportunities brings more of those billions of potential innovators to bear on equal standing within a global network of collective learning. Ultimately this means that if we survive long enough into the Anthropocene without disaster, collective learning will accelerate still faster, and complexity will catapult itself through several more thresholds of complexity.

For better or worse.

The Anthropocene

The Anthropocene is a theoretical geological period which follows the Holocene (the period that began at the end of the last Ice Age). The term is derived from *anthropos*, the Greek for human, (see also misanthrope and philanthropist) and ultimately implies that we now live in the geological age of the human. That is because by several metrics humans are now the dominant environmental and geological force on the face of the Earth. Not since the Great Oxygenation Event 3 to 2.5 billion years ago, have biological organisms had such a profound impact on the Earth's evolution. So profound is our impact that it shows on the fossil record.

There is a debate about when the Anthropocene truly begins. Some date it to the start of agriculture 12,000 years ago (thus the Anthropocene would largely replace the Holocene) when the immense deforestation from clearing land for farming fields may already have increased carbon emissions, and when humans began terraforming landscapes and domesticating and breeding millions upon millions of new animal species. Most proponents of the Anthropocene concept do not consider these changes significant enough to constitute an entirely new geological era. Others date the start of the Anthropocene at the beginning of the Industrial Revolution circa 1750 or 1800 due to the increase of carbon emissions and the role of technology transforming the environment more than ever before. Others still date the start of the Anthropocene with the Great Acceleration, since most human growth has happened since 1945, and because of the commencement of nuclear weapons testing, which has actually disrupted the atomic clocks of decaying isotopes around the world. Still more scholars dispute the Anthropocene as an accurate geological term, claiming that it exaggerates the influence of humans and ignores the extremely short time in which we have been active on massive scales upon the face of the Earth.

That said, the Anthropocene is certainly not an attempt by humans to pat themselves on the back for their power or influence over the Earth. Instead the term "Anthropocene" is usually negative in connotation, referring either to our excessive growth and consumption, or to the fact that long term humans may completely devastate the biosphere. Indeed in terms of pure annual rates of extinction, humans are evidently responsible for an extinction rate as fast as any of the five mass extinctions that have occurred in the past 550 million years (about a thousand times the average rate), causing some to say that humans are driving a Sixth Mass Extinction in the Anthropocene. Beyond that, human use of freshwater has increased by ten times since 1900, which may threaten to completely dry up the Earth's aquifers upon which both humans and other life depends. We have successfully mutilated or destroyed about 70% of the world's coral reefs. In the past 70 years, we have increased the carbon dioxide content of the atmosphere to over 400 parts per million, which is higher than anything in the past 3 million years. A lot of this seems to imply a tremendous influence on the Earth system, and none of it seems to bode particularly well.

On the issue of climate change, we have increased the average global temperature by about 1 degree Celsius since the start of the Industrial Revolution, and we are approaching the same average temperature as the Medieval Warm Period a thousand years ago. If we cross the threshold of more than a 4 degree increase in the average global temperature, we run the risk of melting the frozen methane stores in the oceans and in Siberia, kicking off a runaway greenhouse effect that could take us to 5 or 6 degrees increase. In the long term these increases could reduce arable cropland, starving the population, obliterating still more biodiversity, and over centuries flooding many highly populous regions with rising seas.

There is a diverse range of estimates for, one, how quickly rising carbon dioxide actually affects climate, and two, how quickly the change in climate affects the biosphere, and three, how quickly changes in the biosphere would devastate human societies. The difficulties of prediction arise from the fact that both the climate, biosphere, and human society are all extremely chaotic and complex systems. And layered on top of each other it is difficult to know what will happen, and how fast. If you wish to influence government policy in order to cajole action, it pays to give credence to the most shockingly rapid and devastating forecasts. The result of this has been a vast demoralisation of the public. We now live in an age of anxiety and alarm that has significantly depressed the average future outlook compared to just 30 years ago. If at the end of the Cold War you had asked the average person what humanity's prospects were, the forecast would more frequently be filled with buoyancy and hope. Now I can testify firsthand that the majority of students seem to think that doomsday is coming and cannot be stopped. This is perhaps counterproductive, since such forecasts produce just as much (if not more) apathy as they do proactivity.

Another concern in the Anthropocene is the sheer growth of the human population. In the mid-twentieth century, population growth appeared to be skyrocketing equally across the world, leading scholars like Paul Ehrlich to predict that hundreds of millions of people would starve to death in the 1980s. Happily industrialisation seems to slow down population growth in developed and developing economies alike. Nevertheless, the world population is set to reach 9 billion people by 2050, and somewhere between 10 and 13 billion people by 2100. With most of that population growth happening in regions of the world that are poorest and least equipped to deal with overpopulation – primarily Sub-Saharan Africa. This raises a lot of problems. Either we slow population growth by rapid industrialisation, or we don't industrialise (good luck convincing Africa, India, and China) and we run the risk of a Malthusian disaster occurring in regions already nearest to the margins. Already 65% of the world's current global emissions are produced by the developing world. The only solution seems to be technologies like hydrogen fusion which would flood the world with cheap sources of energy that had comparatively little environmental impact, so that the world's poor could industrialise and raise their living standards to their heart's content, without risking a global meltdown.

From a Big History perspective, of course, it is supremely unsurprising that the first burst of growth following a new threshold of complexity should be followed by a period of strain. We saw it shortly after the adoption of agriculture. As foragers, we had to compensate for such strain by extensifying out of Africa and across the Earth. In every stage of evolutionary history, species have exhausted their environments and had to compete for resources and energy flows by adapting their traits. And ultimately complexity guzzles all energy flows in the Universe until energy is used up and complexity itself dies. The question for humanity in the Anthropocene is whether we can innovate in time to avoid another collision with the carrying capacity and another period of horrific decline and mounting death. Whether in this Golden Age we shall ascend to even further heights, or descend into an Iron Age of war, or a new Dark Age of obliteration.

But that brings us to a discussion of the future, which we shall attempt in the final chapter, both in terms of the next few centuries, and for the next trillion, trillion, trillion years up to the death of complexity in the entire Universe.

Essay Writing Exercise

For this exercise, consider the following essay question only:

What is the single most important theme you have discovered in 13.8 billion years of Big History?

Engage in free-writing for 15 minutes. Take a break, watch TV, go for a walk, do two or three shots of tequila. Whatever suits you. Then on the basis of what you've written try to devise a clear thesis statement, a set of clear topic sentences for each major argument, and a preliminary list of evidence you will use to support each argument.

Lay the outline aside, and wait 6 to 24 hours. Without looking at your outline, try to reconstruct the thesis statement, topic sentences, and list of arguments. Then engage in 15 to 30 minutes of free-writing. At this point you should be well on your way to finishing your essay. Arm yourself with your books and research notes and try to finish the job! Congratulations, you may well have written the majority of the final essay for this course.

Further Reading

Allen, Robert. The British Industrial Revolution in a Global Perspective. Cambridge: Cambridge University Press, 2009.

Archer, Christon, et al. World History of Warfare. Lincoln: University of Nebraska Press, 2002.

Ashton, T.S. The Industrial Revolution, 1760-1830. London: Oxford University Press, 1948.

Baker, David. "Collective Learning: A Potential Unifying Theme of Human History" Journal of World History vol. 26, no. 1 (2015) pg. 77-104.

Bayley, Chris. The Birth of the Modern World: Global Connections and Comparisons, 1780-1914. Oxford: Blackwell, 2003.

Berg, Maxine. The Age of Manufacturers, 1700-1820: Industry, Innovation, and Work in Britain. 2nd ed. London: Routledge, 1994.

Bin Wong, Robert. China Transformed: Historical Change and the Limits of European Experience. Ithaca: Cornell University Press, 1997.

Black, Jeremy. War and the World: Military Power and the Fate of Continents, 1450-2000. New Haven: Yale University Press, 1998.

Chaisson, Eric. "Using Complexity Science to Search for Unity in the Natural Sciences" in Charles Lineweaver, Paul Davies and Michael Ruse (eds). Complexity and the Arrow of Time. Cambridge: Cambridge University Press, 2013.

Diamond, Jared. Guns, Germs, and Steel: The Fates of Human Societies. London: Vintage, 1998.

Headrick, Daniel. The Tools of Empire: Technology and European Imperialism in the Nineteenth Century. New York: Oxford University Press, 1981.

Maddison, Angus. The World Economy: A Millennial Perspective. Paris: OECD, 2001.

Marks, Robert. The Origins of the Modern World: A Global and Ecological Narrative from the Fifteenth to the Twenty-First Century. 2nd ed. Lanham: Rowman & Littlefield, 2007.

McNeill, J.R. and William H. McNeill. The Human Web: A Bird's-Eye View of World History. New York: W.W. Norton, 2003.

Overton, Mark. Agricultural Revoution in England: The Transformation of the Agrarian Economy, 1500-1850. Cambridge: Cambridge University Press, 1996.

Parker, Geoffrey. The Military Revolution: Military Innovation and the Rise of the West, 1500-1800. 2nd ed. Cambridge: Cambridge University Press, 1996.

Pomeranz, Kenneth. The Great Divergence: China, Europe, and the Making of the Modern World Economy. Princeton: Princeton University Press, 2000.

Ringrose, David. Expansion and Global Interaction, 1200-1700. New York: Longman, 2001.

Smil, Vaclav. Energy in World History. Boulder: Westview Press, 1994.

Wrigley, E. Energy and the English Industrial Revolution. Cambridge: Cambridge University Press, 2011.

CHAPTER 13

THE NEAR & DEEP FUTURE

Or,

WHERE WE TRY TO FIGURE OUT WHETHER ALL EXISTENCE IS SIMPLY AGONISING AND POINTLESS OR WHETHER THERE IS ACTUALLY AN OBJECTIVE POINT TO THE WHOLE GRAND NARRATIVE

???

Threshold 9: ???????????????? – happening ??? years from now

- *Wherein ???*
- *??????????*
- *??????????????????*
- *And complexity rises on the same scale as the invention of agriculture or industry.*

Timeline

- **The Human Population Reaches 11 to 15 billion people (22nd century AD):** Current rates of population growth have us reaching 9 billion people by 2050 and a range of 11 to 13 billion people by 2100. Presuming that population growth does not immediately halt, this made add another 2 billion people by 2100. Naturally there are a vast range of possible growth trajectories, each determined by a massive amount of variables affecting birth and survival rates. And the whole forecast gets thrown out if we encounter some horrific disaster that wipes billions of people off the map. It is also an open question whether all these people will have decent education and opportunity to engage on equal-footing as potential innovators in a network of collective learning. From that perspective, these massive numbers could be either very good or very bad.

- **Human Extinction/Evolution/Migration (300,000 to 5 million years from now):** On these timescales there is always a strong possibility that *Homo sapiens* will be wiped out. If it is not, then on timescales as long as humans have been around to roughly the period of time that separates us from our last common ancestor with chimpanzees, we will likely to have evolved naturally into something else. This speaks nothing of whether such evolution would be sped up by genetic manipulation or the transition to a transhuman species that combines organic components with mechanical components, and human intelligence with artificial intelligence. The final possibility on these timescales we will have quite simply left Earth for the wider solar system or galaxy. In which case we are likely to evolve into several different species, whether naturally or artificially.

- **A Mass Extinction Event Occurs Again (Maximum of the next 100 million years):** We have already discussed how humans might be causing the Sixth Mass Extinction since the Cambrian Explosion. However, regardless of what we do, there will be another Mass Extinction on Earth within the next 100 million years. On average, supervolcanic eruptions happen every 100,000 years, asteroid impacts happen every 100 million years. Natural disasters are inevitable. Things will not remain hunky-dory on Earth forever.

- **Life Will Start to Die Out on Earth (the next billion years):** The Sun will begin to age and grow and exert a lot more solar radiation upon Earth. This will make most forms of C4 photosynthesis impossible, killing off a great deal of flora and fauna. More complex food chains will be strangled out of existence. Although life will continue on Earth for another two billion years in a reduced form, from this point forward life on Earth will increasingly struggle against decline and death.

- **The Sun Boils the Earth Dry (the next 3 billion years):** The Sun will continue to age, exhaust its fuel, and grow as a red giant. The increase in temperatures will increase the surface temperature of Earth above the boiling point and evaporate most of the Earth's oceans. All life except perhaps a smattering of extremophile single-celled bacteria and archaea will be killed.

- **Andromeda Collides with the Milky Way (the next 4 billion years):** Over the next few billion years, Andromeda will draw closer and closer to the Milky Way until the two galaxies combine. Unlike the previous events, this collision is the least likely to be disastrous since stars are separated by many lightyears. Though one cannot rule out some disasters happening in various regions of the combined galaxy – either collisions or some solar systems being hurled out of the galaxy altogether.

- **The Sun Engulfs the Earth (the next 5 billion years):** The Sun continues to grow in its red giant phase, and after engulfing Mercury and Venus, it will completely destroy the Earth. At this point, any extremophiles that have managed to survive will be obliterated. So will end the story of our planet, aged 9.5 billion years. It is also probable that the Sun will engulf Mars, but will not grow larger to engulf any of the other planets in the solar system.

- **The Sun Dies (the next 7 billion years):** The Sun's fusion reactions will stop completely and will collapse into a white dwarf. It will no longer be a star capable of supporting any complexity in the solar system. After which it will remain for a few more billion years until completely flickering out leaving only a broken husk behind.

- **The End of the Golden Age of Astronomy (the next 200 billion years):** Dark energy will continue to accelerate the expansion of the Universe so fast that the light from other galaxies will no longer reach us and we will no longer be able to detect Cosmic Background Radiation. Any civilisations comparable to ours that is alive at that time will think that the Milky Way galaxy (or rather the Milky Way-Andromeda conglomeration which I shall dub "the Milo Galaxy" because I feel like it) is all there was or ever will be. This would prompt a reversion to the steady-state model that most cosmologists accepted before the Big Bang Theory was sufficiently proven.

- **The End of the Stelliferous Era (the next 100 trillion years):** The Stelliferous Era simply refers to the long epoch in which there are stars. At this point, all star formation has stopped in the middle of galaxies, and all stars have finally exhausted their fuel and burned out. This includes even the smallest, coolest burning stars that theoretically could continue to burn for 100 billion years apiece. At this point the Universe no longer has the standard source of energy flows and what remains of planets, asteroids, and comets, will wander in a cosmos that is nearly "pitch black".

- **The Heat Death of Matter (the next trillion x trillion x trillion years, plus pocket change):** The radioactive decay that allows us to measure the age of various things by looking at the decay of isotopes will have reached its endgame. All elements will decay back into hydrogen and then hydrogen itself will decay back into the energy from which it originally formed. This is the death of all structure, complexity, and matter in the Universe. What remains is an eternally expanding orb of radiation, with little energy flow, hovering a few percentages of a degree above Absolute Zero.

- **The Heat Death of Black Holes (the next trillion x trillion x trillion x trillion x trillion x trillion x trillion x trillion x trillion x trillion x trillion x trillion x trillion years):** The vast lumps of matter that bend spacetime with their immense mass will finally give off their last burst of radiation and evaporate. It is possible that after the death of stars, complexity could potentially gather weak energy flows from black holes. But at this point, there are no more sources of energy flows anywhere in the Universe and the cosmos will reach an almost equal distribution of matter and energy. This is the literal end of history, because from this point there will be no energy flow, thus no "work", thus no change, thus no events to dot a timeline. Although the Universe will continue to expand for eternity, time will have lost its relevance as a historical metric, and one epoch will drift blandly into another without a noticeable change. In a sense, time will be so devalued that it will become a worthless currency, because it no longer represents anything. This is true death and oblivion.

Predicting the Future

Central to the unifying patterns of Big History is the concept of complexity: a measurable set of phenomena that includes systems as simple as stars to systems as intricate as living cells or entire societies. In short all the "stuff" out there that isn't just space or weak radiation nearing Absolute Zero. Anything with energy flow, anything with structure. Looking at the Universe with this wide lens, we can see a pattern. Energy flows and structures have been intensifying in tiny pockets of an increasingly cold Universe. Increasing complexity is a common thread that unites 13.8 billion years of history, and places human history in direct sequence with the tooth and nail of biological evolution and the slow churning of stars and galaxies. It is a pattern that tells us the history of everything. By studying how complexity rises, we understand how stars, the biosphere, and humanity have continued to thrive. By studying how complexity falters in a star, species, or society, it tells you a lot about how things die. In essence, if you understand how complexity behaves throughout Big History, you can have a reasonable grasp on how it might behave as it continues to increase in the near and deep future. But ultimately everything dies, and so complexity also tells us a lot about how the history of humanity, the Earth, and the Universe will end.

The Near Future and the possible obliteration of humanity is difficult to forecast, given it largely depends on the actions of such a chaotic and complex system like human society, with billions of variables and moving parts. And therefore billions or trillions of slightly or drastically varying outcomes. The field of strategic foresight is still able to illuminate those outcomes for the next 100-200 years and classify them within four broad scenarios. But the deep future on the timescale of billions and trillions of years is easier to forecast because it is driven by the decidedly less complex and more predictable forces of physics in the inanimate cosmos. With current data, we have a fairly good idea of when the Sun is going to die, and furthermore when all matter of the Universe will decay back into energy. The data could be updated, which may change what we forecast in the deep future, but for now I will deliver an account of what is currently deemed likely to occur.

The purpose of looking into the future on long timescales in Big History is that the outcome of all things can tell you a lot about the overarching patterns and trends that have carried us thus far. Whether we are looking at the trajectory of the human race after 300,000 years of our history, or the thermodynamic trajectory of the Universe itself, by peering into the distant future we learn much about the distant past, and vice versa.

Nor is this future one merely of scientific curiosity, since it influences us a great deal philosophically. Where we are likely to end up can have a profound influence on how we view ourselves and what we consider worthwhile human endeavours in the present. Perhaps even driving us to question whether or not there *are* any worthwhile human endeavours in the present.

The Field of Strategic Foresight

Foresight is a mixture of a science and an art. It relies on our understanding of current scientific data and consensus, and also the strict and disciplined methodology of science to keep our speculations in order. That said, it is inescapable that when predicting the future one will require a large amount of intuition and imagination – which is what makes it an art. But tight methodical reins must be kept around these artistic elements in order to avoid the exercise growing disorganised. You must not predict one future. You must predict *several* futures. And then assess each scenario based on their plausibility.

These multiple futures, regardless of their content, fall on a spectrum. Futurists have been developing a method of classification for each future scenario for over forty years. I employ the model refined by fellow big historian, Joseph Voros. During a standard survey of the future, one may start with the most plausible or probable scenario, but in order to properly account for contingency, one needs to branch further out to see the other variations of decreasing levels of plausibility. At the very edges of this spectrum of scenarios are those where we cannot exactly imagine how they could be brought about, i.e. they require knowledge we currently do not have, or they seem to defy our own current knowledge of the Universe. The model has been described as a cone created by a spotlight, where the most probable sits in the middle, but with other scenarios around it being illuminated.

Within the field of Big History, this multiple futures methodology is what I use to trace where long term trends we study over 13.8 billion years of the Universe (increasing complexity) or 300,000 years of humanity (collective learning, i.e. knowledge accumulating generationally) where may go in the future. It is a staple of the Big History genre to spend some time analysing the Near and Deep Future after surveying the grand narrative of the past. This methodology allows for more systematic study of the future than the binary between environmental apocalypse and the author's prescriptions to avoid it that typifies much of Big History work. Or the fatalism that surrounds the end of complexity on the longest possible timescales. As such this methodology, or one like it, is indispensable to our narratives of the future.

I have boiled the classifications of the future down to the essential four. There are others, such as the "preferred" future, which is the scenario that the analyst finds desirable, or the "predicted" future, which is simply the scenario an analyst claims will happen. The former is an area that can generate bias on part of the analyst, the latter is quite a reckless thing to do in strategic foresight, and as such very seldom is anyone so bold. After all, the only truly predicted future scenario is the one in which some, if not all, of our predictions turn out to be wrong!

More fundamental to analysis are the following four. Number one is the <u>projected future</u>. Here things play out how current trends suggest they play out. It is "business as usual" where we assume no major change to variables or behaviours, and no dynamic discoveries. The projected future may not even be the most likely future, since new discoveries and changes in variables do eventually occur, but it forms an important baseline for our forecasting. For instance, a projected future would involve the outcome of greenhouse gas emissions and global industrial growth continuing at current rates.

Number two is the <u>probable future</u>. Where variation or change within the bounds of known science indicates where trends might go. For example, if the current rate of population growth on a graph is a projected future, then the low and high lines for changing rates in growth are probable futures. The probable future is the projected future's "margin for error" or "margin for variation". Change can occur but not beyond what science knows *for certain* could happen. So a world takeover by Artificial Intelligence or a commercially viable transition to nuclear fusion do not go in this category, because we have not fully discovered how those things would successfully work yet. Instead a probable future refers to something that science already understands but hasn't yet come to pass, e.g. a transition to and heavier reliance upon solar technologies and lesser reliance on fossil fuels.

Number three is the <u>possible future</u>. Where a discovery yet unknown to science alters a future outcome. This classification is useful because big historians are not visionary engineers capable of predicting technological progress 200 years from now. One could imagine how difficult it would be to predict the existence of the internet in 1800 AD, or its societal effects. A possible future allows us to investigate outcomes without knowing all the details of the causes. It has an unknown variable like an algebra equation: "present + x = outcome". In fact, like an algebra equation, we can use the known variables to get a clearer picture of what the value of x actually is. Major advances in AI, or nuclear fusion, or the majority of "singularity" or "threshold" moments would fall into this category.

Number four is the <u>preposterous future</u>. Where an outcome seems to openly defy the laws of known science, contradicting all available data or understanding. It plays an important role in prediction because it clearly defines what a possible future is by mere contrast. It also forms an important category for mind-blowing leaps forward that analysis does not anticipate. Given the many astounding forms of emergence in Big History, from the origins of life from inanimate matter to the many technological breakthroughs of humanity, seemingly preposterous things do happen. The moon-landing might have seemed preposterous to someone in 1800 AD before rocketry or even human flight.

In fact, on a long enough timescale, complexity can turn the preposterous into the possible, then the probable, and even projected. If nothing else, the only way to figure out the limits of the possible is by going beyond them to the impossible.

To sum up the four categories even more succinctly:

- *Projected*: what science says is happening

- *Probable*: what science says could happen

- *Possible*: what science might discover

- *Preposterous*: what science says won't happen

As mentioned in the introduction, it is easier to predict what will happen in the deep future than the near future. The reason why it is easier to predict the future on the timescale of millions, billions, and trillions of years, is we know the physics and how the Universe behaves at large scales. We can estimate how much fuel the Sun has. We can estimate how long it will be before all matter decays back into energy. All that cosmology largely falls into the *projected* and *probable* futures.

At the present we have fairly reliable predictions on how long the Sun will live or when the Universe will die. However, if the Universe were expanding faster than we know to the point that the atoms of galaxies were ripped apart before they could decay, then this new discovery in our knowledge makes the Big Rip (instead of the Big Freeze) a *possible* future. If tomorrow the Universe transformed into a giant rabbit, or if humans learned to defy the Second Law of Thermodynamics, that would be a *preposterous* future.

Conversely, the Near Future is much more difficult to predict because we are looking at much more complex systems than the inanimate Universe. Biology and culture. Way more variables and contingencies. A way faster pace of change. It is why forecasting the next step of cultural evolution and human history is pretty difficult. But it also is what makes cultural evolution and human history such a great catalyst for rapid and unforeseen change. If any preposterousness is likely to arise it will be here. Even potentially altering the natural projected future of the Earth and Universe if such complexity continues to grow in power and intensity.

Analysing the Near Future

Even though the events of the next century are difficult to predict, all the possible outcomes of the Near Future over the next 100-300 years fall into four broad categories. These were conceived by James Dator in an attempt to allow for a structured survey of where society might go in the future based on whether it continues to grow unabated, reaches equilibrium in order to ward of disaster, is gradually unravelled to avoid disaster, or will in fact encounter a disaster. From these four directions for the future of human society (up, straight, slowly down, rapidly down) without being further cluttered by detail, we allow a wide diversity of scenarios to be slotted into those broad categories. The purpose of this model is for greater organisation to aid in analysis of plausibility, despite the vast array of different possible outcomes.

In terms of the connection to Big History, the four categories relate to whether human complexity rises, stabilises, gracefully decreases, or collapses. Throughout human history, there have been major breakthroughs and a gradual building of smaller innovations that in the blink of an eye in terms of evolutionary time have raised the complexity of human societies. Either in terms of structural intricacy of the human web, or in raw terms of the thermodynamic density of energy flows that creates, sustains, or increases all forms of complexity in Big History.

Please note that the purpose of these categories is not to make any definitive statement about the future, but they exist for purposes of organisation. There will be some observers who will wish to blur the line between the categories, or replace them entirely, and modification is the prerogative of any analyst coming from any discipline and body of research. But in order to have a fairly well organised approach to the Near Future, one needs to be able to group together the potential thousands of varying scenarios in some form of classification by their common characteristics. In Big History, the Dator model works most effectively given how well it dovetails with our unifying theme of complexity. The four categories for the Near Future are as follows:

Technological Breakthrough – where human society does not hit a limit to its current modes of production in the next 100-300 years and rates of innovation keep pace with growth of the human complex system. Innovation has on hundreds of historical occasions fallen behind the growth of the human system only for society to struggle or collapse until a breakthrough lifts the limits on human growth once again. These limits to growth may be imposed by overpopulation, or contemporary modes of production degrading the environment, and many other possible factors. A technological breakthrough can lift the lid on growth, the most dynamic and notable being the first adoption of agriculture c.12,000 years ago, or industrialisation c.200 years ago. There are of course less dramatic innovations that also "lift the lid" such as the proliferation of legumes and four-crop rotation in 17th and 18th century Europe.

But in this particular category for the Near Future, the "technological breakthrough" is confined to the most notable and dramatic thresholds analogous to the impact of the rise of agriculture or industrialisation on human lifeways and complexity. Whatever the next breakthrough, complexity continues to rise, perhaps even dramatically. This broad category would include all scenarios that involve a major jump in energy use, production, or a major threshold moment in increasing complexity. Perhaps it involves the economically viable distribution of nuclear fusion power, making energy cheap enough even for the poorest countries to develop, with an exponential increase on the limits of energy and production globally, and without the corresponding degradation of the biosphere that comes with fossil fuels.

But such a breakthrough also includes those scenarios where humanity hands the reigns of future complexity to a completely different system or entity (such as in multiple scenarios with AI) resembling the shift from biological evolution to collective learning being the main driver of increasing complexity. I liken the shift from biology to culture to a highway overpass looming over older roads and would liken the shift from culture to AI to airplanes soaring 30,000 feet over the highway. There is a presumption in this category that structural complexity will increase, as will the average free energy rate density (erg/g/s) or FERD of human society. The latter of these is the only quantifiable metric we currently have for complexity devised by Eric Chaisson, and employed by multiple big historians including myself. As a result of these breakthroughs, human complexity (structural or thermodynamic) is symbolised by the arrow pointing up.

To be even more succinct, a major revolution in technology "saves us at the 11th hour" and allows humanity to continue to produce, develop, and grow and similar or higher rates without the present danger such rates present to the environment and the global population overall. It is a necessary category to contain all the plausible and implausible "miracle cures" to the current predicament humanity finds itself in the 21st century stemming from the continued acceleration of technology and scientific progress.

Green Equilibrium – where human society over the next 100-300 years does not develop a "singularity" or major technological breakthrough in the Near Future (by no means a guarantee since the first agriculture and Industrial Revolution are over 10,000 years apart) and live within their means to avoid total degradation of the biosphere. This may include technological innovation at a smaller scale along with some good planning, government policy, and a shift to more sustainable forms of production. Human complexity does not increase significantly but does not decrease either. The defining characteristic is equilibrium.

Instead of waiting for a brilliant set of inventions saving humanity at the 11th hour and to be free to continue developing our economies at the same or higher rate, this category presumes some tightening of consumption and production to environmentally sustainable levels. In a way this category resembles theories in environmental economics about "prosperity without growth". The object of this carefulness is to avoid the exhaustion of the human complex system and the Earth, and a decline of complexity analogous to a star burning out its fuel, a species overpopulating an ecosystem, or an agrarian society hitting the population carrying capacity.

For those analysts who would be skeptical of a purely technological solution to the 21st Century Crisis outlined in the first category, the second category of Green Equilibrium presents mixture of technological and non-technological solutions. These may be innovations in doctrine, policy, or method. Or they may involve a cultural shift. Or they may harness existing renewable technologies in a more efficient way. As such this scenario incorporates a great many "mixed" solutions that involve some form of conservation and sustainable behaviour, as opposed to breakthrough and a relatively unrestrained rate of growth. This category also contains the majority of prescriptive solutions or "positive" futures outlined in previous major works in Big History, from Christian to Spier. One suspects this is the case for the prescriptive or positive future outcomes discussed in other fields. Since complexity neither dramatically increases nor dramatically declines it could be symbolised by the arrow pointing straight forward.

Creative Descent – where human society is in danger of exhausting the Earth's ecosystems with potential blowback on human society, and so invokes a form of environmental policy that actually reduces human production and consumption in order to ward off disaster. It is a deliberate unravelling of human complexity. Examples of scenarios within this category include radical population control and reduction, dismantling of heavy industry, restrictions on car and air travel, restrictions on energy consumption and production rather than their replacement with renewable forms, rationing of food and clothing, etc. This category can be temporary or long-term. Over a long enough period of descent, human complexity (whether structural or thermodynamic) more closely resembles the agrarian civilisations of 300 years ago than society today. It is a conscious retreat of complexity from the limits of the Earth (temporarily or permanently). It is a decline of complexity without collapse symbolised by an arrow going gradually down.

The purpose of this category is to contain all scenarios (whether mostly positive or negative in tone and presentation) that include humanity "living within its means" but with those means being by necessity significantly lower than current rates of production and consumption today. For example, the restriction on air travel to, say, 10% the current volume in order to reduce carbon emissions. This would have a tremendous effect on people's lifeways and many economies.

What makes *Creative Descent* differ from *Green Equilibrium* is that the latter category does not require such drastic reduction, or else would furnish an alternative (e.g. non-emitting aircraft, etc). Some Creative Descent scenarios are not as dramatic and require only slight reductions (e.g. reduction of air travel to 90% of its current volume) but the key feature that it does involve some reduction to reach the level at which society can "live within its means".

Collapse – involving every conceivable doomsday scenario. While most apocalyptic warnings that currently fill most Big History content concern potential environmental disaster, it also includes every manmade and natural cause from nuclear war, to superbugs, to an asteroid impact, to a super-volcanic eruption, etc. The reader is likely to have imagined a few of them. This category covers every scenario where human complexity dramatically declines regardless of the cause. The beauty of this approach is it puts all forms of collapse and doomsday under one banner forming one quarter of the total analysis. This reduces the preoccupation with doomsday that can overwhelm analysis. Instead of the binary of apocalypse-survival, one has four categories to soberly evaluate for probability. The general trend of complexity in this category is rapidly down. And it is here that we encounter our first possible "end of the world".

Take a moment and ask yourself which future do you think is the most likely? Why?

Subtleties of Interpretation

There are some important things to note with these categories. First, that all of them contain potential hardships for the individual humans living through them. While some categories may contain more "negative" scenarios than others, there is not necessarily a purely "positive" category in terms of human well-being. *Collapse* obviously will involve human suffering, as will potentially any draconian measures necessary to achieve *Creative Descent*, even if the resulting standard of living improves in a stripped-down and simplified society a generation or so down the line. But *Green Equilibrium* may also involve telling the developing world currently responsible for 65% of all greenhouse gas emissions to stop industrialising either temporarily or permanently, thus curtailing the increase of their standard of living. And a *Technological Breakthrough* may at first glance seem like the consistently "positive one" but many scenarios may also include individual human suffering. The most obvious example is the numerous scenarios where humans hand the reigns of complexity over to AI resulting in human irrelevance, unemployment, deprivation, starvation, or extinction. An increase of complexity should not be confused with an increase with human well-being, just as the Industrial Revolution sometimes caused a great deal of human suffering with depraved factory conditions, or indeed as the invention of agriculture caused a decline in health and the rise of disease. In fact from the explosions of supernovae, to the bloody tooth-and-claw of evolution built on the brutal death and extinction of millions of species, increased complexity has always engendered some form of destruction and, in latter phases where there is consciousness, suffering. We must not confuse the simple empirical trend of increased complexity we have observed over 13.8 billion years with more Whiggish notions of historical progress.

Second, a scenario in one of the four categories may actually lead subsequently to a scenario in one of the other three. For instance, *Creative Descent* could occur 2050-2200 AD and then be followed by a *Technological Breakthrough* or *Collapse*. Or a *Technological Breakthrough* may result in a *Collapse*. There is nothing about this system of analysis that locks one particular scenario and one particular category in for the entirety of the Near Future. There is always the possibility of oscillation in terms of whether complexity continues, slows, or reverses, just as it has throughout human history, and more widely in the Big History of 13.8 billion years.

Third, once we start looking at the "Middle Future" on timescales of thousands of years, there is an important point to consider. As long as humanity continues to exist without total annihilation of the human species, it becomes increasingly likely that another *Technological Breakthrough* akin to the first agriculture or modern industrialisation will occur. If we look to past examples of oscillations, in the era of agrarian civilisations c.3000 BC to 1750 AD, civilisations underwent periods of population decline, pandemic disease, sociopolitical instability, or total collapse. Yet collective learning (the human ability to accumulate more innovation with each generation than is lost by the next) continued to accumulate despite the deaths of thousands or millions. Even in the most extreme cases, where the devastation was so thorough that some collective learning was lost (called a Tasmanian Effect) after a few centuries or millennia the knowledge was generally recouped and surpassed. In a *Green Equilibrium* scenario, human complexity will hold firm along with the general number of potential innovators for collective learning and the connectivity between them. A breakthrough in collective learning is assured (though the timing of this breakthrough is open to question). In a *Creative Descent* scenario, human complexity is deliberately unravelled, but the collective learning required to rebuild that complexity is not forgotten and potential innovators still survive. After a great duration of time, and with the reconstruction of the necessary research and development infrastructure, the retained knowledge could again be utilised and advanced. In a *Collapse* scenario, millions might die but collective learning might be retained. Or in more extreme scenarios a Tasmanian Effect may occur but on a long enough timescale of thousands of years for recovery, knowledge may be rediscovered in a long lost archive or database or simply reconceived. Only in the most extreme *Collapse* scenarios involving the annihilation of every single human being on Earth does the eventual advent of *Technological Breakthrough* become impossible.

Evaluating Feasibility

Concerning the four broad categories of *Technological Breakthrough, Green Equilibrium, Creative Descent,* and *Collapse,* we need a way of evaluating the likelihood of the many scenarios contained within them. In Big History, we are currently developing such a method in a few books, articles, and educational courses. In a framework that forecasts for multiple futures, we are able to assess what degree of feasibility a scenario has compared to the others according to available data. We can then evaluate each scenario either systematically or in wide-ranging discussions with peers, students, and public audiences on the basis of the *projected, probable, possible,* and *preposterous* futures outlined above.

A Big History treatment of the Near Future in a course or book then involves an assessment of many different scenarios. For *Projected Futures,* the big historian interrogates why current data and trends seem to be heading this way. For *Probable Futures,* the big historian assesses changes within the bounds of realism and current human knowledge would be necessary for those outcomes. For *Possible Futures,* the big historian explores what kind of discoveries would be necessary to achieve that outcome and try to elucidate what that might look like. And for *Preposterous Futures,* the big historian has to justify why those outcomes are so outlandish – even on a long timescale.

Further, classification of different Near Future scenarios and a rating of their feasibility is becoming an area of greater scholarly debate. For instance, many "preferred" future scenarios in major Big History works fall into the category of *Green Equilibrium.* It would be interesting to know whether scholars rate these preferred futures as the most likely scenarios. Further, another scholar may come along and rate most *Green Equilibrium* scenarios as *Preposterous Futures* because they deem human nature incapable of maintaining itself at equilibrium or accepting a model of "prosperity without growth" at either an individual or a governmental level. At least not without one of the greatest revolutions in human behaviour in 300,000 years. If a scholar deemed the "preferred" futures of prominent big historians to be little more than pipe dreams, this might kick off a flurry of scholarship in response. Similarly, scholars could discuss whether *Collapse* scenarios are *Projected Futures,* whether *Creative Descent* scenarios are *Probable Futures,* and the extent to which *Technological Breakthroughs* are *Possible Futures.*

The Projected/Probable Deep Future

Analysis of the Deep Future falls within two broad streams. The first stream is the "natural" *projected/probable* futures of the Earth and the Universe, where higher complexity like biology or society have no impact on the processes of cosmology. The second stream is a series of *possible/proposterous* futures where complexity continues to increase for millions, billions, and even trillions of years beyond the current point of human technology on Earth to the point where the wider cosmos are actually affected and manipulated.

Regardless of what happens to humanity, the actual end of the world is more certain a prediction, flowing from the more regular and predictable laws of physics. Provided we have the right data, we can make fairly concrete assertions and estimates about cosmology at the wider scales. These predictions may shift as data becomes more refined or as physical theories are updated or replaced, and as such the narrative presented below may not remain the same in coming years.

1 billion years from now: Death of the Biosphere

In the "Middle Future" of the next few thousand or million years, it is true that supervolcanic eruptions and major asteroid impacts strike Earth and obliterate a great deal of life every 100 million years on average. But so far they have not yet succeeded in "ending the world", just wiping out a large percentage of existing species. The Deep Future is much more certain. In about a billion years, the Sun will begin to exhaust its fuel. It will start to inflate like a dead cow in a wet field. Its luminosity will increase, CO2 levels will decrease, and this means plants on Earth over the following years will find it harder and harder to do most forms of photosynthesis and thus sustain complex life on our tiny rock. Life would struggle and decline from the 1 billion year mark onward. Life has existed on Earth for 3.8 billion years. It has 1 billion years left before decline starts to set in. That's roughly twice the amount of time that separates us from the Cambrian Explosion, but only roughly 25% of the time that life has existed. In a sense, life on Earth has already had its midlife crisis and is already approaching retirement age.

3-5 billion years from now: Death of the Sun and Earth

At the 3 billion year mark, the Sun will grow larger and larger until it boils the surface of the Earth dry. Once we get to an Earth's surface with a temperature greater than 100 degrees Celsius, we can be pretty sure that's it for life on Earth. Perhaps some single-cell organisms could still exist in the cracks of the Earth, but that is a clear decline of complexity and the end of the tale in our biosphere. A few hundred million years later, the Sun will grow so large it will engulf the Earth, burning and absorbing whatever is left. The planet itself will be destroyed. The Sun may also bloat up to destroy Mars. But it will never get so large that it goes beyond that, leaving the asteroid belt and the gas giants largely unscathed.

The Sun will continue growing, until in about 5 billion years it will shrink back and become a small, dense little star. A shadow of its former self. After a few more eons, it will run out of fuel and snuff out completely. In that sense the Sun is already middle aged. We currently exist at the halfway point in its life. Here is a quite literal and scientifically projected "end of the world". If human beings have evolved meanwhile into some sort of sci-fi super-civilization, we will have long since fled the place of our birth.

The next 200 Billion Years: The End of the Golden Age of Astronomy

As dark energy continues to accelerate the expansion of the Universe past the speed of light, we would no longer get to see the light from other galaxies. If we were to lose the knowledge of Big Bang cosmology, our galaxy would be all we'd see. Or think exists. We'd revert to the idea that the Universe had no start-date, is static, and eternal. The Milky Way would be our entire Universe. That is why a number of scientists refer to the current age where we *can* see evidence for the Big Bang, and *can* see other galaxies, as the "Golden Age of Astronomy".

The next 100 Trillion Years: The End of Stars

All stars have a life expectancy. Giant stars die within a few hundred million years. Middling stars like our Sun last a few billion years. The dimmest, flickering, slow burning stars can last for much longer. Perhaps many tens of billions of years. But like all candles in the Universe, ultimately they waver and flicker out. By the time we reach 100 trillion years from now, there will be *no more star formation*. All the dense hydrogen clouds capable of forming stars will have been used up. The lanterns will go out. The rubble of the Universe will wander in a cosmic graveyard. An eternal darkness will descend. Nothing but ruins and ashes will remain. Eventually even less than ruins and ashes.

The Next 10^{40} Years: Heat Death of Matter

The average organism lives a few years or decades. The average species sticks around for a few hundred thousand years. The average star lasts a few billion. But these are highly complex arrangements of building blocks. What happens to the building blocks themselves? The atoms? Not only do corpses rot, not only do stars die, but atoms themselves will eventually melt and fade away. This is what will occur in approximately 10^{40} years after the Universe has gone many trillions upon trillions of years in the darkness. Atoms will decay into energy, radiation, which will be stretched out across the Universe like too little butter on a giant slice of bread.

In Heat Death, or the "Big Freeze", the entire Universe will become an empty orb of weak radiation, cold and dwelling in the darkness, in a Hades made real. At this point there will be little to no energy flows in the Universe. Complexity will cease to exist and will never rise again. It will be physically impossible. All the work of the past 13.8 billion years will be erased as if it never existed at all. A blank eternity, with no change, no events, no history. Not just the end of the world, but the end of our story. The end of all history.

The Next 10^{100} years: Evaporation of Black Holes

The only thing that will remain in the Universe besides weak radiation are black holes. And they will exist for longer only by virtue of the fact that they are so dense that they take longer to dissolve. But they too emit radiation. They too will decay. In 10^{100} years, even they will be gone. Dissolved into nothingness. Even their hum of radiation smeared out into an almost equal distribution of energy. According to the laws of physics as we understand them, this fate is inevitable. This is our projected future. This is the end of things.

The Possible/Preposterous Deep Future

There are a few possible/preposterous scenarios in the Deep Future that are entirely natural and do not require the intervention of advanced complexity. An old *projected future* from previous years was the <u>Big Crunch</u>, where it was thought that the gravity of the Universe would eventually stop the expansion and suck everything back in on itself within a few billion or trillion years, where the Universe would end in the fireball it began with. Maybe it would even just repeat the process and set off another Big Bang. It gives rise to the poetic idea of death and rebirth on a cosmic scale. However, the scenario is now the least likely. It would require the Universe's expansion to slow down at some point. But the expansion of the Universe is not slowing down, it is accelerating. The Big Crunch falls into the category of a *possible future*, since it would require the revision of current cosmological data.

Another possible scenario is slightly more likely, <u>the Big Rip</u>. If the Universe expands and accelerates more rapidly than it currently appears to be doing, then not only the space between galaxies but also the space between atoms within galaxies will grow larger, eventually overpowering the nuclear forces that hold atoms together. Essentially, the Universe would be expanding so rapidly that in about 20 billion years, the atoms of the Universe might actually be torn apart. Complexity would end a lot sooner than the decay of atoms back into energy trillions and trillions of years in a Big Freeze scenario, and a lot more violently. In that sense, it is almost fortunate that the Big Freeze is the *projected future* because it gives the continued life of complexity a near eternity to develop with all the surprising shifts and threshold moments that may occur, as opposed to just 20 billion years. Currently the Big Rip remains only a *possible future*. If further data implies the Universe is accelerating catastrophically fast, the Big Rip will become the *projected future*.

A possible/preposterous future involves the continued increase of complexity and the rise of supercivilisations that alter the fate of the Universe in a <u>Big Save</u>. Essentially take the accelerated progress of science and technology over the past 200 years and continue it for thousands, millions, and billions of years into the future. While not an entirely unreasonable premise which is worth exploring, it is a bit more difficult to illuminate what such a future may look like.

This chapter will propose one more methodical system by which we can elucidate the contours of the future. We may not know the details of the highly complex systems, but we can see the direction of the arrow of complexity. If we have a way of deciphering and quantifying what that arrow means, we can construct a semi-algebraic equation about the future, where we have unknown values symbolised by *x* but also the sum of that equation. This can be achieved by adapting the Chaissonian metric central to Big History to forecast the future.

Eric Chaisson's Free Energy Rate Density (FERD) is a measurement of the energy flows of a complex system in a certain amount of mass in a certain amount of time (erg/g/s). It has been used as a rough metric for complexity in multiple Big History works. The Chaissonian metric has particular value because it strikes to the root of what creates, sustains, and increases all complex systems: flows of energy. Every single star, new element, new organism, or human manufactured product, etc., would not exist without an initial burst of energy flow to create them. Without further energy flows (fuel) a star would die, an organism would starve, and an artificial machine would shut down. And without a further increase in energy flows it is highly unlikely we could make the leap from single-celled life to multi-celled life, or from an agrarian to an industrial society. Hence the intensification of free energy rate density concurrent with the rise of complexity in Big History.

Complexity Average based on Free Energy Rate Density

System Complexity (ranked from lowest to highest)	Free Energy Rate Density (erg/g/s) (Averages)
The Milky Way	0.1
The Sun	2
A Red Giant Star near to supernova	120
Algae (photosynthesizing)	900
Cold-Blooded Reptiles	3000
Warm-Blooded Mammals (average)	20,000
Australopithecines	22,000
Human Foragers (average consumption)	40,000
Agricultural Society (average consumption)	100,000
Industrial Society (average consumption)	500,000

Modern Society (average consumption)	2,000,000

Estimates for Future Kardashev Civs, carrying on from Modern Society Average (Baker):

Type I Civ (Planet)	2,600,000
Type II Civ (Star)	70,200,000,000
Type III Civ (Galaxy)	14,000,000,000,000,000,000,000,000
Type IV Civ (All galaxies)	6,000,000,000,000,000,000,000,000,000,000,000,000
Type V Civ (All universes)	Above x 10^{500} sets of physical laws multiplied by slightly less than an infinite number of universes with those laws

A quantifiable metric for complexity that demonstrates an increase of numerical values for complexity during its cosmic evolution over 13.8 billion years is useful for projecting further increases in complexity in the future. Particularly once we start taking averages for human societies. Any metric that relies on a quantifiable pattern and takes us beyond short-term speculation is an improvement in how big historians approach the question of the future.

For the rest of this chapter, let us conduct a simple thought-experiment, aided by some simple arithmetic to gain an impression of a *possible/preposterous* Deep Future in which complexity continues to rise. Please note I do not make predictions as to when any of the major thresholds outlined below will occur, but simply supply a very wide and feasible window of time in which each of them could occur. To start, if we take the FERD average for modern society as a baseline, we can project into the future for a potential *Technological Breakthrough* scenario. In this scenario, we will temporarily assume the breakthrough establishes humanity as a Type I Kardashev civilisation. That is to say, a society that controls the equivalent of all the energy flows of a planet. Currently humanity can be estimated as a 'Type 0.7' to 'Type 0.75' Kardashev civilisation, allowing for the nearly 40 years increase in energy capacity. That is *not* to say that a breakthrough will allow humans to control 100% of the planet's energy flows, from wind power to the geothermal energy from deep in its core. Instead it is the *equivalent* of the energy flows of an entire planet to give us a realistic FERD value to assign to technological progress over the next 100 to 1000 years (depending on whether delay is imposed by some global disaster or a failure of human society). That brings the average FERD of human society up to approximately 2.5 to 2.6 million erg/g/s to sustain its own complexity.

We now have a FERD score as a baseline with which we can run some fairly simple numbers from cosmology. Let us say human or post-human innovation continues to advance and accelerate anywhere on the timescale of hundreds to millions of years and leads to society being a Type II civilisation, harnessing the equivalent of the energy of a star. It would increase our average FERD to 70.2 billion (if we calculate what fraction of the Sun's radiation is captured by the Earth, harnessed by the biosphere, harvested by humanity, and simply add in the rest). This far outstrips the increase of complexity of anything that came before it. We are talking about a nearly "godlike" civilisation (there aren't many other words that portray that kind of power), probably transhuman, and capable of large scale "environmental manipulation." Perhaps intricate changes at the quantum scale, perhaps even manipulation of the fundamental forces of the Universe themselves.

If we increase in FERD to the level of a Type III civilisation, or one that controls the *equivalent* energy flows of all the stars in a galaxy, complexity would experience even more phase-shifts. Simply multiply a Type II civ by, say, 200-400 billion stars, and you get huge FERD values of 14-28 septillion for a Type III civilisation. When we consider that it might take a thousand to a million years of increasing complexity to achieve a Type II civilisation, and (barring faster-than-light travel) it would take approximately 5-50 million years to colonise every solar system in the galaxy, this is a comparatively short time in terms of 13.8 billion years of Big History, or the roughly 100 trillion years before the end of the Stelliferous Era. Comparing complexity, modern society will look as quaint as a hydrogen atom. Who knows what miracles it would be capable of?

Moving along into realms of even greater preposterousness, a Type IV civilisation that harnesses all the equivalent of energy flows of all the galaxies in the visible Universe increases FERD values into the undecillions with corresponding levels of structural intricacy and environmental manipulation. Essentially the entire Universe is united into one single complex system, with all the corresponding potential for astounding changes being wrought at rapid speed. The corresponding structural intricacy and environmental manipulation is largely beyond the human imagination. Even "godlike" might not describe it. Nevertheless, at this point it is a fairly safe assumption that all constraints of the Universe generated by the fundamental four forces of physics, the space-time continuum, or the laws of thermodynamics can be manipulated and/or overcome.

A Type V civilisation that (somehow) unites a theoretical Multiverse into a single complex network involves 5 googolplexes of possible sets of physical laws that would animate those other universes, and an almost infinite number of universe that would come out of cosmic inflation. The corresponding FERD and levels of structural intricacy and manipulation are similarly beyond human comprehension. And in order to establish a Type V civ, the constraints of physics would *already* have to be overcome.

Notably, the ability to travel faster than the speed of light or to break the fundamental laws of physics all fall within *preposterous futures*, and thus so do Type IV and Type V civilisations. At the very least, Type II and Type III civilisations require inventions that are not yet known to science, and so are at the very least *possible futures*. Yet complexity does have a way of making the preposterous possible.

There is one more thing to consider in regard to feasibility. The current *projected future* of the Universe is the <u>Big Freeze</u> or "Heat Death". That is, if things continue to proceed with "business as usual" eventually all energy flows will be used up and eventually all matter will decay into weak radiation many trillions upon trillions upon trillions of years from now. With the breakdown of matter in approximately 10^{40} years and the evaporation of black holes somewhere in the neighbourhood of 10^{100} years. A *possible future* is that a <u>Big Rip</u> may occur in 20 billion years, if the expansion of the Universe is happening faster than what current data suggests. In these scenarios, whatever happens to biological or cultural complexity has no bearing on the huge inanimate forces that govern the fate of the Universe.

Consider a *preposterous future* for a moment. If levels of complexity continue to increase from our current society to a Type I, II, III, or IV, and this continues to accelerate on the timescale of hundreds of millions or billions of years, then the endgame of the Universe may not be a Big Freeze or Big Rip but a <u>Big Save</u>. Whereby an advanced super-civilisation has such powers of environmental manipulation that they can stop any natural scenario from happening. And we know the level of environmental manipulation of such super-civilisations would be considerable. Thanks to increasing complexity, we would essentially save the Universe from dying.

Then we have to ask ourselves, if the pattern of increasing complexity over 13.8 billion years continues somewhere in the cosmos (not necessarily with us) uninterrupted for trillions of more years, will a "Big Save" scenario always be a *preposterous future*? Or one that could gradually transition to *possible, probable,* and *projected*? In a "Big Save" scenario, you do not have the same separation between inanimate complexity and animate complexity. Instead, it is the culmination of a narrative where very small and complex systems begin to affect the very large cosmic systems from which they emerged. Perhaps even altering the fate of the Universe itself. In a "Big Save" scenario, the traditional partition between the Near and Deep Future has less importance, because what happens to complexity in the Near Future on Earth ultimately might affect the Deep Future. When considering the fact that the secular scientific projection for the "end of the world" or Universe tends to depress audiences with a grim projection of Heat Death, here is a somewhat intriguing thought that magnifies present attempts at survival in the Near Future. And if you can find a glimmer of hope at the end of the Universe, you can find one anywhere.

Essay Writing Exercise

With all the previous preparation and exercises we have conducted it is now time to write your final Big History essay:

What is the single most important theme you have discovered in 13.8 billion years of Big History?

Once you have finished writing your essay, take it, earn a Nobel Prize, or less ambitiously submit it for a High Distinction. Or show it to your Nan. I bet she'd think it was cool.

Conclusion

In my opinion, I once summed up Big History the best in a series of monologues I wrote for John Green in the tenth episode of *Crash Course: Big History*. Unfortunately, he had a cold on the day of shooting, and so all my carefully crafted words that were designed to encourage and comfort were delivered with a stuffy nose and a gravelly voice! But I'll give you the sum and total of it here without as much grandiose language. The matter of the Universe actually congealed from pure energy shortly after the Big Bang. All the ingredients for your body and mind were around 13.8 billion years ago. Since then, as the First Law of Thermodynamics states, matter and energy have simply continued to change form. In that sense, you are a manifestation of a long continuum of evolution and change. Just a wave of a particular shape in the ocean at a snapshot point in time. It will not be long before the ocean rolls along and your wave will be subsumed by the wider waters and change shape again. It is also fairly easy to view a single wave as inextricable from the wider ocean. In the same sense, you *are* the Universe. Except you've got the privilege of being a small part of the Universe that can temporarily look at itself, as if the cosmos were viewing itself through a mirror. A beautiful (and true) notion.

If you have any sort of anxiety about where you will go after you die, remember that we have an evolutionarily instilled fear of death – if we did not, we'd be a pretty lousy species. We may not like the idea of one day losing our consciousness. But the building blocks of your complexity will carry on through the Universe, for all eternity, continuing to change form. In a way, that is something of a marvelous fate for any of us. It is a more practical form of immortality. We continue the adventure eternally without having to be conscious of it forever, which might get extremely tiresome, boring, and even maddening. Imagine having to watch 100 trillion years crawl by. Instead it is a blessing to have a few moments in our existence to reflect upon our journey.

Very seldom will a Big History narrative alone provide you with a "meaning of life". And I would be very suspicious of any Big History that claimed to do so. Instead history teaches more subtly, and lends the experience of past lifetimes to our own wisdom. Without history, we live one life. With history, we live a thousand lifetimes. When you apply the same logic to Big History, you multiply the number of lifetimes across the clash and thunder of billions of years. Hopefully something about this story has enriched your perspective. Perhaps this enrichment will help you in the pursuit of a meaning of your own, or at least the pursuit of your own happiness.

Anyway, if complexity is ultimately tending toward a "Big Save" scenario, perhaps I'll see you when we are both immortal cyborgs floating around some distant galaxy. Or if this entire Universe is a simulation, I suppose I might see you in the game lobby for the next round once this one is over.

Good luck. Be good to people. And try to make good use of the time that has been given to you.